PROTEST:

PACIFISM
AND POLITICS

James Finn

PROTEST: PACIFISM AND POLITICS

Some Passionate Views on War and Nonviolence

RANDOM HOUSE, New York

Acknowledgment is hereby made for permission to quote from *Partisan
Review*, Summer 1965, © Copyright, 1965, by Partisan Review; and
Denise Levertov's *The Sorrow Dance*, © Copyright, 1966, by Denise
Levertov Goodman and reprinted by permission of New Directions Pub-
lishing Corporation.

Library of Congress Catalog Card Number: 66-22249

Manufactured in the United States of America by
The Colonial Press Inc., Clinton, Massachusetts

Designed by Kenneth Miyamoto

To My Mother

Acknowledgments

Ordinarily, one would thank the principal contributors to a volume such as this. But this book belongs in a real sense to those whose conversations are here recorded and I would feel it presumptuous to thank them. But I would like to express appreciation for what is not evident in the book: first, the almost unfailing courtesy and generosity I encountered even when I disrupted very crowded schedules; second, and more important to me, the experience which the composition of this book became. This second point may merit elaboration.

My initial plan was to provide a topography of contemporary protest, an emotionally neutral undertaking. But the issues that have inspired the protests are of profound importance and the people with whom I discussed these issues have developed strong attitudes and opinions. I initiated the conversations with some few opinions of my own which, to indulge an oxymoron, I held with a measure of passion. In the course of the discussions some of my attitudes were confirmed, but some were considerably modified. The preparation of this book has provided for me an education I had not anticipated but for which I am grateful.

I have attempted to transcribe the recorded conversations faithfully, eliminating obvious redundancies and lapses. I have retained apparent irrelevancies where I judged them to be suggestive.

There are a number of people whom I do wish to thank. My colleagues at the Council on Religion and International Affairs have, over the years, helped me to explore many of the issues that are raised here. For assistance on particular sections of the book I am indebted to James Douglass, Alan Geyer, Dennis Hale, Michael Harrington, Richard S. Hartigan, Robert Pickus, Ralph Potter, Quentin Quade and Roger Shinn.

In addition there are three people who were concerned with the book from its initiation to its conclusion. Susan Woolfson's indispensable assistance at every stage of the book, including the transcription of the conversations, saved me from a number of *gaucheries*. The debt that I owe my editor, Alice Mayhew, is one my vanity seeks to minimize. To my wife, who not only offered needed encouragement but who at the same time bore us a child with considerably less outward anguish than attended the parturition of this book, I owe deep and affectionate gratitude.

J.F.

CONTENTS

Introduction ix

RELIGION AND PACIFISM

PROTESTANTS

John C. Bennett 3
Paul Deats 17
Paul Peachey 36

CATHOLICS

John L. McKenzie, s.j. 43
Gordon Zahn 59
Philip Berrigan, s.s.j. 72
Justus George Lawler 84

JEWS

Arthur Gilbert 94
Everett Gendler 111
Steven S. Schwarzschild 124

THE ORGANIZATIONS

RELIGIOUS

Daniel Berrigan, s.j. 141
Abraham Joshua Heschel 154
Richard John Neuhaus 163
James Forest, Tom Cornell and David Miller 176

PACIFIST

A. J. Muste 193
David McReynolds 206

Staughton Lynd   223
Jack Bollens   246
David Reed   257

POLITICAL

Jack Newfield   279
Julian Bond   292
John Lewis   310
Robert Speck   319
Bayard Rustin   328
Arnold S. Kaufman   342
Stanley Millet   355
Dorothy Day   372

CO'S AND THE JUST WAR

Arlo Tatum   385
William V. O'Brien   399
Paul Ramsey   415

COMMITMENT WITHOUT LABEL

Frederick Franck   431
Tom T. Stonier   443
Joan Baez   454
Mitchell Goodman and Denise Levertov   463
W. H. Ferry   480

Politics and the Spiritual Nobility   493
Bibliography   513
Index   519

INTRODUCTION

Those Americans who protest against the war in Vietnam are a statistical minority. But there is scarcely an aspect of American life that the protest leaves untouched. It passes through the halls of Congress, the centers of education, the religious communities, the labor unions, the civil rights movement, the intellectual and artistic communities, rousing and disturbing even some of the most alienated and disaffected members of the society.

In the surge of movement back and forth between those who defend U.S. policy in Vietnam and those who criticize it, there have been coarse and unproductive acts on both sides, and each side has displayed its share of "organization men." Witnesses have been called, quite gratuitously, before the House Un-American Activities Committee only to call the members of that Committee, equally gratuitously, "coward yellow-belly racists." Faced with an independent and rebellious protest of youth, many older people approached the bewilderment actually attained by Representative John Buchanan, who said, in a remark that deserves to be preserved in amber for the purity of its incomprehension: "When I was in college, we didn't grow beards and throw ourselves in front of troop trains. We swallowed goldfish." Some of the protests have quite obviously been marked by great emotional intensity and a low level of political sophistication. But all this is the froth and the fringe of the protest; in the dense and entangled matrix of protest activities there is present, however incompletely formed, a body of critical judgment and positive insight that is too rooted to disappear and too valuable to ignore. It would be an adventuresome person who would try to demonstrate that all the protest activities had checked the steady development of U.S. actions in Vietnam to any degree. But it would be a foolhardy person who concluded that the protest activities were therefore trivial, irrelevant or wasteful. Though apparently—and in some instances actually—directed at politics as it is practiced in our society and the specific policies thereby developed, the protests are more frequently directed at the society itself.

It is in times of crisis that our proclaimed beliefs and commitments are tested; even those of us who usually slumber are pressured to examine those standards that we have formed, inherited or passively accepted. The war in Vietnam is such a crisis for the United States. We will be tested by it not only as individuals but as a people; by the nature of our engagement we will declare the priority of our values.

Who are the protesters? How do they define the basis of their protest? What relation does it have to foreign policy, to domestic policies, to the conditions of our society? Why is it ultimately involved with questions of race and poverty? Does it tell us anything about the problem of violence, which has been well described as a central problem of our time? What brings the protesters together and what divides them?

These are some of the questions with which I began my investigation. In the process I tried to distinguish what was ephemeral from what was of lasting value in the present phenomenon.

This book explores the current protest in the United States; the inferences which are drawn extend far beyond that protest.

RELIGION AND PACIFISM

PROTESTANTS

JOHN C. BENNETT

"The escalation of the war in Vietnam makes it difficult to be an American."

This is a hard statement that not all Americans would subscribe to. It is the kind of statement that one might expect from an ardent and troubled pacifist, from a member of the radical Left, or even from a moderate critic of U.S. foreign policy caught up in a heated discussion about Vietnam. In fact it is none of these things. It appeared in *Christianity and Crisis*, probably the leading Protestant journal of opinion in this country, as the opening sentence of a considered editorial written by the chairman of the editorial board, John C. Bennett.

Educated at Williams College, Oxford University and Union Theological Seminary, and ordained to the Congregational ministry, Dr. Bennett has taught in seminaries since 1927 and has lectured on campuses around the world. He has worked steadily to relate Christian ethics to contemporary social problems, as the titles of some of his many books indicate: *Christians and the State, Christianity and Communism Today, Nuclear Weapons and the Conflict of Conscience* (ed.), and most recently *Foreign Policy in Christian Perspective*. He played an important role in the discussion of social problems at the Oxford Conference in 1937 and at the World Council Assemblies at Amsterdam (1948), Evanston (1954), and Geneva (1966). He has been president of the American Theological Society and of the American Society of Christian Ethics. He has also served as vice-chairman of the Liberal Party of New York, a post he resigned in 1963 when he became president of Union Theological Seminary. This does not sound like the background of either a radical or an irresponsible social critic.

It is a brisk, sunny day when I visit Dr. Bennett in his office on Morningside Heights. He is especially pleased that morning because he is to have lunch with some Jesuits from Fordham University to discuss the possibilities of a cooperative venture. Although joint Catholic-Protestant activities are increasingly common, they were, a few years back, both rare and suspect. John Bennett is one of those pioneers in the ecumenical movement who strove against severe resistance to break down the barriers, and he now has the special pleasure that comes to those who see their judgments corroborated by time and their efforts multiplied by others.

With his dark, smoothed-back hair and his low-keyed, shy but lively manner he appears much younger than his sixty-four years. His horn-rimmed glasses and dark suit lend him a sober appearance which, when he addresses himself to a serious question, can seem even severe. But his face easily and frequently breaks into a wide smile. He speaks very readily with an occasional pause, sometimes backtracking to be sure he hasn't said something more definite and absolute than he intends.

Christianity and Crisis has recently celebrated its twenty-fifth year, and the occasion dramatically exposed the crisis which the journal and the country are currently suffering through. For the anniversary issue Dr. Bennett had written an article "From Supporter of War in 1941 to Critic in 1966," but the principal speaker for the anniversary dinner, a long-time supporter of the journal, is a foremost spokesman for U.S. policy in Vietnam, Hubert Humphrey. I begin by asking Dr. Bennett about the background of the editorial policies of *Christianity and Crisis*.

BENNETT: Well, *Christianity and Crisis* was formed at a time when the great threat was Hitlerism, and it seemed that a good deal of the pacifism in the American churches became allied with political isolationism. This doesn't mean that the pacifists were personally isolationists, but they made common cause with the isolationists, and it was this tendency that aroused the greatest amount of polemical opposition from Dr. [Reinhold] Niebuhr, for example. And it was Dr. Niebuhr's thought that was

John C. Bennett

primarily back of *Christianity and Crisis* at that time. It seemed necessary not only *politically* to support those in our nation who favored a strong readiness to oppose Hitler, even by force if necessary, but *also* to clarify the situation of the churches where there had been this strange alliance between even the America First type of isolationism and pacifism. I don't want to give the impression that the pacifists at that time were themselves of the same turn of mind at all as the other isolationists. You get this converging sometimes, politically, of people with different motives.

FINN: Well, this indicates there is a possibility that pacifists are sometimes—I'm not sure this is the proper term—used by political movements.

BENNETT: I think, in their point of view, that they often think they can use the political movement. Because, after all, if your main idea is to prevent war, then any political movement designed to preserve neutrality is better than one that seems belligerent. This is a situation the pacifists find themselves in quite frequently. *Christianity and Crisis* was established *partly,* I think, because *The Christian Century* represented this semi-pacifist attitude toward the crisis of the late thirties, having to do primarily with Hitlerism. And it turned out that a very large number of the people who had been pragmatic pacifists out of revulsion against the First World War and were sure that war was the greatest possible evil, during the thirties began to feel that the combination of Hitler's type of totalitarianism with military aggression—or rather the *extension* of totalitarianism by way of military aggression—was the worst thing that was going on.

FINN: So your own thinking about the situation today does not come out of a pacifist background but rather out of one in which you were called upon to examine pacifism in order to show its inadequacies.

BENNETT: Yes it does, actually. And when one takes the pacifist position out of the Sermon on the Mount, for example, or out of an absolutistic New Testament ethic, *I've* always said —and I think this is in line with many others—that the love ethic should not be focused entirely on nonviolence. I mean, it's quite true that in many, most, perhaps even nine tenths of the cases nonviolence has a claim. But at the same time I think that love is a superior command to any *particular* command, like the command to avoid violence, and therefore the love for the neighbor would involve seeking to *protect* neighbors against other neighbors. This is really what it comes down to finally: the protecting of some neighbors against other neighbors. Now you have to be very careful that in protecting some neighbors against other neighbors you don't destroy them all, or that you don't just loose forces that are going to do vastly more harm than good in the long run. But this is a historical, pragmatic kind of judgment—not an absolutistic judgment.

FINN: How do you counter the statements that you often must hear, as you said recently in an article, from pacifists with whom you are sympathetic?

BENNETT: Well, there are really two grounds. One is that no government that is responsible to an existing nation *can* adopt a pacifist policy. Of course there are some nations that may be nonmilitary, because they don't have the *power,* but they do depend upon stronger powers to defend them. After our experience with India's accepting the use of force in several instances—not least of all in the Pakistan conflict—it's very doubtful if we can imagine a nation that is *in principle* absolutistic in its pacifism, however it may withdraw from the use of military force in most situations. Then, secondly, I cannot renounce the use of military power absolutely in principle because I do think you have to have a certain balancing of forces in the world. I can't give up in *advance* all moral right to balance, or at least to check, what seems to be an aggressive and tyrannical form of power. I have to live with the possibility of this balancing of forces, even though I may be very critical of the way it's generally done, and would want to keep the uses of force involved very much limited.

FINN: There's nothing in your reading of the Bible or of the traditional development of Christian ethics which precludes violence as a possibility for a person in his own life or his domestic national life or international affairs? There are *some* occasions when violence seems to be, even in terms of a love ethic, the best alternative which is presented?

BENNETT: There are proof texts in the Gospels which can be used, but I think *that* is a tendency to take love and reduce it to a very specific law of nonviolence; I think nonviolence should be under criticism of love which is an *indefinite* kind of responsibility for the neighbor which might involve protecting the neighbor against aggression or oppression. Now I realize that these excuses for the use of violence are very old and they're too readily used, and that in the present world, with the kinds of power the nations have, we should be very sparing in our use of it.

There has developed within historical Christianity a philosophical doctrine of the "just war," that under certain conditions a government can justly engage in war, and the theory attempts to set forth the limiting conditions of that engagement. To the extent that it succeeds, it provides a framework for the historical pragmatic judgment that Dr. Bennett mentioned. While he thinks the just-war concept has a limited usefulness, he himself rejects the "somewhat stereotyped and legalistic conception of just war." How then does he arrive at his strong position on the war in Vietnam?

BENNETT: Well, I feel, just in terms of the familiar conception of the proportionality in what one does, that the destruction of people in South Vietnam and the destruction of villages is itself a very evil thing. We don't know what's being destroyed in the North in human terms very much—we hear about railroads and bridges and so on. But in the South even, it seems like overuse of force.

Pushing the thought a little further, it seems that what we're doing is likely to be self-defeating. This is partly from my rather, oh, non-absolutistic approach to these things, but it's *partly* a matter of timing. If, for example, at the time of the Baltimore speech* Johnson had been able to pull off some negotiations, this might have justified what had been done up to that time to a certain extent. I mean, I wouldn't have been so clear about it. But this has been going on for years and years, the stepping up of violence with a kind of momentum in the military process that nobody seems to be checking very well. This seems to me to be something which is self-defeating, both in its weakening and destroying of the nation we're trying to save, in driving all the communist forces together on the other side, in weakening the role of both North and South Vietnam as possible checks upon *Chinese* communism. But perhaps in the long run the most

* At Johns Hopkins University, April 7, 1965.

self-defeating thing will be for the United States to end up with a half a million or so military men, forces, on the continent of Asia, representing the whole imperialistic West. The United States has not on the whole been, at least in the usual sense, an imperialistic power, but now it's *the* great power in the West, and all the sins of the past are stuck to it. There's no question about that, and I think this white force on Asian soil cannot but be the source of new resentments.

Without disputing Dr. Bennett's judgment here, I recall that the leaders of some countries in Southeast Asia say they welcome the U.S. presence because it does operate as a check on expansionist communist forces. It's true, he says, of a number of small countries but more problematic of Japan, India and Pakistan. And we nevertheless must be concerned about the provocativeness, "the ultimate meaning of this *for* China." When I suggest that his remarks parallel some of those recently made by Senator Fulbright he only partially agrees.* There are many signs, he says, that "The Americans are anything but arrogant in this matter"; they are eager to bring the conflict to an end and, according to recent polls, to accept arbitration by a third party such as the U.N.

Among those people who share many of Dr. Bennett's opinions and judgments a special burden falls on one group—those young men eligible for the draft who judge the war in Vietnam to be unjust. If the issue is to be faced squarely it must not be turned into a matter of political judgment only—"What makes him think he knows better than the government?"—but must be seen as a question of conscience. At what point can a citizen refuse to be coopted by the government in the service of an action he judges to be unjust and immoral? The issue is not simple, and the memory of Eichmann, and of all the others who defended their crimes by invoking their subjection to authority, hovers over the present discussion.

FINN: Let me ask you what you think should be or *can* be the position of our government when faced with the problem of the selective conscientious objector, someone who's not opposed

* The comments to which I refer are quoted on pp. 201–2.

John C. Bennett

to all war but who does accept the judgment you yourself stated? At present there are no laws which protect this person or give him a right to opt out. Nor do I think the churches have any; I can't think of any church which has attempted to support *this* particular case.

BENNETT: I think actually it's implied in the statement of the Vatican Council. Since absolute pacifism is *not* a Roman Catholic position, for the Vatican Council to call for laws that *do* take account of conscientious objection I think must point in this direction.*

FINN: It's exactly the application of just-war principles, with some scrupulosity, which poses the problem acutely today.

BENNETT: It's quite true. Selective conscientious objection is a great problem. You can look at it in two ways. You can say that administratively it's almost hopeless. The hopelessness of it is indicated when people say "Well, people can't choose the war they fight in." That rather trivializes the problem, I think, but that's the way it's often put, and anyone can see the difficulties. On the other hand, if you have a *large* number of people who can be so classified and we find ourselves sending them to jail, we will find ourselves also being *fed up* with sending them to jail and try to find accommodation.

It might be a safety valve to loosen up the alternatives a little more, make some kind of rigorous peace corps service an alternative, and just by making it available reduce the range of the problem. It seems to me that's perhaps the most hopeful way to proceed at the moment, and not try to solve the problem entirely in principle.

* The statement to which Dr. Bennett referred is found in one of the major documents that issued from the Second Vatican Council, *The Constitution on the Church in the Modern World*. In ¶79 of the *Constitution* the right of government to engage in legitimate defense is recalled and it is asserted that "those too who devote themselves to the military service of their country should regard themselves as the agents of security and freedom of peoples." But in addition to these traditional positions the *Constitution* also states that "it seems right that laws make humane provisions for the case of those who for reasons of conscience refuse to bear arms, provided, however, that they agree to serve the human community in some other way."

Since today, as in the past, there are Catholics who are absolute pacifists, the Catholic position is slightly more complicated than Dr. Bennett suggests, but he expresses without doubt what is generally understood and accepted as Catholic teaching.

Dr. Bennett has devoted much of his time and thought to the ethical and political problems that flow from the possession of nuclear weapons. He was, in 1950, one of the signers of the Dun Report on "The Christian Conscience and Weapons of Mass Destruction," a report which declined to say that the U.S. should not use the hydrogen bomb first in a war. At that time he thought that the greatest threat to peace was communist aggression and that communist uncertainty about U.S. intentions would inhibit a conventional attack on Western Europe. But conditions have changed since then, and so has Dr. Bennett's thinking. Today he is no longer satisfied with that position.

BENNETT: We must ask whether or not unilateral withdrawal from *all* nuclear power by the United States would on the whole be disastrous. For one thing, maybe the best chance of getting a multilateral withdrawal from nuclear power does depend upon our having this balance at the present stage. But I realize *all* the dilemmas here, and I know that the one who uses this power will probably destroy all he tries to defend by *having* it.

FINN: But the argument for the present deterrence system is that it is designed *not* to be used.

BENNETT: That's too optimistic, I think. We have to recognize that the dangers of unexpected escalation might cause it to be used, and all the things you hoped for would be lost.

FINN: There are people who say that if we do have a weapons system such as this it *will* be used, that we have not had, in history, any weapons designed for military use that *haven't* been used. I don't know what kind of judgment is implied in that, whether it's a reading of human nature or of history or a combination, but people do seem to be divided on this particular point.

BENNETT: Divided. But then I suppose you could say against this judgment that we've never had a weapons system that was so irrational, so much of a threat. I think this degree of threat may gain *time* for us, but if we do nothing in this time to reduce the tensions and reduce all *temptations* to use it, we will not survive.

FINN: And, I presume, along with this should go efforts to reduce the armaments system itself. . . .

John C. Bennett

BENNETT: I think that three things have to go on at the same time: one is reducing the *occasions* for conflict, at least for this kind of all-out conflict; second, reducing the armaments system itself *multilaterally,* with many unilateral risks on the way, per- haps—I wouldn't for a moment deny the importance of uni- lateral steps; and third, providing other sorts of security, which is very difficult but still absolutely necessary.

FINN: There *are* people who describe themselves today as nuclear pacifists in the sense that they would say that some wars are justified but no nuclear war would be. And they say "no nuclear war" because they believe that once you use nuclear weapons as tactical weapons, there's no possibility of *stopping* the escalation—or at least the likelihood is so great they're not willing to risk it themselves. Do you think that is a *sound.* . . .

BENNETT: Well, I'm inclined to agree with that, Jim. There are two things we should avoid in as absolute a way as is pos- sible in history. One is the attack on population centers. (And I know there are all kinds of marginal problems there.) And secondly, the initiation of a nuclear stage of a war *regardless* of the political temptation to do it. Now that doesn't answer the final question: what you do if you are the victim of a nuclear attack. I think probably it's irrational to retaliate. But I *do* think you do have at this moment in history to preserve this nuclear balance with all the qualifications I've surrounded it with.

The problem of tension between foreign policy and moral- ity has long occupied statesmen and moralists. A number of thinkers and practitioners have attempted to dissolve the ten- sion, most brutally by attempting to substitute moralisms for rules of political conduct or by positing a political autonomy which is almost antiseptically free from moral directives. John Bennett, who addresses himself to problems in the political order from a specific Christian tradition, has insisted on maintaining that tension. I recall an article in which he said that Christian ethics do not provide rules but that they do provide a perspec- tive with which to view foreign policy decisions. Can he suggest what these perspectives are?

BENNETT: Well, I think that the perspectives are both theo- logical and ethical. They have to do with one's seeing all nations under God's love and care, and therefore avoidance of absolute conflicts between any peoples. I think also that Christian love *does* call for the concern for all neighbors, and this means the neighbors on the other side of our conflicts as well as those whom we may think we're trying to defend. It also means that we should be very self-critical, that we should see the way in which we ourselves are involved in the evils we often criticize others for. I don't mean here that one should say, "A plague on both your houses." But I *do* think that Christian ethics *does* involve —or Christian theology involves—trying to see oneself or one's own nation as it appears to other nations and from outside its own bias. I also think that there is in the Christian perspective a warning against national idolatries, against holy wars and ideological fixations on one's own side as well as the other side. I think one of the *resources* here is the universal church, too, which helps Christians in one country to see the world from the point of view of Christians in other countries.

FINN: Something which *does* transcend the national boundaries . . .

BENNETT: National boundaries, although I recognize a proximate and relative place, very important place, for a wise view of national interest. I don't see how from the Christian standpoint the national interest can ever become the only criterion. I think that it's often a very good guide, and particularly a good guide when it comes to *limitation* of what we do, so that we don't try to act on the assumption we know what's best for everybody else.

FINN: I think this is one of the things that *both* Reinhold Niebuhr and you have pointed out in your writing, that national interest, contrary to what many people think, provides *limitations*.

BENNETT: I think it also is true of Hans Morgenthau and George Kennan. I learned much of it from them.

FINN: You mentioned the responsibility we have to our neighbors, even neighbors who are on the *other* side of the conflict. But is there such a thing as a degree of neighborhood, that some neighbors have more right to expect our help than others? We tend to think of this in our own lives. I mean, our family may have a greater claim upon us than the people next door. It doesn't prevent us from being neighbors; it's just that our obligations are different.

BENNETT: I think it's a very dialectical thing. In a sense we *do* have, because of a kind of division of labor, we do have a special responsibility to our near neighbors. But at the same time, the moment one tends to make too much of this, it becomes a source of a very strong partisanship and encourages a tendency to take our group of nearer neighbors and make far too much of this group as against other groups. I think it's a very dialectical thing. I would recognize the preliminary responsibility for the nearer neighbors, but I would regard it only as a *preliminary* responsibility.

FINN: You suggested that the just-war concept was, in a sense, too legalistic, too absolutistic, for your own approach to some of these problems. The other evening I was with a group of people who are very well informed about just-war theory as well as very interested and informed about the present situation. And they felt—many of them—as a very real problem, whether, under some set of circumstances, it would not be proper to bomb cities, using the law of proportionality. I wanted to ask whether there was, in your terms, anything which would be an absolute moral prohibition against the bombing of cities?

BENNETT: Well, I have difficulty with absolutes, I have to admit, and the bombing of cities is *partly* evil because of the presence in them of the individuals who are quite . . . innocent isn't the word to use, but I mean they're noncombatants who should be protected. But, secondly, the moment you begin to bomb cities you begin to get outside what is proportional in dealing with the problems; you're going to *start* this. Therefore I think I would keep the rules very strict on the side of such bombing. Especially now with the nuclear situation, the thing is bound to accelerate so; no limit to it. But I don't think that means it was right before, in the Second World War. I think it was a kind of a corporate moral fall in the Second World War —our bombing of Dresden, Tokyo and Hamburg and so on.* This was a very *bad way* of beginning a nuclear age.

* It is instructive to recall the destructive force of these bombing raids. According to a report of the U.S. strategic bombing survey, 42,600 people were killed in Hamburg as a result of the first fire storm produced in the Second World War. (July 27–28, 1943.) In Tokyo the fire bomb

FINN: I think this is the kind of problem which this group which I was with *did* continue to explore. It *was* pointed out that there was, as you said, a corporate fault here, but we realized it only with the bombing of Hiroshima and Nagasaki because this seemed so extreme—not that the damage was greater, but it was. . . .

BENNETT: No, that's right, but we got a bad start in the nuclear age because we'd already begun to bomb cities before, and therefore it wasn't too difficult to decide to bomb these cities. There's probably no political cause that justifies this kind of massacring. The ideological causes and the holy-war causes certainly don't.

FINN: Well, there have been people who've pointed out that out of the bombing of Hiroshima, which they regarded as unnecessary and immoral, some good consequences have come.

BENNETT: Well, I think you can always say—now this in theology is being used as a kind of example of divine overruling —that God can rescue good out of things, even though we should not do these things. I mean, this is a traditional doctrine of the Church.

FINN: This is the point that I would really like to get at because it *is* a teaching of the Church. Is it not difficult to argue on *historical* terms that what we regard as evil means cannot have good ends?

BENNETT: Good consequences may come out of evil means, certainly. I've no doubt that that's true. But I don't know that we should put ourselves in the place of God and therefore be *reckless* about this. I mean . . . I think. . . . I stumble here because I realize the difficulties. Take, for example, such a matter as torture. This is a simpler matter than bombing cities. I've always said, "Well, certainly to torture an individual, force that

---

raid of March 9–10, 1945 killed 83,700. Dresden contained no military targets of importance. Nevertheless on the night of February 13–14, 1945 in the most harrowing, destructive raid of the war, British bombers created a fire storm that was visible for two hundred miles. In the morning American Flying Fortresses continued the attack while accompanying fighters strafed the survivors. As a result 135,000 people died. By contrast the atom bomb dropped on Hiroshima killed 71,400 people. The story of Dresden is told in detail in *The Destruction of Dresden* by David Irving (New York, Ballantine Books, 1965), from which most of these statistics are taken.

John C. Bennett

individual to go against his own conscience by your pressure, is an evil thing; it's a *very* evil thing." Then you get up to the question whether there's some perhaps *limited* form of torture in the case of individuals. You could save a lot of other people from being tortured. And there's no way out of that problem. On the other hand, when your society starts this process, it's a deeply corrupting thing, it seems to me.

FINN: So in your own thinking you would establish warning points. They may not be absolutes but they're strong cautions.

BENNETT: That's it. Very, very strong warning points, I would say, rather than absolutes is what I'm governed by. Even when it's overrun, one shouldn't disregard the warning and therefore one should *mitigate* the thing which one does, in the light of the warning. That's my objection to situation ethics as presented. It seems too often, as Fletcher* presents it, it is decided in a particular case that love causes you to put aside the rules. Well, maybe that's true in terms of external behavior, but then the rules still must be operative; there should be *pressures* from the rules *on* you, in the situation.

FINN: I take it this is what you were saying in the recent exchange you had with Paul Ramsey, when you said there were some actions in the Vietnam war that were morally intolerable. Nevertheless you could not say that because of this the total action, the entire war, was unjust.

BENNETT: Yes. I think what Ramsey's doing is what I think the moral theologians have done. He's trying to work out a system by which you can do things without any guilt; you can find some thing to do which is *morally approved*.

FINN: And which the politician, in this particular set of circumstances, would like to feel as a moral possibility as well as a political, military necessity.

BENNETT: Quite. Even when one does that thing which might be the lesser evil, it's still very, very evil, and I think somehow that's *lost,* some of the thinking.

* Joseph Fletcher, Professor of Social Ethics at Episcopal Theological School, Cambridge, Massachusetts, is the author of *Situation Ethics and Moral Responsibility: Situation Ethics at Work.* He has become a leading proponent of the subject delimited by these titles.

FINN: I presume, John, that you would regard most warfare as evil, even if . .

BENNETT: Certainly

FINN: There *is* a tradition which says that war is not the lesser of two evils, but is really a good.

BENNETT: Yes, well, I wouldn't buy that.

PAUL DEATS

Paul Deats was born in 1918 in Graham, Texas. He received an A.B. from Southern Methodist University, a B.D. from Union Theological Seminary and his Ph.D. from Boston University, where he is now Professor of Social Ethics in the School of Theology.

Before he got his Ph.D. he found time to be director of the Wesley Foundation at the University of Texas and to direct, with his wife, an interracial work camp in Rio Grande Valley. He is co-author, with H. E. Stotts, of *Methodism and Society: Guidelines for Strategy*. He also serves as vice-chairman of FOR (the Fellowship of Reconciliation).

As he comes down the hall to greet me, Paul Deats gives the impression of a lively, energetic person. The familiar, academic horn-rimmed glasses fail to conceal his light eyes. With his dark checked jacket, the deep-red bow tie and bright, wide smile he appears younger than his years, and it is only later that one notices his graying temples. Because we have not seen each other for a few years we spend a few minutes reminiscing, but he is between a class and a faculty meeting so we get to the business at hand.

DEATS: I have for almost thirty years been identified with the Fellowship of Reconciliation and have identified myself as a pacifist, as an *absolute* pacifist. I still am sure that I personally could not participate in war. I mean by this, taking an active part in the military service. I'm sure that all of us *are* involved in the "war effort." One of the things that's affected my thinking is that I'm sure all of us are to some extent involved in preparation for war—by the payment of our taxes, by support of the draft. And it's very evident these days simply by being a faculty person and turning in grades which will then go to Selective Service we give some kind of consent to national policy, say, in Vietnam.

FINN: The machine doesn't let anybody escape.

DEATS: That's right. On the other hand, I think that my concern has been to move from just a personal witness and a personal decision—that I not be any more identified than I can help with the war machine—to ask how I develop politically responsible positions that can be debated in the marketplace of ideas and that might affect public policy. And so I really am torn between my personal witness as a pacifist and how my attitudes toward what's going on in the world affect public policy debates.

FINN: This means that one pole of this tension is the necessity to be politically responsible in such a way that you'll be understood by, and will possibly affect, a large body of people —at least those people to whom you address yourself. I mean, you have to be able to make yourself listened to and understood by more than pacifists.

DEATS: That's right. This gets us outside of the fallacy of the group soliloquy in which we just keep talking to ourselves.

The group soliloquy—the phrase pinpoints what is both a strong temptation and a recognized danger not only for pacifists but for all those engaged in some collective and organized protest. The temptation, of course, is to talk to those who will understand and accept one's own terms of debate; the obvious danger is that of becoming progressively isolated, alienated and ineffective. To move out of the group soliloquy, however, is to engage in debate and possible cooperation with people who do not share many of one's own basic beliefs and opinions. It is to run the risk of compromise, of losing the purity of one's position, of becoming political.

FINN: Does this mean that you have to accept a kind of political framework that is not pacifist and therefore doesn't flow from your own pacifism?

Paul Deats

DEATS: Well, I'm sure that all of us take our final positions ethically on other than the rational political and analytical grounds with which we may argue them with other people. There is a place in my decisions about *any* ethical problem, particularly in the area of war, which I probably finally hold on an intuitive ground. Although I would try to articulate it and defend it and criticize it on rational, philosophical and political as well as biblical grounds.

FINN: Which, it is presumed, *will be* sound reasons.

DEATS: But they are more critical and justificatory than they are constitutive of my ethical argument.

FINN: Well, does this lead to the possibility that what you've called your intuition comes from your own personal background and in such a deep way that it's hard to analyze or discern?

DEATS: I'm sure this is true. I wouldn't want to imply that *only* on an analyst's couch could I understand myself and only with the analyst's help could I do anything. I think I *could* change my mind, and the more this has been brought into my consciousness the more able I am to make my rational reflection *affect* my position.

FINN: Do you think there is such a thing as a pacifist mentality or personality? Maybe it's not a good question.

DEATS: I think it's very good. I don't have any data. I think that there may be some experiences, some personality sets, that are more important than logical arguments, than reason, in why people become pacifists. I don't think we know enough about it to say, and I would hope that these are at least open to change. I know some *very* different personality types who are pacifists.

FINN: I suppose if we could answer that we could also talk about other people in the same terms.

DEATS: You mean, are there then people who would be secretaries of defense? But how you would put Forrestal and McNamara* into the same personality picture presents quite a problem.

FINN: So you'd probably have the same difficulty trying to type pacifists as you would others.

* James V. Forrestal, first Secretary of Defense (1947–49) and Robert S. McNamara, present Secretary of Defense (1967).

DEATS: I would want to recognize the play of psychological and emotional factors without saying these are all explanatory.

FINN: Well, what kind of background did you come from? Would one expect it to lead to pacifism?

DEATS: I doubt it. I was raised in a small community in Texas, as a Methodist—fairly conservative, individualistic, pietistic religion, the kind that both of the Niebuhrs have been protesting against since the beginning of their writing. My call to the ministry, for example, was a very emotional one. I went to an agricultural and mechanical college, was involved in ROTC. In the middle of the 1930's the most strenuous paper I wrote tried to take apart Harry Emerson Fosdick's position that you can't end evil by doing evil. And I said how wrong he was. Then I switched schools and came into contact not only with certain other ideas. I met Kirby Page, Marshall Steel, who was minister of the campus church there, Paul Schilpp, and others who exerted tremendous influence upon me. I was doing some reading in sociology and politics, and I confess also that there were some people of my own age—my fiancée, for example—whose ideas and influence were much more subtle. And I did an almost about-face which involved a whole new conception of what religion was. I revolted against the pietistic background; religion *had* to have some concern with the world in which I lived. This affected the relationship toward problems of war and peace, it affected my conception of the ministry. I became *then*—oh, I think about 1939—a pacifist.

FINN: The pacifist position at that point obviously had a real bearing upon the possibility of American participation in the war. Now one of the criticisms that's made of the pacifists at that time is that their efforts prevented the United States—and this is obviously made by people who supported the war effort —from developing, as effectively as it could, the material which was needed once our country entered war. Is that a sound political judgment? Did it stand in the way of such development?

DEATS: Much of the pacifism that I heard was isolationist-pacifist. This was not true of A. J. Muste, I think I'd have to say. For Kirby Page a lot of it *was*. This may sound very strange, but I heard Kirby Page in 1939 talk about the distance our bombers could fly. Since you could not fly across the Atlantic

Paul Deats

Ocean without refueling, he said, there's no need to get worried about European problems. Now this obviously involved some very, very temporal, technological developments. It was to this extent isolationist, because he thought we could stay out. And so *if* you say—I don't accept this yet—but *if* you say finally, "We *had* to come in," pacifism was malfunctional because it did not help us prepare for what we finally had to do. This probably affected the way in which we were maneuvered, led, manipulated by Mr. Roosevelt, who, while appealing to the isolationist sentiments—"I will never send American boys to fight on foreign shores"—was at the same time involving us in commitments.

I think we were a *very* confused people, and the pacifists were as confused as anybody. I remember statements in a debate, a *vigorous* debate, in a Methodist student conference. One young lady got up and said, "Are you willing to face God with blood on your hands?" Now this is the *purity* of your individual soul. This was important to me, although at that time I was already beginning to change.

Now the third thing that I think is tied in with both of these: there was really no sense of alternative political strategies. What do you do with the emergence of a Hitler, other than ignore him, other than retreat into an isolationist America? I think this was a part of the whole intellectual climate, the whole religious climate, of the pacifists. We were not seeking any *alternative* options, either to Fascism and Nazism, and we were probably uncritical enough that we were willing to be drawn along *for a while* by thinking that these weren't very bad ideas in opposition to the Soviet Marxism. (I'm not talking now about Kirby Page, A. J. Muste, and a few others.) But I'm saying we were *not* developing the alternative political strategies, and for the pacifist movement there was not very much sense of the need for viable alternatives to war, of facing the problems which we obviously have to face in the 1960's—of emerging nations, of wars of national liberation, of underdeveloped peoples.

FINN: Do you think there is a possibility that the pacifists to-day are using, or are being used by, those who criticize U.S. participation in Vietnam from other than a pacifist viewpoint—those who are, say, on the far left, some who have leftover feelings from the thirties when they had sympathies with the Communists, or those who are neo-isolationists, or simply those who adopt pacifism as a tactical political position?

DEATS: That's a complicated question, Jim. I guess I'd have to start off by saying I'm *sure* that all of us—pacifists, non-pacifists—*are used* by various groups of people. I'm sure that many people are being used, for example, by government. Some of us have noted recently, here in the Boston area, that it's awfully difficult to get really highly placed and highly trained persons to defend publicly Administration policy in Vietnam, people who are themselves involved in government research contracts. They will not debate. Many of us feel they themselves have some reservations about it, but they are so deeply involved in government-sponsored research projects, Defense Department or other, that they feel they cannot afford to take a public position. There are lots of us being used.*

And here the conversation veers off slightly to a discussion of attitudes that pacifists have toward neo-isolationism, collective security and peace-keeping efforts. It is not isolationism, Deats says, to reject, as he does, NATO, SEATO and other security commitments that the United States has with over forty countries. It is not isolationism, that is, if with such rejection there is a recognition of the need for some international police force. It is because the more responsible pacifists do recognize the need for such a force that they resist the arms race and some of the arms control proposals that come out of ACDA (Arms Control and Disarmament Agency). "They don't see any hope for developing genuine international police forces as long as there are national police forces."

DEATS: Collaboration with some of these groups is not isolationist insofar as it accepts—and this is a significant change for a number of us in the pacifist movement—accepts the necessity for police action and says, yes, armed force will have to be used. Now some of us have some real questions when we're asked, "You mean you'd give nuclear weapons to an international agency?" You probably boycott these; this at least is where I'm thinking now.

We could very well have been accused twenty-five years ago, say, of calling for peace at any price, and there may be some times when we could be accused justly of saying this right now.

* Deats here opened a subject that became, during and after the summer of 1966, an issue at several universities.

But I'd say there's been a new awareness in the pacifist movement of the fact that you have to deal with questions of justice. And insofar as you deal with questions of justice, you face the necessity for some kinds of coercion, and probably violence getting out of hand. We recognize our implicit or explicit involvement in situations where violence may have to be used to make changes. All this means that the pacifists are much less isolationist, those that I know, than they were before.

I suspect that there's a very different attitude toward Communists, not only abroad in the country, but among pacifists. There were *many* pacifists, led by A. J. Muste with his close affiliation with Trotskyite groups in the late twenties and early thirties, who were so careful that they would not come close to anything which had any Communist taint at all, because they felt this would tar and feather them. Now, across the country, I think men like John Bennett are helping lead the way, recognizing, on the one hand, much more splintering in the Communist political spectrum and, on the other hand, much more maturing of Marxist thought itself in Communist countries.

What Deats expresses here may be true of a number of people, but many do not share his attitudes. If the polls are reliable, American Catholics are still imbued with a strong anticommunism. (There are some notable exceptions, and John Bennett likes to recall an editorial in *Commonweal,* a weekly journal of opinion edited by Catholic laymen, that said: "Communism within Russia should be looked upon as an experiment that deserves a chance to succeed.") And the issue of cooperation with Communists is one of the points of contention between the New Left and the old in this country.

FINN: How does the pacifist reconcile his own position with this recognition that there may be need for a police force to insure justice, particularly in areas of the world where some kind of violence seems almost inevitable?

DEATS: Again, I guess I have to put a disclaimer in, that there are some pacifists who would have no part of a police force. I use a local illustration. We had some pacifists protesting at the Boston army base back in March. They were not adequately protected by the police. Some of us formed a committee to ask for better police protection. Some of the *very* committed and *very articulate* young men, who were themselves beaten, said they did not want police protection because they didn't *believe in* police protection. They felt there was some necessity to confront their attackers face to face, because only through their voluntary acceptance of suffering and their confrontation with the attackers was there any way to get through, that the use of police came between them and their attackers. There *might* be an element of masochism in this kind of a thing. I don't know. At any rate, I have a thorough respect for these people. On the other hand, I start by recognizing the local community. When it exists under a community of law, under some accepted authority, then there's a necessity for police power. One of our great troubles that I see now as a pacifist who accepts the use of police power is that we are so used to violence that we think it takes an awful lot of violence to deal with problems. I say I don't think I could participate in an army. I think I *could* participate in a police force and be *armed*. Now this may mean I'm no longer a pacifist.

I am now willing to go up the scale of coercion, depending upon certain conditions: in whose name and under what authority the force is used, that the minimum force necessary be used and that it stop *far short* of the escalation of military hardware present in the arms race today. And I think that with some genuine international agreements there could be a police force. I don't know what level the military hardware would take, but something less than what some of the people talk about in terms of tactical nuclear weapons. I *recognize* the dilemma there: what do you do if a nation state itself holds on to tactical nuclear weapons? Don't you have to have the predominance of arms on the side of the police force? And this is a good question.

FINN: What you have stated is a hopeful situation which is posited sometime in the future. But we do now have an apparent balance because of nuclear deterrence systems. To what extent do you support or criticize the possession of nuclear deterrents by the United States?

DEATS: I wish I knew empirically, rather than hypothetically, exactly how much of the uneasy truce that we've had rests upon mutual deterrence. It has been argued, and argued very persuasively, that one of the things we pacifists ought to be very grateful for is that we have had *rough parity* of nuclear weapons, that this *is* the basis on which our uneasy truce rests. I think I have always to weigh over and against this at least one or two considerations. One of them is that we're always under the threat that this might break out, through accident, through miscalculation or through over-threatening behavior—as we may well have come awfully close to in Cuba. I am also impressed when I hear Thomas Schelling and some other people talk about the extent to which there's also a basis of trust—not institutionalized, very informal, but operating as a tacit understanding that we won't do this if you won't do that. I'm not sure that this *rests* upon possession of certain weapons. It *may be* that this could be achieved at lower levels. At any rate, whether it follows logically either from my political analysis or from my pacifism, I would have to say I think the arms race itself is an unstable phenomenon; we must develop not only controls in the sense of stabilizing the arms race at a certain level but disarmament procedures which *de-escalate* the arms race and *shift* the burden from national to some kind of multinational agency. I don't think this is necessarily so very far in the future. When you get a Secretary of Defense saying in Canada* that our peace doesn't depend on just military hardware, he is saying that there is, at least in *his view,* some hope for some other kinds of instruments for the control of aggression, for the reaching of. . . .

FINN: Well, he said it didn't depend on hardware *only.* He didn't exclude that, did he?

DEATS: No, he didn't exclude it. But there seemed to be a system of priorities that this might not be the most important item. I have a suspicion that our policy started out with a notion of deterrence, and that this basic presupposition has then dictated both where we would go in terms of multinational developments, international developments, and where we would go in developing alternatives to nuclear weapons.

FINN: I presume it would be the responsibility of a pacifist of your own position to work toward and support those alternative measures.

* In a speech delivered in Montreal before the American Society of Newspapers on May 18, 1966, Robert S. McNamara said: "We have come to identify 'security' with exclusively military phenomena; and most particularly with military hardware. But it just isn't so."

DEATS: Yes. With unilateral initiatives at least, in [Charles] Osgood's phrase.*

FINN: Are you willing to say how far your own support for unilateral initiatives would go? Osgood has a whole system in which he thinks that unilateral initiatives will be met by response from the other side. But suppose they're not, how far would *you* be willing to carry this?

DEATS: This is really one of the ticklish questions, because I personally would be willing to carry it much farther down the road than I think American public opinion would be willing to go. But I think here we get into a tactical question of how Americans debate the issues, and I think we need much more clarification of the differences between depending on this mutual deterrent system and exploring what the initiatives would be. I think Americans could come to understand the relative costs of the deterrent system, both in terms of its present economic demands *and* in terms of the risks that they're running.

What disturbs me in this is the "of course," and the "naturally" attitudes of so many of us in America, that of course you couldn't do this because. . . . We assume the response of the other party. It may be that you have to take two steps before you get the reciprocation that Osgood is talking of. Maybe you have to take three steps. And I think there has to be some exposure to risk.

We had talked of the Boston unit of the CNVA (Committee for Nonviolent Action) which I had visited the preceding day. Not many weeks earlier some members of the CNVA staging a protest in South Boston had been set upon by a group, mostly high-school students, who slugged and kicked them, yelling, "Shoot them! Commies! Kill them!" *Time* magazine reported that a veteran police captain said later: "Anyone foolish enough to commit such an unpatriotic gesture in South Boston can only expect what these people got." I ask Paul Deats what he thinks of such demonstrations and of such a response to the demonstrators.

DEATS: It seems to me police as citizens have a right to their own opinions. But they have a duty to protect people, even

* In *An Alternative to War or Surrender* (Urbana, University of Illinois Press, 1962).

Paul Deats

people doing unpopular things, and I certainly was *most* disturbed in Boston in March, and I'm disturbed now when a police lieutenant says this kind of thing 'cause it sounds like Selma to me when the police are completely *against* the minority's legal rights.

Let me say about the Boston situation that some of us went in immediately after the attacks in March to talk to the Mayor. And the Mayor said, "It is clear in the training manual for Boston police that they protect the rights of *any* minority for peaceable assembly no matter how unpopular the cause may be." And he went on the air to make a public statement to this effect and reissued orders to the police department. And I have to say that immediately thereafter we had *excellent* co-operation from the police in Boston. I recognize that there is also—hopefully a minority—a group who are most antagonistic to those who demonstrate for peace. There were longshoremen involved, there were adults involved in that beating, so this response is part of a general American response. And I have to say—back to what the psychiatrists were saying before the Fulbright Committee yesterday—that part of the price of involvement in a war is the attitudes that the war builds up, that you can't demonstrate because it gives aid and comfort to the enemy. "Why don't you go with the Vietcong if you really feel so strongly about the Vietcong?" And any kind of criticism is unpopular with a lot of people—particularly those who have suffered some *personal* misfortune in the war, who have lost a son, lost a brother, lost a father, something like this. I would hope we would have moved beyond this, but we haven't. And it seems to me it's a part of the public responsibility of leaders, mayors, presidents, if you please, to insist that we *need* this kind of criticism.

FINN: I presume that the President would refer to some of these people as "nervous Nellies." It doesn't help to calm the kind of violent reaction which is visited upon them.

DEATS: No it doesn't, and he's done this two or three times. But when he includes in his nervous Nellies everybody from the CNVA people to Hans Morgenthau and J. W. Fulbright, then he's covered a pretty good range of territory. I think you have to ask what are the grounds upon which people make their protests and have their demonstrations? I'm sure that there are kooks with the pacifist movement, and with the protesters.

I'm sure that there are people who are interested in protesting, and they'll take any banner that's handed them. This is *not* true of a vast number of people, though, who are critical of the Vietnam policy, and I would hope that the pacifists among them try to maintain some sense of balance and responsibility.

How do you evaluate the demonstrations? My wife and I have had some *real* arguments on this one. Both of us have a very warm, sympathetic, immediate response to the kind of courage and to the fidelity, the faithfulness of the witness of these boys in CNVA. I don't particularly like some of their methods, their haircuts, their beards, and so on. These simply don't *help* their protest. I'd like something much more *strategic*. And I can't take *as* absolute a position as they do, as John Phillips takes when he says, "I simply want no police protection, I want to confront my attackers." This may assign them a vocational pacifist role, and I'm not happy with this. I think the problem a lot of us who are interested in protesting face is how do you get the public to think about issues? I think it's David Riesman who said that in an age when people no longer are interested in ideas you have to have the shock of events to make people think. Now in the civil rights movement we learned about the shock of events. The Aldermaston Marches and all this sort of thing have been attempts to call people's attention to the evil, to get them to think. Now I'm not sure—we've done no empirical testing that I know of—we need people to ask about the effect of a demonstration. I'm not sure that these things are really conducive to better public discussion. But we don't know *how* to get better public discussion.

Let me comment specifically on one thing. In the Oregon primary race for a U.S. Senate seat, Mr. Duncan attributed part of his victory to the fact that there was no alternative presented. He said *nobody* who's protesting our involvement in Vietnam ever presents an alternative policy. I think what he and what the President and what Mr. Rusk mean is that they don't present an alternative policy that we can buy. But there *have* been alternative policies.

FINN: Alternative policies that the President and Rusk can buy?

DEATS: Yes, and I think they dismiss these too easily. On the other hand, I confess to you that the most telling criticism that I think the protesters have had made of them is this: if

Paul Deats

the academics were to give as much serious attention to alternative policy proposals as they have to drumming up protest activity on its own, then they would be making a much more significant contribution.

FINN: You said earlier you didn't read much pacifist literature. I take it this means you don't look for the development of ideas or even support of your own position in the pacifist material that's written.

DEATS: I find some of the pacifist material intended, it seems to me, for public relations purposes, for recruiting purposes. I don't get very excited about this. Some of it is doctrinaire; I don't get very excited about this. Some of it is more anecdotal, and I don't even get very excited about this. To say I don't read the pacifist material does not mean that I give a lot more attention to reading material by Paul Ramsey or by the radical nonpacifists. I try to read material from some social scientists and others who are trying to do empirical and theoretical work on problems of human behavior which ought to cast some light on problems of war and peace; then I try to reflect theologically and ethically on what these kinds of things say. I think, for example, I can get some guidance from Herman Kahn, although I don't read him regularly. But I think Osgood and Jerome Frank, those men who are appearing today, can offer some good insights about what kinds of things we ought to be taking account of in our planning.

I guess I'm caught really in a marginal man's role on this. I have resisted involvement in the Church Peace Mission, where a group of representatives from the peace churches get together to ask how we'll make a better theological attack upon nationalism, upon the aggrandizement of the nation state, and this kind of thing. This seems to me to be a part of the group soliloquy we were talking about a while ago. On the other hand, I've had uneasy feelings whenever I've been involved in CRIA [Council on Religion and International Affairs] because it seems to me CRIA—if you'll forgive me—has given too many hostages to obtaining influence, to being in on the councils of power. And I find only a scattering of people who are, as I am, committed for a long time to seeking pacifist and nonviolent alternatives but who try to resist doing this in a doctrinaire manner and try to learn from a variety of sources to which we can turn to get some really imaginative and creative possibilities for new developments. Because I don't think the old pacifist/nonpacifist debates will get us very far.

FINN: Have you found any place *to* turn?

DEATS: I think one of the most amazing developments, for example, is *Christianity and Crisis,* especially the anniversary issue that they put out. Here was a journal founded twenty-five years ago to find an alternative Christian social involvement which was not pacifist; this was its presupposition. And now it takes a *lead* in the struggle, journalistically, against our involvement in Vietnam. Some of the nuclear pacifists, it seems to me, are most helpful. John Bennett seems to be really wrestling with the problems and every once in a while comes up with a *new* idea. Howard Schomer's a pacifist I'm willing to listen to, a long-time pacifist. But all this is to say that I find the *Christianity and Crisis*-John Bennett *kind* of orientation these days much more congenial to my way of thinking than it used to be. And I'm sure this means both of us have moved.

FINN: You said you reflect ethically and theologically upon some of the statements written by those who are working as scientists or social scientists. Robert Tucker at Johns Hopkins University has written on the just war, and in one of the manuscripts he prepared recently he said that—and I'm recalling what you said earlier about the position you attacked before you were a pacifist—he said that you cannot find on historical grounds any proof that you cannot achieve good by doing evil. He said at least it's open to serious debate and contention. If you believe that evil means never produce good ends, you're arguing on faith, not something open to empirical investigation and proof. Is that a statement you would accept?

DEATS: This is a very involved question. First, I don't know many cases where you have completely evil means and a completely good end; rather, you've probably got mingled good in ends and means. And this makes the historical sorting out much more difficult and much more complicated. I think I could adduce some historical evidence, but at least my commitment is to the belief that you've got the interpenetration of ends and means, and you can't just use any old means to achieve ends because the kinds of means you choose will affect the ends that you do achieve. Therefore it seems to me there is a moral obligation upon us to select *those* means which are most consistent

Paul Deats

with—in intent and in practice and in consequences—with ends we're seeking. The conscious selection of evil means will even further corrupt the ends.

FINN: This is a point that I think would be worth coming to because, after stating that, Tucker said that the nation acts on the basis that nothing is superior to reasons of state. Therefore, faced with some concept like the just war, if the state finds what it regards as its real interest in conflict with an essential principle of that concept, the politically prudential judgment will rule in favor of the state.

DEATS: This has all the earmarks to me of a mythical statement. That is, this is the way nations do operate, therefore—and it tends to be a prospective myth—therefore whatever the security of the state, whatever the interest of the nation demands, we will do it. And there is a presumption that you can separate one nation's interest and one nation's good from the interests of other nations. Now it seems to me both ethically and I think to some extent empirically there is hope that persons *can* detect, discover, an interest which transcends this state, the interest of a particular nation, and there is at least some hope that persons can act with the larger interest in view.

And with these comments we have come to the threshold of an issue on which people markedly and emotionally differ— the concept of national interest. About this Hans Morgenthau has written: "The controversy which has arisen since the end of the Second World War around the concept of the national interest differs from the great historical debates on American foreign policy in that it raises not necessarily a specific issue of American foreign policy but the fundamental issue of the nature of all foreign policy and of all politics as well."* There are two general approaches to this concept that represent two strongly opposing types of political morality. Although some political theorists disclaim allegiance to either school and some are consciously trying to transcend them, one can, with a degree of justice, assign most political theories to either the "realist" or the "utopian" tradition. The basic conflict between adherents to

* *Politics in the Twentieth Century*, Vol. I: *The Decline of Democratic Politics* (Chicago, University of Chicago Press, 1962), p. 79.

these schools admits of no ready compromise, for it derives from varying ideas of man and the nature of his society.

Briefly, the realist tends to emphasize the limitations and weakness of man and the temptations to which he is prey. The conflicts inherent in individual behavior are magnified in group behavior and the restraints are fewer. The realist appeals to history both to support his contention and to find measures that will help check and balance the inevitable conflict of interests. The utopian or idealist stresses the potentiality of man to realize that just society which his reason can elaborate. Injustices will yield to increased understanding and better planning. Universally abstract principles will inform moral and legal codes superior to those of ages past as there is an increasing realization that this is the political destiny of man.

Among the people commonly regarded as realists—in addition to Hans Morgenthau—are Dean Acheson, Reinhold Niebuhr, and George Kennan. After professional immersion in foreign affairs for over a quarter of a century Kennan wrote that one of the greatest deficiencies in the legalistic approach to international affairs "is the inevitable association of legalistic ideas with moral ones: the carrying over into the affairs of state of the concepts of right and wrong, the assumption that state behavior is a fit subject for moral judgment."* (It is because of statements like this that many people find Kennan an exceedingly fit subject for moral judgment.) But it is salutary to see how he invokes the concept of national interest. He wrote, for example, that if we are to get away from the dangerous goal of "total victory":

"It will mean that we will have the modesty to admit that our own national interest is all that we are really capable of knowing and understanding—and the courage to recognize that if our purposes and undertakings here at home are decent ones, unsullied by arrogance or hostility toward other people or delusions of superiority, then the pursuit of our national interest can never fail to be conducive to a better world. This concept is less ambitious and less inviting in its immediate prospect than those to which we are so often inclined, and less pleasing to our image of ourselves. To many it may seem to smack of cynicism and re-

* *American Diplomacy, 1900–1950* (New York, Mentor, 1960), p. 87.

Paul Deats

action. I cannot share these doubts. Whatever is realistic in concept, and founded in an endeavor to see both ourselves and others as we really are, cannot be illiberal."*

There are many who write in opposition to these views, but one of the sharpest expressions of difference I have found is in a work of political philosophy by a young, vigorous thinker, Leslie Dewart. He writes: "The conditions that have made international justice indispensable to the continuation of human life demand a somewhat broader conception of the right order among human beings than was possible at a time when, for instance, international justice and some type of war were not incompatible. . . . Henceforth we can only be guided in international politics by the widest loyalty to the whole of mankind. We have become one world. What we need to do for our own good, collectively and severally, is to recognize this truth and to act upon it. This is the political vocation of the Christian citizen in our time." †

Variants of these positions were to appear in the conversations I had with other people. It should be noted that one cannot always infer the policies a person will support from the school to which he belongs. Morgenthau, for example, has become a favorite spokesman for many pacifists because his analysis of the Vietnam war in terms of our national interest dictates a policy which, from a quite different vantage point, they find praiseworthy. Alliances such as this are temporary, shifting as the political scene is reordered.

While the realists have been in the ascendency for years, there is now a growing dissatisfaction with some of their "pessimistic" formulations. But the lessons they have taught have been learned too well to allow an easy return to the inadequate moralisms of the past. It is this uneasy dissatisfaction that Deats has been expressing.

DEATS: I think I have to back up and say something in answer to the question you've just been pushing. We've been operating for the last thirty-five years in ethics, I guess almost everyone in the Christian world, with an underlying notion of Reinhold Niebuhr's contrast between moral and immoral society—that

---

* *Ibid.,* pp. 88–89.

† *Christianity and Revolution* (New York, Herder and Herder, 1963), pp. 284–85.

really men acting in groups consider only the interests of the group and there's no viable way of transcending it. Now I just have a suspicion—maybe it's a hope—that this is not all that can be said about group life and group activity. I *know,* on at least some levels, that groups can enable people to do things against what they take to be their own interest. And maybe groups can enable them to do things against the interests of the group, *if* they have a conception of a more inclusive loyalty, a more inclusive group to which they're committed. I see no reason *in principle* why the nation state is an exception to this.

One of the things that bothers me is that people who have taken this *most* seriously—the moral man-immoral society thesis —are those who argue on the basis of interests of state. There are people who argue on the principle that order is the primary value. If I may refer to the discussions the American Society for Christian Ethics had on wars of national liberation and the papers which you reprinted in *Worldview*—in the discussion I tried to challenge Paul Ramsey and said, "Paul, it seems to me that the basic assumption that you work on in most of your ethics is that order is *the* primal value." He said, "Yes, this is true."

FINN: He didn't say that it was order for the *sake* of justice?

DEATS: No, he said order is primary. I guess if you had pressed him he would have gone on to say "You can't have justice without order," but it becomes the *basic* value. And this, I think, is at least operational even if it is not professed. Now I'm saying the bias *toward* order really corrupts a lot of our analyses; we assume that things have to go on as near the way they are as possible. I tried to suggest also that in the notion of a responsible society which the World Council of Churches has been exploring (though it hasn't explored it very much in terms of what it means in the international area) involves freedom and justice and equality as well as order, and involves some procedural restraints which you might call counsels of prudence. But it may be that once you break the myths—or as Harvey Cox would say, once you de-sacralize the myth of order—you have a place for people to say "All right, the particular order which we know now, which we cherish and to which we have some commitments, may have to go, it may have to be changed —because we also really believe in freedom, we also really believe in equality, and there's a tension between these. And there-

Paul Deats

fore the order, or the disorder of the present world, which leaves us with such tremendous military power in this country, is an enemy of equality, an enemy of freedom, and finally, an enemy of justice. And therefore we may have to recognize that there are going to have to be some *serious curtailments* of American power and influence."

I've taken your question a long ways around, I know. I guess what I'm saying is that I resist assent to Tucker's thesis if it's a statement of descriptive fact that nations tend to act on the basis of interests of state and tend to value order more than they value certain other goods.

FINN: Well, do we have any historical example of a government endangering its own security because of some proclaimed moral principle?

DEATS: I simply cannot answer the historical question at the *state* level, but I think probably it's at the nation state that the immoral-society thesis really comes home. Let me refer in terms of the industrial realm. In a recent speech one of the executives of the Xerox corporation, Sol Linowitz,* said, "Xerox is coming to recognize that its viability as an economic institution depends on certain political decisions and the way these political decisions are structured. Therefore we have a *stake* in a world in which orderly change is possible and in which the development of underdeveloped nations is made possible. Therefore it's a question of our asking: 'What is the kind of a world in which there will be a possibility for growth and development of Xerox as a corporation?' " He did *not* say, "What is the interest of Xerox?" Now it seems to me this phrasing of the question is very important. If a modern industrial corporation can ask this question, I see no reason why a nation state can't. What's the kind of a world in which there's the best hope for the people of this state to have a viable existence?

FINN: Yes, of course that's what Dean Acheson and Dean Rusk both say, but. . . .

DEATS: But we come out with radically different ideas on this.

* Sol M. Linowitz was later in the year given a double government assignment. He is serving as Ambassador to the Organization of American States and as President Johnson's representative in the Inter-American Committee for the Alliance for Progress.

PAUL PEACHEY

The historic "peace churches" in the United States are generally considered to include the Mennonites (instituted in sixteenth-century Switzerland), the Friends or Quakers (seventeenth-century England) and the Brethren (eighteenth-century Germany). Because of their emphasis on nonviolence they have traditionally provided the most consistent resistance to war, the most unrelenting criticism, and, of course, the greatest percentage of conscientious objectors.

Paul Peachey, a Mennonite, was born in Elk Lick, Pennsylvania in 1918. After receiving degrees from Eastern Mennonite College in Virginia, he continued his graduate studies at the University of Pennsylvania, the University of Basel, the University of Frankfort, and the Sorbonne. He received his Ph.D. *cum laude* from the University of Zurich. These years of study were interrupted by postwar emergency relief work in Belgium and Germany. He has traveled not only in Western and Eastern Europe but in the Soviet Union, East Asia and Japan.

A professor of sociology and church history, he has taught in a number of universities including the University of Maryland and the Catholic University of America. In addition to his many articles he has written *The Church in the City* and has translated from the German Heinrich Dumoulin's *A History of Zen Buddhism*.

At the time I speak with Paul Peachey he is executive officer of the Church Peace Mission,* a small national agency engaged

* The sponsoring groups of the Church Peace Mission include the American Friends Service Committee, Baptist Peace Fellowship, Church

Paul Peachey

in interdisciplinary studies and workshops on churches and international problems; but, he tells me, he is soon to accept a position as executive secretary of the Mennonite Committee on Peace and Social Concepts.

Peachey ascribes the formation and strength of his present pacifist beliefs first, to the fact that he is a Mennonite and was brought up in a classic peace-church position, and second, to his experiences in the Relief Program of the Mennonite Central Committee in Europe. Both of these facts were connected with the scholarly and academic interests he pursued during and after World War II.

During the thirties a German Protestant research society had begun a systematic program to publish the sixteenth-century documents of the Anabaptist movement, which includes the Mennonites—largely documents of religious dissent. The war brought a halt to this project in Germany, but it also "occasioned a good deal of reflection and discussion about whether we were really a peace church." When Peachey went to Europe after the war, he completed his dissertation on the sociological aspects of the origin of the Anabaptists and worked with people who were "creeping out from the ruins of war." He lived for twenty months in Belgium, where he spent long hours with people who suffered under the Gestapo, before he went to work and study in Germany.

In distributing food and supplies to Germans through the Mennonite Committee, Peachey and others formed friendships with German clergy out of which developed continuing discussions about "the whole problem of church and state in Germany—the close tie between church and altar, and the fact that there is a demonic potential in the state." Two other things happened at this time. First, representatives of the Quakers, Mennonites and the Brethren who were working on relief teams began to meet periodically "to share experiences, frequently dealing

of the Brethren Service Commission, Disciples Peace Fellowship, Episcopal Pacifist Fellowship, Fellowship of Reconciliation, Five Years Meeting of Friends, Friends General Conference, Friends Peace Committee, Lutheran Peace Fellowship, Mennonite Central Committee, Reformed Church Peace Fellowship, United Church of Christ Peace Fellowship, United Presbyterian Peace Fellowship, and Southern Presbyterian Peace Fellowship.

with questions of war and peace." Second, the World Council of Churches was formed in 1948 and recognized as a sizeable problem the fact that the members of different denominations had difficulty meeting in intercommunion but were "perfectly prepared to go out and shoot each other."

The peace churches urged the National Council to consider seriously the problems of war and peace. Dr. Visser t' Hooft, then General Secretary of the Council, said, in Peachey's paraphrase, "O.K. Bring us a theological document that can become the basis for discussion." In response the three peace churches and the Fellowship of Reconciliation produced separate statements and put them in a pamphlet entitled "War Is Contrary to the Will of God." Visser t' Hooft said, "That's fine, but if you peace churches can't get together, what do you expect me to do?" The peace churches then decided that their differences were so great that a common statement was impossible. But the small group that had been working together in Europe accepted this as a challenge and produced, under Peachey's authorship, a pamphlet entitled "Peace Is the Will of God." This was not only sent on to Council in Geneva but it became the stimulus for the continuing Puidoux Conferences (named after a town in Switzerland) that involve the peace churches and mainline Reformation churches.

In our conversation Peachey had talked about the demonic potential of the state. But other people, as he knows, have talked as readily about the demonic potential in the churches, pointing out that the church is sometimes able to act with arrogance and pride and to assume a superiority which it doesn't have and hasn't earned and which, when it intruded into political affairs, can often be harmful. I ask him if this is seen as a problem within the Mennonite tradition.

PEACHEY: The question is unresolved in our own group. So far as the ecclesiology of the Anabaptist and Mennonite movement was concerned, this issue was really very central to the whole protest at the time, and in modern times we've had a great deal of agony over this. It is sobering indeed that even our very small Mennonite community—small compared, say, to the Catholic Church—has exactly the same problem with the demonic that larger bodies may have.

Paul Peachey

And this point is crucial for Mennonites. You see, originally there was a good deal of distinction made between those functions of a political nature which are related to the sword. It was to these that objection was raised initially, and not to the state in toto. But when the state began suppressing the movement by violent means, then the positions hardened. Mennonites began to say, "We'll have nothing to do with the political, period." In modern times there are Mennonites who are quite gullible in economic affairs, unaware of the demonic dangers in economic organization, in corporations; they are safe because they are not "political." But they would get up on their hind feet if a Mennonite would hold a political office or become active politically, even though this could be a very limited and justifiable kind of operation. Thus the demonic potential is ignored not only in the churches but in all nonpolitical spheres.

FINN: Speaking earlier you mentioned a group that wanted to have the best of both possible worlds, where political demands and moral imperatives would nicely dovetail or coincide; what was morally desirable would also be politically desirable. And you mentioned liberal Protestant ministers who thought this was a possibility. I presume from your own comments that you do not see this blooming as an immediate historical possibility.

PEACHEY: No, but this doesn't mean that one doesn't work at it, or that in limited ways progress is not possible. I think that it's a tragedy of the inter-war pacifism—the pacifism of the thirties—that it succumbed to optimistic temptation which is part of the American ethos. I remember a book of Donald Meyer, *Protestant Search for Political Realism*—it's the best thing I know on this period—which analyzed the commitment which the Protestant clergy made in the 1930's when many thousands signed pledges that they would never again support a war. Meyer observes that while these men signed sincerely, they nonetheless signed on the assumption that they would not again face the temptation to support a war. To sign was further to forestall this danger. And I think it's something that would figure in this discussion: the extent to which people either become pacifist or take a pacifist position on a particular issue on the assumption that it will be possible, in an idealistic fashion, to coordinate moral considerations and policy imperatives in such a way that we can have the best of both worlds. I think this is a very great peril.

What it means is that people have an oversimplified view of what the political possibility is; they don't recognize the real dangers. They don't realize the price that is really involved in radical Christian commitment. This is harmful both in terms of what the Christian witness is about and in terms of power politics at the point where it is operating, and operating in some real sense outside the lordship of Christ. I do not know, and we may not know for several years, how moral and prudential considerations intersect at this point.

But I think that anyone seriously concerned about the relation of the churches to the international struggle, whether pacifist or nonpacifist, should give serious attention to the question that a few people are beginning to raise now: Is this new pacifism in danger of the same kind of superficiality that became the bane of the movement in the thirties? And I'm not in a position at all to make a judgment on it. I'm sure that the immediate specifics surrounding this movement are different. People are more outraged about a specific issue. Nor is their opposition to the war in Vietnam rooted in a utopian scheme of human betterment, the kind of thing which was prevalent during the interwar period. Perhaps in the end my fear may not be justified.

If there's any purpose in a pacifist-nonpacifist conversation today, it would certainly be at this point. Because I think here, from both sides, we could begin to smoke out some basic issues. In other words, a nonpacifist, particularly in the old hardheaded realist tradition, would be able to put hard questions to the new pacifists and the old and discern the points at which their pacifism might be a superficial sort of growth.

But on the other hand, it's pretty important that the nonpacifists recognize that there are times when a moral change is possible, and that a society may be even in more danger of a doctrinaire repetition of "Remember Munich" in order to justify what's going on. I'm just as much afraid of that as I am of softness in pacifist thought. In purely practical terms, this illustrates the necessity for reviving what we haven't had for some years now, a really serious pacifist-nonpacifist conversation.

FINN: What do you see as the benefits of a good, fruitful pacifist-nonpacifist conversation for the society at large?

PEACHEY: I think it would be of value in various ways. One would be to clarify the issue for people who are concerned with these things and who make decisions. But mainly—having lived

Paul Peachey

these five years in Washington and occasionally participating in discussion and conferences—I am much disturbed at the way in which to use a shorthand expression, "realism" (Niebuhr) has gone to seed among some theorists. As nearly as I can tell, the formula that Reinhold Niebuhr and his associates worked out in the thirties and forties has become a kind of arid record that's laid on and played over and over again. I'm reminded of the observation of historians that the generals always prepare to fight the previous war, and so we hear a doctrinaire repetition of ideas like "Remember Munich"—we've heard a great deal of this from Secretary Rusk lately. From a Christian, theological point of view, I'm convinced that the tragedy of the pacifist-nonpacifist split is that it always ends debate when it is only at the point of deadlock that a real exploration could begin. Only at that point can we begin to understand the profound and complex dimensions of human history, of human destiny. And if at the point where we disagree we assume that ends the conversation, we cut off the possibility of a breakthrough.

John C. Bennett did this in his book on *Nuclear Weapons and the Conflict of Conscience.** In the introduction he comments that he didn't include a pacifist in the book because we know what his answer is before he begins. That observation has troubled me ever since because I think it's a mistake. But it also means that the pacifists have been sufficiently abstruse or ineffective in what they have done, that they haven't been a fruitful conversational partner. I think this is disastrous for everybody.

FINN: You say that responsibility for what you regard as an obvious failure is shared here?

PEACHEY: Right.

FINN: Now what would you yourself foresee as possible? What would you regard as progress? Not only in terms of conversations between pacifists and nonpacifists; what would you regard as progress for those people who share your own position? What, realistically, do you think you could hope for in terms of a program?

PEACHEY: I don't think that I would relate my commitment to a formula of an overall kind in which I could say, "Well, if we pursue this policy long enough we can have a warless world."

* New York, Charles Scribner's Sons, 1962.

I don't think that this is a framework that one can find in the biblical materials which I would hope to live by and be informed by. I think that a great deal of progress is possible. Working for the peaceful resolution of conflict, developing the instrumentalities for it, removing the occasions, solving the problems that lead to war—these are all things that in a non-utopian fashion we have to work at. And in these tasks, Christians ought to count.

I accept, however, the biblical assumption that somehow, whatever it is, the "Fall" is a reality, and history certainly demonstrates this repeatedly. We take this realistically so that what we need is a recovery of the biblical way of thinking about power. I'm surprised at the paganism of all of us in this respect —or call it secularism or what you will. We talk a great deal about power. We talk about our Judeo-Christian heritage. But the principal categories, and the depth dimensions underlying these concepts and categories, are largely absent from our discourse. That's one of the things that we have been working at a bit in the Church Peace Mission. Progress is enormously slow, but we do have a small project under way at present in which we are working with *Interpretation,* a biblical quarterly published in Virginia. Papers are to be written by biblical, theological and behavioral scholars as an attempt to see whether some of the recent language about power in biblical studies can be translated into the contemporary political idiom. The Bible, after all, is an intensely political book.

CATHOLICS

JOHN L. MC KENZIE, S.J.

An English Catholic philosopher, J. M. Cameron, has commented that Catholics tend to be devotees of a political fetishism that "gives to the commands of the state, notably where matters of war and peace are in question, a sacred and unchallengeable character, with the result that in this area of political life there is a tacit understanding that traditional moral principles are not to be applied . . . where the security of the state is held to be in question (held to be in question, that is, by the political authorities themselves), too often a guilty silence descends. General principles may still be enunciated, but awkward or potentially treasonable applications are avoided."

Does this statement apply to American Catholics? There is much evidence that it does. There is not, within modern Catholicism, the strong pacific current that one can find within Protestant and Jewish traditions. This is not without tangible political consequences. According to a Gallup poll of September 1966, Catholic support for the President's Vietnam policy significantly exceeded Protestant and Jewish support.* In addition, while many influential and highly placed Protestant and Jewish leaders have early and vigorously dissented from Vietnam policy, Catholic bishops have been reluctant to do so.

*	Approve present policy	Disapprove	No opinion
Jews	41%	41%	18%
Protestants	39	43	18
Catholics	54	31	15

* This statement is not meant to imply unanimity where none ex-

Thus, Catholics who criticize present policy in Vietnam are running against an even stronger tide than are other Americans. One of these Catholics is Father John L. McKenzie, S.J. This is not the only tide that John McKenzie has breasted, as his remarkable career illustrates. Acknowledged dean of American Catholic biblical scholars, past president of the Catholic Biblical Association and current president of the interdenominational Society for Biblical Literature and Exegesis, he has no degree in scriptural studies. Born in Brazil, Indiana in 1910, he entered the Society of Jesus in 1928 and was ordained in 1939. After receiving a doctorate in theology he was Professor of the Old Testament at West Baden College, and the Jesuit theologate for the Chicago province, from 1942 to 1960. For the next five years he taught at Loyola University and then became visiting professor at the University of Chicago Divinity School, the first Roman Catholic priest to have the position.

The war prevented Father McKenzie from attending the renowned European centers for scriptural studies, but not from mastering twelve ancient and modern languages and the tools of biblical scholarship. He has published highly acclaimed books

---

ists. Within limits there has been a range of opinions expressed. Cardinal Francis Spellman at one time recalled with approval Stephan Decatur's, "Our country right or wrong," a disastrous principle. Cardinal Richard Cushing of Boston has spoken out in support of U.S. policy. Cardinal Lawrence Shehan of Baltimore has publicly recalled the need for moral restraints in war, but he did not suggest that they had been transgressed in Vietnam. Archbishop Paul J. Hallinan and Bishop Joseph L. Bernardin of Atlanta, Georgia, issued a pastoral letter on "War and Peace" urging Catholics to speak out and protest "whenever there is danger that our conduct of war will exceed moral limits," but did not presume to comment on the conduct of the present war. Bishop John J. Wright of Pittsburgh is a co-chairman of the National Inter-Religious Conference on Peace, which has spoken out strongly on Vietnam.

During the summer of 1967, a small number of bishops voiced their protests openly. Four bishops—Archbishop Paul J. Hallinan of Atlanta, Bishop Victor Reed of Oklahoma City–Tulsa, Auxiliary Bishop John Dougherty of Newark and Auxiliary Bishop James Shannon of St. Paul–Minneapolis—endorsed Negotiation Now, a national drive that calls for "new initiatives to bring about negotiations" and an unconditional end to the bombing of North Vietnam. Bishop Wright supported but did not sign the statement of Negotiation Now. Quite independently the flamboyant Bishop of Rochester, Fulton J. Sheen, called for the immediate withdrawal of U.S. troops from Vietnam.

John L. McKenzie, S.J.

on both the Old and the New Testament and an impressive 800,000-word *Dictionary of the Bible*. Most recently he published *Authority in the Church,* in which he argues that the prestige of ecclesiastical authority has been lost because of, for example, the conflicting positions of American bishops on segregation, the refusal to discuss the question of birth control openly and to allow laymen a serious voice, the covert and irresponsible censorship, and the great institutional pomp and accumulated wealth of the Church.

All priest-scholars must have their work read by appointed censors before publication; McKenzie's are also first read in Rome. "The practice of censorship," he said, "is basically immoral and irrational." Such tart observations are frequent in his disciplined, aphoristic writing. In his scholarly work on the New Testament he comments that the student who compares the treatment of chastity found there with that in modern literature "may be tempted to ask himself whether chastity has not replaced charity as the basic Christian virtue." With such credentials it is not surprising that John McKenzie has himself been a subject of controversy. He is a man of convictions, arrived at through observation and reflection—and faith.

The campus of the University of Chicago is familiar from my own years there and I have no trouble finding Calvert House, the center for Catholic student activities, where Father McKenzie has a study. He remembers his appointment but he momentarily forgets with whom or for what purpose. As he settles into a chair I set up the recorder and recall the intent of our meeting. He is prepared to plunge into discussion, and I learn almost immediately that he will say what he thinks, directly and incisively. He tends to speak in phrases; there are pauses for thought and then a rush of words.

MC KENZIE: I think that war is essentially irrational. And immoral. It's essentially irrational because violence, by definition, is not a solution of *human* questions. It might defend me against a wild animal, but unless I reduce the human being to a wild animal, I'm not settling any issue that exists between us. The human way to solve human problems is rational discourse. Violence is used on the assumption that rational discourse *won't* solve the problem, and it won't solve the problem because one or both of the parties refuse to engage in it. Now I'm not sure that this assumption is verified.*

FINN: So you're saying that we really had not exhausted resources that were available before we resorted to war in the past.

MC KENZIE: Cynically, I'd say we haven't even begun to tap them, let alone exhaust 'em. But let's keep the rhetoric out of it. Simply that war is by tradition and modern theory an extension of politics. And it's accepted that way. So it's a use of means which, in civilized countries, have long been abandoned as a means of settling *personal* differences. I do not see how it is any better as a solution of *national* differences, since it does involve the refusal of rational discourse and puts the issues not on any reasonable or moral basis, but simply on the basis of brute strength.

FINN: But if one party in a dispute does act in this irrational way, does refuse any discourse because he thinks the only way he can gain is by violence, what is left open to the other contending party?

MC KENZIE: Well, there are two ways of looking at it. One way would be to think that the party which does believe in rational discourse has an even greater obligation to sustain it. The other way is to say that because one man refuses to engage in discourse, or is alleged to refuse it, I am therefore excused from continuing to act rationally and may drop to what I say is *his* irrational level myself.

FINN: You are *not* excused?

MC KENZIE: Well, what does a nation say when it refuses discourse because it says the other party will not join, except to say that because *he* is irrational it is now rational for *me* to be

* Some time after this interview I encountered in an essay by Walter Stein, a leading English pacifist, this quotation from Machiavelli: "You must know, then, that there are two methods of fighting, the one by law, the other by force: the first method is that of men, the second of beasts; but as the first method is often insufficient, one must have recourse to the second." Mr. Stein observes that "we owe Machiavelli some gratitude for never confusing the names of things." Walter Stein, ed., *Peace on Earth: The Way Ahead* (London, Sheed & Ward, 1966), p. 2.

John L. McKenzie, S.J.

irrational too? Because he won't rise to my level, I'm going to descend to his.

FINN: Well, is it necessarily *irrational* to resort to what you know is an irrational action. I mean, I think most people would agree that war is evidently irrational.

MC KENZIE: Um . . . yes, they do, by the way, nobody challenges that. They say we *have* to do it.

FINN: Yes. And most people today, even people who are drawn toward a pacifist position or *see* the irrationality of war and see the possibilities of utter destruction, still keep World War II in mind as a challenge to or restriction on their sympathies here because they see nothing else that would have stopped Hitler's expansion.

MC KENZIE: Um huh. Well, if anybody wants to give me World War II as a way in which international problems were rationally and humanely resolved, I'll be glad to listen to an explanation—but not very long. Let us say that if the price of the war and its consequences were what you had to pay to get rid of Hitler, it might have been better to sit down and think whether he could have been tolerated. This is not to say that there is anything very defensible, I'm afraid, about National Socialism. It wasn't. But the idea that you could divide the world into National Socialism on one side and all the good guys on the other is . . . well, it's just so stupid, you can't even laugh at it.

FINN: And I presume you say it's equally stupid to say this about dividing the good guys and bad guys on the basis of communism, anti-communism, with some neutrals in between?

MC KENZIE: I'm not very well *satisfied* with the way that it's dealt with. If one wanted to talk about, say, the containment of communism—not the use of violence but the calculated threat of violence—as a citizen who is supposed to take responsibility in what his government does—or at least used to be supposed to, I'm not so sure the government still thinks that I *should*— I would have to say that the containment of communism, as a policy, is something completely out of whack. I can't possibly rationalize it. It's not being contained, really; they don't know what containment means. They've drawn an artificial line, which I suppose originally was drawn more or less by agreement with these beastly Communists. Neither side has seemed to be satisfied with it, but each feels that they ought to *honor* the engagement—which, quite candidly, I think most historians in the future will view as an agreement between thieves.

FINN: It may be foolish to ask you how you would resolve a situation that is already as messy as Vietnam, but do you have even a kind of general suggestion about the *direction* that a policy could take?

MC KENZIE: Well, I don't know whether as a responsible citizen I have to think up a foreign policy. I should think that to produce a foreign policy I should have at least some of the resources the President has to produce one. So you ought to elect me President and give me my choice of Secretary of State and his staff. I will then make an effort to come up with a foreign policy. At the moment I am in the position of the voter who says, "I don't like it and therefore I'll vote against it."

FINN: Do you think that is the position of most citizens today? Most of us do *not* have resources anywhere near what the President or Secretary of. . . .

MC KENZIE: Of course not. And that's why foreign policy suggestions made by amateurs *don't* sound very impressive. They are made usually from a very slender basis of information. Let us not forget that one reason why the basis is slender is because the government has consistently lied about Vietnam since 1954. How is a citizen supposed to be informed when that's the kind of information or misinformation he gets from his elected leaders?

No government is immune to the corrosive effects of widespread distrust, but a democratic government is more susceptible than others. And charges of evasion, deception and lying have been brought against the present Administration so pointedly and so consistently that Ambassador Arthur Goldberg speaks of a "crisis of credibility," and others of a "credibility gap." Is this simply confirmation of U Thant's comment that "in times of war and hostility the first casualty is truth," or is something more involved? Something involving *this* war and *this* Administration?

The issue is not simple. When Arthur Sylvester, then Assistant Secretary of Defense for Public Affairs, stated after the Cuban

John L. McKenzie, S.J.

blockade of 1962 that the nation had a right "to lie to save it-self," he stirred up a hornet's nest of reaction. Yet he only stated, in however impolitic a fashion, what every political leader of a great country has acted upon in times of stress. Every country must, on occasion, conduct some of its operations in secret. The Cuban missile crisis is an excellent example. In order for the U.S. to bring to a politically and militarily successful conclusion the strategy it had outlined, an array of misleading statements was released from various government sources. And those members of the press who learned of the operation maintained secrecy. For these statements and actions both the politician and the moral casuist have more palatable terms than the harsh description of "lies" that Mr. Sylvester employed.

It is easy, and common, to say that such lies are necessary, and therefore right. It is almost as easy to say that such lies are wrong, and cannot therefore be necessary. Untroubled by qualification or nuance, both positions are dangerous. Accepted as unqualified principles, the first statement leads to cynicism and contempt for the citizenry, the second to a continually frustrated moralism and contempt for the government.

It is essential, for any adequate approach to these problems, that the citizen have a general understanding of the conditions within which they must be considered and judged. But there must also be an understanding, running from the President to the citizen, that no set of conditions will justify a continuing series of official statements that are intended to deceive not only other nations but the country's own citizens. It is this understanding that the Johnson Administration is charged with violating.* These are some of my reflections on the issues raised by

* The list of those who have accused the Johnson Administration of deception is impressive both in number and quality. One of the strongest accusations by a responsible and knowledgeable critic was made by James Reston in the *New York Times* in the spring of 1966. "The Johnson Administration may finally get over its agony in Vietnam—it may even achieve its military objective in the end—but it will probably never regain the confidence it has lost in its judgment and veracity.

"With the bombing of targets on the outskirts of Hanoi and Haiphong, it has now done almost everything it said or indicated it would not do except bomb China, and the end of this melancholy chapter in American history is not yet over. . . . Even when allowances are made for the uncertainties and moral ambiguities of warfare, the guile of this

Father McKenzie and the basis of some of my questions to him. But as we discussed the relation of the Christian citizen to the state I was to find that his reading of the Bible led him to political judgments much more stringent than my own.

FINN: What is the possibility of a citizen who *wants* to be informed playing any proper, responsible role?

MC KENZIE: Well I don't know how he's going to make himself informed. Most of us have to work for a living and we can't make this a full-time job. You hope that the citizen can handle this thing if he's a reading man by reading some newspapers and journals which are respected and getting enough of a variety of opinion for him to weigh one opinion against another. On this question that's been extremely difficult. Extremely difficult.

FINN: I presume when you said earlier "if one is dissatisfied with our present foreign policy and wishes to vote against it," it appeared to you that there is little choice in voting.

MC KENZIE: Oh, definitely. You really have no place to go— at least it hasn't appeared *yet*. Consequently people who are opposed to it are pretty much limited to the use of publicity. In other words, what they try to do is to alter the popular consensus. Now this is a process which ought to be recognized as a constitutional, law-abiding thing and all that, but I understand that people who make too much noise in trying to alter the consensus find that they have troubles that they didn't *suspect*.

FINN: Do you have any optimism about the influence of peace movements or peace groups in the country?

MC KENZIE: Well, not much. No. It's always been a very minor group. It's got a bad name. I don't think it deserves it. The fact is that it has it. It's regarded as a form of extremism, like total

---

Administration, exercised in the name of high and noble principle, is hard to match. . . .

"This question of confidence in the good judgment and good faith of the U.S. government is really more important than anything else. The specific arguments about bombing the oil refineries are not vital. Honest men can obviously differ about the wisdom of the decision. Nevertheless, the fate of Vietnam or the United States does not hang on any of these specific arguments. But a great deal does hang on whether the American people can trust the pronouncements of their government, whether they can remain united on purposes they understand and respect. . . ."

John L. McKenzie, S.J.

abstinence or vegetarianism or the Anti-Vivisection Society, all of which are taken very seriously by some people. But not by many. So pacifism, actually, is a very harmless activity in this country, except, of course, in wartime. And while I s'pose that the government is still willing to let the conscientious objector object and serve his term in a nonviolent capacity, it's very much less sympathetic toward any *expression* of *views* on the subject which would go beyond that, and quite unsympathetic to any *activity* which would go beyond it. Theoretically, of course, Congress is supposed to be the place where the issues are debated —and *have* been debated too.

FINN: I think Senator Fulbright has suggested that he had a certain responsibility which he *didn't* fulfill by bringing this debate before the public earlier.

MC KENZIE: Well, I think so too. But . . . Fulbright's like the rest of us. Federal government is Big Daddy and you don't question Big Daddy. He knows best.

FINN: There are a number of people who are beginning to question our policy in Vietnam. As it goes along there are more people dissatisfied today—this is an estimate on my part—than there were a year ago.

MC KENZIE: In my judgment, it is so *patently* irrational and unsuccessful that even the *unthinking* are beginning to wonder about it. What is it *supposed* to produce in the first place, and *is it* producing it in the second? I don't even know, and I don't know whether any spokesman for the government can tell us what it's *expected* to produce.

FINN: I wonder if I could shift a little bit. What is your judgment about the *possession* of present nuclear weapons and the whole nuclear weapons system which, I presume, raises this irrationality to a high degree?

MC KENZIE: Well, I do not think that nuclear weapons can be morally acceptable on any terms. *Any* terms. Even the possession of them. It's so purely theoretical that it just is sheer nonsense. One of the most expensive things we've got is nuclear bombs. I just do not believe in all that money going to producing museum pieces. They tell you they're not to be used; they're there as a deterrent. Well, that is the most arrant nonsense. How can anyone say that sincerely, unless he is wooly in the head?

FINN: Well you do have, I'm afraid, history on your side. When weapons have been introduced they have been used—with the *possible* exception of poison gases which we have not yet used.*

MC KENZIE: Quite right. Very possibly that's what will keep the nuclear weapon from being used. Well if it isn't going to be used, here is a place where one would hope that the statesmen of the world would be as capable of rational discourse . . . as I am with the man next door whose dog keeps me awake at night. But they're *not*.

FINN: Well, this is the hope, of course, of people who would defend the deterrent system, that the irrationality of the use would be *so apparent* to even the most arrogant national leader that he would not resort to these weapons.

MC KENZIE: Well, that's nice. I would think, being trained in an old-fashioned logic, that if it's irrational to use it it's irrational to threaten to use it.†

FINN: Would you yourself uphold, as a reasonable restraint on the part of those who *do* accept violence as a proper way to control international affairs, an attempt to limit destruction? Would you uphold or accept the traditional just-war theory, or do you think it has any applicability?

MC KENZIE: I have not had any use for the just-war theory for about ten years. And it just came all of a sudden—there was nothing to it. It's a kind of theoretical and totally impractical moral thinking that moralists just like to engage in every now and then. It has no reference to the real world at all. As one

* This statement demands elaboration. Critics have pointed out that tear gas, touted as a humane weapon, is used to flush the enemy from cover to face fragmentation bombs. But children exposed to large doses are harmed.

In September 1966, twenty-two scientists, including seven Nobel Laureates, wrote to President Johnson, protesting the use "of anticrop and nonlethal anti-personnel weapons in Vietnam." They also asserted that word had spread through the scientific community that secret research financed by the government is attempting to develop biological weapons with total destructive power. All reports indicate that their protest was not acknowledged as serious, but the issue is one that is likely to assume greater importance.

† This point is considered by Paul Ramsey, who would also claim allegiance to "old-fashioned logic" but who comes to a different conclusion.

John L. McKenzie, S.J.

who dabbles in history, I would be inclined to say you can't show me a just war. And the theory of the just war . . . well, actually it goes back to the efforts of the Christian community to reconcile itself to a practice which it *really knew* in its Christian heart of hearts that it couldn't countenance. And so I put the ethics of the just war in almost the same boat with the ethics of the just adultery or the just murder.

FINN: Have you always held the position that war itself was so irrational as to be immoral?

MC KENZIE: No, I came to it because I had the job of teaching the Bible to students. It's not a philosophical position. It's not a theological position, in the usual sense of the term. It's a biblical position. But, of course, if I talk in those terms I limit myself quickly to the Christian community. And I cannot very well discuss this with a person who is outside the Christian community—or within it—like the secular humanist who feels that the Christian community has nothing meaningful to say any longer. I suspect that one of the reasons why he thinks this about the Christian community is because it had been so strangely silent on the question of war and so very *articulate* on such things as contraception, which the secular humanist, I think, regards as a less urgent moral question than the question of war. In this, I think his moral judgment quite good.

The last sentence, I realize, Father McKenzie added for my benefit lest I miss the irony implicit in his tone and smile, the same tone in which he had referred to the "beastly Communists." But no one familiar with Father McKenzie's works would have doubted the order of priority he himself would assign to two of the questions which plagued the bishops during the Second Vatican Council, the questions of contraception and of modern war. One of the many quips that circulated during the sessions of the Council was that "Those who are for the Pill are against the Bomb and those who are against the Pill are for the Bomb." A crude distortion, but one that does not obscure a real insight.

MC KENZIE: When you come to the New Testament, you are dealing with, well, a Gospel, which is proposed *in* the Church and is to be fulfilled by the individual person in the Church. Well, this sets up, we think, an entirely new scheme of human

relations and an entire new attitude toward other persons. Now the New Testament says nothing about politics, in general. In the Roman Empire, all the politics was handled by the government, so the question wasn't pertinent; it was not being *asked*. However, the whole Christian thrust against evil in the Gospel is pretty well summed up under the main phrase—nonresistance. It *never* suggested that the Christian can resolve the problems of evil which we encounter by what we call resistance. I mean, of course he doesn't yield to it, but he doesn't apply *violence* to it. He suffers it.

Now how can you apply *that* to a nation? You only apply it to a nation by saying that the nation is not a Christian entity. And in pre-Christian times—or post-Christian, it doesn't make any difference—the fact is the Christian ethic has nothing to do with the way in which national decisions are made. And you remove that whole area: the Gospel doesn't touch it . . . and it seems to me if you do that you remove most of life. Because man does not live as an isolated individual, and if he can't fulfill himself as a Christian in his national community I'd like to know where he's going to. And there are such restrictions in the impractical quality of Christianity, as is alleged in almost every social context. Pretty soon you have about what we do have, and that is a fine Christian ideal which, effectively, is fulfilled habitually by no one. So when people ask me whether Christianity is old I would say, "No, it's very, very young. Quite possibly it hasn't even been weaned. It's *not* mature."

FINN: I take it you have *hopes* for its maturation.

MC KENZIE: Well I believe in God, the Father Almighty, and in Jesus Christ His only son, Our Lord. I do believe it, yes. And in the power of the Gospel. And very, very much also, I'm convinced of the ability of man to not so much refuse it or resist it as to drown it in a sea of molasses.

FINN: If the Christian ethic has nothing to do with the ethic of the state, how does the individual Christian resolve this for himself? Or, can he have two sets of ethics, one for his individual life and one for his public, social life?

MC KENZIE: Right. He has had two sets of ethics, and every now and then he's aware that they don't quite jibe. But most of the time it doesn't bother him because it's the ethics of reason

John L. McKenzie, S.J.

and nature which govern by far the greater part of his existence. So the Christian ethic is just drowned in molasses.

FINN: If someone *does* understand and *does* follow the Christian ethic, is he necessarily going to be a-political or nonpolitical? How will he develop any political participation in the nation state?

MC KENZIE: I don't have the answer actually—and it's one of the things, of course, that the critics have pointed out—although I think it's just a little bit unfair to ask me to do in a year or two some unfinished work that goes back about 1,500 years. On the other hand, if I don't want to do it I guess I shouldn't even raise the issue.

FINN: But it may still be a question which *can* be answered in a number of years.

MC KENZIE: Well, here I go back again to the New Testament, which gives us the picture of the original Christian community living in a secular state. And—it's the New Testament times—getting along. And they got along with the secular state until the government of the secular state all of a sudden realized that this Christian business was totally incompatible with the Roman way of life, and that if they did not destroy it, it would destroy them. So they attempted to destroy it *but* not too hard, not too long and certainly not successfully. Then, of course, Gibbon is quite right: Christianity *did* destroy the Roman Empire, because such a secular state could not really endure if all of its members were to be Christians. Now we think we're back to the secular state.

We have no Christians in politics. We never have. Never had a chance. When the states of Europe became Christian, well, they remained kind of Roman in their politics. So that's when they cooked up the ethics of the just war and a few other related things and, oh, tried to put political power on a moral basis, whether as an absolute or something else and. . . . So what does a Christian do in a state? I'm afraid that on this point the Church, up to now, has not given him very explicit directions. If you look at the New Testament, Jesus lived in a pretty un-Christian atmosphere. He doesn't refer to it very much, really. But he doesn't seem to think that there was anything as Christians they could do, and he never takes anything off—you know, never tempers the wind to a shorn lamb. This is the Gospel. This is a new life which is yours to live.

FINN: It's clear from what you said that you would have some reservations about the statements in the *Constitution on the Church in the Modern World* that apply to war and peace. But do you think that those statements and recent papal statements on war are moving in a *direction* which is favorable to your own position?

MC KENZIE: Well, I thought that. . . . I'll tell you this, what [Pope] Paul said at the United Nations at first surprised *me*. I didn't think he'd be as candid as he was. I sometimes wonder whether he realized how candid he was being, and whether he might not when he got back say to himself, "Maybe I said too much." You know: "Stop it right now. Don't plan to stop it, just stop it!" Otherwise you've got this, well, *planned* reduction of armaments. In a sense it's like giving up smoking.

FINN: You either stop it or you don't.

MC KENZIE: Well, I haven't stopped it. I've stopped it several times.

FINN: It's probably unfair to take out of context one or two sentences, but I would like your comment on another statement in your book on the New Testament. You've written that what really determines the state to be un-Christian is the basis of its ethics. And you say the ethics of the state are the ethics of survival and states live in a moral jungle.

MC KENZIE: Right. I think that statement ought to stand up pretty well. A moral jungle. Yes.

FINN: And is it part of the question which you say you haven't answered for yourself yet to see whether the states can, or *how* the states could, move out of a moral jungle?

MC KENZIE: Well, I don't know why they can't move out of a moral jungle the same way a man would move out of a moral jungle. But, of course, what would you say . . . Here's one man who *has* principles, but finds himself in a moral jungle and *can't* leave it. Well, there are two things he can do. One is to surrender to the moral jungle, and the other is to get the moral jungle to surrender to him. If he does the second thing he becomes a great hero. If he does the first you never hear of him again. Certainly in a, at least I hope, a Christian scheme of things, even the most warlike Christian would have to say that in that situation it would be his duty to try to change the jungle, not to let the jungle change him. But for states, no. No state is obliged to do what's right until every other state has done it first . . . because survival is the answer. You see, what's un-Christian about this is that no one individual, no person and no group has an inalienable right to survive. You can only survive as long as conditions are favorable for your survival. There are times when it's no longer morally possible. Most people admit *that*.

FINN: Most people admit it for themselves as individuals but not for the state.

MC KENZIE: Right, not for the state. In spite of the fact that historically, while states have longer lives than persons, we don't know any one *yet* that has successfully defied mortality. They might say, of course the state recognizes its mortality, but don't expect us to plan for it. You'd say, no, a man plans for death but he doesn't plan to bring it about. But he *does* know that there are some things he may *not do* to insure his survival. Society won't tolerate some things. You know, like killing your parents to get the inheritance, and stuff like that. We frown on that. You might feel an honest conviction that that was a key to your survival. And I have said, facetiously, it sometimes happens that murder is practical. It does solve problems.

FINN: It brings them to an end.

MC KENZIE: And so does war.

FINN: And so does war. Your contention is that. . . .

MC KENZIE: You don't adopt solutions just because they're practical. Unless you live in a moral jungle. It may be a solution, but it's irrational. If a person creates a problem for me, I can certainly solve that problem by removing that person. I may not solve others and I may even—probably will—create new ones. But on the short-sighted view, you can think of murder and/or war as being the solution of this immediate problem. Personal and international violence are on the same level, under the same moral judgment.

FINN: Can I ask you how your students react to this presentation? Are they taken aback, as most people would be, at something which runs counter to what society offers?

MC KENZIE: Well, oh, the reaction is mixed. Sometimes it's hostile and remains so, other times it's favorable and remains so, and some people go from, well, they go from hostile to favorable; after they hear me they don't go the other way. So I would say that in the long run I don't lose anybody by this presentation. If the presentation is properly made, it seems to me that it's pretty hard to resist. Actually the most resistance comes from people who are trained in theological thinking . . . using the word loosely.

GORDON ZAHN

Gordon Zahn was born in Milwaukee in 1918. He attended the College of St. Thomas and the Catholic University of America, from which he received his doctorate in sociology in 1952. His dissertation was "A Descriptive Study of the Social Backgrounds of Conscientious Objectors in Civilian Public Service During World War II." While his dissertation was properly academic, it was also informed by personal experience, for Zahn himself had spent time in C.P.S. camps from 1942 to 1946. After receiving his Ph.D. he continued his studies at Harvard and at Julius Maximilian University, Würzburg, Germany. For the year 1964–65 he was a John Simon Senior Fellow at the University of Manchester, England. He is presently on the faculty of the University of Massachusetts.

As a sociologist Zahn has been heavily influenced by C. Wright Mills; he wants his work to be scholarly and methodologically sound, but he also insists that it make value judgments and have contemporary relevance. His major publications show that he is concerned with questions that are not only relevant, but urgent. The reaction to these works shows that he makes value judgments that a number of reviewers find unpalatable. Zahn has contributed chapters to *Morality and Modern Warfare* (edited by William Nagle) and *Breakthrough to Peace* (foreword by Thomas Merton) that are imbued with his pacifist convictions.

The scholarly product of his year in Würzburg was a book entitled *German Catholics and Hitler's Wars*. After acknowledging the murky context in which these judgments are made, Zahn concluded that, "in World War II, the leading spokesmen of the Catholic Church in Germany did become channels of Nazi control over their followers, whether by their general exhortations to loyal obedience to legitimate authority or by their even more direct efforts to rally these followers to the defense of *Volk, Vaterland,* and *Heimat* as a Christian duty." * Zahn's analysis did not end with this conclusion, for he was most interested in asking why German Catholics did give almost complete support to Hitler's wars, why there were so few conscientious objectors, and—his original inspiration for the book—why the Friedensbund deutscher Katholiken (German Catholic Peace Union), which had 40,000 members before the war, had collapsed.

The controversy swirling around this volume had not been stilled when Zahn published *In Solitary Witness,*† a volume devoted to Franz Jägerstätter, an Austrian peasant. He had first heard of the remarkable life and death of this man while working on his previous book and returned to learn the full story. The story of this peasant is extraordinary and moving. Although a member of no political organization that would seem to support his views, Jägerstätter publicly declared he would not fight in Hitler's wars because he considered them unjust. Against the strongest personal and institutional pressures—from family and friends, local officials, the parish priest, his bishop—he endured. After a military trial he was beheaded on August 9, 1943. Zahn inquires into the general implications that can and should be drawn from the example of this most singular man.

Zahn's appearance, in combination with the geographical area of his studies, has led more than one person to think that he himself is German. He is of medium height and build, with a rather square face, close-cropped graying hair and the seemingly inevitable horn-rimmed glasses of the scholar. He is a frequent lecturer and agrees to spend some time with me if we can both cope with his voice, which is exhibiting the strain both of too much speaking and of laryngitis. He does admirably, although I find missing from his voice the intensity that I have

* New York, Sheed and Ward, 1962, p. 203.
† New York, Sheed and Ward, 1964.

Gordon Zahn

previously noted when we have discussed points of disagreement on questions of war and pacifism.

I ask his opinion, as a sociologist, of the magnitude of the problems posed, both to church and state, by the particular-war objector. He sees the problems as great indeed and would include educating the average citizen as one of them. He offers an immediate example of what he means. When his book on Jägerstätter was published, Zahn appeared on a television program that is conducted by Irving Kupcinet, a highly respected columnist in Chicago. On the program he praised Zahn's book, which he obviously liked. Yet in his column sometime later this item appeared:

> The American Civil Liberties Union tripped over its civicism in urging that young Americans who view the Viet Nam war as "unjust" be excused from the draft. That would be, as the saying goes, a helluva way to run a railroad. It also implies that youngsters can determine whether a war is "just" or "unjust," a matter over which historians have argued for centuries.

Although in subsequent correspondence with Zahn he acknowledged more complexities than this brief note in his column suggested, many people would probably agree with that column, and it is those people that Zahn thinks should be educated. And, Zahn adds, the particular-war objector poses an exceedingly difficult problem to the Selective Service officials. Furthermore, "if a great majority—or a sizeable number even—of young men make this decision, it is quite reasonable to expect that a war effort would be in some trouble."

We turn to Zahn's own position and how it was shaped. I ask if he would accept the designation of absolute pacifist. He agrees, but suggests that "absolute religious pacifist" would probably be better. His position has varied over the years. Although he was familiar with Scripture and the teachings of the Catholic Church, he would not describe himself as an educated Catholic when he began, in high school, to think of himself as a pacifist. His education in the Church's traditional teaching on war began during the war.

ZAHN: I came into Civilian Public Service as a conscientious objector, feeling that I would be almost alone as a Catholic in the program. I hadn't even heard of the *Catholic Worker,* for example, until after I had had my first tussle with the draft board. In other words I'd gone, applied as a Catholic for this conscientious objector's classification, and was told by the local Catholic pastor, who I believe was chairman of the draft board at that time—or at least sat on it—that it was absolutely impossible for a Catholic to be a conscientious objector. I imagine largely because of his position on this my first classification was turned down and I had to go to appeals. And it was while this appeal was in process that somebody pointed out to me there was a group of Catholics that took the same position and were publishing a paper in New York. And that was the first I had *heard* of other Catholics who held this position.

And so when I got into Civilian Public Service, in the Catholic camp, my position is the one that I've described as integralist. It was a humanitarian type of Catholicism; you had on the one hand the nature of war, the spirit of war, the genius of war if you would call it that, and on the other hand the genius or spirit or nature of Christianity. And I just made a judgment—largely emotional, part intellectual, I suppose—that the two were irreconcilable. Then when I was in camp I *met* educated Catholics who began pointing out that I was holding an untenable position in their eyes, and they instructed me in the traditions of the just war, and quite converted me at this point into a traditionalist Catholic pacifist.

FINN: Why did they regard your position as untenable?

ZAHN: Because they felt it was unorthodox. To be orthodox you had to cite the conditions of the just war, and so forth. And most of them at this point were what we would call today limited pacifists. They felt that *this* war, for various reasons, was an unjust war, but that no Catholic could hold that *all* war was unjust and wrong—as I did. I held that *all war* would be wrong. And so I did have something of a conversion to their position during my days in C.P.S., but since then I've come back to something approximating my original position—which is very much, I think, in keeping with the new theology and so it's probably quite up-to-date. In other words, it's based on Scripture but not on an exegesis of any particular line in the Scriptures. Just trying to take the *whole meaning* of the Gospel message.

Gordon Zahn

FINN: Do you feel the changes which are taking place within the Church now lend any more support to your position?

ZAHN: Much more support to my position, I would say. I don't know if it's only the changes that are taking place in the Church itself; but changes that have taken place in war have made my position much stronger in arguing with others. I have a very good friend, for example, who is a veteran, and we've argued this point many times. Of course I like to chide him about such things as *Pacem in Terris,* the recent Council developments, and he usually comes back and says "Well, don't take any credit for *that.* It's the way war has changed that has *forced* this type of position on the Pope and the Council Fathers and so forth." *

FINN: Of course the positions of both Pope John and Pope Paul do certainly allow war, just war, to be fought, and say that —as Pope Paul said when he spoke in New York—as long as man is the weak and wicked creature that he is, war will probably be an instrument of political relations.

ZAHN: Yes, but I still would not interpret these, Jim, as what we might call even a negative endorsement of war. And this would include Pius XII in the Christmas message that has been such a thorn in the pacifist side. Even he was restating the traditional conditions of the just war, and it still is a matter then of individual judgment as to whether they apply or not.† And I'm perfectly willing to grant, shall we say, the theoretical possibility of a just war even today. But in terms of *practical* pos-

---

* It is relatively easy to find evidence to support Zahn's view. In addition to the documents we discuss, he could point to statements made by a number of leading European prelates. For example, a news item that appeared about the time of this interview:

"Modern armaments create such injustice that the old theory of the 'just' war is no longer tenable, Cardinal Bernard Alfrink of Utrecht asserted here (The Hague). The head of the Dutch Catholic hierarchy said in a speech that in a certain sense, any act of violence is a violation of the precepts of the Gospel. He added that in the world of today there is a natural incompatibility between the Gospel and war."

† The Christmas message to which Zahn refers and which has troubled many pacifists is that of 1948, in which the Pope said that among the goods of humanity "some are of such importance for society, that it is perfectly lawful to defend them against unjust aggression. Their defense is even an obligation for the nations as a whole who have a duty not to abandon a nation that is attacked. The certainty that this duty will not go unfulfilled will serve to discourage the aggressor. . . ."

sibility or even the remotest likelihood of such a thing occurring, this I would deny.

Although Zahn's own position is perfectly clear, I find the several preceding statements, taken together, rather confusing. To grant the theoretical possibility of a just war but to deny totally an actual possibility is to make of it—adapting T. S. Eliot —"an abstraction/ Remaining a perpetual possibility/ Only in a world of speculation." But Popes Paul and John did not, presumably, intend their comments simply to encourage a high level of speculation. The only conclusion, which Zahn might accept, is that his individual judgment differs markedly from the judgment expressed by these two popes. But Vietnam presents the current test for just-war concepts and we turn to that. Prescinding from the political considerations, I ask Zahn if he believes such a war *could* not be fought justly because of the military conditions?

ZAHN: Yes, I think this would be true. To win a modern war one must use modern techniques. A nation which would limit itself to what *I* would consider legitimate means—and thereby meet the traditional condition that the methods employed be just—would have very little hope of success. That would violate *another* of the conditions. It seems to me that modern war—and this goes before nuclear war, which is merely the icing on the cake as far as I'm concerned—is intrinsically unjust. I think that the type of strategy, and to some extent the type of weapons employed in our own Civil War, already were of a nature that would have to be viewed as unjust according to traditional theory.

I ask Zahn to be more specific, pointing out that the Administration claims that the war is being fought with a good deal of restraint. He agrees that in their terms that's true, but their terms are unacceptable. The napalm bombing of villages, where discrimination between combatant and noncombatant is impossible, is immoral, as are the delayed-fuse bombs designed to surprise and kill the civilian labor gangs that repair damaged roads, bridges and paths.

Gordon Zahn

ZAHN: The civilian is not a proper target. For example, take the bombing of Dresden. The first wave was immoral enough, but the *second* wave was absolutely unthinkable. Not only had they *calculated* the amount of bombing that would have to be done to create the firestorm that happened accidentally at Hamburg, but the second wave was timed precisely to catch the fire fighting equipment from other surrounding areas and thereby get *them* and make sure that nothing could be done to stop the firestorm from having its total effect. This is, to me, absolutely immoral. Anything which carries even by *implication* the intention of destroying civilian life would be a violation, I think.*

FINN: Would you make this distinction so hard that there'd be a proper military target where the aim *was* to destroy something that was essential to the war effort but where a small number of civilians would be killed inevitably?

ZAHN: Well, I could conceive of a *totally* military target being the object of a bombing attack. I could see in terms of those who do not buy my point of view that this *would be* a legitimate target under the strict application of the Thomistic conditions of the just war. But then the question is: How *many* of the accidental or incidental killings are going to be taken into account? And the first thing you know, you *might* end up with a morality by numbers rather than a morality by principle.

FINN: Well, numbers have to enter in if you want to say that a *small* number of civilians are killed. It seems another way to define proportionality according to the just-war theory. According to your application of just-war principles, I assume that the nuclear weapons systems that we have now, the large deterrent system on which our security supposedly rests, could not be used justly.

ZAHN: That is true. I would hold that position.

Zahn then added that the mere possession of these weapons might be the greatest threat to our security today, conditioning us for the "situation which *seems* to demand what is absolutely forbidden." And he expresses scorn for the view advanced by

* This is a point which is at least debatable in the view of William O'Brien (see pp. 405ff.) and Paul Ramsey (see pp. 421ff.).

two people in a London conference he had recently attended: "The air force simply would not obey an order to release these bombs."

This would seem a point too obvious to contest, except that there are still a number of people, apparently, who would like to comfort themselves with the illusion expressed by these two people. They are very much like the English bishop, mentioned by Herbert Butterfield, "who said that if we totally disarmed he had too high an opinion of human nature to think that anybody would attack us." It is this kind of person who gives the term "idealist" a bad odor.

It is the declared policy of Western powers to use the weapons at their disposal as the circumstances require—and this includes the full range of weapons. For a number of sound reasons Robert S. McNamara has regularly placed on the public record the general lines of American policy on war and has given a general estimate of American war potential. On February 18, 1965, for example, in a formal statement to the House Armed Services Committee, he discussed general nuclear war in terms of "situations involving strategic exchanges between the U.S. and the Soviet Union alone."

In the course of that statement he said: "In the event of general nuclear war, attacks might be directed against military targets only, against cities only, or against both types of targets, either simultaneously or with a delay." Mr. McNamara continued, "it seems reasonable to assume that the destruction of, say, one-quarter to one-third of its population and about two-thirds of its industrial capacity would mean the elimination of the aggressor as a major power for many years. Such a level of destruction would certainly represent intolerable punishment to any industrialized nation and thus should serve as an effective deterrent."

For some people this might still leave open the possibility that such attacks would never be made. In Britain the issue was put and answered in its bluntest form. At the British Official Secrets Trial of February 1962, Air Commander Magill responded under oath to the question:

"Would you press the button you know is going to annihilate millions of people?"

Gordon Zahn

"If the circumstances required it I would." *

It seems fair to say that only those people who have acknowledged the conditions under which modern war is presently conducted—that is, the nuclear deterrent—have earned the right
to a hearing. It is unlikely that the others will deviate into sense.
We return in our discussion to the question of just-war principles which Zahn rejects.

FINN: The just-war principles, however much they are violated in practice, do attempt to use a degree of rationality in this
fundamentally irrational enterprise which is war. Do you see an
alternative to them? Isn't it better to use whatever rationality is
possible than to discard it entirely even in preparations for war?

ZAHN: Well, I see the just-war principles, the whole formula,
as something of a compromise from an earlier tone or tradition
in Christianity which would not have allowed for *any* war, which
would have held war as an essentially un-Christian type of endeavor.

FINN: How did your own investigations in Germany support
or modify or complicate your views on pacifism?

ZAHN: Well, I don't know if they had any great impact upon
my own views on pacifism. What they did do was reinforce the
conclusion I've already stated, that the whole tradition of the
just war is irrelevant to the fact of war—certainly to the fact
of war as it's been fought in the past couple of centuries. No
one is *going* to apply these things. In fact, one theologian prepared a little pamphlet in which his answer to the men who
picked it up in the churches was: Now is not the time to *raise*
the question of the just or unjust war; one just does his duty now.
Faith in the cause of his folk.† We can find Catholic theologians

* Walter Stein, "Would You Press the Button?" James Finn, ed., in
Peace, the Churches and the Bomb (New York, Council on Religion and
International Affairs, 1965), p. 20.

† In rereading sections of Zahn's *German Catholics and Hitler's Wars*
I encountered a quotation from the pamphlet *Was Ist Zu Tun?* by M.
Laros. In Zahn's translation: "Now there is no point in raising the question of the just war and introducing all sorts of 'ifs,' 'ands' or 'buts.' A
scientific judgment concerning the causes and origins of the war is absolutely impossible today because the prerequisites for such a judgment are
not available to us. This must wait until a later time when the documents
of both sides are available. Now the individual has but one course open

today who probably aren't quite as crude about stating it, but think it would be rather pointless to disrupt the national effort by raising such inconvenient questions as to the justice or injustice of the war in Vietnam.

While Zahn said "theologians," he would probably be willing to extend his statement to include all Catholic clergy. And he could find positive as well as negative support. For example, on September 22, 1966 Archbishop Patrick H. O'Boyle of Washington issued a directive to all the priests under his jurisdiction regarding masses they would celebrate during October, which had been designated as a period devoted to the cause of peace. The directive read in part: "Under no circumstances should they express the individual priest's views about the foreign policy of our government in conducting the war. It is everyone's right to have his own opinion about the issue, but our private views are never to be made the subject of sermons for our good people who may hold contrary views about the government's policy."

Such an admonition must, however, be read in its context. Apart from matters of sex and education, debated political issues are rarely topics of sermons by Catholic clergy. The priest who wishes to express his views will find different outlets. The ban here confirmed general practice.

The general practice of avoiding debated political issues does not completely prohibit the priest from addressing himself to the subject, as the Archbishop's own example makes clear. On October 4, at a mass for peace that was attended by President Johnson, Chief Justice Earl Warren, scores of high government officials and Roman Catholic and Protestant clergy, the Archbishop recalled the various teachings of the Church that recognize the right of legitimate defense, that is, just war. He did caution that even in a just war some means are not permitted. His entire sermon, however, could be regarded as a cautious endorsement of present policy.

---

to him: to do his best with faith in the cause of his *Volk*. For this, one cannot demand mathematical proof. This would no longer be faith but, instead, a reckoning; and service to the *Volk* is based on faith and trust not calculation. Today that is self-evident to all patriots." This was published in Germany in 1940.

Gordon Zahn

The Archbishop did step outside the realm of general principles to say that the U.S. "has tried every form of persuasion to get its adversaries around the conference table." Some people would regard this not as a descriptive statement of fact but as the presentation of a "private view."

FINN: Are you surprised, or dismayed, that there are few Catholic theologians or bishops who have made an outright condemnation of either the nuclear weapons system or the war in Vietnam?

ZAHN: I'm *very much* dismayed, but not at all *surprised*. We're still bound very much, too much, to the state. What we really need is something of separation of church and state from the *other* side than that at which the issue is usually presented.

FINN: You spoke about your own experience when you chose Civilian Public Service and thought that you were practically the only Catholic to do that. How has the situation in our country changed since then for Catholics?

ZAHN: I think it's changed significantly. I still believe that the great majority of Catholics, including priests, bishops, would look somewhat askance upon Catholics who took this position. But for the most part I think there's *more awareness* of the fact that, first of all, there *were* conscientious objectors in the last war—this is something *we* could not look back upon. The only reference I could find when I did my research at Catholic University on Catholic CO's in World War II, the only reference to *World War I* I could find was that *one* man apparently took this stand. And if this is true, this fantastically small number who were in C.P.S. with me, less than two hundred all together, was still a great upsurge for the intervening period. And now I understand that there are this many or more indicating at least interest in the position each month.

I ask Zahn if he thinks the pacifists are having a political effect in this country. He says they are not winning acceptance of their position, even in the peace groups, but the great news coverage given to the various demonstrations does introduce a cautionary note into the discussions. The demonstrations have impact. They act as a deterrent upon the hawks who call for escalation.

We turn to the treatment Zahn was subjected to in C.P.S. He says that although there were some built-in injustices—since they weren't paid, men with families were almost automatically excluded—the treatment was quite good. And he suffered only minimal unpleasantness because of his stand as a CO. I recall the frequent demonstrations at which CO's had been beaten during the year and ask him to comment on the differences.

ZAHN: Well, as far as I know there was nothing like this at the time I was a conscientious objector. This is probably because we didn't do the demonstrating that these young men are doing at the present. Perhaps we should have. It might have been better *had* we been beaten up a little and gotten more press coverage so that others would have known there were people taking such positions. As it was we were hidden away, and actually we were hidden away in a convenient cubbyhole set up by the whole conscription system. In a sense we *were* doing our bit for the war effort whether we liked it or not. I don't think the young men today would be putting up with that. I think they'd have far more camp demonstrations.

I ask Zahn about his position on the use of violence and nonviolence in domestic affairs. He starts with the premise that the ways of violence are now forbidden. He suggests that a disciplined, organized, nonviolent program of civil disobedience and non-cooperation provides one alternative to violence. This possibility has not yet been tested, he says, rejecting the Indian case as being an insufficient test, but it is the Christian's responsibility to investigate it.

FINN: Gordon, how much of what you have said about your own position would be relevant to people other than Christians, people of no religious belief at all?

ZAHN: I would say to the extent that my position includes the emotional and intellectual bases I mentioned, that they should be generally attractive or at least open to these other groups. When you get to the third base, the specific theological position, well then obviously people of different religions would have different theological approaches to it, and people of no religion would probably just stay at the humanitarian level.

Gordon Zahn

But I think we must recognize that the bulk of the peace movements, as we have known them recently, has not been predominantly Catholic, that it *is* something that has been carried on by people of other faiths and, to a large extent, of people who quite explicitly state that they have no religious commitment but are just interested in the welfare of their brothers.

FINN: Are you generally satisfied with the statement of the *Constitution on the Church in the Modern World* on war?

ZAHN: Yes, I would say that when it was first proposed to bring these issues to Vatican II, I was somewhat against it, expecting that anything that would come out would be something I wouldn't be too pleased with. But I must confess that, with some misgivings, I find the Constitution *very much* along my inclinations as far as its position on peace and war are concerned.

FINN: And therefore, I presume in your thinking, an advance upon previous official statements?

ZAHN: Oh, yes, if only in that it's a much more official statement than even some of the previous statements by John XXIII and the other popes.

FINN: And open, I would presume, to what you think would be a *proper development* of the Christian position on war.

ZAHN: This is essential. It's now left to us to activate what has been set for us in that Constitution.

PHILIP BERRIGAN, S.S.J.

Because Philip Berrigan and his brother Daniel have both become known as "controversial" priests, because they share many of the same interests and commitments, and because these interests frequently project their names into the news, their acquaintances have sometimes tried to distinguish between them by saying that Philip is the activist and Daniel the poet-intellectual. This distinction seems inadequate at best, and their friends most frequently resort to pointing out that they belong to different orders: Philip Berrigan, S.S.J., is the Josephite; Daniel Berrigan, S.J., is the Jesuit.

Nevertheless Philip Berrigan *is* an activist. He is a member of an American order dedicated to the service of the American Negro, and Father Berrigan has spent seven of his eleven years as a priest in the deep South working and demonstrating with civil rights groups, with CORE, the Southern Christian Leadership Conference, the Urban League, and SNCC (the Student Nonviolent Coordinating Committee). He has also worked with peace groups like CNVA (Committee for Nonviolent Action), SANE, the Catholic Worker, and the FOR (the Fellowship of Reconciliation). For the FOR he has served as theologian in the Triple Revolution Convocations that have been held across the country from Portland, Oregon, to Washington, D.C. He writes for a variety of publications and lectures around the country on race, American poverty, and Vietnam. One item in his background does not seem to fit the pattern suggested by these activities: Father Berrigan, who was born in 1923, served for three and a half years in the Army during World War II, and received an overseas commission as Second Lieutenant in the infantry.

At present Philip Berrigan is a curate in a Negro parish in Baltimore, Maryland, but we meet at the Free Library in Philadelphia. Here, at the invitation of the Church Peace Mission, he and I are to speak to a group, mostly clergy, on aspects of the war in Vietnam. (Arlo Tatum, the executive secretary of the Central Committee for Conscientious Objectors, later speaks to the same group about CO's, and it is these comments that Father Berrigan refers to in our interview.) Tall, with a sturdy, athletic build and graying crew-cut hair, Father Berrigan establishes a notable presence.

After this session and dinner I go with Father Berrigan to visit some friends of his. It is not long before a number of other friends stop by, and as the group grows and the conversation mounts, Father Berrigan and I retire to the kitchen. I prop the recording set up on a washer and the microphone on a child's yellow high-seat and pick up the threads of the discussion we have been carrying on most of the day. He speaks in a strong, slow but unstudied manner.

P. BERRIGAN: Well, it might amount to this, Jim. I would agree almost wholeheartedly with Pope Paul that peace is the issue of our day. I think that peacemaking as a course of both thought and action for the Christian has to literally invade all of the areas of human life today. Maybe reductively, every human situation, every problem, has to be seen in terms of peacemaking or Christian reconciliation. And when one considers— well, first of all there's the overriding concern about war, then there is the racial problem operating not only in this country but in the world, and then there's the reality of poverty, with our own people domestically and also in the world—one can discover in these three issues common threads and common problems, and one of these is the violence done the human person.

FINN: You're saying that all of these things—poverty, racism and war—inflict violence upon the individual, the human person.

P. BERRIGAN: Yes. And when one reflects upon a document like *Pacem in Terris,* which deals with not only personal rights but also community rights and national rights, and then the whole world community, you can see how many of the things that are critical in the world today are poles apart from the picture of mankind that John XXIII possessed. We have to start approaching these world problems and domestic problems just from the sheer position of what a man has a *right* to, and then of course react accordingly as well as we can.

FINN: Does this lead you to a position that you could describe as pacifism, or would you allow some areas in which a measure of coordinated violence might be necessary in order to prevent further disorder, further harm?

P. BERRIGAN: Yes, I remember your considering the variations of pacifism in your talk this afternoon. To my mind the term is almost wholly inadequate because it's open to so many connotations. And in some kinds of pacifism you do not have nonviolence accepted as a way of life. So one is thrust back upon the Gospel definition of a peacemaker or the Pauline conception of minister of reconciliation. And this I find to be much more consistent with what I believe Christianity to be. It is moreover much more workable and much more effective and, it goes without saying, much more adaptable to a greater variety of situations. I think it's no more than realistic, and perhaps we might agree on this, to say that the burden of proof lies with those who are convinced that war is an extension of political process today. In a nuclear age, such a thought is viciously absurd. I would go along with Pope John when he said that no longer can war be thought of as a solution to international conflict.*

* The statements Father Berrigan refers to are found in Pope John's encyclical, *Pacem in Terris*. The first passage (¶126) states: "Men are becoming more and more convinced that disputes which arise between states should not be resolved by recourse to arms, but rather by negotiation." There was some initial confusion about the translation, and therefore the meaning, of the second passage (¶127). In the edition of the National Catholic Welfare Conference the passage reads: "Therefore, in an age such as ours which prides itself on its atomic energy it is contrary to reason to hold that war is now a suitable way to restore rights which have been violated." In the section on Just War it will be made clear that there are three traditional reasons for recourse to war. The one which has been left standing as a legitimate recourse today is *ad repetendas injurias* (to resist injury or armed aggression). This remains untouched by the statement in *Pacem in Terris* which would, however, rule out as moral enterprises wars undertaken to liberate already subjugated nations. Father Berrigan's reading seems to extend the scope of that statement.

Philip Berrigan, S.S.J.

I think that war, even a brush war similar to the India–Pakistan affair, really alerts the nations of the world to the dangers that are implicit in such a struggle; and really I would say the whole world reacts against this, just as the whole world is reacting to what is going on in Vietnam today. I think it is literally true that we do have the majority of men *against* us in Vietnam— not because they are anti-American but because they are pro-peace, and they see Vietnam as a very, very definite threat to world peace and maybe the springboard for World War III.

There are probably more people who would dismiss this opinion than would dispute it. That is, they would discount the importance of anything that sounds like a reference to "world opinion," a concept they find too nebulous to be useful. Nevertheless it is an opinion that finds increasing support from those who report from other countries either professionally or casually (I posit a difference). I was to hear Tom Stonier voice similar sentiments on his return from Italy. (See pp. 449ff.) And late in the year the chief of *Newsweek*'s Paris bureau made much the same point.*

Television has brought the cruelest and most repellent aspects of the war directly into cafés and living rooms. The reaction is frequently immediate, personal and emotional, outside of political considerations or ideology. But the revulsion might well be translated into political terms, and they would probably have to be totted up on the debit side of the ledger. There is raised here, once again, the question of the general social climate out of which political decisions emerge.

FINN: Is the situation such today that war is no longer a logical enterprise? Has it ever been a logical enterprise, or is it simply that the possibility of utter devastation allows us insights into the irrational and unhelpful nature of war that we didn't have previously? I don't mean to put words in your mouth.

P. BERRIGAN: No, I think that's an entirely fair question. The little reading I've done on the history of war, and the ambiguity of the Christian Church in face of it, seems to argue that war has really never solved human problems; rather, it has

* Joel Blocker, "Through European Eyes: You're on Your Own," *Newsweek*, October 31, 1966, pp. 34–35.

complicated the human situation and resulted in an infinite variety of problems of much greater depth and wider extension than the original problems that war purportedly solved. And I'm speaking here of the Crusades, I'm speaking of the religious wars in Europe, I'm speaking of the great wars, two of which we have had in this century, and now of course the Vietnam war and the prospect of World War III. So I think it is arguable that today, in light not only of the history of war but in light of the wholesale destruction that a nuclear war would create, that we have to start from the utter conviction that no longer are there any alternatives to peace and that, if necessary, national sovereignty must yield before this new conviction. The *Pacem in Terris* convocation in New York in March '65 seemed to bear on this common thesis: that the only thing that would secure the peace finally would be a system of world law and government, and that the nations of the world, of course using the United Nations as a first step in this direction, must start along these lines.

FINN: But we clearly do not have today world law and government. We have neither a system of external laws to which various nations will give allegiance nor an authority to see that they would be followed. How do you react to those situations today which have given rise to conflict or seem like they might —clearly Vietnam, but you also suggested earlier Rhodesia and South Africa? What kind of policies should the United States follow, for instance, in South Africa?

P. BERRIGAN: It seems to me that we must analyze the South African situation in much the same basic terms that we analyze our own problem of segregation here at home, and we must investigate just what supports it and keeps it continuous there. For example, there's a question of American investments in South Africa. Now it wasn't many years ago—it was within the last decade—that the South African government was pretty much on the ropes economically and at this point appealed to the nations of the world for succor and support. The American support was almost immediate, not only investment in gold interests there but also diamonds and sheer capital investment through banks like Chase Manhattan. It would seem to me that it would be only realistic on the part of this government to withdraw from the things that basically and essentially keep apartheid going in South Africa—and here we're speaking of

Philip Berrigan, S.S.J.

the economic factor which makes it a very, very profitable enterprise indeed.*

FINN: I wonder if you would state how you arrived at what is a very critical attitude toward U.S. policy in Vietnam.

P. BERRIGAN: It perhaps happened while I was in New Orleans, and I would like to think—though I don't really know —that it became possible simply because I was at least somewhat acquainted with the human dimensions of the civil rights struggle. But I came on information that was entirely new to me, a study of civil defense and its inadequacies published by *Progressive* magazine. I not only learned something about the potential violence that we had in overkill capacity at that time, with Strategic Air Command on alert and constantly patrolling the skies of the world and the measures that we were taking to increase this, but in addition to that some of the President's— President Kennedy at that time—proposals for national protection against nuclear retaliation on the part of the Soviet Union. And it was conclusively proven to me that we were ready—at that point and later in a variety of critical situations—to initiate nuclear war in spite of the fact that if a retaliatory strike came,

* Some months after this interview, in a report of the special committee on apartheid to the General Assembly of the U.N., not only the United States but a number of other countries were accused of encouraging South Africa to "persist in its disastrous course." Marof Achkar, representative of Guinea and chairman of the committee, accused the United States, Great Britain, France, West Germany, Japan, Italy and other countries of greatly increasing their economic interests in South Africa precisely when the U.N. was calling for sanctions.

He stated that if no peaceful solution were found in South Africa the only alternative was obviously violent conflict. He then said, "The question which causes us great concern and which we pose clearly in this report is the question of the attitude of these powers in case of an explosion involving the lives of whites as well as blacks." *New York Times,* October 26, 1966, p. 3.

Some idea of the attraction of the economic factor that Father Berrigan mentioned can be gained from a promotional brochure prepared by Union Acceptances Limited, a merchant bank in South Africa. Capital invested in South Africa from abroad cannot be taken out, *but* companies are permitted to transfer profits in various forms. The risk need not be great because, as the brochure indicates, return on capital funds of foreign subsidiaries has averaged 25 percent in recent years. A 50 percent return is not rare, and a 100 percent return in the first year of operations has been known. The suggestion that mere persuasion will cause the business community to resist this attraction invites skepticism.

according to the testimony of our own leaders, we would have to bear casualties that would hover around one hundred million people. This was six or seven years ago. I was utterly appalled by that, and I began to read further and I began, from that point on, to be anti-war. Then I was able—through reading and discussion and contact with people in the peace movement—I was able to see some common human threads operating in the other great social issues and able to connect them to a degree. So, it was perhaps a process of education.

FINN: You said you were appalled by the nuclear weapons system we had and the *apparent* willingness of people in government to employ that weapons system. What kind of a judgment would you make of our deterrent system today? What courses are open to those who actually have to make decisions about military systems in the United States?

P. BERRIGAN: I would reject the possibility of unilateral disarmament simply as an impractical course. It just won't happen that way. People won't agree to it, nor will this country, nor will the Soviet Union. Theoretically I would go along with the judgment that it is immoral to even possess these weapons. It's immoral for a variety of reasons. First of all the weapons themselves have built into them the intention to use them under certain circumstances. . . .

FINN: That's not what's claimed for them, of course. They're placed in different categories, in the minds of some theorists, from other weapons. They are designed *not* to be used, to moulder into obsolescence.

P. BERRIGAN: Yes, well, I can at this point just refer to the statement on the part of the Red Chinese that they would never use their nuclear weapons first—a statement that we have never matched, and never dared to match. And then if you trace the historical record of our use of nuclear weapons, it seems to counteract what theorists might say about the sort of built-in obsolescence of nuclear weapons. I think that we are very, very ready to use them. I remember the very powerful suggestion on the part of Admiral Radford, on two occasions, to give the French nuclear weapons in the Indo-Chinese war. The fact that President Eisenhower overruled him does not argue against the fact that in certain military quarters they were ready to be used.

Philip Berrigan, S.S.J.

FINN: Well, I'm not disagreeing that they might be used; there are people prepared to use them. But what *is* the best course for government to follow?

P. BERRIGAN: Initial concessions, relative to nuclear disarmament, even if they are unilateral ones, because the Russians are just as suspicious of our good intentions as we are of theirs. And I am fully convinced that they have as good reason to be suspicious of us as we have to be suspicious of them. And then, too, there's the whole climate of fear, hatred and suspicion generated by the Vietnam war.

FINN: Do you think the actions of the United States government in Vietnam are continuing and developing, fostering, what you call "war mentality"?

P. BERRIGAN: Very definitely. In perhaps the second last speech that Fulbright gave he went into this in rather accurate and certainly emphatic fashion. He said that the national conscience is just being deteriorated, a very definite war hysteria is developing among our people. And the possibility of reckless consensus on the part of the American people will perhaps even demand that this war be ended quickly—particularly in face of the increasing number of American bodies that are being brought back to this country. This is the type of thing which is being generated and increasingly is a factor in the struggle.

FINN: You mentioned our present policy as being part of an entire system, but the system also is part of the entire society of the nation. Do you regard the present policy as flowing out of the general conditions of our society, or is it some aberration?

P. BERRIGAN: It's a very, very good question. I think that there are strong elements of injustice operating within the American framework today.

And then Philip Berrigan develops those ideas that support and bind together all his observations. We are, as a country, willing to expend much energy, talent and money to arm ourselves, but we neglect the real enemies within our society: poverty, ignorance, brutal materialism. Under analysis "it's really quite a horrid picture," he says.

FINN: I take it you would accept what Eisenhower described in his farewell address as the "military-industrial complex" which is growing up, or maybe what C. Wright Mills called "the power elite."

P. BERRIGAN: Yes, and of course one of the more fearsome aspects of it is that the larger universities in this country have been bought off, too, to a very, very large extent through massive grants and through the enticements that industry offers them for their best graduates, and which they are very, very ready to channel into research, and so forth.

FINN: You said that our policy in Vietnam should be one of withdrawal but not immediate or precipitate withdrawal. Is that right?

P. BERRIGAN: Yes, I don't think we can in justice abandon a country and a population that we have ravaged for about twelve years now. I think we have a definite moral obligation there and that any military withdrawal—and of course the last test of our good faith will be military withdrawal—has to be a phased operation. The military in turn has to be replaced by a considerable number of technicians, social workers, medical people, the general run of services of all descriptions in order to serve a people that has been decimated in its manpower and fractured in its total economy, its agriculture, its industry, all of the rest. Oh, yes.

FINN: A little bit of a shift. You said earlier you do *not* reject the idea that violence under some circumstances might be called for. There are a number of people today—and I'm not speaking only of the Communists who support what they call wars of national liberation—who think that their first task must be to tear down the existing structure. Frantz Fanon, in his book *The Wretched of the Earth,* speaks of the necessity for violence, the rejection of all that colonialism and imperialism and Western civilization have imposed upon others. Do you think that those who think they must make positive constructive efforts are obligated to oppose this kind of violence by other violence?

P. BERRIGAN: This is a very, very thorny question because it's right at the heart of not only many national situations in Asia but also Africa and Latin America. One is reminded, for example, of a man like Camillo Torres who, after he went from

Philip Berrigan, S.S.J.

political organization to join the revolutionaries, was killed in action with them.* Torres, from the best information I can gain, was pretty well convinced that since the political and social system of his own country was essentially violent in tone, and since the poor, the masses, were forced to live under this climate of violence from the moment they were born until they died, that the system could only be confronted in violent terms, and so he joined the revolutionaries. I would not agree with this —at least at this stage in my thinking. I haven't heard enough of a theological justification of this course of action.

FINN: Would you support—not only sympathize with, but support—the person who, faced with the war in Vietnam, comes to the conclusion that this is an unjustified war in which he cannot morally engage? If you were presented with this as a pastoral problem, how would you react?

P. BERRIGAN: Well, I'd be very, very interested in understanding why he is opposed to the war. Under scrutiny, the reasons for opposition of the war, this particular war, on the part of many—I would say not many, but a few young pacifists—really do not stand up. The rights of conscience are not absolutes, in the sense that they usually have to be dictated by the common good or by a higher good than the evil that is being shunned. And so it's a question of investigating with a young person the reasons why a war should be shunned, then going into a system of pastoral counseling following that.

FINN: Are you generally pleased with the direction that the Catholic Church seems to be taking in its approach to questions of war and peace? I'm speaking—if I can put it broadly—of the sentiment that seems to pervade *Pacem in Terris* and the *Constitution on the Church in the Modern World* as it relates to questions of war.

* Camillo Torres is a name well known in countries of Latin America and increasingly among some groups in the United States. A priest in Colombia, Camillo Torres was officially laicized in 1965 by the Colombian Church after the hierarchy had severely reproached him for his political attitudes. ("The Church stands with those who have economic and political power, because the Church of Colombia is rich," he declared.) He subsequently joined revolutionaries who he thought were fighting on the side of justice. While engaged in a military operation in the state of Santander, Colombia, he was killed. By his example he has harshly questioned the generally accepted relations of the priest to political activity, of the Church to revolution.

P. BERRIGAN: No. Maybe I am overidealistic, but I feel a tremendous amount wanting in the general attitude of the Church toward the question of war and peace. In fact, the Catholic Church has been and still is one of the most powerful institutional allies of war. Personally, I would prefer the reaction of, let's say, Cardinal Ottaviani after the Pope returned to Rome from the U.N. From the Council floor, he called for an outlawing of war, all war, on the part of the Church and received rather substantial support from some of the Council Fathers, including the Patriarch Maximos. It would seem to me that in light of the nuclear weapons, the arms race, and because of limited wars which are, nonetheless, total in nature—the Vietnam war to my mind is a total war—that the Church ought to justify itself in a course of faith and come out for a rejection of war. And I think that eventually the Church *will*. I just wonder if it will be too late to make any difference.

FINN: You're saying, Philip, that the Church *can* and *should* make such a statement, without concern for the political problems which then must be faced by the statesman or military leader or whoever, in order to be true to itself.

P. BERRIGAN: I would say almost that, Jim. Now certainly such a decision *would* be made in light of the political climate in the world. The Fathers of the Church, and particularly the men who sat through four sessions of Council, are not so politically naïve that they would come out with such a statement to the utter disregard of political realities. But no foreseeable curbs upon the escalation of the war in Vietnam and its possible consequences and/or the arms race have been so far injected into the world situation by any structure of international moral authority and international affiliation. And the Church is all of these things. The Church is supposed to speak right from the heart of the Gospels, and it is very, very hard to imagine that Christ would view the situation today except in terms of severe denunciation. And then too—one last note—what *is* the meaning of Paul's advice, and it *was* an imperative—war, war never again, never again war—in his U.N. speech? And what does this suggest to international Catholicism?

FINN: He *did* say that, but he also said, when he spoke about the situation in Vietnam, that his own position was not that of pacifism, which overlooks relative rights and duties in that conflict. That's not a quote but that's in substance what he said.

Philip Berrigan, S.S.J.

And he also said in the U.N. that as long as we are weak men prone to error, unfortunately we may need to possess arms in order to maintain the structure which will better enable justice to be brought about. They're not contradictory statements, but . . .

P. BERRIGAN: Yes, they are spoken from different approaches to the question, I'm sure. Well, I'd be inclined at least partially to disagree with one or two of them that I know Pope Paul made, and Pius XII in his time. And I remember that John XXIII, on occasion, accepted the rights of nations to bear arms and to wage defensive war according to what amounted to the just-war theory. But I think that such statements must be interpreted in terms of the reality we have to live with, and what we seem to be moving toward. I do believe that the chances of avoiding nuclear war are less than even today.

FINN: *Less* than even today?

P. BERRIGAN: Oh yes. Yes, I would say this.

JUSTUS GEORGE LAWLER

The title of Justus George Lawler's most recent book is *Nuclear War: The Ethic, the Rhetoric, the Reality*. The title indicates a good deal about the author, for Mr. Lawler is a practiced rhetorician who is intent upon discerning in the welter of conflicting opinions those issues which most merit serious attention and ethical judgment. Those who take him on in debate are unlikely to forget the experience, for he is capable of pursuing a contested point with tenacity and increasing refinement of analysis. I was particularly interested in speaking with Mr. Lawler because he had, in his book and in subsequent articles, established his position as that of the nuclear pacifist, that is, a person who believes that nuclear weapons can have no sanctioned use, that the intrusion of such weapons into a conflict is morally unacceptable.

Lawler, who was born in Chicago in 1927, has taught in a number of schools in the Midwest. He has been a Fellow of the Committee on Social Thought at the University of Chicago and of the Faculty of Letters at the Sorbonne. He is a member of the Board of the Institute of Judeo-Christian Studies and a Fellow of the National Council on Religion in Higher Education. Among his books are *The Christian Imagination: Studies in Religious Thought* and *The Catholic Dimension in Higher Education*. He was, for four years, editor of the quarterly *Journal of Arts and Letters* and is presently editor of *Continuum*, an independent quarterly sponsored by the Saint Xavier College in Chicago, where he is now Professor of the Humanities.

Because a trip out to the College presents a few complications

Justus George Lawler

for me, Lawler kindly offers to meet in midtown Chicago. I am surprised, as he enters my rather indifferent hotel room, to see someone so young, for I have known him by reputation for years and have some vague expectation of greeting an older person. With his brown hair and clothes of differing shades of brown and tan, he provides a study in gradation and tone. As he relaxes into the armchair he seems not so much tall as long.

I have recently refreshed my memory by referring to a *Continuum* editorial in which Lawler had analyzed an address by a Catholic political scientist who had written critically of pacifists. The editorial read, in part: "Pacifists, nuclear pacifists, those who accept the just-war theory as valid but condemnatory of American nuclear strategy, those who believe the just-war theory is obsolete—all are globally grouped together and bombarded by this overkill rhetoric. Like the weapons systems he approves . . . [the author] does not seem able to discriminate between the combatants and the noncombatants, between the cities and the launching pads, between the clearly defined and significantly different positions, for example, of Gordon Zahn, Leslie Dewart, Thomas Merton, James Douglass, Robert James Fox, Archbishop Roberts, and a great number of others who have questioned the morality of the present deterrent. All are massed together and assaulted under the noisome rubric 'pacifist.' "

I ask Mr. Lawler to make some of the distinctions that are appropriate.

LAWLER: I would never see myself as a radical pacifist. In other words, I don't find even the philosophical and the historical grounds for saying simply that all war is evil. But I do think that, given the presence of such extraordinary weapons, it is quite certain that any conceivable major war in the future would be a nuclear war. And *any* use of nuclear weapons—even on a target which is military—constitutes an immoral act because once these weapons have been brought into play the *proximity* of the total war is heightened immeasurably. And as I said in the book [*Nuclear War: The Ethic, the Rhetoric, the Reality*], I *know* that this can't be logically certified, but there are scores of things in human life that aren't logically demonstrable.

FINN: Would you say the same thing would be true about the introduction of chemical and bacteriological war?

LAWLER: I would think, only because it doesn't have, at least to one's knowledge, the widespread effect, that it presents a different kind of problem. I don't think I would say simply yes or no. You know, I base this thing on a kind of convergence of probabilities, which is a phrase of [John Henry Cardinal] Newman's. No single reason would justify the conclusion that *any* use of nuclear weapons constitutes an immoral act. But the whole history of past warfare and the passions that would have to be ignited before the bomb would be dropped—all of these factors build a kind of picture that I would say gives you a basis for judging just the one act of dropping a nuclear weapon as simply immoral. And that's what I would define as the position of a nuclear pacifist.

FINN: Did you come to your position as a nuclear pacifist by using concepts of traditional just-war theory?

LAWLER: I do believe in the theory of a just war, but I think the theory is perhaps negated when it comes to prosecuting a just war through the use of nuclears.

FINN: You said earlier that a better case could have been made in 1965 than today for the U.S. prosecution of the war in Vietnam. What has changed within the last year that would make your judgment change?

LAWLER: I'm not too sure whether events have changed radically or that I have begun to look more closely at the sequence of events that may have started as far back as a year or two. But I suppose it's now much clearer that what we're supporting is not a government of the people, and this by itself would seem to weaken our case. I'm convinced that all we're doing is fighting to save face. And you can make a kind of a vague political case for the desirability of this, but it doesn't convince me. Basically, I think the war is being prosecuted immorally, and this is certainly clearer now than it was, say, a year ago—at least to me.

FINN: Because of the instability of the regime?

LAWLER: Yes, this is one basis, but also because I think it is now quite clear that there's a tremendous mass of evidence that we've been destroying civilians with a good deal of abandon. Without any definite certitude that these were combatants, and so on. In fact, one has the impression—though this may

Justus George Lawler

again be a prejudice—that the notion of noncombatants is almost nonexistent in this war. We're not going to bomb major civilian centers because this is too visible, but as far as bombing anything that's in motion, under the assumption that anything that moves is the Vietcong, this we're doing. I would say this factor would have changed my opinion. I suppose that I had great hopes a year ago that Johnson was going to negotiate from strength, that he was going to use a more considerably restrained strength than in fact he has. I think I would say too that the use of SAC, all of this escalation, is drawing nearer and nearer to the ultimate weapon and therefore an occasion for increasing the danger of a major catastrophe.

FINN: Of course the Administration continually suggests that it's operating with a good deal of restraint and that the targets are *not* indiscriminate and, as the papers today suggest, the Administration is coming under attack from people like Congressman Ford and Senator Goldwater because indeed they *are* showing such restraint.*

LAWLER: Yes, but I think that these are very relative terms, and what would strike Goldwater as excessive restraint would strike somebody else. . . . I mean ultimately there has to be a kind of faith in one's own prudential judgments, and there's nothing in the background of Goldwater that would indicate that you would think of him as being worthy of prudent trust. The military mind, say, is so intense in the inbred circles in which the government is administered that they have no concept of what the ordinary citizen or the ordinary humanist would view as restraining. In other words, they think it's exercising great restraint not to bomb Hanoi yet. This would be a

---

* This statement applies specifically to mid-April, 1966, when this interview was recorded, but a train of similar claims and counterattacks was to follow. On August 31, 1967, the Senate Preparedness Investigation Subcommittee urged President Johnson to accept the advice of high-level military leaders, to abandon his policy of (in Secretary McNamara's term) a "discriminating bombing campaign," and to widen the air war against North Vietnam. The military leaders included the chairman and members of the Joint Chiefs of Staff. Senator Stuart Symington of Missouri, a strong advocate of air power, commented that "if the position as presented by the Secretary this morning is right, I believe the United States should get out of Vietnam at the earliest possible time, and on the best possible basis; because with his premises, there would appear no chance for any true 'success' in this long war."

considerably serious infraction, I would think, or rather a frightening escalation.

FINN: I would suppose from what you said that you would think there would be a good basis for those people who *are* taking a position of selective conscientious objection.

LAWLER: Had there been enough theological sophistication at the time of the First World War to have pursued the principle of conscientious objection to its most *elementary* conclusion— that is, to its basis in freedom of conscience—then the right to selective objection would be clearly implicit in the present situation. In other words, it's only now that we *have* this theological, maybe political, refinement to recognize that conscientious objection is an absolute *right*.

FINN: Do you think official members of the Church are called upon to make open judgments about the morality of the present war?

LAWLER: Yes, I think so. Since we're talking about a moral issue, I don't see how you can let them sidestep it. I would think that there probably hasn't been enough agitation of the type that strikes the minds of bishops. In other words, the action of Catholic kids burning draft cards is not going to speak very cogently to the hierarchy. But I think that conscientious objection would be fostered by the bishops if they would realize the implications of the decree on religious freedom, that this decree directly implies the right of the free spirit to exercise its own judgment in a mature society, given a comparable maturity on the part of the individual. And I don't see how the bishops could avoid going along with this to the degree that it can be presented to them properly, making due allowance for the relative novelty of the notion in most secular and religious circles. I think they would then speak forth on their own. You know this little thing that we did in *Continuum,* where we got— it wasn't much—nine to come out against the bombing of civilian centers. This was at least a statement.

The "little thing" to which Lawler refers is an informative editorial "On Consulting the Episcopate in Matters of Practice." (The reader was expected to recognize the parallel to John Henry Newman's "On Consulting the Faithful in Matters of Doctrine.") The principle that noncombatants are immune from

Justus George Lawler

direct intended attack has been challenged recently,* and [then] Under Secretary of State, George W. Ball, had made a statement (July 13, 1965) that North Vietnam could not regard its capital city Hanoi as sanctuary against U.S. air bombardment. The *Continuum* board prepared a declaration disavowing the bombing of civilian centers such as Hanoi and sent it to the bishops of the U.S. so that those who approved the declaration would sign it.

The declaration was modified so that all who signed were satisfied. The total number of bishops who signed was nine.†

As we discuss the possible effects of such ecclesiastical statements, about which Lawler is not euphoric, I ask his opinion about newly formed organizations such as the Clergy Concerned about Vietnam and the First National Inter-Religious Conference on Peace (since then renamed the Inter-Religious Committee on Peace). The latter, a conference with heavy attendance, did turn out a number of papers‡ with specific suggestions for the implementation of policy concerning Vietnam, China,

* See O'Brien, pp. 405ff.

†   A DECLARATION ON THE THREAT OF BOMBARDMENT
                OF CIVILIAN CENTERS

The recent warning by Under Secretary of State, George W. Ball, to the NATO organization (July 13, 1965) that North Vietnam could not expect its capital city, Hanoi, to be viewed by the American government as a "privileged sanctuary" against air bombardment provides an occasion for raising a moral question on which we as Americans and as bishops of the Catholic Church must speak out.

Unlike other clouded issues concerning the war in Vietnam on which there is necessary and justifiable debate, the possibility that either side may bomb any purely civilian center would entail a clear and direct violation of Christian ethics and must be denounced as an immoral action.

Henry J. Grimmelsman	Walter W. Curtis
Bishop of Evansville	Bishop of Bridgeport
Marion F. Forst	Mark K. Carroll
Bishop of Dodge City	Bishop of Wichita
Hugh A. Donahue	John J. Russell
Bishop of Stockton	Bishop of Richmond
Maurice Schexnayder	Charles A. Buswell
Bishop of Lafayette	Bishop of Pueblo
Robert J. Dwyer	
Bishop of Reno	

‡ Homer A. Jack, ed., *Religion and Peace: Papers from The National Inter-Religious Conference on Peace* (Indianapolis, Bobbs-Merrill, 1966).

and the problems of intervention. Such groups, Lawler judges, have great potential value, but they are as yet too untried for anyone to make a firm evaluation.

FINN: I was talking with a pacifist recently, a Catholic pacifist, who suggested that on a question as serious as Vietnam, there's a certain dereliction on the part of a Church that's not able to make a statement about the morality or immorality of that war which would *call* for general approval by Catholics. Do you think that it is a reasonable judgment that such action *is* possible?

LAWLER: Churchmen are not going to be any more enlightened than the generality of their advisers. And since there's an obvious disparity of view even among fairly reputable people, I doubt that you could expect the churchmen to know which judgments to follow and therefore to make a clear-cut statement. I would think that you could expect something from them comparable to what the Protestant bodies have produced in which they would come out very strongly for a negotiated settlement. And even to have this said would be a considerable achievement if it were said by the full hierarchy; to come out against, say, escalating any further—well this might be more dubious—but as far as descrying the war itself as moral or immoral, I can't see how they would have the basis for a judgment. I can see an individual *bishop* who may have studied it, like any other individual Christian coming out with "this is my opinion," but I couldn't see the hierarchy making general statements.

FINN: To shift the topic slightly to the position of nuclear pacifism. Do you think there will be *more* Catholics who will come to see that as a sound position, or is that simply too speculative?

LAWLER: I don't really think this is speculative at all. I think it's a gradual drawing together into one strand of a number of loose threads; and I think this is something that will be born in the whole experience of the Christian community. And at *that time* I would think that you could expect the Church, looking at the sentiment of the body of the faithful, to make a statement which would come out clearly for what now would be called nuclear pacifism—that *any* nuclear war would be immoral.

Justus George Lawler

FINN: On the basis of your last comment, I would take it that you think Americans generally, and Catholics more particularly, will be able to develop what you regard as a more adequate response to the problems posed by modern war.

LAWLER: Yes, I would think that part of this would simply be an aspect of the whole enlightenment coming from the Council and above all from a thinking through of the decree on religious liberty, which is the basis for everything on conscientious objection in the text on warfare. This probably did happen in France during the Algerian war. You know, they had a kind of heightened awareness of the meaning of selective pacifism, if this is what it's called. And I suppose because now the major focus for moral concern is Vietnam, that the American people, and therefore American Catholics, *would* be expected over a period of years to contribute somehow to a kind of new assessment of the question of the morality of wars of national liberation.

FINN: What do you see as the political possibility for a country like the United States initiating significant *steps* toward unilateral disarmament?

LAWLER: Well, practically speaking, I would say probably very slight because of the whole climate now. If you have a government that can justify the war in Vietnam on the major ground that we're holding back communism, if this type of mentality prevails—which is basically a kind of troglodytic mind set —then you can't expect much enlightenment on even more liberal questions.

FINN: But if a significant body of people in the country came to think, and declare, that all nuclear war was immoral—something in which they themselves could not participate—it would create *for* the country a kind of problem which it hasn't previously had to face.

LAWLER: It's very utopian to think that many people are ever going to really come to this kind of articulated understanding. Perhaps one could hope that to the degree that it is felt by the whole community spokesmen will come forth and voice the concern. But I simply think that the whole anti-communist mentality, the holy-war spirit that prevails in the country, would make almost impossible any kind of introduction of accommodations on our part. I could see accommodations being brought about mainly by the influence of whatever it is we feel is pressuring us. In other words, I could conceive of some sort of bilateral arrangements with the Soviet Union.

FINN: Well, do you think that the pacifists today, including radical pacifists, nuclear pacifists, selective pacifists, have much political effect? Do they keep options open for the government, do they make it more difficult, or do you think they have any particular effect?

LAWLER: Well, I'm not sure that one would put it in terms of people who are one or another type of pacifist. I would think the political effect will come from people who, whether or not they'd made a judgment on themselves being able to serve in this war, are nevertheless critical of the war. And I think that there's no doubt, if one has any hope for this kind of politics, that this is bound to have a certain effect, even under a government as tightly enclosed within itself as ours is. But I think this will come not from pacifists as such. . . .

In fact I think that the political impact of most of the demonstrations has been unfortunate in that they made the voices of Senators Church and Gruening and others a little less attended to—perhaps because they began to be identified with this sort of public agitation, perhaps because they were afraid of being identified with it and therefore tended to mute their own witness. One can conceive of a much better vehicle for venting one's disgust with what is going on in Vietnam than massive marches. One can conceive of some sort of massive person-to-person doorbell campaign or something—things that have not been tried. Because I think the marches tend to antagonize the great mass of the people, which then confirms the government in the wisdom of what it's doing—although this would be, I suppose, a question for somebody to take a poll on.

FINN: In your discussions with people who differ with you about the morality or about the *basis* of United States presence in Vietnam, and who *also* claim the argument from the just-war theory, do you think that this is a matter of having different information? Or do you think there is a different understanding of just war, or is the just-war theory simply being tortured out of its proper application?

LAWLER: Well, I would say probably both groups have the same concept of the just war. I think that the one group—that is

Justus George Lawler

to say, those who are in favor of what's going on in Vietnam—must view itself as having a larger political vision, and therefore see Vietnam as merely an adjunct to a more important strategy, which is the containment of Red China, and so on. Whereas I think the other group would come up with historical analogies that would allegedly prove the Administration strategy wrong. They therefore are concerned immediately with the direct violation of a moral code; they can find *no* justification for Vietnam, no matter how *grand* the strategy used to rationalize it. And I would end up saying, I suppose, that probably you do then say that the one group *has to be* torturing the just-war concept out of its true context, while perhaps not really *knowing* that they're doing it; they're doing it so subtly or deviously. But I think that this distortion has to do with the approach to what is seen as the larger political thing. The question for just-war people and everybody else is whether any strategic program, however grand, can justify the kind of destruction going on in Vietnam. I would say no.

JEWS

ARTHUR GILBERT

Arthur Gilbert was born in Philadelphia in 1926. He received a B.A. from New York University in 1947 and four years later his M.H.L. and Rabbinical Degree from the New York Branch Hebrew Union College-Jewish Institute of Religion. He spent the next three years in graduate studies at the National Psychological Association for Psychoanalysis.

From 1953–60 he was director of the National Department of Interreligious Cooperation of the Anti-Defamation League. He represented the concerns of the Jewish community before Christian organizations and worked with them to combat not only anti-Semitism but social and religious discrimination generally. He was director of a four-year project on Religious Freedom and Public Affairs conducted by the National Conference of Christians and Jews. At the completion of that project he returned to the Anti-Defamation League where he was mainly concerned with the religious content of public and church schools, universities and seminaries. He is presently on the faculty of Marymount College in New York.

Rabbi Gilbert has addressed many Protestant and Catholic groups on Jewish-Christian relations. He was, for example, invited by Hans Küng, a highly influential Catholic theologian, to be the first lecturer at the Catholic Ecumenical Institute at Tübingen, Germany, and he was the sole Jewish observer at Billy Graham's World Evangelical Congress in Berlin in October-November 1966. He has been a productive writer whose articles have appeared in a wide number and variety of magazines and books. When I visit him in his office he has just re-

Arthur Gilbert

ceived advance copies of his newest book, *A Jew in America.** In addition to these professional activities Arthur Gilbert was also president of the Jewish Peace Fellowship from 1961–66 and is editor of their publication, *Tidings.*

We begin by discussing the Jewish Peace Fellowship and its implications. Gilbert is of medium height with a solid but rounded figure. He has a smooth clear voice and speaks in low even tones at a pace that suggests we have time at our disposal and should not sacrifice the nuanced response for the sake of efficiency.

GILBERT: A Jewish Peace Fellowship was organized during World War II in an effort to provide counsel, assistance and fellowship for those Jews who wished to serve as conscientious objectors. In those days the law required a clearly recognizable *religious* affiliation; so the Jewish Peace Fellowship became *the* agency inside the Jewish community to serve such Jews. Our numbers were never very large. The membership and board of the Jewish Peace Fellowship, however, included both Jews who were pacifists and Jews who were not; all acknowledged the right of Jewish conscientious objectors to their position—the legitimacy of their selecting from the Jewish tradition that which is pacific in impact. The board and membership of JPF, from the beginning to this day, consisted very heavily of rabbis of all denominations—Reform, Conservative and Orthodox.

FINN: But all *religious* . . .

GILBERT: Yes, almost all religious. We have a considerable number of lay members, non-rabbis, who sympathize with the purposes of the organization; but they too have come to JPF out of religious influence and commitment. JPF has issued an annual publication called *Tidings* in order to let people know that there is such an organization, to keep the members in communication with each other, and also to raise the bare minimum of funds required to keep the organization alive.

FINN: About how many Jews were registered as CO's during the Second World War?

GILBERT: It is hard to know exactly, but it was never a large number. Our best estimates are that there were approximately

* New York, Sheed and Ward, 1966.

one hundred fifty Jews both in alternative service programs and in jail for radical noncooperation. There are now two thousand supporters of the Jewish Peace Fellowship. It's a very small organization, and it has met with significant resistance inside the Jewish community.

FINN: Does this represent a division within the Jewish tradition?

GILBERT: Yes, it does. But, in addition to the religious teachings, there are historic and emotional factors to be kept in mind. For example, JPF was organized during World War II. Hitler's maniacal attack on *Jews* made many feel that any Jew who was a conscientious objector was a traitor and disloyal to his people.

FINN: As a matter of fact, Jewish conscientious objectors had a heavier burden than other objectors at that point.

GILBERT: Yes. Jewish religious law recognizes two kinds of war: a war in which it is obligatory for everyone to participate and wars that are voluntary. Among the obligatory wars are those described in the Bible for the conquest of the Holy Land —these, of course, are in the past. Such wars of conquest are never to be obliged again. But also within the category of obligation is that war where the enemy *clearly intends* to destroy the Jewish people, completely. Such an opinion would probably be held were all the Arab nations to attack Israel with the pronounced aim of driving the Jews into the sea. The defense of the land and, more importantly, saving the lives of the people would fall within the category of obligatory war.

In World War II the overwhelming majority of the Jewish community throughout the world recognized that Hitler's attack on German Jews was a personal attack on Jews in general. Over and beyond their national loyalties as Americans or Canadians or English or French, they were being attacked *as* Jews, and therefore they had an obligation to fight Hitler. The Jew who was a conscientious objector *then* had a much more difficult situation than the CO of this day; and therefore he had all the more need for the support of Jewish religious leaders. We could say to the CO: "There is a pacific tradition in Judaism; we recognize a man's right, in conscience, to come to this position; and we extend the hand of fraternity to you." But there was a hostility directed against these CO's. Jewish laymen who were on the draft boards would usually deny the request of the

Arthur Gilbert

Jewish conscientious objector; they could not believe that a Jew in his good senses could be a conscientious objector.

FINN: Because it was opposed to law and tradition?

GILBERT: Well, there was an additional factor at work. Many Jews feared that Jews would be considered disloyal to our country were there many conscientious objectors and that such disloyalty would be used by anti-Semites against us. In order to prove that Jews are *loyal* we have to send a greater percentage of our men to fight.

FINN: They have to be more than one hundred percent patriotic.

GILBERT: That's right. There was a difficulty then for the CO and there still is today. In fact Jewish agencies and organizations have not yet made arrangements to provide alternative service for Jewish conscientious objectors. It is very hard for JPF to place a Jewish conscientious objector who wants alternative service in a Jewish agency.

We have strayed from Rabbi Gilbert's exposition of the kinds of war recognized in Jewish law and the corresponding obligations imposed by them. Since there are Jewish pacifists and they do find some support, however minimal, it must derive, I suggest, from Jewish law.

GILBERT: Yes, I said there were two categories of war in Jewish rabbinical writings. One was the obligatory war which I described. Now there was also a second category of war: voluntary wars. These were wars for the defense of the nation, wars in defense of the national integrity of the Jewish state or in protection of the right to religious freedom. One was not *obliged* to serve in such a war. If such a war had to be fought it had to be declared by the appropriate political and religious authorities. Exemption had to be made for those who did not wish to engage in that war. As one can anticipate, rabbis disagreed with each other over what was a just war. Many rabbis believed that it was proper to fight for religious freedom but that it was not really important to fight for Jewish political integrity. They reasoned: even if Jews lost their political integrity they might have the right to worship God, and in that event one is not obliged to fight a war. For political sovereignty is not as significant as the freedom to serve God. On the other hand, some rabbis felt that it was important, it was *just,* to fight for political freedom.

FINN: But even the second group allows the separation of the religious and the political.

GILBERT: Oh, yes. Political independence and religious freedom did not always have to go hand in hand. Many rabbis also concerned themselves with the *methods* of warfare within the category of just war. For example, the question was raised: Can one take offensive action as a form of defense? The majority opinion answered in the negative. If the Jewish people were fighting for their political integrity then it was clear that the war had to be defensive in character. Jews would not strike first. Furthermore, even in the course of the battle itself, the state officials were obliged to keep the channels of communication open and make offers of peace. Peace overtures were obligatory at *all times,* even in the course of the war.

FINN: This has its parallels, of course, in the just-war tradition which has developed historically within Christianity, which also insists that the means to the ends have to be recognized as just.

GILBERT: Yes. Rabbis went into that issue at great length. For example, we were enjoined against destroying the earth. A scorched earth policy was prohibited.

FINN: I wonder if this would apply to defoliation.

GILBERT: Indeed. Jews were specifically prohibited from uprooting trees in the course of war. And furthermore, supposing you were to lay siege to a city. It was Jewish law that you could only surround the city on three sides, because the objective was the conquest of the *city,* not the *murder* of its inhabitants. By Jewish law we were required to allow the besieged to escape and save their lives.

Now of course such legislation derives from a day when military armament was of a different character; nevertheless it still influences many Jews who see that even today within the Jewish category of just war there are moral inhibitions regarding the nature of war. In a day of nuclear weapons, the inevitability of total destruction would *seem* to compel a pacifist position. It's impossible to engage in contemporary war without the murder of civilian population and the destruction of the land. In other words, the means of war have reached such horrendous proportions that we can no longer apply the concept *just* to nuclear war, or easily apply humane limitations.

FINN: The total war is obviously out.

GILBERT: Yes.

FINN: And even the kinds of limited war that modern nations are prepared to engage in?

GILBERT: In Asia, where war assumes a guerrilla nature, it means that we have to look upon civilian populations as soldiers; and, therefore, the way to fight war now involves us in the burning of forests, the destruction of whole communities, the murder of men, women and children. I find it hard to justify a sustained, country-wide war of such a nature that leaves the victors in worse condition than they could have even imagined.

FINN: We've accepted the statements of Chinese theorists—of Mao, specifically—that if, in guerrilla warfare, people are the sea in which guerrillas swim, it may be necessary to somehow withdraw the sea which is the peasantry. Sometimes this clearly means damage to that peasantry.

GILBERT: But there is yet a profounder Jewish conception regarding war, and it is that conviction which is truly the basis for the pacifist tradition in Judaism. War, even when fought for just reasons and in just ways, is considered sinful.

FINN: It is sinful to engage in a just action?

GILBERT: Right. The paradox in the Jewish religious tradition is exactly this: to take the life of another human being even in a just war is considered sinful. Under *all* conditions. Although a Jew might have had to go to war for a legitimate reason, still he was obliged to feel that the taking of human life was a reproach before God. Before going into battle he had to bring a sin offering or make atonement. There are a number of liturgical rites still performed in contemporary Jewish practice that repeat this ancient message of remorse over the human life ravaged by war—even that of the enemy. During the Passover Seder, for example, the ten plagues are recited—the plagues that were inflicted upon the Egyptians—and the Jewish participants spill a drop of wine from their cups at every mention of each plague.

The cup of wine in Jewish tradition has a symbolic meaning as the cup of life. The lesson learned is that one is not to enjoy a full cup because God's creatures were slaughtered in the plague and suffered anguish; the Jew's own joy is to be diminished in his compassion for Egyptian suffering. Although Jews regard Egyptian suffering to have been justly imposed because of their hard-heartedness in not permitting the Jews their freedom, nevertheless if human beings have to be killed, whatever the reason, something is wrong. War, bloodshed, violence—these violate God's wish for mankind, and we are enjoined to feel the pain of human brutality and repent.

FINN: Well, it sounds as if there is support for both the Jews who participate in war and Jews who are pacifists. As a matter of fact, it sounds like there should be for *both* a real tension.

GILBERT: In the long course of Jewish history both pacifists and nonpacifists have found support in the religious heritage. Historic factors were the decisive influence. Once the Jewish state was crippled in 70 A.D. and no longer maintained the trappings of government and army, it became evident that resistance to Rome, which continued deep into the first century, would only bleed the people more and more. It became clear, increasingly so as the Jews recognized themselves to be a weak minority scattered throughout Europe, Asia and North Africa, that we could not defend ourselves against hostility by physical means.

Jews have a custom of making a virtue out of necessity. And so there developed a pattern of Jewish religious thought that recognized a virtue in the fact that we had to find other ways of defending ourselves. We justified the nonviolent ways of reacting to a hostile environment as the superior means for resolving human conflict. The strong pacific tradition in Judaism emerged as a virtue, but it was a virtue that grew out of necessity; it was a function of our powerlessness. This situation prevailed throughout most of our history in Christian civilization. There were scattered instances where Jews resisted the Crusaders, fought back against the pogroms, or retaliated against their oppressors. But more frequently it was considered nobler to die a martyr, to risk and give one's life pronouncing the Holy Name, than to kill another, even the enemy. In our condition of helplessness we found those sources of accommodation—spiritual resistance and life-affirmation—that made the pacific approach to the reso-

Arthur Gilbert

lution of human problems a supreme virtue and a workable theory. For 1,500 years Jews were, by far, the largest community of pacifists that have ever existed in Western civilization. Then this situation changed. It changed as a result of two circumstances: first, the cruel pogroms in Czarist Russia in the late 1800's—a time of emergent nationalism and social revolution—and second, the establishment of the state of Israel.

In Eastern Europe Jewish communities were ravaged regularly. Jews under the influence of the revolutionary, nationalistic and socialistic theories then circulating in Russia heaped ridicule upon their co-religionists who accepted the attacks without resistance. Many of those Jews fled Russia, came to Israel and there organized self-defense units to protect themselves from Arab hostility.

In the period immediately prior to World War I and thereafter the Russian Jewish immigrants who had migrated to Palestine found themselves physically threatened by Arab terrorists who even then recognized a danger to the Arab hegemony over Palestine in this Jewish settlement. But these Jews, unlike their fathers in past centuries, organized the first Jewish self-defense units in almost 1,700 years. Through every means of mass communication and by appealing to the concepts of patriotism and heroism, the image of the pioneer who carried a gun, the watchman at night, became the predominant Jewish symbol. Soon it became the absolute *need* of the Zionist movement—with its trappings of statehood and power—to glorify the image of the soldier. This marked the end of Jewish pacifism as a central phenomenon of Jewish communal existence.

The issue has erupted again in a most painful way in the debate over whether those Jews who walked obediently to the gas chambers, singing, "I believe in the coming of the Messiah," were indeed more noble than the resisters in the Warsaw ghetto who fought violently against the Nazis and killed their full measure. I would say that the predominant view in Israel today, particularly among the young, is that the heroic battler is morally superior.

There is yet another aspect to this issue. Obviously there is pain in accepting the image of oneself as victim. It is horrible to think of so many Jews being slaughtered by the Nazis. It is comforting for some Jews to think of themselves as *having* power, of being able to kill another. That need has stimulated and supported a revolution in Jewish thought today: the emergence of the soldier as a hero. This is even more important to some in the Jewish community than the image of the Jew as scholar or martyr. I believe that this revolution in values has also been supported by a Christian world that is uncomfortable with the guilt that must be engendered at the movie clips of starving concentration camp victims and the sight of instrumentalities of mass destruction. If the Jew can be depicted as soldier, hero, victorious battler over evil, if he too can demonstrate some measure of human brutality, extremism in violence, then Christian guilt is abated. We all become human, sharing in judgment under God and in our sinfulness. The Jewish pacifist is harder for the Christian conscience to accept than the extremism of the Israel Irgun gang.

FINN: This revolution in Jewish values has been helped by the formation of Israel as a state. The nation state tends to support the militant aspects that are within the Jewish tradition.

GILBERT: Of course. Today militarism and pride in physical power are part of the trappings of Jewish statehood. But, of course, such a transformation of values is not unique to Jews. Passive resistance was fine during the days of Gandhi, but now, if China were to attack in Tibet, India has an army prepared to engage in military battle. Military power is part of the accoutrements of statehood in all time and for all people. It was so in the biblical period and it is the same today. Even so, many Jews were shocked when, in 1956, the Israeli Rabbi led the Israel army into the Sinai desert with the Torah scroll. I, for one, believe that this was a distortion of our religious tradition. The rabbi made it appear as though he were giving a religious sanction to the war. In my opinion, even if the Sinai campaign is to be considered just—in light of the offensive weapons seized— still it is the duty of the religious leadership to make us feel *ashamed* that we have had to engage in such battle, to feel regretful for it. Religious symbols must never be used to glorify war or to sanctify it.

Religious leadership ought always to serve as a restraining force on man's inclination to violence. The Torah must pronounce judgment upon the need for war. It must be made clear by all religions that when man wages war, even for reasons he considers just, the war is an expression of the bankruptcy of human striving. Man must always feel humiliated and shamed that his problems had to be settled that way. In Israel today, many, many Jews believe that war will not be necessary if a more sincere, concerted effort at peacemaking will be pursued. This always remains the problem: we don't pursue, with sincerity and diligence, the ways of peace. Finally, when we must reap the harvest we have sowed, which is violence, we expect all men to join in. War hysteria allows little room for the loyal dissenter.

FINN: You don't think that man's nature is such that he must necessarily form institutions or get involved in movements which lead, almost inevitably, to conflict. It's the fault of imagination or perception or intelligence . . .

GILBERT: The normative view is that war is a consequence of man's nature, his proclivity to violence. There is some validity in that position. The fact that Jews maintained a concept of obligatory war, in defense of the survival of the people as a whole, indicates that even without believing in a physical Satan, the Jews recognized that there was a diabolic element, a pervasive evil in the heart of man that could erupt at any time. And so we are instructed by Jewish religious tradition to "remember Amalek," the nation that attacked the helpless Jewish pilgrims wandering in the desert. Amalek was, thus, prototypic of the senseless cruelty of which man is capable. Jews are aware that from time to time this diabolic element erupts in history; but its eruption is an *unusual* event. We should rather believe that in general men can be reasoned with and accommodations can be found. There are values that survive defeat. There is a way of life that conquers the enemy, not by overpowering him, but by converting him. The real challenge to our civilization is to increase the numbers of those who can enjoy its benefits, and particularly the colored races of mankind.

I fear those who consider communism to be Satan, and fail to see the human being in the fact of the communist. That view of the world makes war. It is better to believe that even as men respond to fear with violence, so will they respond to justice and compassion with love. The need for human community is part of God's gift to all men.

We have discussed the two alternatives of violence or nonresistance in the face of threat or attack. I ask if the concept of nonviolent resistance has gained much attention within the Jewish community. Have historical circumstances intruded this as a concept to be taken seriously?

GILBERT: Only for those Jews who have begun to experience it through their participation in the civil rights movement. The Jewish community is still not involved in the discussion of the third alternative in those terms. Since the end of World War II a great part of the Jewish community would hold that no further wars are really required if we would only vigorously pursue the proper political and economic alternatives for the making of peace. That is why a tremendous amount of Jewish emotional support goes into the United Nations and still continues to support those political efforts that will establish channels of communication with Russia, with China, with North Vietnam. The Jewish pacific option is not now seen in terms of martyrdom for a noble faith as victims of prejudice, but rather in the ongoing task of pursuing peace through methods that are political, economic and social; these are the proper alternatives to be followed. The overwhelming sentiment in the American Jewish community *today* is in support of *this* alternative to war.

FINN: That's not a pacifist alternative. If these things don't work, war may be the outcome, an outcome in which you would participate.

GILBERT: Right. If America were attacked by China or by Russia, then the chances are that most Jews would say, "Well, we tried. Now our country is under attack; to defend ourselves is moral." The majority would assert their patriotism by being part of the military; but a small part of the Jewish community, as heretofore, would say, "No. As an individual I would rather witness to my ideals by seeking alternative service, if it's available to me. Rather than kill others I would register as conscientiously opposed to war." Now with regard to the Vietnam war, however, Jewish sentiment is more evenly divided. For in that case the morality of our position and the defensive need of the war is not at all so clear.

FINN: Can you estimate, Arthur, how Jews divide on Vietnam?

GILBERT: The Jews are split right down the middle. In every open major debate that has taken place inside the Jewish community, the rabbis have been largely in opposition to American policy in Vietnam, and the laymen were in good measure in support of the policy. And when the votes were counted, the division was sharp; it's down the middle.

Arthur Gilbert

Gilbert's estimate here is particularly interesting in the light of two events which were to follow this interview by some months. The first is President Johnson's alleged dissatisfaction with the support his Vietnam policy receives from the Jewish community. After a meeting with the President, Malcolm H. Tarlov, newly elected commander of the Jewish War Veterans, reported that the President could not understand why so many influential Jews oppose present policy, especially if one considered the assistance the U.S. has given the State of Israel.

The remarks, as reported, could only nettle—and they did. Ambassador Arthur J. Goldberg met in an unofficial, off-the-record conference a group of Jewish leaders who were top officials in nineteen national Jewish organizations, religious and secular. He explained that the President had been misunderstood, that the Administration fully understood that Jewish opinion was divided on Vietnam, that it respected dissent, and that Vietnam and Israel were connected, in the President's mind, only as small countries that merited protection from aggression. The *New York Times,* which editorially labeled this conference unfortunate and unnecessary, was typical in questioning the validity of the concept of a "Jewish community." Like other American citizens—Protestant, Catholic, atheist—Jews go their own way as individual citizens.

In a letter* taking the *New York Times* to task, Steven S. Schwarzschild rejected what he termed the "old chestnut that there is no unified Jewish community." He asserted that there is and "furthermore, this is how it should be. Americans do not only act as individuals but also as 'intermediate social groups.' In the case of Jews this is due not only to perfectly correct sociological causes . . . but also to what must minimally be called a religiously derived ethical orientation. Is this not one of the chief functions of religion?" He asserted that of course Jews do oppose the war in Vietnam in a disproportionately high degree, and that this is something they should be proud of, whatever President Johnson's reaction.

The second item that casts light on Gilbert's estimate is the

* The *New York Times,* September 25, 1966, "Letters to the Editor," p. E 11.

Gallup poll * which was released soon after the Goldberg conference, showing Jews evenly divided on Vietnam policy, 41 percent approving, 41 percent disapproving, 18 percent having no opinion.

GILBERT: The Jewish Peace Fellowship has never received so many inquiries from parents and youngsters of draft age. The whole climate has changed. Whereas in World War II you had to be some kind of an extremist to be a Jewish pacifist, at *this* moment, Jewish pacifism or conscientious objection is a very much alive option.

FINN: Do you think this is a temporary, passing phenomenon?

GILBERT: Well, I'm prejudiced. I just cannot believe at this point in the history of the world that there can be, or that there will be, another major world-wide war that I would consider just.

FINN: Of the young people who come to inquire, is the objection to Vietnam on *that* particular war or does that particular war *raise* the question of total pacifism?

GILBERT: It's both. Many young men are opposed specifically to the war in Vietnam and on that ground they wish to register as conscientious objectors. But by the nature of America's draft law, they must make their case on universal grounds, they must be opposed to all wars; and it would be better for them if they were to give a religious justification for their objection. However, once these men start reading in their faith and consider the problem in all its complexity, many begin to feel compelled to make judgments that *are* more universal and ethical and spiritual rather than simply political in character; thus they come ultimately to a Jewish pacifism rather than a limited political judgment with regard to one war.

That which gives purpose to the existence of Jewish peoplehood is of course, religious; but in today's America it is possible for the Jew to be a loyal and devoted member of the Jewish community and yet never set foot in a synagogue, never resolve the problem of his faith or work out a system of beliefs.

FINN: As you stated, it isn't always recognized as a problem.

* See p. 43.

Arthur Gilbert

GILBERT: That's right. But it is a problem today for a young man. Suddenly here comes the draft law. If a man wishes to be a CO he has to reveal his religious training; he has to consider what might have been the religious teachings that influenced him. What does he believe about God and how does his conception of God shape his decision? Now we don't teach Judaism through theological principles in our religious schools. We teach Judaism in terms of our connectedness to a people and its history; we teach Hebrew and customs and ceremonies. Theology is implicit in all of this but we do not make it explicit. Unfortunately, therefore, it is possible for a Jew to be confirmed in the Jewish religious community and yet never to have worked out a theological conception of the meaning of one's Jewish identity. Thus, Jewish young men desperately need religious counseling as they consider the morality of participation in war.

FINN: I assume it is particularly difficult for the Jew who has to explain his position to the draft board?

GILBERT: Yes. The Jew is burdened by the fact that he has to make his case in religious categories that obviously reflect a Christianized conception of religion.

FINN: The present draft laws and the present exemptions are under examination—and under attack—partly because of these difficulties. Is there within the Jewish community any effort to clarify these laws and develop them so that they will more properly take account of the difficulties faced by the Jewish CO?

GILBERT: Well, the Jewish religious position on this issue would be cast in terms of obligatory and voluntary war; and a judgment would be legitimately allowed in each circumstance. Therefore, the Jewish religious position would be that a man shouldn't have to profess, at the age of eighteen, a once-and-for-all-time position on the morality of war. He should be given the right to make a judgment in good conscience with regard to his predisposition at *that* moment and with regard to *that* war. If a man believes American participation in the Vietnam war is unjust or immoral, that person's judgment and conscience should be respected. He should be given a conscientious objector status no different than that granted to a person who attempts to make a judgment with regard to the nature of all war.

FINN: Is the Jewish Peace Fellowship working with this end in mind?

GILBERT: We rarely engage in political activity seeking legislative redress. On the other hand, individual rabbis who belong to the Jewish Peace Fellowship are always the ones, at their various rabbinical association meetings, who head up the resolutions that do press for political goals. The right of an individual to make selective judgment with regard to participation in each war is an issue that will be coming up at the rabbinical conventions. I feel confident that this position will be supported by the rabbis of the United States.

FINN: That would be a very significant voice and pressure.

GILBERT: Yes. But it represents authentic Jewish thought. There is a clear Jewish teaching on that subject. Whether you consider a war just or unjust is a matter of the individual conscience. But the *right* to make a decision at each point is a right accepted by all.

Is there an increasing convergence of views on this question? I recall the conversations that I have had with Jews, Christians and people with no religious commitment. They too would assert the right of the individual conscience to make such a decision for itself. This may not seem remarkable, but the inevitable and necessary tensions that exist between an individual and the communities to which he belongs—with their complementary rights and obligations—have not always been resolved in this fashion, even in theoretical terms. To admit such a right as absolute would, it is frequently contended, be an invitation to anarchy.

One need only recall the liberal columnist, mentioned by Zahn, who thought it would be a "helluva way to run a railroad" to let every youngster make such a decision for himself. Or the Manhattan judge who, in sentencing Terry John Sullivan to jail for refusing to carry his draft card, said he "found nothing in young Sullivan's background that would qualify him as an expert in foreign affairs." * These voices surely represent a respectable body of opinion in this country.

* The *New York Times,* July 30, 1966, p. 54.

Arthur Gilbert

But even some people who are in accord with the view expressed by Gilbert question whether it can be legally implemented; they judge the technical difficulties of dealing with a group of people who would be selective conscientious objectors as practically insurmountable. At present, objectors who base their opposition to a particular war on religious grounds are legally indistinguishable from nonreligious "political objectors," and the latter group finds little favor in Congress.*

Is it possible, I ask Gilbert, that the problem will resist all efforts to cope with it adequately?

GILBERT: I cannot accept that. In my view, if the rights of the minority *cannot* be protected, then the values of the majority are subject to serious question.

FINN: But there are historical parallels for this. The state has decided, for instance, that polygamy is not allowed even though a particular religious group would have adopted it. And it has decided that it will levy taxes on everybody, some of which will go to the war effort even though some people object. There are certain *limits* and they sometimes seem to be defined by the size of the minority.

GILBERT: I am not prepared at this point to defend each one of these actions. But a protest by a significant minority ought to give the majority some cause to consider whether they are really correct. If there is not an overwhelming consensus of the people who feel that a war is just, then maybe the chaos that would result when the minority expresses its resentment is a judgment on the majority.

Gilbert has said that a large percentage of Jews in the U.S. were opposed to "even conceiving of a nuclear war." I ask how those who are informed by and adhere to the Jewish traditional teaching on war cope with the problems presented by our nuclear weapons systems. It has been argued that they are now stabilizing factors, promoters of peace, however uneasy.

GILBERT: I think that's a myth. The political judgment that peace has been achieved through balance of power is a distorted

* These points are discussed in more detail in pp. 426ff.

reading of the facts. The profounder dimension is that it is also horrendous to the mind of man to invoke an instrumentality of destruction of such proportion. And if we didn't feel that horror before the bombs were thrown upon the Japanese, well, the realization we have today of war's total destructiveness ought to be enough to convince us. In other words, it is not only a fear of each other or for ourselves that keeps the peace. Rather it is a positive revulsion at the idea that we would ever again destroy life in such massive proportion. It is human compassion. Now if this judgment of mine is correct, there is an openness that men everywhere feel to alternatives to peace; there is evident a certain rational hope, a prayer, that ways can be found to deal with international conflict without using maximum force or violence. What started out as awe at our destructive capacity has now become hope in our human ingenuity.

EVERETT GENDLER

"Anyone observing the current Jewish socio-religious scene is bound to note an interesting phenomenon: in relation to the momentous issues of war and peace two rather distinct sets of attitudes appear within the community.

"One we might designate that of the Establishment. This, represented by the majority of statements issued by individual rabbis, rabbinic groups, and respected (and respectable) community spokesmen, portrays Judaism's attitude toward the life-and-death issues of our time in somewhat the following manner:

"Judaism prizes peace highly and sees it as that condition of life fitting and proper to man. At the same time, however, Judaism is 'realistic,' not 'pacifist.' . . . Though aware of non-violent motifs within the Jewish religious tradition, Establishment Judaism today seems to have little trust in such schemes, and the terms and categories of its analyses are notably similar to those of any *realpolitik* analysis.

"The other attitude within the Jewish community today we might designate the Dissenter position. The Dissenters are, roughly, those many Jews, young people especially, in sympathy with and active within . . . peace groups. . . . By their participation in petitions, peace marches, picketing, and other forms of protest as well as affirmative activities, these members of the Jewish community implicitly challenge the propositions of Establishment Judaism.

"They question whether even life itself, let alone human values, can be preserved by mass violence in this advanced technological age. They question the validity of the sovereign state as a social organism, and they are radically skeptical of its claim to defend either ideals or persons. . . .

"Despite its sketchiness, this characterization of the polar points of view within the Jewish community appears to me sufficiently accurate to serve as the basis for a very important, though seldom asked, question: Which point of view, that of the Establishment or that of the Dissenters, is closer to the moral mainstream of Judaism?"

This is from the translator's introduction to what is itself an extremely interesting article, "Politics and Passion: An Inquiry into the Evils of Our Time," by Rabbi Aaron Samuel Tamaret (1869–1931).* The introduction and the translation from the Hebrew are the work of Everett E. Gendler, rabbi of the Jewish Center in Princeton, New Jersey.

Everett Gendler was born in a small town in Iowa in 1928. He received a B.A. from the University of Chicago and began advanced work in the Department of Philosophy. He received his M.H.L. and rabbinic ordination from Jewish Theological Seminary and he has done graduate work in History and the Philosophy of Religions at Columbia University.

He has served congregations in Mexico, Venezuela and Brazil, among others. He has been teacher, youth counselor, discussion leader, and a participant, not only in conferences which demand words but in demonstrations which require action. He is a member of the Fellowship of Reconciliation, the War Resisters League, the Jewish Peace Fellowship and, he would want me to add, the Jewish Vegetarian Society.

I had known him to be an able and articulate social critic and I was eager to speak with him about the question he had posed: is the point of view of the Establishment or that of the Dissenter closer to the moral mainstream of Judaism? Since his answer was implied, what I really wanted to probe for was the basis for his answer.

Rabbi Gendler greets me at the door to his office; because he is unexpectedly called away for a few minutes I have time to look at his bookshelves—my usual first impulse—and glance

* In *Judaism,* Vol. 12, 1963, pp. 36–56.

Everett Gendler

around his neat but obviously busy office. In one corner, but not inconspicuous, is a familiar poster of several Negroes, one with a long, lean uplifted arm touching the lower edge of the single, stark word NOW. It is the same poster that I had seen in the dilapidated headquarters of the Boston CNVA when I had talked with David Reed, and was to see later in the neat, efficient headquarters of SNCC in Atlanta.

In addition to the Hebrew texts on the shelves are Herman Kahn's *On Nuclear War,* John Bennett's *Nuclear Weapons and the Conflict of Conscience,* Jean Lasserre's *War and the Gospels* and related books. There are also books by people as diverse as Buber, Hammerskjöld, Keats and Wilfred Owen.

Rabbi Gendler returns with a light energetic step. He has a slight, trim build and firm, refined features. His wavy, wiry hair sits close to his head, thinning on top and fuller and graying at the temples. His movements correspond to his lively expressions and his gestures are both strong and graceful.

GENDLER: My personal feeling today is that for understandable reasons Jewish spokesmen and even many rabbis don't express the tradition as I think it existed throughout most of the other centuries, at least most of the post-biblical age. I think there was a great striving for peaceable accommodation with all men. I think that there was an *abhorrence* of bloodshed—and there's no term that should be used that is less strong than that. I think there was cultivated in the *shtetel* community and in the Talmudic tradition an *abhorrence* of even the instruments and the implements of war or bloodshed.

It's explicit in the Talmud that while items of ornamentation can be worn on the Shabbat and not transgress the prohibition against carrying, anything associated with military exploits is by *no construction* to be regarded as ornamentation. And you find the rabbis of the classical age constantly reinterpreting the war episodes of the Bible. "Who are these mighty armed warriors? These are the learned men armed with the teachings of Torah." You have it all the time, and part of it I think is hyperbole, part of it is fantasy, part of it is very profound wisdom. But this streak, this whole attitude of peaceableness and the refraining from injuring others, has been very much criticized by people like Hannah Arendt and Bruno Bettelheim.

Particular circumstances in Central Europe, and the rise of

Nazism, made this whole attitude seem somehow irrelevant to political and social life today. There was an appalling loss of life, and I think that Bettelheim's treatment of it in *The Informed Heart* is not patronizing and not hostile; he raises some very deep questions about whether an inner attitude may not invite or at least permit the harm, the destruction of an individual.

FINN: And this inner attitude is one that had been prepared for many centuries.

GENDLER: Right. Now, I think that what's happened is that most spokesmen today for Judaism appreciate that denying reality, turning one's back on evil, may be disastrous; instead of asking what means we have for resisting evil that are consummate with this tradition, they abandon too much of the tradition and adopt what was already brewing earlier in the century within the Jewish spirit, a kind of militancy which quickly becomes a kind of military spirit.

I find, for example, that in any discussion of current issues, it is *not* possible to sustain a discussion without flipping back to 1933 and 1939 and through '45. It's understandable, but if it's tragic for a general to fight the last war, it's even more tragic for a religious people to fight the war before last. But that's how I would account for the fact that someone like Tamaret, who seems to me just typical of the whole beauty of the Eastern European Jew, is *much* despised by many of the modern Israelis but still has a great beauty and I think a great relevance for our time. I think that accounts for the fact that he seems so strange and so deviant, whereas all of us who will temporize and make out a case for expediency seem like the normative Jews today.

FINN: Would Tamaret be more readily acceptable by Jews in America than he would by Israelis?

GENDLER: I think that certainly the young radicals among Jews in the United States would find him more acceptable than comparable radical or alienated elements in Israel. But I don't think his teachings would meet with much reception on the part of many people who are perhaps more committed to a comfortable kind of middle-class materialism, even though they are within the Jewish community and often members of synagogues. He would seem terribly strange and the sort of Jewish phenonemon that needs revision to make Judaism up-to-date.

Everett Gendler

FINN: How close is Tamaret, in your own thinking, to what in the long tradition is the mainstream of Jewish teaching?

GENDLER: He seems to me very close. You know, I try to argue, in what some regard as a somewhat biased introduction to the article, and [with a slight laugh]—I admit it; sure it is, but it's a fair bias. I try to argue that he represents a visionary application of many a traditional teaching, that most of us are too shy to take as seriously and as semi-literally as he does.

FINN: You suggested that Jews should look back on their tradition to find other ways of resisting violence which are not military and not completely pacifist. Well, are there alternative ways which Jews *have* used in the past?

GENDER: Yes, I think one of the important cases is the description in Josephus of the massive nonviolent resistance of the Jews to Caligula. And it's a very moving story. It's reprinted in *The Quiet Battle,** but it's also in Josephus.

Gendler recounts briefly the story of the ten thousand Jews who, in order to prevent the installation of Caligula's statue, throw themselves in the path of the Roman soldiers. Their lives threatened, they reply that while they live they can allow no such desecration of the Temple. The soldiers are chastened, other circumstances intervene and the Jews triumph. Gendler acknowledges that the "other circumstances" help determine the outcome, but then, he adds, they do in violent conflicts as well. (As editor of *The Quiet Battle,* Sibley comments on this event: "Although certain Jews living at that time did espouse principled doctrines of nonviolent resistance, the Jewish community's behavior during the incident . . . seems to have been motivated by its helplessness in a military sense, rather than by any articulated set of beliefs.")

FINN: You've already cautioned about reverting to the thirties as a touchstone, but nevertheless the thirties *are* important, and of crucial importance for Jews, because *no one* would suggest that this particular technique would have worked with Hitler. I presume—although I say it confidently—I'm presuming that's the case.

* Mulford Sibley, ed., *The Quiet Battle* (Garden City, Doubleday and Company, Inc., 1963), pp. 111–15.

GENDLER: Well, I'm not sure. You see, there are so many considerations. Let's ask, what would have worked with Hitler? Now partly the question is, at what point are you willing to begin working? I think this really is crucial. First of all you have to ask: What sorts of resistance might have mattered in the early days of Hitler? A friend of mine asks the question: What would have happened if in '37, '38—I don't even remember the exact dates—in Austria, at two o'clock in the morning when the Nazis knocked on the door, instead of Jews saying "Shhh, don't make any noise; what will the neighbors think?"—and there were Jews who did this—if instead there had been a certain facing of the foe? It could have been nonviolent; it might have been *terribly different*. Bettelheim asks the question, and I think it's a valid question in the extreme situation, why were there so few attempts to escape on the long marches? Now there had already been a terribly long process of human destruction and people had been brutalized. But perhaps the real question is: How did it happen that people didn't resist? I don't want to throw out the modern criticism of what may have been undue passivity—not just pacifism but undue passiveness—throughout the ages. A kind of reliance on a supernatural force intervening from outside is not, I think, what any of us would advocate. And I think what's striking about Tamaret writing fifty or sixty years ago, is that he doesn't take refuge in that, but finds within the texture of human life those dynamics which may contribute to defense, though nonviolently. But I think a lot of the modern criticism of the tradition is a rejection of passivity, and I'm sympathetic to that 'cause I'm all in favor of much activism. But I think that one musn't confuse the passivity then with the selection of appropriate means.

FINN: Let me ask if you think, on the basis of what is obviously historically limited experience, whether the way in which Jews in Israel appropriate the main traditions of Judaism differs markedly from the way Jews in America do?

GENDLER: I think that there may be differences. And I'm not sure entirely what may account for the differences. Some of the articulate Jews today in this country will, in my opinion, represent the tradition at its best. Some of them find their chief areas of concern in the civil rights struggle, and the particular application of nonviolence in this area at least appears promising. There's been more experience of person-to-person con-

Everett Gendler

frontation and personal demonstrations. I think *confrontation* is the key word here. I think that activist Jews who are sensitive to the tradition which asks that we seek life, choose it, that we also not stand by silently at the blood of our neighbor—I think that there is a kind of human tradition of how we meet one another face to face which is available and which can be put to use.

I suspect that activist Jews concerned with pressing problems in Israel think most immediately not of what can be done with Yemenites and Arabs within Israel. The question probably is what can be done to defend the borders against external pressure. And since the effective application of nonviolent techniques to this kind of political clash is almost nonexistent, it would take a *particularly* visionary person or group to involve themselves with it. My expectation is that most of the young Israelis will sound very much like the realistic politicians in any nation state power.

I think also, insofar as Israel and its neighbors are not technologically so advanced in war-making potential, to that extent there is still great possibility for the application of nonviolence. It becomes harder and harder as human beings become more removed from one another, and as 8,000 miles and the missiles and the pushbuttons and the computers intervene. So that while I think it not likely that most of the Israelis I'm aware of are going to be active in this development, I think they have a tremendous possibility.

FINN: You talk of this as something which would be exciting, but how likely do you think it is that the Israelis would adopt some of the experiments you talked about? We really do not have, historically, a people who are themselves invested with the power and responsibility you mentioned taking that risk. They can risk their own lives but not that of the nation state.*

---

* This statement would benefit from qualification. For example, Donald Armstrong invokes the history of Carthage:

"Twenty-one centuries ago, a certain nation so loved peace that no price to keep the peace was too exorbitant. It faced a ruthless enemy, but it abandoned war as an instrument of policy. It tied its hands by giving 300 young noblemen as hostages to prove its peaceful intentions. It surrendered unconditionally when the enemy declared war. Finally, on the enemy's demand, it disarmed unilaterally. Appeasement could go no further."

After repeated concessions, Carthage finally resisted. "Alas, for Carthage, the amazing will to resist Rome's aggression came too late. The

GENDLER: Right. . . . Just the way you phrased the question suggests, in a way, part of the answer. Insofar as Israel the political state—not Israel the concentration of Jews, not Israel as a cultural, religious, economic center—insofar as that Israel was a creation of a certain kind of political dynamism which has been identified with the military as its primary means of defense, I think it very *un*likely. I think it would depend, though, on the possibility of Israelis reclaiming certain traditional elements within Judaism now that some of the "practical problems" are at least more under control. But I think that in some ways the desire for a nation state represents a spirit which is not always defensible by nonviolent means.

You see, I criticize those who are busy reworrying 1933, but I admit that there's a tendency in me to go back to '47, and I keep wishing that Judah Magnes and Martin Buber and Henrietta Szold and Ernst Simon had been the spokesmen, or been recognized as the true spokesmen. I'm still sorry about the partition, I'm still sorry that a bi-national state wasn't established. I think rapprochement will ultimately mean some kind of extended national unit where the same kinds of human problems will have to be faced, where Jewish-Arab rapprochement will be the issue. And I think it would have been somehow easier in '47 than in '67.

FINN: To get closer to home, you've talked about younger Jewish radicals who are in movements like SDS and Turn Toward Peace and SNCC. Do these people have conscious ties to Judaism as a religion? I mean, do they feel part of the *religious* Jewish community or would they say they are simply part of a *Jewish* community, or would they even feel community ties?

GENDLER: Perhaps one could say *most* don't feel identified with the synagogue. Some of them feel identified with values in the tradition. Many of them, I suspect, feel close to the prophets, though many of them seem to find all of this irrelevant for their particular commitments. Or it's relevant in a kind of inherited and subconscious rather than conscious way. A lot of them recognize as a kind of sociological fact their being Jewish.

enemy's creeping advances, the deterioration of Carthaginian will during the cold war, their modest hope to maintain the status quo, combined to ensure the death of an empire." From "Unilateral Disarmament: A Case History," *Peace and War*, Frank R. Barnett, William C. Mott and John C. Neff, eds. (New York, Anchor Books, 1965), pp. 5–13.

Everett Gendler

They make of it little, and sociological facts without any other meaning probably shouldn't be made too much of.

I hope that we'll be at least wise enough, if we haven't encouraged and supported these radicals, to draw on them for the future of this community. They're a real challenge to the synagogue. What I hope is that rather than leaving the synagogue ranks they'll pull us all along. My assumption is that with all of the good to be found in this society, there is still a fattening over—as Isaiah puts it—there's a fattening over of the faculties, which impoverishes the human being. And I think that a lot of kids have the potential for recognizing that satisfaction is not found simply in passive enjoyment of things or comforts.

But I think there is not just social unrest in and because of the slums and the urban ghettoes; I think there's enough spiritual unrest so that there are real possibilities of an awakening. And I think that it could happen partly because of the comfort. I mean, the comfort both breeds the dissatisfaction and at the same time provides a base on which the dissatisfaction can operate without jeopardizing the minimum needs of people.

This may be pure wishful thinking, and if my wife were here she would say "Och, listen to him." I'm saying it could happen. In fact I think there are possibilities for real breakaways, but much depends here on the clergy, and since none of the radicals do you think these few are?

FINN: And few of the clergy enter the radicals. How valuable do you think these few are?

GENDLER: I think all of them are valuable. First of all, they tend to support some of the currents within the clergy which may not always have their out. Look, we're human and we're often shy and we're often scared and we're often uncertain; maybe it would be nice if we weren't, but we are, and we get support from one another. So all of this activity, all of this social concern, all of this protest, however mild—and some of it seems to me much too mild for the investment of time and energy—all of it, to the extent that it represents religion speaking to current issues, is valuable at that level.

Now the question—and I think you've raised pertinent issues in *Worldview*—the question of in what terms shall these groups speak, seems to me quite important. I'm sympathetic to all of them, but it seems to me that insofar as these groups function as amateur political science assemblages they probably accomplish little. I think that there are still the remains of a moral tradition in the West, a moral tradition that has found embodiment in some respects in the just-war doctrine, in other respects in still a stronger pacifist position, and I think that this tradition has to be brought to bear on the political issues of today. I don't like to see clergy groups simply sponsoring candidates for the House or the Senate. I don't like to see them dealing excessively with issues of strategy, though one cannot avoid the question of the consequences of one's action. But the real burden at this point is to affirm and reaffirm some of the old clichés—I mean the sanctity of human life, that ends do not justify means, that application of slogans does not thereby sanctify any particular course of action.

I think that severe moral criticism, not disguised political criticism but the kind of way-out criticism which the prophets and the saints have made, is what ought to be offered by these groups. And I think that to take these generalities still yields a kind of discourse different from political strategy and is valid, terribly valid, in determining any kind of national policy.

FINN: Are there any people that you would pick out who are offering the kind of way-out criticism you said the prophets and saints did?

GENDLER: Ahhhh. Yes sir, friend: James Douglass and Daniel Berrigan and Philip Berrigan, just to name three. Maybe I think of them just because we've spoken of them earlier—but they speak the Gospel, the text. They don't merely speak generalities, they apply them. But the applications are, I think, on religious not simply power-political grounds. Steven Schwarzschild: A perfect example. Steven speaks preposterously and I think truly. These are all figures within the religious community, but I'm not even mentioning people like A. J. Muste. Dave Dellinger I would mention especially because while he speaks in political terms he's one of the few people I've heard in any of the teach-in situations who really deal with the moral issues. He is a moralist in the good sense of that term, and I think he speaks both truth and morality to power. And that seems to me the crucial religious function.

FINN: What would your own moral and political judgment be about Israel's getting greater arms and using reactors to develop nuclear weapons?

Everett Gendler

GENDLER: I'm slightly hesitant about answering because, not living there and not being immediately involved, I hate to prescribe for someone else. My personal attitude toward nuclear weapons is that under no circumstances and for no end may they be used. That seems to me almost a categorical imperative.

Gendler has said that he is committed to nonviolence. I ask him a question that troubles many pacifists. There are in Latin America, for example, or in Africa, countries in which most of the people suffer great deprivation while the ruling minority is comfortable or rich. Do they have a right to violent revolution?

GENDLER: Have people the right to use violence? While I'm sympathetic to the need for radical change, some prerequisites are necessary if a violent revolution is to have any meaning at all. And if these prerequisites are there, might there not then be some possibility for the use of nonviolence? I don't know. Let me say that I cannot feel quite the same about the oppressed South African striking out as I do about our heavily armed planes flying over peasant territory in Vietnam.

FINN: There are a number of people in civil rights groups— Martin Luther King is a good example—who have been criticizing our foreign policy *after* they have established their authority in terms of civil rights in this country. Do you think this is a sound extrapolation?

GENDLER: Personally I do. I think that there is a continuum. I think there's great validity in a moral approach to human issues at home being applied to the international area. I think in fact it's one of the really hopeful things that's happened, because too often we've been able to make moral judgments within a society but not between societies. The international area has been really a kind of open banditry area, and now *if* these moral judgments are applied—not simple-mindedly but with sophistication, and taking due note of all the issues—and if the basis for the judgments is partly the civil rights movement and this kind of personal experience with people here, it seems to be something that all of us should welcome.

From the point of view of the civil rights movement, I think it is, on a short-term basis, poor. I think they will suffer by it.

I admire their willingness to suffer for it, and they earn greater respect from me because of it. I think it's a perfect case of a moral act in which some of the immediate consequences are unpleasant but in which the real contribution is substantial. But as I say, I'm not under any illusions. That's *murder* for the civil rights movement so far as *immediate* support from some of the established white element. But the real issue *is* whether the civil rights movement will simply buy its way into this society or whether it will be the means by which the society can be significantly transformed. Personally, I hope for the latter.

FINN: How did you come to hold the position that you do? Did you find it primarily in what you regard as the teachings of the Jewish tradition, or in the humanistic tradition, or simply in what's available to everybody today?

GENDLER: I think personally for me it was a combination of many things, and I would start with temperament. O.K.? When I was struggling with the question of whether I should be available for the military chaplaincy, I remembered asking myself if this were a newly-arrived-at struggle—though for a number of years I had been associating with Friends and had been involved in work projects and so on. And I could remember when we were just moving to Des Moines and the Second World War broke out and I was quite young, the question came up, would I kill somebody. And at that time I understood the Ten Commandments to mean "you shall not kill." Now, later subtleties suggest that it means "you shall not murder," but at the time, in a very simple-minded way but instinctively, that seemed to me what it was saying. And the strong peaceable tradition within Judaism, reflected in rabbinic writings, had a *lot* of effect on me because I became acquainted with the prophets when I was in high school. But I also became acquainted with Thoreau when I was in high school, I also heard of Gandhi—so it was a combination, it really was.

FINN: Is there such a thing as a pacifist mind or a pacifist temperament? People use, correctly or not, "the military mind" and think that it has some meaning.

GENDLER: I wouldn't talk about the pacifist *mind* if I were to try to deal with this typology, pacifist, and I'm not sure that it's valid altogether. But I think that one *might* find a particular. . . . No, I'm trying to think now of individual pacifists I know and, you know, I can't even say that pacifists are necessarily less hostile than the ordinary human being bumping about. It *could be* that different individuals come to it by different paths. It *may* be some of the psychoanalytic criticism suggesting that this is simply a defense against an excess of inner hostility is true in some cases. I think that—not wanting to judge but just reacting—there are pacifists who seem to me to exude a kind of hostility. I think there are others who are deeply appreciative of the gift of life and this earth and other people and who really can identify with others—not just humans, but trees and vegetation, all that. *But* I also know nonpacifists who are deeply receptive to Creation.

I have often heard Rabbi Gendler stress the value of life and the Creation which supports it, and I recall a beautiful and severe quotation he had included in an essay I have recently read.

> In the hour when the Holy One, blessed be He,
> created the first man,
> He took him and let him pass before all the trees
> of the garden of Eden,
> and said to him:
> See My works, how fine and excellent they are!
> Now all that I have created, for you have I created.
> Think upon this, and do not corrupt and desolate
> My world:
> for if you corrupt it, there is no one to set it
> right after you.*

* Ecclesiastes Rabbah 7. In *". . . therefore choose life,"* a pamphlet published by the Center for the Study of Democratic Institutions, Santa Barbara, California.

STEVEN S. SCHWARZSCHILD

Dr. Steven S. Schwarzschild has the distinction of being the only American rabbi who is a member of both the (Reform) Central Conference of American Rabbis and the (Conservative) Rabbinical Assembly of America and of important commissions of both. On the day he came to my office he was scheduled to fulfill a formal invitation to speak to a group of Orthodox Jews. If we can divest the term of the Christian habiliments it has donned in recent years, this was an ecumenical achievement of no mean proportion.

Born in 1924, Dr. Schwarzschild received a B.A. in philosophy at the University of Cincinnati and degrees as Bachelor, Master and Doctor of Hebrew Letters at the Hebrew Union College-Jewish Institute of Religion in the same city. He has served as rabbi to the Jewish Community of Berlin, and to the Federation of Jewish Communities in the Russian Occupation Zone, 1948–1950, as well as to communities in Fargo, North Dakota and Lynn, Massachusetts. He has taught at Brown University and at Washington University, where he is now. The author of *Franz Rosenzweig—Guide to Reversioners,* he has also written a large number of scholarly articles. He is presently editor of *Judaism,* a quarterly journal sponsored by the American Jewish Congress and regarded by many as the most significant journal of Jewish religious thought in the world today.

My first and continuing impression of Steven Schwarzschild is that he is a man in whom force and energy and passion have found a home. His dedication to what he considers important and his conviction that he has a serious and sound position

Steven S. Schwarzschild

allow him to override the frequent worry that one will, in discussing matters of war and peace, seem emotional or, what's worse, irrelevant.

Since I have last seen him he has trimmed down what are still a fine full mustache and goatee, which are as dark as his strong, black hair. After introducing him to James Forest, who is just leaving, and picking up some loose threads of past conversations, we turn to the agreed-upon topics.

FINN: What are the major elements of doctrinal pacifism, as you described your own position?

SCHWARZSCHILD: Well, in the first place, obviously, principled opposition to any war by anybody at anytime under any conceivable set of circumstances—in fact, under all circumstances, for anybody. Another element is that I derive it, with some difficulties I grant and at the cost of some exertion, but I derive it from what I believe to be authoritative and mainstream Jewish sources—which would make it doctrinal in another sense of the word. I believe, and want to believe, that not only is the pacifism to which I subscribe congruent with, I even want to go so far as to claim that it is *identical* with authoritative, normative Judaism. However, what I'm saying is that to prove this involves me in some admitted difficulties.

FINN: Do you think that you have at this point intellectually overcome these difficulties? I meant in terms of the mainstream of Judaism, because there are, of course, a great number of. . . .

SCHWARZSCHILD: Jews who would disagree with me.

FINN: Yes. Historically and presently. And with support from the Bible.

SCHWARZSCHILD: Lots of people as knowledgeable and more knowledgeable than I, would agree with what you said just now. This however having been said, I think that you and they are entirely wrong. In the first place, the Bible is not authoritative Judaism. Talmudic law is authoritative Judaism. Another way of putting this is to say that the Bible as read by the Talmud is authoritative Judaism. And therefore the problem of pacifism, like every other problem that is to be dealt with Jewishly, must be dealt with in terms primarily of Talmudic law, not in terms of the Bible. Now the way the Talmud reads the very passages that you presumably had reference to in the Bible tends to be very different from what the uninstructed and unenlightened and unguided mind will see in the pages of the Bible.

To give you only one example, all, virtually all of the law, all of the narratives of war in, and for that matter *beyond,* the Pentateuch that people usually refer to—I believe it was Aldous Huxley who once spoke of the Bible as "that bronze age document," with all the barbarism and belligerency and the bloodthirstiness of it—virtually all of those wars are, in Talmudic law, referred to as *Milchamot sheva goyim,* the wars of the seven peoples—the seven peoples being the seven aboriginal Palestinian populations.

Talmudic law says that with the disappearance in history of these seven aboriginal Palestinian peoples, everything said about that kind of war automatically lapses for all eternity thereafter. So that they set absolutely no precedent, but *none whatsoever* —legal, moral, theological or what have you. This is regarded in Jewish law as a closed chapter which has absolutely no bearing on anything that anybody is ever going to do again in the history of mankind. Which eliminates one entire section of what I presume you may have had in mind.

FINN: Would you think that there would be one reading of the Talmud that would be more correct than another, that pacifism would be what is recommended? Or are there alternatives of which pacifism is one which would be equal with others?

SCHWARZSCHILD: Well, you said something earlier on about the historical and theological predisposition which many people think they perceive in the Jewish record which does not seem to be doctrinally pacifist. Now one thing, whatever casuists and theologians and philosophers and ethicists may say about Jewish theory with respect to violence, one thing I think is absolutely indisputable: namely, that two thousand solid years of *actual* Jewish history—and the hell with all the theorizing—is quite *unqualifiedly* de facto the most extraordinary exemplification of persistent practiced pacifism in the history of the human race (with the possible exception of what the American Negro community has been doing in this country in the last ten years).

FINN: Well, two points concerning what you said about the two thousand years. One is—and here I put forth an opinion which a number of Jewish spokesmen have themselves given to me—the Jewish pacifism for those two thousand years was not a doctrinal pacifism—not even pacifism so much as passivism. Jews were passive when they did not resist. I mean they did not resist nonviolently; they did not resist at all.

SCHWARZSCHILD: Now as to some of the other things we've been talking about I understand that I hold a very small minority view. And though I think I'm right, obviously I must grant that the people who disagree with me can make a very good case which one has to take seriously. What you quoted just now I find to be theoretically, morally, and if I may say so even scientifically obnoxious—not just wrong, but obnoxious.

FINN: You would say this most specifically, I presume, about the experience of the Jews in Germany during World War II?

SCHWARZSCHILD: That's only the last thirty years. You know, obviously that's sort of the climax of it all. But on the other hand there are, as I say, two solid millennia that are in complete accord with what happened in Nazi Europe. It is not only false, but it is profoundly revolting and obnoxious to say that they didn't resist. They certainly *did* resist. They resisted in a more grandiose and, literally, ineffably magnificent way than anybody has ever resisted in the history of the human race, in the name of heaven. You mean to say that the people who were in the concentration camps and who, like some of my teachers, taught Talmud and philosophy and theology and ethics and literature weren't resisting? Ernst Simon, a teacher of mine who's head of the Department of Education at the Hebrew University, wrote a little book about the Jewish school system in Nazi Germany, and the subtitle I believe was "Self-education as Spiritual Resistance." I mean to say Goethe and Schiller, but particularly Schiller, who couldn't be taught any more in the German schools by Germans to Germans, was being studied by Jews at the hands of Jewish teachers in the midst of a spiritually and intellectually and morally completely degraded and denuded Germany. And this is not to speak of the Jewish subject matter they also taught.

FINN: Well, what happens when the Jews who have done this are then simply killed, completely wiped out?

SCHWARZSCHILD: You know, this is the Hannah Arendt syndrome. I'll say this on the record. And I think her Eichmann book has been much misunderstood. I think there are some things in it that need to be taken much more seriously than in fact they were. For example I don't think it's a germanophilic book as some people have said. But she, like Attorney General Hausner of Israel, have fallen prey to that insidious Western, European, Occidental, Greek question, which is the question that you're now also raising: Why didn't you fight back? Why did you let yourself be led to the slaughter like sheep?

Well, the fact of the matter is they didn't let themselves be led to the slaughter like sheep. They studied, they prayed, they made their confession of faith—even those who hadn't had the faith before they were led to the slaughter—in the hour of their death. Now we have a long tradition also in Western culture that the martyr, as the Greek work etymologically indicates, is a witness to the truth, to *his* truth. Well now they certainly are martyrs and therefore, by definition, they witness to a truth. And if that isn't nonviolent resistance I don't know what is. If one dies for a truth, then one certainly isn't being passive, is one?

It's incidentally interesting that among the Jews, it's usually people like Hannah Arendt—for whom, I want to repeat, I have a good deal of respect—and Bruno Bettelheim, for whom I have very little, the almost completely Westernized, de-Juda-ized Jews, who make that accusation of passivism. There is a vast literature by now—unfortunately for the rest of the world mostly in Hebrew and in Yiddish—it's come to be known as the Holocaust literature, which gives the lie to this entire view which indicts Jews for their supposed passivism. I know you're right, that some people do say this—namely, that Jews for the last two thousand years have been pacifists because they had no alternative. Just like these individual Jews who may have been martyred as Jews although if they had had an alternative would've been very eager to choose it. To say that Jews didn't fight back because they had no alternative and that therefore they weren't martyrs is to say something about one's own dis-belief in Providence and in the God of History. I think anybody who is slaughtered is automatically a saint. I don't care *what* he has previously been. So that I would maintain my original position that there is a factual history of two thousand years of Jewish pacifism, I repeat, the likes of which I do not believe can be found anywhere in human annals.

FINN: Is this tradition compromised or modified or compli-cated by present-day Israel? And does this present theoretical-intellectual problems for someone who has your position?

Steven S. Schwarzschild

SCHWARZSCHILD: It certainly does. But I hasten to add that the fact that difficulties are being created for me, theoretical difficulties, and for that matter even very practical moral and political difficulties, does not lead me to try to cut through the Gordian knot—I don't want to be misunderstood on this—by simply rejecting pacifism or the actions of the nation state of Israel if they are in conflict with each other; I want to try to work out those problems.

As we talk it seems clear to me that for Steven Schwarzschild pacifism is simultaneously a passion, an intellectual conviction, and a prism through which he can view vast historical events. For him it is a solid reference point, a means to illuminate and clarify much that is murky, disturbing and uncertain in human affairs. I ask him as I have asked others: in a society which does not greatly honor the pacifist, how did he come to his position? What biographical or psychological preparation was there?

As usual, and not surprisingly, the answer is partial and tentative. His father is a socialist who participated in the heavily pacifist German revolutions at the end of the First World War, and he has some sympathetic admiration for that background. But in 1941, when the United States entered the war, he was only seventeen and since he was soon enrolled in the seminary he did not have to make the crucial decision of accepting or refusing military service at that time. He speculates that the fact of not being in the war may have induced him "to find a good reason for this," but we both agree that without supporting reasons any "rationalizations" would soon have collapsed. And when the full horrors of the Nazi wars were revealed they did not drive him, as they did some World War II pacifists, to reject or temper his pacifism; that revelation strengthened his growing convictions.

How do his present convictions help him to cope with some of the problems presented by the Second World War? Is it possible, retrospectively, to make judgments about the opposition of the U.S. and England to Hitler's Germany? His response is accompanied by a laugh which acknowledges the apparent arrogance which informs his reply, but he is quite serious.

SCHWARZSCHILD: I confess that I try to think about such questions, starting from given philosophical and theological and Jewish starting points, and I try to work myself forward to the historical facts. Now if that be metaphysics and old-fashioned idealism and all sorts of other things which aren't very fashionable anymore these days, well, make the most of it so far as I'm concerned.

FINN: To make the most of it is simply to say, "Well, where does this lead you?"

SCHWARZSCHILD: One of the main justifications which I think I have for being prepared to face the hard questions once you reach the actual historical situations—or for that matter the empiric situations individually speaking—is that I watch what the other people do who claim to work in the opposite direction: namely those who start with "them thar facts." You know, this kind of realism, it seems to me, has led to an absolutely incredible abyss of compromise, and even of treason—moral treason and religious treason.

FINN: I'm not sure I understand you exactly. People in religious and nonreligious groups have certainly been led to support the present nuclear weapons system because, in their thinking, the international scene largely exists in a law of nature; that is, without any governing body. And therefore the individual— in this case the individual nation state—has taken upon itself to make a judgment of what is right and proper because there *is* no other alternative.

SCHWARZSCHILD: There's the law of God.

FINN: But how does this operate on the political scene? Those who start with the facts don't immediately go to the law of God. We have nations who are likely to come into conflict. Given these facts we want to reach a certain level of what is right and proper on the international scene with as. . . .

SCHWARZSCHILD: I believe the phrase is "a realistic appraisal in the light of Christian ethics." I mean among the theologians that you're talking about.

FINN: Yes. What is wrong with that as an approach?

SCHWARZSCHILD: Oh, I think just about everything. In the first place I don't think it's the job of the man of faith to make

Steven S. Schwarzschild

the compromises that the politicians inevitably and lamentably make.

FINN: Well, you can be both though.

SCHWARZSCHILD: No, I don't think so. I think the man of faith has only religious politics to practice, not secular politics. And by religious politics I mean, for example, pacifism, which I consider to be religious politics.

FINN: I really don't understand that. Religious politics as dissociated from. . . .

SCHWARZSCHILD: The politics that people practice who derive their sanctions and take into account facts *other than* or in addition to religious imperatives. In other words—may I put it in Barthian terms?—I don't care about the Brunnerian *Ansatzpunkt* and I don't believe that the truth comes from the world. It comes only from the law of God. And my job as a believing man—whatever that phrase may mean—is to try to live in accordance with that law of God. And if that law of God doesn't seem to be in accord with historical realities, *tant pis* for the historical realities. And I think that's one thing wrong with this kind of realism. But another thing which I find even more objectionable is what I've called Niebuhrianism. I think in *Worldview* once I called it the theological wing of the Pentagon with a bad conscience. They do exactly everything that the Pentagon does except they proclaim their bad conscience in doing so all the time. Well, to the devil with that bad conscience!

FINN: In your views, however, it would be almost impossible for the believing person to have a sense of high political. . . .

SCHWARZSCHILD: Relevance. Yes, I know. Isn't that just too bad.

FINN: I think it is too bad. If it is the case I think it is too bad, yes.

SCHWARZSCHILD: Well, I have to say two things about that: I do not believe that—let me not quote the usual standbys because I'm tired of the appeal to the prophetic biblical tradition which is one of the gases of contemporary lingo—I do not believe that the articulators of the religious imperatives down through the ages, until our time, primarily asked themselves: "Now am I going to be 'relevant' to the actual situation?" They ask themselves primarily: "Am I going to be relevant to the demand that I believe God makes of me and of my fellow men?" I've just come back from a long discussion about the dubious nature of the demand for relevancy in our time. That's a subject well worth exploring, I think. So that the first *caveat* which I would stipulate is that one would have to talk a great deal about what one means by relevance and whether that really is the final arbiter of all value nowadays, as so many people seem to think it is.

But in the second place, in a profounder sense, I think that we—and by we I mean the radicals, not the realists, I mean the utopians if you please—are being infinitely more relevant than anybody else. The so-called realists, as that article by this chap Dibble* makes crystal clear, have invariably, when the chips were down, gone along with whatever the Establishment wanted them to say and do—with such minor qualifications that they didn't amount to a helluva pile of beans. *Commonweal* has had absolutely *no effect* on American public opinion so far as Vietnam is concerned because it's constantly straddling the fence.† It wants to be prudent, it wants to be careful, it wants to be literate, it wants to be polite. So nobody pays any attention to them and they're right. On the other hand this young fellow that just walked out of your office, and the Catholic whatever they call themselves . . .

FINN: Peace Fellowship.

SCHWARZSCHILD: . . . Peace Fellowship, and Dorothy Day's paper the *Catholic Worker,* and even *Ramparts.* Thank God they've had to pay attention to Sergeant Duncan‡ and to the people that, out of Dorothy Day's group, even kill themselves. These radicals I would say have had a noticeable effect on American public opinion. Why? Because they make their position clear, they state it, they try to work it out. But even if it can't be worked out, that's still where they stand, and now—to switch

---

* The reference is to an article which criticized the group of theologians who are presently most prominent in discussions concerning the ethics of war. The article, entitled "Military Strategy and the Hard-Nosed Theologians," was written by Ernest F. Dibble, who is on the faculty of the Fort Benning, Georgia, branch of the American University.

† Subsequent to this conversation, *Commonweal* took a strong editorial position critical of U.S. policy in Vietnam.

‡ Sergeant Donald Duncan returned from Vietnam combat with the Green Berets to give a very moving and critical account of the effect of the U.S. presence on the entire life of the Vietnamese people.

Steven S. Schwarzschild

to a Protestant phrase—"I can do no other." I think that's *very* relevant. We're pulling them in our direction. The guys in the middle, they're pussyfooting.

Schwarzschild says that the time of acceptable uncertainty about the war in Vietnam is past; there is enough available information for anyone to make a sound decision. I suggest that President Johnson is high on the list of those who want the war brought to an end. He responds, "Yes, on his terms," but Johnson, he adds, has done nothing to bring the war to an end.

SCHWARZSCHILD: Some friends of mine at my school, Washington University, have just put out a so-called Citizens' White Paper on Vietnam.* The main thesis of that report is that the facts seem to indicate—I would say in fact do indicate—that every time there's been any possibility of negotiation or even contact, invariably something has happened which pulled the ground out from underneath its feet. And that, of course, has been our experience long before the Vietnam war; you know; U2 flights and all sorts of things at opportune moments in our recent history. I think it is perfectly clear what the interests of the American Government are in Vietnam, in Southeast Asia, and unless these interests are achieved I don't believe that any-

---

* The White Paper to which Dr. Schwarzschild refers has since been published in hardcover by Beacon Press and in paperback by Fawcett under the title *The Politics of Escalation in Vietnam.* Although the document was produced by scholars at the University of California at Berkeley, and Washington University in St. Louis, it lists as co-authors Franz Schurmann, Peter Dale Scott and Reginald Zelnik. The subtitle suggests the emphasis that Schwarzschild makes definite: "A Study of United States Responses to Pressures for a Political Settlement of the Vietnam War: November 1963–July 1966."

In a prudent foreword Arthur Schlesinger, Jr. describes it as "a careful analysis, executed by disinterested scholars and based necessarily on public sources, of critical stages in the development of this policy [American policy in Vietnam]. The questions raised by this analysis are questions that historians must answer some day—and which, in a democracy, policy-makers should answer now."

In an afterword explaining the origin of this book, Lindsay Mattison says that the Citizens' White Paper, with a supporting letter signed by a number of prominent citizens, was sent to the President. With the exception of a remark by Under Secretary of State George Ball that the White Paper was "just not true," no reply had been made by the time of book publication in October 1966.

body in the government today has any slightest intention of doing anything that might bring the war to a premature conclusion.

FINN: Well, how would you yourself define these interests?

SCHWARZSCHILD: The forceful and weighty American presence in the politics, economics and military status of Southeast Asia. The world-wide political and economic, and indeed military, interests of America require that it dominate as much of the world as it can.

FINN: Are you hopeful about any change in the international scene so that conflicts will be settled by other than military force? You described yourself as a utopian.

SCHWARZSCHILD: I consider myself essentially a utopian revolutionary. I do not believe that, given the present society, there is anything to be hopeful about. But I do believe in the revolutionary possibilities of the truth and the law of God as it becomes effective in human beings and in human societies. And he who is a utopian believes that the solution to the problems of America, Southeast Asia and anything else that you might want to mention, reside precisely there.

FINN: Well, how would that apply precisely to Vietnam? I mean, how does this come to bear politically? You see, part of the problem for me, and I would guess for religious pacifism, is to see that indeed it does have some bearing upon human affairs and to see that whatever weight it has is indeed brought to bear. And the difficulty, of course, for many people is that they don't see how this is done. One of the reasons that some people hesitate to become pacifists or act as pacifists is that they think it will make them politically irrelevant and they do not want to be politically irrelevant. I mean simply as citizens.

SCHWARZSCHILD: Well, you know, I said before, I don't think that this is being irrelevant. To the contrary, I think that everything else is really being irrelevant. I think, for example, that to refuse to bear arms in Vietnam is a very real and very relevant act of religious politics.

FINN: But it doesn't change the situation—or does it?

SCHWARZSCHILD: If enough people do it, it might. On the other hand it's obviously true that religious politics aren't exhausted by pacifism. There are lots of other things that go into the making of it.

FINN: I presume, given the views you've expressed, that you find no justification for a nuclear weapons system upon which some people say the international scene now is stabilized?

SCHWARZSCHILD: That's correct.

FINN: What would you suggest that a nation has a right to keep? Enough armaments to police an international scene? You said earlier that you might support a police action.

SCHWARZSCHILD: No, I said I can understand that some people might support this. *I* do not. No, I think weapons defeat the nation as well as the individual that holds them. I don't believe that nations are a legitimate object of concern for the political scientist or for the man of faith, whatever that may mean. I think human beings are.

FINN: Well, let me put it like this: I know very well that part of the order of my own life depends upon the fact that the United States is this rich, powerful, relatively stable nation of which I am a citizen. If something would happen to make that unstable, if we engaged in large-scale war, or if we were told to disarm, the structure of that society would be changed considerably, and I, my family, friends, everybody could indeed have their lives affected.

SCHWARZSCHILD: That might be good though.

FINN: That's of course a possibility, but it might not. That's the whole problem. So if *I* want to start with the end which you suggested—not the nation state but the individual—I will go through this thing that people have gone through: the relation of the individual and the community.

SCHWARZSCHILD: Don't think that I'm an anarchist. I'm not. I think there's a legitimate function for government obviously and for national government for nations. There's a magnificent phrase somewhere at the end, I think, of the second paragraph of the Declaration of Independence, something about when government no longer serves this function it is the right and the duty of the people to alter or abolish it. I hope I'm not being misunderstood nor that I'm being insufficiently clear about this. I depend as much as you do obviously on the smooth functioning of the structures of American society. But only insofar as they serve human and humane purposes. And that is therefore the criterion, not the nation state *qua* nation state.

FINN: Well, that brings us back to the question I asked earlier: if, for instance, we could consider the possibility of the United States disarming to such an extent that it would not be able to exert on the world scene the influence it does, you would yourself be willing to accept the consequences which inevitably would flow from this.

SCHWARZSCHILD: Yes.

FINN: The comment you made about people who wanted to make their religion politically relevant would extend to those theologians, ethicists—people like our friend Bill O'Brien—who are engaged, say, in just-war theory or in attempting to devise ways to limit war once it is initiated. I mean, they are, as far as you're concerned, . . .

SCHWARZSCHILD: Finks [with a laugh]. Whom is Bill O'Brien kidding? In the first place, after what he has, in his thinking, granted the government, there is nothing, virtually nothing, *in fact* nothing, that any war-waging power needs to ask for further, quite apart from the fact that even if there were an excess that he delimits as being off base, he knows perfectly well, surely, that no military command ever has, and none in the future will, in the event of war, pay the slightest attention to what he is saying. So what sort of guides has he provided?

FINN: Even if much of what he said was perfectly valid, in the actual practice this is ignored?

SCHWARZSCHILD: It always has been. I mean, we were talking before about a doctrine of legitimacy of the torture of civilian prisoners. After that, where else can you go? What else can anybody ask for?

FINN: You do have a number of military men to support your view.

SCHWARZSCHILD: And the historical record surely. And as a matter of fact, if I were a military man I'd say the same thing. The only thing I object to in Bill O'Brien is not what he's saying—I mean I object to it on moral grounds—but the logic of it, in and of itself, is completely, I think, impeccable; the only

Steven S. Schwarzschild

thing I object to most strenuously is that he claims that it's a logic of religion, theology, morality, and so forth. If he came right out and said, "This is the logic of military warfare," that I could understand.

We had discussed Hans Morgenthau, whose enlistment in the forces of those opposed to the war in Vietnam had bemused Schwarzschild as it had many others. He welcomes the support of a leading political "realist" who argued that present Vietnam policies did not serve the nation's interest, but he recognizes that the alliance is not permanent; on another issue the pacifists and Morgenthau could easily part company. I recall a comment Schwarzschild had made earlier about students at the university who had been uncertain about the relation between conscientious objection and a political objection to the war in Vietnam. Does he, I ask, place much reliance on the stability of the students' political judgment?

SCHWARZSCHILD: Oh, I have much greater confidence in them than I have in Hans Morgenthau. For one thing, I always have greater confidence in college students than I have in their elders. For another, they are still trying very hard to work this out, whereas Hans Morgenthau, of course, has a stabilized theory. And thirdly, the students must be given time to work their ideas out. As young Forest said, these youngsters have seen America at work only in their own lifetimes, and their own lifetimes are pretty much circumscribed by the end of the Second World War as the *terminus a quo* and today—whatever today may be—the *terminus ad quem*. And that presents a pretty monochromatic picture I think.

FINN: Well, it leads to some of the difficulties of what is called the peace movement today because the peace movement is composed of people who would hold a position similar to your own or exactly like your own, people who would have a position similar to Hans Morgenthau's, people who have positions like the students that you are counseling, groups making really political protests but who are not at all pacifist, for example, The Clergy Concerned about Vietnam, for which you expressed dismay.

SCHWARZSCHILD: For moralizing or preachifying.

FINN: Right. Do you have any judgment about the possibilities of a religious politics, or just the peace movement, being effective? Do you have any hopes for this?

SCHWARZSCHILD: Yes, with some qualification my hopes are largely centered on the nonreligious radical movement. I think SNCC is considerably more effective than SCLC, and I think that the political protest movement against the Vietnam war, which is pretty secular and political in nature, is considerably more effective than the religious peace movement, such as it is. I think that's where the action is and I think that's where the hopes are.

THE
ORGANIZATIONS

RELIGIOUS

DANIEL BERRIGAN, S.J.

Philip Berrigan's book *No More Strangers,* which deals with racial strife, war and the effects of poverty, carries the dedication:

> *"To my brother, Father Dan, S.J., without whom neither my priesthood nor this book would be possible."*

This is only one testimony to the kind of influence Father Daniel Berrigan can have, and since it is offered by his younger brother, probably not remarkable. But as I talked to people in the peace movement and his name kept cropping up, it was evident that he had an influence on many, and many different kinds of, people. One was as likely to hear of him standing with Norman Thomas or Dr. Spock on a platform in Washington protesting U.S. policy in Vietnam as leading a peace vigil before the U.N. or giving a talk to some student group in the Midwest. He seems ubiquitous and, if current fashion has not pulverized the term out of meaningful existence, he has charisma.

Daniel Berrigan is a poet, essayist and theologian and presently editor of *Jesuit Missions* magazine. He entered the Jesuits in 1939 and was ordained in 1952. He has studied at the Gregorian Institute in Rome and in France, where he also did parish work. His poetry and prose have appeared in a number of magazines such as *The Atlantic, Poetry, Saturday Review* and *Commonweal.* He has published three volumes of essays and five of poetry. His poetry is favorably regarded by a number of poets, including Marianne Moore who has said that she reads "with reverence anything that Father Berrigan writes."

Father Berrigan is an engaged person and his multiple activities have caused him to be described as "a leading voice of dissent in this country." At one point, apparently, that voice impinged upon the ears of his superiors in a way they found unpleasant. The official story reads that their displeasure had nothing to do with his withdrawal from the national debate, that Daniel Berrigan was sent to Latin America as a part of a normal journalistic assignment. That story failed to convince a number of people who thought that he was being penalized for his activities in the Clergy Concerned about Vietnam. Students demonstrated outside Cardinal Spellman's office in New York, and over a thousand priests and laymen signed an advertisement which appeared in the *New York Times* demanding his return. When he returned he took up his activities where he had left them.

It is a number of months after this that I visit Daniel Berrigan in the Jesuit Missions House on the Upper East Side of New York. The housekeeper shows me from the cool, quiet, cavernous foyer into the waiting room. Berrigan comes in brisk and lively from the chill outdoors, but as he responds to my questions there is an air of reserve, of withdrawn inwardness, of self-communing, as if his statements were directed to himself as much as to me. His voice is low and intense with a slight breathy quality.

His own position on the war in Vietnam is clear. He has publicly referred to "the immorality of our current effort in Vietnam," and has said that it fails to satisfy Thomistic requirements of a just war on three counts: (1) The United States has not explored every other means for a settlement; (2) United States forces have exceeded justifiable employment of force; they rely upon "torture of prisoners, execution without trial, defoliation of crops" and have practically erased the "crucial distinction between the nonviolent noncombatants and the guilty"; (3) We have not attended to the rights of self-determination of the entire Vietnamese people.*

* Quotations are taken from an interview printed in the *National Catholic Reporter,* September, 8, 1965, p. 2.

Daniel Berrigan, S.J.

When I ask Daniel Berrigan what were the most important factors in the development of his judgments about war and peace today, he separates out from the many which he acknowledges three that seem most crucial.

BERRIGAN: I think the first factor would be the civil rights movement. The light it shed upon, first of all, the human person himself, the new light it shed upon the creation of persons and the creation of community, the way this kind of new building of human life and the human person had to come about by way of the acceptance of suffering—I think that was very important —a kind of symbol of a universal attitude toward man, not just a national attitude toward a minority.

Then, I can remember, really to the day, when I read a certain article by [Thomas] Merton which landed in my brain like a bullet; it exploded there and really helped me very greatly to bridge the difficult gap between this national movement and an attitude of nonviolence toward man in general, man in the world. I remember being profoundly disturbed by the article and finally writing him, not really expecting an answer. But he did answer at some length and helped me to clarify what I had tried to say and suggested some reading and so on.

And then, thirdly, I would mark the influence of the worker-priests, especially as they had gone through the Algerian experience and the French experience of colonialism and helped, I think, France understand herself as a post-colonial power. I think their contribution solidified my idea that perhaps we had accepted a kind of Marxist mystique without analyzing it, and that we ourselves were unconsciously and perhaps in a betraying sense dedicating our conscience to an ideal of warfare as inevitable.

FINN: We, meaning which people?

BERRIGAN: Christians, I would say. Especially, yes. And it was a great kind of purifying of my own mind just to see that men like that could be peaceable and sources of peace for others, not merely by talking but by the sort of life they had adopted.

FINN: Did your experiences in the civil rights movement have much to do with your own ideas about the uses of violence or nonviolence, or did you even think of your actions at that time in these particular terms?

BERRIGAN: Well, my own experience in civil rights began in the North, which is of course a limiting and very specific factor. Meantime, my brother Philip was operating in the deep South and we were able, I think, to share a great deal, mainly along student lines. I guess I learned a great deal from the university students who were just beginning nonviolent methods in the freedom rides and the picketing and sit-ins, North and South. And without reflecting a great deal upon it, I think it had great impact on me.

FINN: Did you write to Merton specifically about issues involving war, peace, violence?

BERRIGAN: As I recall it now, his article had mainly to do with the beginnings of his thesis that limited violence, strictly limited violence, was practically speaking impossible in a nuclear age, and that therefore the incursions of the United States into Latin America—I don't think Vietnam had really erupted then —that the economic and military adventuring of the United States abroad was indicative of something much deeper in a national malaise, a national kind of loss of spirit and of identity. He said that recourse to violence was an increasingly seductive temptation for us and, as a nuclear power, a particularly dangerous thing. And I remember being struck especially by his analysis of violence as an illness, because I had never really seen it put this way before.

Berrigan had mentioned Merton's analysis which suggested that recourse to violence is an illness. And I recall the *Pacem in Terris* Convocation of February 1965 at which statesmen, politicians, intellectuals and diplomats from twenty nations discussed and debated the way to peace. Only toward the end of the discussion did a participant touch on this question. "No one at the conference," Eugene Burdick said, "has addressed himself to the problem of whether the human animal is pacific. Does he want peace rather than war?"

More recently I had read a passage which impressed me sufficiently to clip it out. Reviewing *A Passionate Prodigality*, G. Chapman's memoirs of World War I, George Steiner wondered whether the noted scholar "was ever again as happy, as wholly alive, as he had been in the mud of Flanders." And Steiner goes on to speculate about the vision expressed in that book,

Daniel Berrigan, S.J.

comparing it with Homer and Tolstoy. "It is a recognition," he writes, "both wry and zestful, of the fact that war matches certain rhythms inherent in man, that battle calls forth potentialities of nobility, of ingenuity, of endurance, left unrealized in the gray routine of ordinary life." I read the clipping to Berrigan and ask for his response.*

BERRIGAN: A quote like that, it seems to me, brings up a great deal of history that has to be confronted. An acceptance of this history, as a fact, you know—that neither the history of Western civilization nor the history of the Catholic Church is a history of nonviolence. You have this kind of marvelous landmark of the figure of Christ, and the imitation of Christ, and then a very early deflection away from that, sort of by-passing it on the part of actual history. So the quote you bring up, it seems to me, is part of an enormously powerful and persuasive folklore which I find almost totally imbedded in the consciousness of modern men. Warmaking is an honorable way of life. It's imbedded in all sorts of national history, in shrines and battle grounds. Perhaps the greatest symbol of it all is the vitality of the Pentagon itself and the thinking there. And I keep thinking, especially flying out of Washington, if only some day this incredible concentration of talent, resources, energy, could be applied to the making of peace. What a day!

But I think realistically, especially after this tour of Latin America, that we are *not* going to have an end to certain kinds of limited warfare, at least in our lifetime. I don't see any real-

---

* The question has, of course, a long and still unfinished history. Quincy Wright in his monumental *A Study of War* cites various theories and mentions as oversimplified those attributing to man a primitive fighting instinct. He does, however, cite a minority of psychologists who hold this view and quotes one, G. W. Crile:

"Soldiers say that they find relief in any muscular action; but the supreme bliss of forgetfulness is in an orgy of lustful satisfying killing in a hand-to-hand bayonet action, when the grunted breath of the enemy is heard and his blood flows warm on the hand. . . .

"As I reflected upon the intensive application of man to war in cold, rain, and mud; in rivers, canals, and lakes; under ground, in the air, and under the sea; infected with vermin, covered with scabs, adding the stench of his own filthy body to that of his decomposing comrades; hairy, begrimed, bedraggled, yet with unflagging zeal striving eagerly to kill his fellows; and as I felt within myself the mystical urge of the sound of great cannon I realized that war is a normal state of man. . . . The impulse to war . . . is stronger than the fear of death." Abridged edition. (Chicago, University of Chicago Press, 1964), p. 320.

istic possibility of it. Nor do I clearly see the alternatives to it, and this is what makes me very tentative and qualified in my own pacifism. Because while I see clearly a Gospel ideal, I think we must also deal with our history and our times. And I talked down there to so many *good men* and revolutionary men, in the *best* sense, who themselves did not see a way out by means of nonviolence. This, of course, throws new light upon my own thinking, at the same time a new perplexity, you know.

FINN: You used the term pacifism about your own position, at the same time saying you didn't see any way out. Without unduly limiting or using too easy labels, can you describe what your pacifist position is? You said it's evolving—so maybe "position" is not even the right word?

BERRIGAN: Well, it's a sort of a stance that one is, I think, obliged almost continually to pause and reflect upon in the light of things that are bombarding his life so constantly. I wouldn't take a stand that is rigid and absolute out of a sense of responsibility. And I would like to see developed or perhaps like to work out for myself a little more clearly a morality that would try to start from the obligations that one senses, say to a person who is right at hand and who is under immediate and violent attack. It seems to me that one's responsibility to repel that is very evident.

My problem right now is to try to understand that in the context of society, especially in some of the countries of Latin America that are really suffocated by an oligarchy and where violence at least offers a very profound invitation. What are the responsibilities, say, to a revolutionary group—let's say Christian revolutionary group—in a country which sees two percent in control and ninety-eight percent permanently destroyed? And can we extrapolate the idea of our individual responsibility to one or two persons to the idea of our responsibility to a society, which might involve one in the necessity of repelling unjust violence against that society? I don't know. I don't know. But to me this is at least a valuable question right now.

And just to be practical I'm trying also to understand, mainly in the midst of our Vietnam impasse, what the role, say, of the nuclear powers would be in revolutionary situations which certainly are going to continue to confront us across two thirds of the world. And I would have to separate my thinking—again, just for myself—with regard to the kind of violence that a people

Daniel Berrigan, S.J

needs in order to become itself within a deprived nation, and
the kind of violence which is allowable to a nuclear power in
its international dealings. And for myself I find these are two
very separate questions.

FINN: You obviously have a position which rejects violence
but nevertheless sees some conditions under which it may be
the best alternative, at least in the minds of the people who
are there presently involved. How do these various factors come
together in your judgment of Vietnam?

BERRIGAN: Well, here we go with something very complex
again. But I was very heartened by this morning's *Times* account of Senator Fulbright's speech, which I considered a very
great speech, in New York here yesterday.* And the cause of
my rejoicing was not *solely* that this senator had so thoughtfully
analyzed not merely our war but our national spirit, our kind
of stance before the world community. More than that even, it
was almost like a recognition scene, because I found gathered
into one there so many of the threads that my brother and I
have been trying to explore and to reflect on and to speak of in
the last six months.

But the biggest single debt that I could point to with regard
to my own kind of moral conclusions on the war would really
be the writings and the whole symbolic meaning of Pope John.
I think that he gave me a kind of universe, an intellectual universe, to walk into where I was able to see this war in a non-
obsessive way; to see it in its context of world need, world development, world hope, and then to see also, by way of ricochet
almost, what I would call the betrayal of those things by this
war adventuring. Almost as though we had allowed a kind of
embolism to appear in the bloodstream and then really to form
a serious blockage to this communication and communion contribution that is our world vocation right now as Americans.

I find public figures like Kennedy and Fulbright, and Morse
to a lesser degree, being able to see more and more clearly not
merely this point of no return at which escalation will perhaps,
and perhaps even shortly, find itself, but also able to look at
this larger picture of what the developing world hopes for from
us, how these hopes are being disappointed. They see how an
enormous percentage of world resources and brains and attention—psychological and spiritual attention which is really irre-

* The *New York Times,* April 29, 1966.

placeable—how all of that is being deflected from, well, the real
war nationally, which is the war against poverty, and the real
war internationally, which is what Dom Helder Câmara called
"the state of pre-violence" in which the third world is presently
condemned to live and die, the pre-violence of deprivation.*

Berrigan had said that nations, as persons, could learn best
from equals. Since no nation is equal to the United States in
terms of power, to whom should it turn, from whom would it
best learn?

BERRIGAN: A nation, if it is healthy, has almost as much to
learn from its enemies as it does from its friends, and the listening in the two directions is important. Friends will almost
invariably tell us what we want to hear, especially if they are
deeply dependent upon us in a material way. But our enemies,
who for various reasons are cut off from us and who bombard
us with unwelcome news, are also rather important to our soul.
I was thinking in this regard of some of the analyses that have
come from China in recent months and which get a little bit
beyond rhetoric and a little bit beyond hate talk and really begin to talk about the profound reaction of the East to our war.
But in any case, this struggle for identity with a great power like
ourselves is, I take it, practically impossible to conduct within
our borders. I don't think that Americans can know themselves
from talking to Americans, no matter how highly placed or how
intellectual or how artistic. I think this has to be a dialogue with
the world. And this kind of exchange with the world is *exactly*
what the war tends to cut off. Our highly placed officials no
longer want to talk seriously, even with our friends, about who
we are, because our friends also are growing increasingly uneasy
about who we are.

France now can talk to us directly and critically because of
a certain native experience, colonial experience, war experience,

* Dom Helder is the Archbishop of Recife, Brazil. The present regime
in Brazil, which has declared war on communism and corruption, has
seemingly added some prominent members of the Roman Catholic
Church to its targets. When Dom Helder issued a statement criticizing
the regime for injustices committed against the workers, he was declared
a "leftist" and a disturber of men and ideas. When the showdown came,
President Humberto Castelo Branco flew to Recife. From that conference, Dom Helder won concessions, but the struggle in which he is involved continues.

and also a certain healthy Gallic dislike for many of our pretensions. But most other countries cannot feel such independence. It seems so utterly foolish, for instance, for us to think that we could really learn something about ourselves from India or, let's say, even from some of the Latin countries. Or, even in any profound sense, from England.

FINN: If this judgment applies to persons and to nations, is it applicable to groups within the nation which are sometimes deeply estranged from each other?

BERRIGAN: Now within our society, of course, I would find a kind of honest irreducible core, an independent, incorruptible core, in civil rights people and the student movements, the New Left, and then hopefully also in some of these public officials that we've discussed earlier. And I have a suspicion that being involved deeply in some aspect of social struggle or social change is a powerful kind of boot-camp preparation for a correct stance internationally. Maybe this is one reason why the Negro has so much to say to us with regard to our war.

FINN: I'm not quite sure I know what you mean—there are groups, civil rights groups, that have criticized U.S. participation in Vietnam, but there are also a large number of Negroes who, like other Americans, either support or at least go along with, without much question or reservation, Administration policy.

BERRIGAN: I wish I had more evidence about this, Jim. You know, I had some evidence in teach-ins in Harlem and in discussing the war with the poor in general, and I find—again, I'd have to be very tentative about this—but I find an extraordinarily high proportion of the *poor* opposed to the war. And also I find that their reasons in general are quite thoughtful and quite eloquently expressed. They have to do with a profound sense of the danger of the exportation of violence. Their ideas also have to do with the experience of spiritual and physical violence which they themselves have endured.

FINN: And these people really *project* to the international scene the things that the United States is doing?

BERRIGAN: They have that sense also. Maybe the *bridge* to that sense is their kind of conclusion about our hypocrisy in announcing two simultaneous wars. That is, a war in Vietnam and a war against poverty at home.

FINN: You mean that we are willing to expend relatively little on this war at home and great sums on what we do in Vietnam?

BERRIGAN: Yes. One cab driver, one Negro cab driver, questioned the hawks at one teach-in that I was at in Harlem. After quoting the monthly figures on the war on poverty and the war in Vietnam, he said: "Gentlemen, I would like to ask you which war are we really fighting?"

FINN: You mentioned the New Left and you mentioned some student groups. Do you think that there is among these students, or among the younger people in this country generally, a more critical attitude than there is among older people?

BERRIGAN: I don't know, Jim, whether I would be able to cut it that clear, you know. Again I want to be very tentative about this. My impression over the last months, in trying to get to all sorts of audiences, is that the line of division is not so much a matter of age or a matter of status or position in the sense of student or non-student or that. It seems to be a matter more of, say, middle class or upper middle class versus, let's say, some form of social involvement; and I want to include in that latter category the poor themselves, those who are really the subjects of social change here.

And it might be a little bit of help to note that the further you go into the suburbs to talk against the Vietnam war, the more difficult it becomes, and the more hysterical the opposition becomes. Whereas in the inner city, by and large, you'll get a better hearing.

FINN: If I understand correctly what you're saying, the judgments that people make about United States participation in a war, such as Vietnam, is a part of a total reaction that they have to their own lives, and to the way in which they participate in, say, their own community and the community which is the nation.

BERRIGAN: I would almost be willing to go so far as to say that. I buy very much the distinction that the editor of the *Saturday Review,* Norman Cousins, made about nine months ago when he said that racial and religious differences are not the

Daniel Berrigan, S.J.

sharpest lines that are dividing the human family, but the line which is most discernibly growing in attitudes toward existence are those that have to do with life and non-life; those who, on the one hand, would agree that man has a future and that human life is valuable and who are willing to work toward that, and those who don't. And how do you favor life unless you've struggled for life?

We return to the discussion of nuclear weapons systems and the possible differing attitudes that people have. In the course of this, Berrigan refers to the "atheism of the state."

FINN: Is it even sensible to talk about the state being atheistic or Christian? Are these good ways of describing a state? Is not the state *necessarily* secular in its actions, no matter whether the citizens themselves are atheists or Christians or Moslems or whatever?

BERRIGAN: Well, I really don't know what to say, except that I find that maybe the religious neutrality of the state gets a little bit thin when we speak of concrete situations in which a given state is demanding certain things of its citizens, among whom are believers. Are they to regard this state, for instance, as neutral if it is demanding their lives in a way which only God has a right to demand them, or demanding a style of life which is in contravention to what their own faith is demanding of them? It seems to me that a state which in principle we could call neutral, can become possessed by the dominations and powers as the New Testament gives us evidence, and may, with regard to *this* community of believers, become an actively evil force.

FINN: The statements of Jesus, of course, seem to apply mostly to the individual. He makes very few about collective actions which apply to the state.

BERRIGAN: Of course, the Gospel that finally got written down is not trying to create a stereotype within a kind of volcanic history that we all knew occurred afterward. And perhaps, as I think you're implying, it would be very wrong to look for precise guidelines that would just take this book across twenty centuries and make it a kind of blueprint for immediate action today. I don't think it's that at all. This would take the freedom and the adventuresomeness out of this whole Christian vocation. But at the same time I have this perplexity: central to the Gospels is the Christian experience of Christ, which is not *solely* the experience of God in this human situation. But this experience is now to be *lived* in *community* and in person throughout history. And as we turn to that experience of who Christ was and the way he responded to human life and human beings, we find that invariably his response was nonviolent and sacrificial. And this was joined to a strong interior freedom which expressed itself in the invitation to discipleship on the part of others. So that he actually, in word and then in work, submitted before the powers of this world and died in order to release new life into human history. And this, to me, is the heart of the matter. This pattern of response to life and to human beings and to violence—at least in its general outlines—demands of us, I feel, such a quality of life and such a quality of resources that we would rather endure violence than inflict it.

FINN: I find it very difficult to ask the question I really want to ask. If that is the case, how possible is it for most men to follow that example? People have said in the past that Christianity is impractical; some people have said it's nevertheless true; and others have said that it's both true and practical; and others say if it's impractical, it *can't* be true—or at least men cannot be called upon to follow something which is impractical because most men will not do that. And I wonder whether one can expect most people to live in a way which they would regard as impractical.

BERRIGAN: Well, I find it very difficult to believe that in a humanity which is governed by the providence of God, which we believe is declared in His Son, there would not be the resources available to man to make this invitation felt. Which is another way of saying that I find it very difficult to reduce this thing to a small knot of people who are lost in the midst of a violent and violence-oriented mass. It seems to me we have something perhaps directly opposite. When we turn outward to the human community we find vast and growing resources of competence and of compassion at work everywhere; the workers of violence and those who really place violence on the line as *the* kind of unique and *impeccable* tool, are in fact themselves a minority.

FINN: Yes, but if we take what the just-war theory of war suggested, it's not an attempt to use violence as the best tool,

Daniel Berrigan, S.J.

but a recognition that man is weak and broken and fallen, that he *will* resort to violence and therefore the need is to place whatever civilizing limitations on violence that one can. It is a recognition of—in theological terms—the fall, or—in psychological terms—an illness or possibly a need for violence in man.

BERRIGAN: I'm just wondering, though, Jim, whether or not that kind of moral theology, again, has to be taken in its historical setting. It seems to me that we were dealing, at the time the concept was elaborated, with Christians who had pretty much lost hold of their Christian roots; a period which was quite decadent with regard to liturgy and to scripture and to the seeding of the ideas of Christ into community, and which was pretty much living off second-rate sources. Even such noble sources as Saint Thomas, it seems to me, were substituting a minimal human conclusion for the call of discipleship. And this, I take it, is our great opportunity today. Since the Council we have these *explicit* invitations to return to the Gospel and to personal discipleship, and to ask not so much, "what are the wise men of Christian history saying to us about conscience?" as "what has Christ our Lord made possible for conscience?" This only the Gospels and our worship and our life together can tell us. What does our life *really* ask of us?

FINN: One more question. Do you think that with enough imagination the United States *could* find ways of protecting its interests *without* resorting to war?

BERRIGAN: Ah, now we're really talking! My answer would be an unqualified yes. I believe that with all my heart. That's the kind of credo I can still give to the American Revolution as continuing, viable, and experimental in the world. And your question also lies at the heart of my protest. I protest because I am an *American* and because I see in this war or other points of violence today the defeat and destruction of that which we had to offer the world and that which we had to offer our own continuing growth. Which is to say, the exportation, the internationalization, of the American experience.

ABRAHAM JOSHUA HESCHEL

In the summer of 1966, there was held in Town Hall in New York a meeting to honor Thich Nhat Hanh, the Buddhist monk, poet and teacher who had come to the United States to speak for peace. Tributes to the man and his mission were offered by Daniel Berrigan, S.J., Abraham J. Heschel, Robert Lowell, Arthur Miller and John Oliver Nelson. The following comments are from the address of Dr. Heschel.

. . . In a free society, all are involved in what some are doing. *Some are guilty, all are responsible.*

There is a deep and awesome communion of the power that kills and the blood that is spilled. They are united in "the voice of the blood that cries from the earth," and the voice of those who die in Vietnam abominates both Communists and Americans.

Is it not true that Communists are fellow human beings first, antagonists second? Politically, the concept of the enemy is becoming obsolete; yesterday's enemy is today's ally. Religiously, the concept of the enemy fills us with dismay.

. . . Our confidence both in the candor of the Administration and in the policy which it is pursuing in Vietnam has collapsed, while the world's respect for American democracy has been profoundly shaken. America's image is tragically distorted.

America has been enticed by her own might. There is nothing so vile as the arrogance of the military mind. Of all the plagues with which the world is cursed, of every ill, militarism is the worst: the assumption that war is an answer to human problems. There are many wild beasts in the human heart, but the beastliest of all is the brutality of arms.

155]

Abraham Joshua Heschel

The State Department and Pentagon behave as if there were a division of qualities: infallibility of judgment in the possession of the State and Pentagon; ignorance, sentimentality everywhere else.

Those of us who disagree with American policy on Vietnam are told by the State Department that since we are not in possession of all the facts, we are not competent to evaluate the situation. Yet some of us wonder whether the State Department alone has the monopoly of wisdom and vision. Is it not possible that the mind of those involved in a certain policy become addicted to it, and hardly capable of undertaking an agonizing reappraisal that may prove how wrong the premises are?

. . . Modern war is a mechanical operation. But peace is a personal effort, it requires deep commitment, hard, honest vision, wisdom and patience, facing one another as human beings, elasticity rather than dogmatism.

Abraham Joshua Heschel was born in Warsaw in 1907. He received a Ph.D. from the University of Berlin in 1933 and in 1934 was graduated from Hochschule für die Wissenschaft des Judentums in Berlin. He taught in Frankfurt, Berlin, Warsaw and London before he came to the United States in 1940. Since 1945 he has been at Jewish Theological Seminary in New York, where he is professor of Jewish ethics and mysticism. He is a very productive writer, the author of over twenty volumes, and an impressive speaker.

We renew our brief acquaintance in his book-lined small office at Jewish Theological Seminary. To a romantic mind Dr. Heschel's appearance and manner might suggest an early prophet in modern dress. He has a full head of wavy, curly gray hair, and a correspondingly full mustache and beard. When he speaks it is as if his voice, soft and low, issued already pregnant with meaning from depths beyond speech and it was necessary to find the words capable of conveying that meaning. He speaks slowly with marked pauses between phrases.

FINN: Dr. Heschel, in one of your books you have written: "Emblazoned over the gates of the world in which we live is the escutcheon of the demons. The mark of Cain in the face of man has come to overshadow the likeness of God. There has never been so much guilt and distress, agony and terror." I infer from this statement that you believe we live in a time which is significantly different from previous times, and that the terrors which are visited upon us now are greater, if not different, than in the past. Part of this terror, I would presume, is the terrible kind of warfare in which people are continually engaged.

HESCHEL: Yes, that is correct, but my statement goes beyond that because I believe we act differently from the way people acted generations or ages ago. It seems to me as if the machine had taken over, machine in many forms. Conflicts, violence in the past would go back to a personal motivation, a clear motivation more or less. Today we are not even properly motivated. In other words, when a man entered the Crusades, he had a motivation. The motivation may have been evil, but it was a personal motivation. Today people who fight don't even know why they fight. It is a sort of depersonalized motivation.

Number two, I claim that the amount of violence, death caused by men, is not only different from the same crimes of the past in terms of quantity but also in terms of quality. In other words, if war in antiquity, in earlier days, was an art, war today is a science—and science is certainly different from art. It's impersonal, unlimited, devoid of any qualitative distinction. I'll give a special example. In the past, even wars were waged under certain rules. There was—I hate the phrase—an ethics of war. For example, civilians were considered immune, protected. I believe this changed probably in Spain in '37 when German bombers attacked a town in Spain.

FINN: Guernica?

HESCHEL: Guernica. If I'm not mistaken—I may be mistaken —it was the first time that a city inhabited by civilians was just bombed indiscriminately. There followed later the bombing of Rotterdam. I remember the shock that overcame the world— many blocks just wiped out. In other words, in those good old days—and I say it sarcastically—in 1940, people were still shocked when civilians were killed. Because there was still the distinction, the respect for some rules of war. This has now, of course, perfectly disappeared as a result, for example, of the extermination of six million Jews and numerous millions of non-Jews by the Nazis. Civilians. And now what goes on in Vietnam is an example. First of all it's frequently waged indiscriminately. Secondly, most of us don't know why this war is being fought.

Abraham Joshua Heschel

American citizens are not really convinced that we should fight the Vietnamese. It's done, let's say, in the absence . . . devoid of all consent and conviction. It's a war waged, so to speak, automatically. It looks as if the computers have taken over the decisions, decisions about international relations. Consequently I just tremble when I look at our civilization. So much guilt. Let's just recall what happened between 1914 and 1918, the amount of bloodshed. And then, from the vantage point of 1945, the First World War looks like a child's play. The world has not learned anything, so what does the future hold for us? But we may not even *speak* about the future; the present is dreadful because we are still the people who failed to hear the screams of millions of civilians tortured to death during the Nazi world war. This is a dreadful world. What happened to our hearts? The guilt is heavy and God is just.

FINN: I find it difficult to think that this war in Vietnam is—I don't know whether it's art or science—is working out scientifically. Few of the predictions that the government has made have been borne out, so if it's science, the experiments are failing continually.

HESCHEL: Perhaps this is precisely the logical fallacy—in assuming that you can fight a war scientifically, or let me say technologically, without taking into consideration the human dimension. After all, we are fighting not automatons, we are fighting human beings. I say "we" with a sense of shame. But I am responsible, as we all are. Now the dreadful mistake is that we are treating with obsolete conceptions of political philosophy a living, dynamic people. In other words, instead of realizing that there is also a human aspect of the situation, all they seem to think of is a cliché of bodies rather than communities of souls who have courage, who have dreams, who don't even understand what we are talking about. There's no communication between America and the Vietnamese. The slogans we use are totally irrelevant to the lives of these people. The Vietnamese have an old-fashioned conception. They don't understand the slogans. Now what they cherish is *life;* they abhor death, they would like to live. Consequently, when we come with the slogans of equality and freedom and democracy, these are issues they do not understand, issues that are certainly secondary to their will to live. All they ask us is "Let us live. Let us have nights of rest rather than nights of fear of being bombed."

FINN: Dr. Heschel, various spokesmen for the government have said that indeed the United States is using a great deal of restraint in Vietnam; it's attempting to be selective and limiting the evils which war does visit on people. From your own statements I take it you would not value those claims very highly.

HESCHEL: Right.

FINN: You also said that we are all responsible for what is taking place there. Are we responsible because we are members of this particular nation state or because we are members simply of the human community and involved in that evil?

HESCHEL: We are responsible as members of the human community. The Vietnamese are our brothers just as much as New Yorkers are my brothers. There's no difference between Saigon and New York. But we are responsible in a very special way, and this is precisely the terrible predicament of our time. Foreign policy is left to a few specialists. Foreign policy and international relations should become as important as personal relations. There is a moral imperative, for everyone concerned, to know that the whole world is one neighborhood. Consequently, what the government does in Vietnam should be as important and vital to us as what the government does to our very homes, right here, Main Street.

FINN: What is it that citizens who *are* concerned, but are not as highly informed as the experts, can do? As one of the co-chairmen of the Clergy Concerned about Vietnam, you clearly have some idea of what a particular group of citizens in this country can do.

HESCHEL: Well, this is a democracy, and if we want the Administration to be aware of the sense of horror we feel when the napalm is used, when civilians are killed, when the motivation for this war and the policy of this war are devoid of convincing argument, then we say "no." And this is, after all, a government *by* the people. Unfortunately, there are very few people who are concerned. If I want to be realistic I would say that by far the largest society in America today could be called a Society Unconcerned about Vietnam. There are tens of millions who haven't even thought about it.

FINN: You have really criticized, in very strong terms, United States participation in this war, and you said you did not like

Abraham Joshua Heschel

the phrase "the ethics of war." Are there wars in which you think the nation states have a right, and at some times an obligation, to participate in order to prevent the visitation of some great evil?

HESCHEL: I am convinced that if we find our very existence threatened—in other words, if an enemy arises, wants to destroy us—then it is our duty to fight against that enemy; in other words, *self-defense*—there's a necessity of human existence.

FINN: A number of people think that the limitation you have just indicated is being urged on nations as they realize the devastation that a great war can bring. But partly, they say, this realization is a result of the nuclear deterrents that we possess, and therefore flows as a kind of good out of that nuclear deterrent.

HESCHEL: I fully appreciate the importance of this argument. However, I feel that this argument is *terribly incomplete* because the assumption is that peace means absence of war. If peace is only the absence of war, then deterrence by nuclear weapons may guarantee it. But it's not so. The human situation is terribly complex. Consequently it requires not only just no wars, it means cultivating peace, cherishing peace, building peace. There's an old prophetic statement: "Peace is the fruit of righteousness and of goodness and of compassion." In other words, the way to build peace is to build it with continuous wisdom, active justice and generosity. Peace isn't just something that comes about by itself when there are no battlefields. The truth is that there are continuous tensions in human relations— private, public, national, international—and unless there is a continuous spiritual effort to make our ultimate insights real and potent, there'll be no peace. There will only be preludes to wars, which may be prolonged preludes because of the power of deterrence.

FINN: You are saying that the concepts that we have, the relations that we have with each other, are important and applicable to politics and to international politics. I recall a statement by Dean Acheson, made almost two years ago in a speech at Amherst, in which he said that the ethics one applies to one's self, to personal relations, are *totally* different from the ethics that one applies to political activities.* Your own statement

* Former Secretary of State Dean Acheson delivered a major address,

would suggest you're in almost total opposition to that view. Is that right?

HESCHEL: Yes, because the way I understand fully Dean Acheson's conception, it posits the autonomous and unique nature of political structures. I'm afraid there are two things that seem to be overlooked in that strong distinction. First, ultimately a nation consists not only of an administration but also of human beings. Consequently the human beings have to understand and have to respond to the kind of policy that is carried out in terms of human understanding and human requirements. Secondly, if this is the case then we have a dreadful dualism—which means that in private relations we are expected to be sincere, honest, generous, cooperative, in terms of reciprocity, of helping one another. On the other hand, in international relations we are expected to be shrewd, try to outsmart one another. This kind of dichotomy undermines the very integrity of human beings. If this is the way we must live, then maybe the human species is not worthy of survival. That's the height of hypocrisy. To my individual friend I'm supposed to be kind, to our whole nation I'm supposed to be calculating. I would just be ashamed to be a human being.

Perhaps what is required is the following. There's a certain intelligibility to what Dean Acheson said, the assumption mainly

---

"Ethics in International Relations Today," at Amherst College in December 1964. The speech, which generated much discussion, was generally understood to be a strong argument for greater realism in foreign policy and a strong criticism of idealist critics of the Administration. "The discussion of ethics or morality in our relations with other states is a prolific cause of confusion," Acheson said, and he went on to suggest what he understood the bases of that confusion to be.

"The vocabulary of morals and ethics is inadequate to discuss or test foreign policies of states. . . . What passes for ethical standards for governmental policies in foreign affairs is a collection of moralisms, maxims, and slogans, which neither help nor guide, but only confuse, decisions on such complicated matters as the multilateral nuclear force, a common grain price in Europe, policy in Southeast Asia. . . .

"A good deal of trouble comes from the anthropomorphic urge to regard nations as individuals and apply to our own national conduct—for instance, the Golden Rule—even though in practice individuals rarely adopt it. The fact is that nations are not individuals; the cause and effect of their actions are wholly different; and what a government can and should do with the resources which it takes from its citizens must be governed by wholly different considerations from those which properly determine an individual's use of his own." *Amherst Alumni News,* Winter, 1965, pp. 2–5.

that the very structure of power is filled with evil, therefore evil cannot be dealt with in a gentle manner. If this is a necessity, if this is unavoidable, then it means that we are somehow laboring under a demonic power. This is a very fantastic and rather blasphemous pagan conception of human affairs. This is a conception that has, of course, its sources in certain systems of political philosophy, but it is one, I believe, which if we accept we write a death verdict for the human species.

FINN: You said we're all responsible for our government's policy, but what of the person in our society who feels that U.S. participation in Vietnam is wrong and protests as strongly as he can, in whatever way he can—does he bear a share of the moral guilt? Is he necessarily responsible for that policy?

HESCHEL: Yes, what I'm saying is such a great sadness. Of course there are many of us who protest. What does it mean? That they have a deep feeling, a tense feeling, and they utter strong words. But that's all. While those who carry out the atrocities in Vietnam don't use just words and feelings, they act, they carry out cruel acts. With all my great respect for words, I cannot assume that words are as impressive as acts. One bomb dropped in Vietnam vitiates many speeches delivered in New York or in Berkeley.

What I miss, to my chagrin, is the realization that this is the most important issue—killing people, murder, innocent Vietnamese people, people I've never seen in my life, people I can't even call "enemy" because I haven't seen them. The cause is obscure. The whole conception of this war is confused. We can never win this war; but this is a political issue. My conviction is that we have already been defeated there. We have made more enemies than friends, in spite of the tremendous things we have done in Vietnam in terms of even life—many Americans have died in Vietnam. We have not won anything, but we have lost a great deal.

There is something to America which is different, at least in the eyes of a great part of the world. America is associated with the dignity of man, with democracy, with foreign aid, with helping the poor, with peace—this was the image of America for many years. For generations this is a new world, not inhibited by ancient resentments and hostility. This was the great vision of America. Within the last few years that image has changed. America does not evoke any more these conceptions of de-

mocracy, helpfulness, peace; on the contrary, it is associated
with aggression. This is terrible, not only for America but for
all of humanity. The beautiful image is now distorted.

The bus I board on leaving Dr. Heschel's office has the
usual array of advertisements and slogans, but I notice especially
one that is meant to advertise nothing but an idea. Next to the
picture of a man standing sadly in a downpour is this legend:

> The rain raineth.
> It raineth on the just and the unjust,
> but it raineth more on the just
> because the unjust have taken the just's umbrella.

And then I turn to read a review of a book that a friend had
mentioned. The review begins:

"In the last one hundred years, nearly 60,000,000 persons
have been slaughtered in wars. They were killed by people like
myself. The most formidable killer I know is an affable English-
man, now in his mid-forties. He's a very decent fellow and a
great family man. In 1943, he made several bombing runs over
Hamburg and helped create the fire storms that wiped out
thousands, many of them women and children.

"My friend is an accountant now and he doesn't think about
Hamburg and its dead. . . ." *

* Franklin Russell, "Why We Should Behave Like Animals," *Life*,
June 3, 1966. The book under review is Konrad Lorenz' *On Aggression*.

RICHARD JOHN NEUHAUS

FINN: You've been one of the leaders in the Clergy Concerned about Vietnam. Does the clergy—say religious leaders but particularly clergy—have a special obligation to be concerned with questions, large political, moral questions, such as Vietnam? Is there any reason for an organization called *Clergy Concerned about Vietnam*?

NEUHAUS: Yes, I think so, although I should say that the national group is officially called Clergy and Laymen Concerned about Vietnam. But if we talk about the religious community and its leadership, whether it be clerical or lay, I think if anything really new is going to come out of all this, it's going to be the renewal of the churches' understanding of what God's intention is in history. I think for a long period of time, perhaps beginning with the Enlightenment, perhaps beginning with the death of Christendom which I would date from that period of time—perhaps with the French Revolution—the Church retreated into an exclusive preoccupation with the private sphere of life, with individual, personal salvation, holding hands with people who have metaphysical blues and answering all kinds of esoteric questions. The church in America, not unrelated to the whole controversy regarding the separation of church and state, has largely accepted this role and has institutionally prospered in carrying out that role. And so we have developed, you know, a kind of American Shinto, as Martin Marty calls it, in which we simply place a halo around the American way of life.

Now I think that what's happening today—and this, of course, would have to be closely related to the civil rights movement which perhaps was the first time that it broke out in large proportions—is that the underground in the church, which had for a long time been saying that the Christian faith is essentially concerned with historical events and with the ordering of society (which means that essentially it's a political movement, if we understand political in the sense that Aristotle talks about political, as that which humanizes interpersonal relations), that this underground has now broken out into the open. And I think that that is for the religious community the great significance of the Vietnam debate and of a lot of consequent issues which are going to be arising in the generation ahead.

The church is going to take the risk of saying that it can be concerned about nothing other than and nothing less than what God is concerned about—which is human welfare, which is Man. And therefore anything which touches upon human welfare, preeminently the question of war and peace, is not only a valid concern of the church in the sense that you can set up a social action committee to take care of one more department, but it is the *central* and *ought* to be the central preoccupation of the religious community. I'm sure this will come as a great shock—it has come as a great shock—to many people who consider themselves to be quite religious but who were trained— and we all must take responsibility for this—to believe that being religious was purely a private kind of commitment.

FINN: Not long before he retired as head of the World Council Visser 't Hooft said that the churches should speak out. But he also said that church leaders were, unfortunately, not prepared to respond as fully and adequately as they should. Do you think that's true of the people who are involved in Clergy Concerned about Vietnam? What is the level of competence that these people should have in order to address themselves to this question and expect to be heard by responsible leaders, government leaders? Do you think they actually have attained that level?

NEUHAUS: Oh no. By no means. I mean I think we're just beginning to break through in this area, Jim, and I'm sure that the vast majority of clergy in America had no training in their seminary period and no *expectation* that their role was a social role in the sense that we're talking about it here. And because the expectation wasn't there, the concern wasn't there; they weren't expected to be concerned. I mean they were given a catechism answer, "Obey the powers that be," Romans 13, and all that, and it was more or less assumed from then on that this

Richard John Neuhaus

was an area where they didn't have to take any particular interest. In fact, that they would be more effective clergymen and more effective manipulators of the ecclesiastical machinery the less interest they took.

So the vast majority of clergy in America are thoroughly unprepared, I'm sure, to understand their role as clergy in the public sphere. Now I think there's a rationalization which has been current a good deal, I think perhaps more in the Roman Catholic circles—Archbishop Cody of Chicago, for example, talks about the distinction between priest as priest and priest as citizen, and so forth. But this, I think, is very, very inadequate, and it doesn't *begin* to touch upon what really has to happen. That is, we have to see that the priest as *priest* is a public person, that he is a political person. Now I think just as a matter of strategy, the church has to be very circumspect, not for its own sake but for the sake of its usefulness to society, in allying itself with the particularities of political movements, endorsing a particular candidate or a particular party or something of this sort. It is not a matter of principle that it ought not to do that, but simply a matter of strategy; that is, how can it be the best steward of its influence. And I think that when the church is in a healthier state, as I hope it will be years from now—which will mean probably that it will also be much smaller than it is now, not nearly so successful as it is now—that then we will see a lot of clergy involved in these particularities of political movements. And that will be a very healthy thing.

But then the mainstream of the clergy will see their role as being the constant guiding of people toward an apprehension of what God intends in the ordering of human society, a constant calling of people—the members of the parish, of the congregation, of the synagogue, whatever—to see that by their participating in the act of liturgy, by their participating in the cultic, that they are also committing themselves to the cultural and that they're committing themselves to certain kinds of directions which, if we are faithful to God, must begin to characterize our age. And I think that the whole movement here is just *barely* under way. And so today most of the church bodies see it as a peripheral thing.

It's part of the syndrome now that people feel very liberal and excitingly relevant and so forth, simply because they're willing to tolerate as a peripheral kind of action some participation in social change. But they certainly do not see the church's primary role as being that of guiding social change, participating in social change, towards the ends that we perceive—always very fallibly but nevertheless at some points rather clearly—to be God's intention. Now Heschel says Clergy Concerned about Vietnam should be called Clergy *Un*concerned about Vietnam.

FINN: Because most of the clergy are unconcerned?

NEUHAUS: Yeah, I think he exaggerates a little bit. I think they're concerned in much the same way that most Americans are concerned.

FINN: What degree of competence do the members of the group have who *are* participating? How politically sophisticated do the clergy have to be to play the role you suggested they should within the church?

NEUHAUS: Well, I'd say they're pretty competent. They're not willing simply to come in with a number of moral principles or whatever and say, "Now Rusk and Johnson and everybody, you know you all love one another and that's how we're gonna settle this." No, I think they're pretty sophisticated. I think they're quite aware of the complexities of the situation. You know, Congressman Rosenthal out here in Queens said that if one reads the *New York Times* each day, carefully, that he knows ninty-nine percent of what Dean Rusk knows—probably a little bit more. That may sound irreverent toward constituted authority, but I think it's probably pretty accurate, and I think that if one reads the kind of predications which again and again, and with all sincerity, the State Department has made about Vietnam, well my gosh it's obvious they don't know what they're doing. And I think that one of the healthiest things is that we're gonna knock away some of the mythology of Romans 13— you know, that they're the powers that be—and then this whole notion that they know more than we do, et cetera, et cetera. Unless one attributes to those who are in the decision-making positions in the government an *extraordinary,* almost *unbelievable* degree of guile and sheer capacity for deception, well obviously they are not only fallible but they're *extraordinarily misled* with regard to Vietnam. And I think that even if they *were* being that guileful, well, one wonders what political or military or whatever advantage it is to them to constantly appear to play the role of fool and misguided prophets.

You know, just the other day, I was reviewing a book called

Richard John Neuhaus

Law and Theology in which Rusk had a paper. This had been delivered about a year ago at a midwestern university, and he was talking about South Vietnam just before Ky took over. And he was going on about how their information indicated that not only military victory but the redevelopment of Vietnam and social reconstruction, was all going ahead apace. Well, I mean, now what *was* the situation there? Was he deliberately misled? Was he misinformed? Was he incapable of understanding what was happening, or was he being deliberately deceptive? I find the last very hard to believe. I don't think that Rusk *is* being that deliberately deceptive. I'm sure that there are points at which government officials, as anybody else, say things which may only be half the truth. But this has been a little bit too much to believe. I mean it stretches my credulity, and I think that of most other people, to believe that the government really knows what it's doing there.

So I think the clergy that are involved are very well informed. I think they're extremely sensitive to the charge that they aren't experts in the area of politics and foreign affairs, and therefore, I think, bend over backward to read, study, join in discussion and dialogue and listen to the other side. No, I think it's quite a virile, intelligent, responsible group of men. At least the guys I've been working with.

FINN: You have suggested that this group, and other groups like it, are properly constituted and should be effective. How would you adjudge the effect that they are actually having in society? I'm talking about all the various groups that may be loosely grouped under the peace movement.

NEUHAUS: Now, maybe there's an unavoidable, inexorable spoiling going on. The Administration is moving in one direction. I think the religious community, or at least the vocal leadership—with the exception largely of the Roman Catholic hierarchy, but I think that it's not going to hold out too long and that we're going to see that change too—is moving in a quite different direction. And the intellectual community and the academic community, the artistic community, all those forces to which a society looks for the shaping of its culture, are moving away from a feeling of participation in the decision-making process as far as our country's foreign affairs go. And of course consequent on this too is the whole development toward the so-called Great Society, the poverty programs and a lot of things here domestically. And I think that this is gonna have a terribly long-range effect. I agree with James Reston of the *Times* that perhaps in historical perspective this will turn out to have been the single greatest tragedy of the Vietnam affair.

FINN: The effect of Vietnam upon the American scene?

NEUHAUS: Tocqueville, in the nineteenth century, talked about why the kind of government that we have in America was possible, that there was a kind of naïve, unsophisticated assumption on the part of the American people that they *did* really participate in the government in some way—a kind of a literalistic faith in government of the people, by the people and for the people—and that it could be trusted. And now there is the open, almost jaded acknowledgment of even the man in the street that of course the government has lied, of course Johnson lies, of course the State Department's not telling the truth, as well as the more sophisticated—although perhaps at times just as jaded—attitude of the academic and maybe even the religious community.

I suppose that finally, for the religious community at least, there is—I'm sure to some it appears to be unsophisticated—but a kind of belief that finally the truth will make us free and that finally men must, for the sake of their own integrity, for the sake of their own soul's salvation, continue to say how they see things, continue to speak the prophetic word where they believe it must be spoken.

America may yet change or even reverse the strategy with which it is attempting to cope with Vietnam and with the underdeveloped world generally, Neuhaus says, but if it does not, if the Administration continues on its present course "all we have to look forward to is a profound alienation." It will be difficult for the Johnson Administration and perhaps successive generations "to enlist the best minds and enthusiasm of deeply concerned people" in urgent domestic programs.

Even though the peace movement may not seem very constructive, it serves, Neuhaus says, to keep alive the alternatives, to point to new possibilities "even as perhaps we head toward disaster. Maybe that sounds too doom-laden, but I don't think the peace movement is changing American policy in Vietnam."

Richard John Neuhaus

FINN: It sounds like a different basis for faith in the peace movement than a number of people who participate would offer.

NEUHAUS: Oh yes. I must say now, as someone who's raised in and lives and breathes the Christian tradition, that I too respond to the kind of thing that Dan Berrigan talks about, the kind of creation of communities of concern, of the formation of a virile and vital subculture in America of those who see the shallowness and the falseness and the dehumanizing factors in the American way of life. Maybe in the new communities of concern there will come a new kind of thing pointing toward man's development, society's development. I believe in that. Fundamentally I believe in Man. I believe that the intentions of God will not be totally frustrated by Man's evil, by Man's capacity for destruction and dehumanizing.

FINN: Let me ask—that's a very large statement you make—what kind of expectation or faith does this give you in regard to the possibility of nuclear war? You spoke earlier about this as a very real possibility. Would an all-out nuclear war be destructive of what you would regard as part of God's plan for Man, or not?

NEUHAUS: We never had an all-out nuclear war so it's very difficult really to talk about what it would be. But to the degree that we can assume that Herman Kahn and McNamara and others have some capacity to envision the consequences of all-out nuclear war, it would seem to me to be a disaster which ought to be resisted at all cost. That is, that there is no value or cause which could justify destroying civilization, millions of human beings. But as to whether it would be the defeat of God's intentions, no it wouldn't be, nor would it be the end of human history. If we respond at all to the kind of vision that Teilhard [de Chardin] and others present—and I do respond to that—Man is just beginning, you know, and therefore we ought not to be so overwhelmed with the immediacy of the present that we lose our historical perspective. And if we think in terms of centuries and even millennia, and perhaps hundreds of millennia, an all-out nuclear war would be looked upon in perspective, I'm sure. In reflection it would be seen as an *extraordinary* retrogression, as a great disaster, but as something through which Man came and through which God's purposes continued

PROTEST: PACIFISM AND POLITICS

to be unfolded. And hopefully Man might learn something from it.

So all-out nuclear war may set back in terms of centuries or millennia the progress of God's creation, but it would not defeat God's purpose. If we believe that God is Almighty and Omnipotent and that finally the Cross—which is probably more of a cosmic symbol than simply a private personal bearing of the cross kind of thing—if we believe that the Cross and the Resurrection are the central realities of our human experience, then we can perhaps see that this may be what is in prospect as far as nuclear war goes. I hesitate to speak of this because I think for a lot of people it becomes a kind of invitation to resign themselves to this possibility, and that of course we cannot do.

FINN: Have you ever been tempted to consider the pacifist position?

NEUHAUS: I think the question today, Jim, is largely *when* a person becomes a pacifist; at what *point* does one become a pacifist? Any rational person is a pacifist in that he is morally, religiously, ultimately committed to a pacific resolution of human conflict. But I think there are times in which war may be the least of several evils confronting a society or a group of societies.

FINN: I presume it's the values you have mentioned that enter into your own judgment about the Vietnam conflict?

NEUHAUS: Yes, I think the Vietnam conflict is an unjust war.

When I ask if he is saying that it is an unjust war in terms of traditional just-war theory, Pastor Neuhaus replies, "Yes, *even* within traditional terms," and he adds that he believes in keeping alive some of the insights of the traditional theory. He has great respect, he says, for those pacifists who, by their actions and attitudes, point toward the future. For he believes that man is at the beginning of an evolutionary development and that we can anticipate a time when conflicts will be resolved by means superior to war. But those of us who are not pacifists, he adds, and who wish to be politically effective need to establish standards of behavior and limitations of action even in war. And it is here that the traditional theory is helpful. It is in terms of that theory that he judges the "policies we are pursuing

Richard John Neuhaus

in Vietnam to be completely out of proportion to the conceivable goals." I ask him how he understands the government to have defined those goals and what means he judges to be disproportionate to their achievement.

NEUHAUS: Well, I suppose that the government understands the goal as being, number one, a demonstration of the credibility "of America's commitment." And to achieve this one must have something that could be called victory in Vietnam. The one thing that is intolerable is that America would, in Johnson's simplistic phraseology, tuck its tail and run. Now the means being utilized to achieve this end are, I think, a very barbaric disregard of the civilian population of South Vietnam and increasingly of North Vietnam; the fringe use of some kinds of chemical warfare; the fact that the government has taken the risk of destroying the whole kind of trust and confidence which there must be in the relationship between the culture-shaping communities in America and the government. In other words, the very fabric of democracy at home is being laid on the line in order to achieve that goal, and I think this is an intolerable thing. I think the very nature of the democratic process makes this quite unthinkable. And beyond that, we are risking—and I think no matter how much one wants to belittle this or how sanguine his viewpoint— we are risking nuclear holocaust. We are certainly taking a calculated kind of step in provoking Communist China and testing the degree of unity or disunity between the Soviet Union and China.

The other great thing which I think is intolerable is that we are alienating world opinion, particularly on this one score of the future of Asia and Latin America and Africa, of the underdeveloped world. I mean certainly *the* great issue of the twentieth century has to do with the unequal and unjust distribution of wealth on the crust of this globe. And if one really sees the revolution of rising aspirations and expectations as being the thing which characterizes our time, well then certainly the Vietnam policy of the American Government not only threatens but is a deliberate rejection of any creative alternative of dealing with this phenomenon.

FINN: Well, to counter that the Administration and the people who support Government policy say that far from opposing this revolution, the conflict in Vietnam and the United States

participation in it supports all those elements—or many of the
elements—that wish to bring about that revolution; that it will
show that a revolution cannot be taken over, controlled and
used for other ends than those which it should properly serve.
This is a contention that has to be dealt with.

NEUHAUS: Right. The whole rationalization, according to the
Rusk mentality, is that we are doing this for the underdeveloped
nations and assuring them that they can rely upon American
strength in the immediate threat, save face from world communism, whatever that may be. Well, I think one must say
that obviously the underdeveloped people of the world don't
see it this way, and that here we are, America, a white European
nation in a sense, telling the rest of the world what's good for
them and telling them that if they don't see it our way, that
they have only our bombs to look forward to. And if there's
anything that's characteristic of any genuine indigenous revolution, it is that the leaders of that revolution and those who support it are not going to accept being told by outsiders—particularly by the conservative and affluent nations of the world—
what's good for them. In other words, they must participate in
the decision-making process, and we are simply denying them
that role.

And I think that, just as with the Negro revolution in America, much of the revolution is generated not by a direct desire or a clearly articulated intention to share a certain amount
of wealth, or to redistribute power, as it is a kind of need, a
kind of cry to find an identity, to find a role in the whole
decision-making process of our century. And so even if one believes, as Dean Rusk does and others do, that America is doing
the best thing for the underdeveloped nations and that Vietnam
is a great sacrifice on the part of America for them, the fact
remains that *they* don't believe it, and we are forcing this
medicine upon them.

But I think that the important thing is that this little, re-
mote Asian peninsula shouldn't assume such gargantuan proportions in our mind. It's not really that important, you know,
who is operating the government of that particular little peninsula. I think that a much more important question is that this
is a precedent which, if it is followed in the years ahead, I
think is going to mean continuing disaster and continuing fissure
in this country and breakdown of any kind of American appeal

Richard John Neuhaus

and therefore American usefulness in the building of world community; that we're going to see continuing Vietnams in Asia and Africa and Latin America, and this I think is really the frightening thing.

FINN: How would you account for the rift which you have already defined, the gap which exists between the community that is concerned and critical about Vietnam and our political leadership which has supported this policy over a number of years? Has the church failed to perform its function in society so that government leaders do not participate in the ethos which should have been formed? Or is it that they have an understanding of political affairs which is different and . . . ?

NEUHAUS: Oh, well no. I'd say that most of our government leaders, most of whom I'm sure consider themselves to be religious people in some sense or another, are not being unfaithful to the religious tradition in which they were brought up and to which they feel they are loyal. It's been the failure of the church that we've allowed them to think, that we've allowed ourselves to think, that religion is preoccupied with this private sphere and that it need not impinge upon political and economic decisions, or decisions regarding world order.

I'm sure that the church has to depart now, increasingly, from the blasé assumption of American righteousness, which it has never been necessary to do before. At least it has never felt itself so compelled because somehow there was always an ability to rationalize—perhaps because what America did was not *that* critical for the whole future of mankind as it is today. And this, of course, has also to do with the technological development and nuclear weaponry and so forth. So I think the church today finds itself in a situation in America very similar to the church in Germany in the 1930's. And I think because we're only thirty or forty years from that experience that we're perhaps better equipped to respond—I'm confident we are—than was the church in Germany. And I think that we will see if Vietnam is the parable of the future as far as American policy goes. If this is true, then we will see increasingly the religious community accepting the role of a minority community and accepting the role of dissent, accepting the role of criticism and of the positer of alternatives in a way that the church in America has never done before.

Is this an example of the "moralizing and preachifying" that Dr. Schwarzschild attributed to the Clergy Concerned as a group? Or is it rather an example of someone who, in Everett Gendler's phrase, "speaks both truth and morality to power"?

It is probably evident from this transcript that Pastor Neuhaus is highly articulate. Concepts, phrases and facts seem equally and readily available to him. There are people who distrust such facility. They wish to see in the speaker's voice and expression and gestures some evidence of the intellectual and moral effort that should support statements as large and judgments as strict as those made by Neuhaus. Nothing of this is evident as he addresses himself to my questions. Anyone glancing into his office as we talked and seeing him seated behind his desk with one leg occasionally draped over the side of his chair might well have thought he was recounting some pleasant trivia of the day. And if they overheard some of his references to the secular obligations of the Church, they might have thought that he was indulging in currently fashionable concepts.

But as a number of facts in his background make evident, Pastor Neuhaus' interest in the political and social issues he discusses cannot be dismissed simply as literary or aesthetic. He was born in Pembroke, Ontario, where his father was a Lutheran minister. After early public schooling he went to high school in Seward, Nebraska, but dropped out to run a self-owned retail business in Cisco, Texas. He then continued his formal education at Concordia Theological Seminary in St. Louis, Wayne State University and Washington University, St. Louis.

Since 1961 he has been senior pastor at St. John the Evangelist, a low-income, predominantly Negro and Spanish parish in the Williamsburg-Bedford-Stuyvesant sections of Brooklyn. He serves as chairman of community and citywide organizations which are active in housing, school integration and antipoverty programs. He has been arrested and jailed because of civil rights activities. Pastor Neuhaus has written on liturgy, ecumenism and social change, particularly as these are related to the metropolis. He is editor of *Una Sancta,* a theological quarterly devoted to the Church's renewal in liturgy, unity and social responsibility.

All of this background makes it easier to understand his

interest in and emphasis upon the way in which social concerns are interrelated. And I wonder as I listen to him speak whether his age is not an important factor in the way he discusses the relation of the Church to society and of the person to authority, whether of church or state. For, since he is only thirty, he has escaped a kind of pastoral training that many clergy are now trying to overcome, and his own education has taken place at a time when the challenge faced by the Church is thought by many to be greater but more exciting than it has been for many years. Whatever the reasons, Pastor Neuhaus believes that the Church is in the world to serve it and he intends to bend his own best efforts in that service. The Clergy Concerned about Vietnam is, for him, one of the channels.

JAMES FOREST, TOM CORNELL
AND DAVID MILLER

The Catholic Peace Fellowship was begun in the summer of 1964 by Catholic members of the Fellowship of Reconciliation and is affiliated with it.* The CPF describes itself as primarily an educational service; its first responsibility is "the introduction of the various traditions of the Church in regard to war and peace to our fellow Catholics."

The activity of the CPF would, I thought, be particularly instructive for several reasons. American Catholics as a group have not been noted for their participation in the peace movement. Yet Pope John was an ardent advocate for peace and Pope Paul has made eloquent and anguished pleas for the cessation of all war and particularly the war in Vietnam. The reactions of Catholics would be an indication of whether a strong moral voice speaking from within a developed tradition would have any influence. One bit of evidence would be the number and kinds of inquiries the CPF received.

Another reason is that, theoretically at least, the Catholic Church has kept in good repair the theory of the just war. The war in Vietnam seemed to be a war which invited the application of those principles and therefore the appearance of a number

* The FOR, an international, interdenominational peace organization, was started in England in 1914, shortly after the start of the First World War. In addition to Catholics, the FOR lists the following as having pacifist fellowships affiliated with it: Baptist, Disciples, Episcopal, Ethical Culture, Liberal (Unitarian-Universalist), Lutheran, Methodist, New Church, Presbyterian U.S., and United Presbyterian, U.S.A.

James Forest, Tom Cornell and David Miller

of selective conscientious objectors, those who judged this war—though not all wars—to be unjust. If indeed this were the case, it should be most noticeable among Catholics.

The CPF is one of the many peace organizations that honeycomb an entire large floor at 5 Beekman Street in New York. It has just moved from smaller quarters and, when I visit, James Forest, the national secretary, is restoring a degree of order to the office. It is colorful and bright; the walls are already partially covered with large, bold serigraphs by Sister Corita, pictures of many supporters and "heroes" of the CPF, letters and cards, slogans and posters of other peace organizations, buttons and pins. When I comment on some of the slogans, Forest says that not everyone is equally appreciative of the contribution they are supposed to make. During one demonstration several of the participants who carried placards reading "Make Love, Not War" and "Draft Beer, Not Boys" were, he said, severely admonished by a fellow demonstrator, a stern little lady who thought the serious nature of the protest should preclude such unseemly levity.

As I am able to observe, Forest himself is capable of answering inquiries with efficiency, confidence and occasional lapses into levity. He is of medium height, with a shock of brown hair, a mustache that has only temporary status, round steel-rimmed glasses, noticeable teeth and a strong, pleasant voice. I ask him about the people who come to the CPF for information, particularly those who want counseling about conscientious objection to war. Have their numbers increased in recent years?

FOREST: Well, I started counseling in the latter part of 1961, when I was on the staff of the *Catholic Worker*. At that time we got at the *Catholic Worker*—which was really the only place the Catholic CO's went to, except for a few who went to the Central Committee for Conscientious Objectors—we got maybe one or two a month. Very few. Of course it was a different period. There was no war in progress. This number gradually started increasing around 1963, and I would attribute this in large measure to the Council and to Pope John—not on guesswork so much as on the basis of interviews with conscientious objectors. And still you hear Pope John mentioned, and the Vatican Council quite frequently. Now what are the statistics? I suppose that the Catholic Peace Fellowship, the National Office, counsels approximately forty-five or fifty a week. You've gone from a few a month to perhaps two hundred or so a month.

FINN: I presume most people who come to you for some kind of advice are those who are facing the draft or soon will face the draft?

FOREST: Well, we do get a few who want to register their opposition to the war, even though they themselves are not, probably will never be, eligible. I'm speaking particularly of professional people who are in their thirties and have a family and children. But some of them *have* filed CO forms just for the record. Some also want to do everything they can to ease the pathway for other Catholic CO's. They feel that by registering they will make another Board aware of the fact that there is such a thing as a Catholic conscientious objector.

FINN: Do the people you counsel tend to get much, if any, support from their pastors, their families, the communities in which they've grown up or in which they now live?

FOREST: Well, that varies widely. The experience that we have had is that conscientious objectors often are very shy about talking to their pastors about conscientious objection. I don't know why the lines of communication are so thoroughly poor between the pastor and the people that he serves. But I think this is the case probably in other matters as well. We always urge them to talk to their pastors, and it's surprising how frequently the pastors are willing, after they have given it some thought, to stand by them even if they don't agree personally with this conscientious objection position.

Forest then says the counseling procedure the CPF follows is fairly standard. First there is the task of getting the basic facts: the person's age, occupation, religious education and allegiance, current draft status, etc. Then the big question: why is he now thinking of becoming a CO? The CPF believes that a Catholic CO should be aware not only of the legal definition of the conscientious objector but of the traditional teaching of the Church on war. This obviously requires some directed study, and the CPF is willing to supply the direction.

James Forest, Tom Cornell and David Miller

FINN: Have most of the people, when they come for information, already determined that they are conscientious objectors, or are many of them undecided and really coming for information and assistance to help them think through the problem?

FOREST: I just remember when I first knocked on the door of a Catholic rectory for instruction years ago, that I had definitely made up my mind that I was going to be a Catholic. I just knew that. Something basic about it. And yet at the same time I felt a great need to know more about what it was. And I think this is the way with a lot of guys who come here. They feel that they have made a decision about it and at the same time they are painfully aware of the need to learn a great deal. There *are* some who come and who just are *not* sure. They're really not sure—very undecided. Some of them become CO's and some of them don't. I think it's probably fifty-fifty of that group.

FINN: Do you follow or get any later information about people that come to you for assistance?

FOREST: Generally, I suppose, it's the bad news that gets to us, when a person is having difficulty.

FINN: What kind of trouble?

FOREST: Well, some Boards are simply hostile to the conscientious objector. There are a few that, well, simply pour abuse upon the conscientious objectors that come to them. I don't think it's as bad now as it used to be for Catholics; I think that it's much more widely known in the draft board these days that the Catholic can *very definitely* be a conscientious objector with no ifs, ands or buts; it is theoretically possible.

FINN: That's a fairly recent victory?

FOREST: Yes. It was true that during World War II all the chancery offices in this country would issue a one-sentence statement to the effect that the Catholic could be a conscientious objector. Period. No elaboration. That was it. It's only in the light of Vatican II, I think, that it has become explicitly clear that a Catholic is formally obliged to follow his conscience, and that the Church has extended its abstract teaching on conscience to declaring formally that a Catholic, that a conscientious objector, has a legal right to this.

FINN: You said that many people have an incorrect or almost caricatured idea of the pastors or bishops they might consult, but you have had some bad experiences, you said, in trying to get help.

FOREST: Well, yes. I mean, there's that fellow that I mentioned in the parish of Our Lady of Pompeii, here in New York. He talked to a priest there upon our suggestion—I think he knew better instinctively. In his case he was quite right. But he did go to one of the priests—I don't think it was the pastor—and said "I decided to become a conscientious objector, and here's why," and so on. The priest hardly gave him a chance to talk for more than a minute. He just exploded in rage, just said "Why don't you burn youself?" And I don't know if he walked out or harangued him further or what happened, but it was terminated rather quickly after that.

FINN: Now there are other Catholic organizations that have been working with problems of peace and international relations . . .

FOREST: Three others. The *Catholic Worker,* the American Pax Association and the Catholic Association for International Peace [CAIP]. For what we would consider, there are four American Catholic peace organizations. I still consider myself a member of the *Catholic Worker* movement. The American Pax Association I organized when I was at the *Catholic Worker,* but I regret that it doesn't cooperate with non-Catholic organizations in any way public or private. They're not very active, they're not very big. They publish a quarterly magazine, that's their main thing. I didn't belong to the Catholic Association for International Peace for years simply because I didn't want to spend ten dollars [laugh]. I recently joined and we *are* in contact with Monsignor Higgins,* who has been helpful to us.

FINN: Do you find Catholics, in the theoretical approach they take to the problems presented by war, in any way distinguished from Protestants or people of no religion whatsoever?

FOREST: I'm not sure. I'm not sure because I think that there's an obvious change that's taken place in Catholic thought, as opposed to how Catholics approached war before. We talked

* Monsignor George G. Higgins is director of the Social Action Department of the U.S. Catholic Conference, formerly the National Catholic Welfare Conference.

James Forest, Tom Cornell and David Miller

about this in terms of the drift away from the just war by the Catholic conscientious objectors. I'm still amazed, as a matter of fact, that we don't have more Catholics who approach it via the just war. Actually I'm disturbed about the lack of interest in the just-war theory. I'm concerned that those Catholics who are *not* conscientious objectors, who are *not* pacifists—you know there's a distinction between the two—and who therefore presumably go along with war more or less, seem to have so few questions to ask about the war in Vietnam. It just seems that you have two attitudes, one of "Any war is O.K." or a total rejection of war.

FINN: Well, this follows from what is a typical American reaction. We are a peace-loving people and we'll do our best to stay out of a war, but once *in* there are almost no rules. No matter what we have said previously, it's all or nothing at all.

FOREST: Well, again it bears out the sociologists—like [Gordon] Zahn's argument about the German hierarchy and the German church during the Hitler years. Basically it was the German church, and it did what the German nation did. And that people generally, in every nation, do that; and that we over-emphasize often how important religion is in the life of man; that it plays a peripheral function rather than a central function. Now I don't think this is true of our conscientious objectors. I think these are people who are *exceedingly* curious about what it means to be a Catholic and what it means to be a Christian.

I ask Forest whether he has any expectation that those who share his views will grow in number; will they ever be more than a minority group?

FOREST: I do recall Henri Fesquet's observation in *Catholicism: Religion of Tomorrow?* that it just might be the rule someday for Catholics to be conscientious objectors.* I think it would

* Henri Fesquet has been covering religious news for *Le Monde* since 1950 and has, in the course of the years, earned a reputation as a learned and penetrating commentator. The passage to which Forest refers reads:
"The future may see it come to grief like every other form of violence, whereas it is hard to see what could kill a doctrine which issues in nonviolence. In this respect, too, Catholicism is still in its infancy. When will Christians finally assimilate the lesson of Gandhi? The atomic bomb could do the West the terrible service of demonstrating the absurdity of armed violence. In all probability, Rome will one day—

be more helpful for me just to say that I don't do anything on the basis of expectation, and so that would be like asking a vegetarian what kind of meat he prefers.

Maybe I should be the first one in line to say indeed we can all be conscientious objectors. Catholicism can be so important to us that at least we're conscientious objectors, not just-war theorists. But I just have no desire even to hold that idea. All I want to do is to see the teaching of the Church in all its varieties presented as often and as loudly and as clearly as possible to as many people as possible.

Still I *do* think the question now is: What does it mean to be a conscientious objector and a Catholic? Under what circumstances *ought* a Catholic to be a conscientious objector, and are there circumstances in which *all Catholics* should be conscientious objectors? These are things which are live questions now.

It was only after I had talked with Forest a number of times that I asked him to give me information about his background. Dictated over the telephone, it came out in the following telegraphese:

Born, Salt Lake City, 2 November 1941.

Father a Communist Party organizer, Mother a Smith College graduate.

Raised in Chicago and Denver until divorce of parents at age five. Moved to Red Bank, New Jersey to live with mother and relatives. Mother works as psychiatric social worker for New Jersey mental hospital.

Lived in rural Negro slum, attended public schools.

Attended Hollywood High School. Received a Richfield Oil Corporation scholarship to attend summer sessions at Long Beach State College. Received Los Angeles County Board of Education scholarship for art studies at county art school. Was officer of class in high school and of the honor society. Editor of school annual.

Dropped out of high school, winter 1958. Went on a cross-country trip.

Joined Navy in May '59; trained at Great Lakes, Illinois.

better late than never—lead a crusade of collective conscientious objection." (New York, Holt, Rinehart and Winston, 1964), p. 205. The reader may wish to compare this statement with that of Father John McKenzie on pp. 52ff.

James Forest, Tom Cornell and David Miller

Was intelligence officer of company. Went on to Navy Aerographers school at Lakehurst, New Jersey; graduated first in class, and was sent to Washington, D.C.

Became interested in Christianity at training school, returned to Episcopal Church in which he had been baptized and confirmed as a child. While in Washington, active with Episcopal parish and diocesan home for emotionally disturbed children.

Became interested in Catholicism, beginning instruction in spring of 1960. Following November received into Catholic Church.

Became interested in the *Catholic Worker* movement at this time and began visiting the New York house and Tivoli Farm. Decided he was a pacifist early in 1961.

By April, sought discharge on CO grounds. After discharge was approved, joined the *Catholic Worker* where he eventually served as managing editor of the paper until February 1962. (During this time attended such institutions as Staten Island Community College and the New School where he took courses in arts and literature.)

Afterwards worked for the CNVA, Catholic Relief Services (where he ran an adding machine for goods lost or stolen between here and the Orient). Then several months working for *Bottling Industry*, a trade magazine, and then a year at *Liberation* as assistant editor. The following year he was a staff writer on a daily newspaper in Staten Island.

In the course of that summer he went to a Christian Peace Conference in Prague (under the auspices of FOR) with Daniel Berrigan. This revived his interest in the peace movement (he had been disgusted with it).

It was during this summer trip that the Catholic Peace Fellowship was created—John Heidbrink of FOR, James Douglass, Daniel Berrigan and Forest were the initiating parties—and the CPF began functioning after that trip. The office opened in February '65.

Since November 1965 he has been on the FOR staff as Assistant Director of Interfaith Activities (the other assistant is Tom Cornell; Heidbrink is the director).

He has written for *National Catholic Reporter*, *Ramparts*, *Worldview*, *Fellowship*, and *Commonweal*.

He and Tom Cornell have edited a "Catholic Worker Reader" which will be appearing.

His pride is his son Benedict, now four years old.

On another occasion I talk with Forest; Tom Cornell, whom he has mentioned; and David Miller, who initiated a new form of protest by being the first to burn his draft card. Cornell is slim, has a narrow intense face, heavy eyebrows over deep-set eyes and straight black hair. Miller, well over six feet, has wide shoulders and a good, loose build, blond hair and an almost conventionally handsome face. He is quiet, possibly shy, as if he held his strength in reserve; but his reserve becomes part of his strength.

Tom Cornell was born into an Irish-Italian family and was raised in a traditional Catholicism. He recalls an incident from the third grade: his teacher showed the class a picture of a young man in the *Bridgeport Post,* a local newspaper. Because he refused to participate in the war—the year was 1943—he was sentenced to jail. Cornell remembers thinking that he'd never have to face that problem because he was a Catholic. Not until his sophomore year in college did it occur to him that the problem might be his after all. Quite by accident he ran across a copy of *The Long Loneliness,* the autobiography of Dorothy Day. The Catholic Worker, the name both of the newspaper and the movement founded by Dorothy Day and Peter Maurin in 1933, is dedicated to social justice, nonviolence, civil rights and personal poverty. Cornell says that he saw "the logic of the Catholic Worker's position on war right away," and saw its relation to "what the Jesuits had been feeding me all these years" about just wars. But he also saw the dilemmas and ambiguities, "and I suppose I have a streak of chicken in me too, and I didn't want to make the decision about being a conscientious objector.

"By the end of college I still wasn't to the point where I could say that I was a conscientious objector. But the draft was facing me and I had to make the decision. I was either going to say yes to all the things that I really believed in or I wasn't. And so I said yes and I applied for classification as a CO, and

James Forest, Tom Cornell and David Miller

it took four years before I convinced the draft authorities that I was in fact a conscientious objector, and I got my 1-0."

Cornell now says that all war is insane and unjust. He believes that what happened during World War II led to a brutalization of sensitivities so that we were, as a society, prepared to rejoice at the horrors of Hiroshima.

FINN: If I understand you, you are saying that in retrospect you think it would be preferable if the United States had not participated militarily in World War II, if it had decided to opt out, and that there are other alternatives that would have been better.

CORNELL: Definitely so. But we did not have the vision to see other ways. Dorothy Day and Peter Maurin had proposed other ways, or at least avenues, which the public could not accept at that point. You know, when the bombs are falling and you're in the middle of a war, especially World War II, how could you talk about nonviolence as a positive technique? No one was prepared to listen, the avenues out had not been taken, the kinds of approaches that should have been used in the 1930's had not been used. We were in the middle of the thing; there was nothing for the pacifist to do, in the mid-1940's, but go to jail or go to those concentration camps that were called Civilian Public Service Camps.

FINN: Now if history had taken a different course during the 30's, if the peace movements had indeed made history other than what it was, what you suggest might have then provided alternatives. But history didn't move in that direction and people *are* faced at particular moments in their lives with decisions where they cannot go back and redo history. And this was what happened to many people—including people in the peace movements. Now, what does a government under these conditions *actually* do, and what was possible at that time?

CORNELL: That's a very difficult question. We say that the United States should have laid down its arms, should have greeted the Nazis and the Japanese with open arms, empty hands, using a completely nonviolent approach. "What little I have you're welcome to." Take California, it was suggested. I think that's O.K., but I know perfectly well that the society is not going to buy a package like that. Nevertheless we will stick by the nonviolent guns and continue to bear the witness, the individual Christian witness. Christianity comes to us as individuals, I feel, even with the society of the Church and the society of the state. If we're convinced, we have to bear the witness.

While we talk, David Miller has been following the exchanges, and it is difficult to associate him, quiet and serious, with the image that floats off the news stories about draft-card burners and the Congressional Record in which their action is denounced.

On October 15, 1965, as part of the International Days of Protest, there was a meeting in front of the U.S. Army Induction Center on Whitehall Street in New York City. Twenty-two-year-old David Miller appeared in the middle of a fairly long program to say that he was not going to deliver a prepared speech. He was, however, a pacifist, opposed to all wars, but particularly opposed to the war in Vietnam and the conscripting of men for that war. Hoping that it would be a politically significant act that would speak for itself, he burned his Notice of Classification in front of the audience—supporters, hecklers, police and reporters.

Not only did Miller set a precedent which others were to follow, but he set off a wave of reaction across the country. For example, it was reported that Vincent Di Mattina, New York State Commander of the Veterans of Foreign Wars, along with several other V.F.W. officers, traveled from New York City to Syracuse, Miller's hometown, to place him under arrest. Since Miller was in New York City, the attempt failed. The New York *Daily News* demanded that "Communist-incited beatniks, pacifists and damned idiots [who] are demonstrating" against the Vietnam war be tried under the treason provisions of the Constitution. Similar reactions were reported across the country.

Miller was subsequently arrested, tried, convicted and sentenced on March 16, 1966 to three years' imprisonment. Execution of the sentence was suspended and Miller placed on probation. As we talk, less than a month after his sentencing, his case is in the United States Court of Appeals.*

* The law under which Miller was convicted is the Universal Military Training and Service Act of 1951 as amended August 10, 1965. Speak-

James Forest, Tom Cornell and David Miller

How, I ask David Miller, did he become a pacifist? What path led him to his present act of civil disobedience?

MILLER: Well, I think it begins when I went to LeMoyne College. I had decided, it was that summer, to attend the freshman retreat at LeMoyne—and to begin to go to confession and mass and communion more often than I had in the past. And I did, and after the retreat, the starting of the school year, I began to read the Gospels and the Epistles at mass and to take theology and some of the other courses that helped me very much. And I began to think in a critical way for the first time in my life—which began, I really think, in the freshman English course. Not long after that I decided I had a vocation to the priesthood. And I lived that way actually for a couple of years, and talked to a spiritual advisor who helped me a great deal— Father Cox at LeMoyne. And Dan Berrigan, certainly, with his writings and his talking at LeMoyne. And my decision actually was to follow wherever this choice would lead me.

FINN: Where was this exactly? Pacifism is. . . .

MILLER: No, pacifism didn't have anything to do with it. It was a religious life. It was to follow wherever the Gospels and

ing for the bill which proposed the amendment, Mr. L. Mendel Rivers of South Carolina, from the Committee on Armed Services, explained its intent:

"We do not want to make it illegal to mutilate or destroy a card per se, because sometimes this can happen by accident. But if it can be proved that a person knowingly destroyed or mutilated his draft card, then under the Committee proposal, he can be sent to prison, where he belongs. This is the least we can do for our men in South Vietnam fighting to preserve freedom, while a vocal minority in this country thumb their noses at their own Government."

Speaking in support of Mr. Rivers, Mr. William G. Bray of Indiana said:

"The need of this legislation is clear. Beatniks and so-called 'campus cults' have been publicly burning their draft cards to demonstrate their contempt for the United States and our resistance to Communist takeovers. . . .

"Just yesterday such a mob attacking the United States and praising the Viet Cong attempted to march on the Capitol but were prevented by the police from forcibly moving into our Chambers. They were led by a Yale University professor. They were generally a filthy, sleazy beatnik gang; but the question which they pose to America is quite serious."

It may be worth noting that the Government's Selective Service witness testified that it was completely irrelevant to Miller's possible induction whether or not he had in his possession his draft card. And that the Yale professor referred to by Mr. Bray is Staughton Lynd.

this teaching and thinking would lead me. And that led me first, actually, to work in Mississippi at the suggestion of Father Cox and Father Berrigan, after I had joined the Sodality at LeMoyne. And I worked six weeks with Negro children, and took the census with several other people from LeMoyne in Natchez, Mississippi. It wasn't until I came back to LeMoyne that I became involved in Syracuse CORE and involved in work with Negro children at my old parish in a downtown section of Syracuse. It wasn't long after that I was arrested actually in a CORE demonstration after participating in several of them. The first arrest took place in September of '63, I think it was. Well anyway, it was the beginning of my junior year in college.

And then I began reading radical things—maybe the *Catholic Worker* once in a while, and *Liberation* magazine, some of the things that A. J. Muste wrote in there and Barbara Deming, and the *National Guardian* among other things. And the more radical ideas appealed to me. The most radical I had read before that was *Modern Youth and Chastity,* and I decided at the end that the best way was to—if you really appreciated all this—to give it up.

Well, the vocation I thought I had for the priesthood didn't work out right away, and I decided to wait for a while and finish my college career, or at least the junior year. And that's why I became involved in CORE and became gradually involved in thinking about pacifism and about nuclear war, and became more and more drawn toward what I thought were radical ideas in regard to pacifism and to the civil rights movement. And I became a nuclear pacifist and then, toward the end of my senior year in college . . . maybe toward the beginning too, an acknowledged complete pacifist at the school. So much so that I would be able to talk about it among friends. And it was during my senior year in college that I became interested in the Catholic Worker, effectively interested in wanting to go down there, by reading *The Other America* by Michael Harrington. At the beginning of my senior year I made the trip down to the Catholic Worker for a week, and then again for a week during semester break in January. And I decided that I was a conscientious objector, but the noncooperator position appealed to me most of all. I was going to go to the Catholic Worker and begin my noncooperation there.

My mother thought I should do this too, so as not to cause too much publicity in the hometown. [laughter] But she was actually very good about it and had gotten used to all these ideas,

James Forest, Tom Cornell and David Miller

little by little, you know, through my first involvement in what she might have thought was religious fanaticism [laughter] when I first started at LeMoyne. And it was at the end of my college career that I just picked up and went to the Catholic Worker and began noncooperating.

FINN: You speak of noncooperating. That's noncooperating with the government in, I presume, its efforts to engage you in military efforts. How did you decide, Dave, that your non-cooperation should extend to the degree of openly and publicly displaying your attitude by burning your draft card?

MILLER: I think draft-card burning is essentially a minor matter in relation to good noncooperation with the draft. As I say, I began in June of '65. At one point I refused to report for induction, but instead picketed outside the induction center at the time I was supposed to be inducted. I think this kind of act in natural, open refusal, in good courtesy, of the draft, is much more meaningful than just the act itself of publicly protesting by burning your draft card.

CORNELL: Dave clearly would have qualified as a conscientious objector under the law and under the Selective Service procedures, but did not apply for conscientious objector status and was given a couple of induction notices. Tell Jim why you refused to apply for conscientious objector status when you clearly qualify.

MILLER: There are many good reasons for that, but the one that comes to mind first of all is that given the situation of our society and the innocence of young men who are called upon to participate in Selective Service and who are drafted, it simply would be unfaithful to them, unfaithful to myself, were I not to take such a strong stand against conscription and against war. It's the best personal witness that I can give. There are many more reasons. The laws are very stringent and the process of going through applying for conscientious objection is made humiliating to the individual who does it. They're just simply not given the benefit of the doubt; they're just not given an opportunity to express themselves, I think.

FOREST: This is a problem, a problem that has tortured the consciences of a lot of guys who, like Dave, clearly qualify to be conscientious objectors under the law without *any problem.* A person who is concerned not only about his own conscience but his communal function, may be very hesitant to take advantage of an exemption when he knows that another guy whose conscience is just as sensitive, who is unable to live with himself and to fight in a *particular* war, is forced to go to jail. The answer to this problem is something which we're just beginning to discover because the problem is at hand and is not resolved.

Now, we have two or three possibilities of people who are taking a fairly well defined just-war position, and we *are* asking bishops and we are asking theologians if they will take positions in support of these cases. I don't know what the results are going to be. I'm *relatively* optimistic about it.

In our discussion of the just-war theory, we have come upon a conversational experience that I think many Catholics and perhaps many non-Catholics encounter in their own conscience and intelligence as they work over the problem of war. Very few Catholics today are thinking seriously, that is the Catholics who are conscientious objectors, are thinking seriously about the just-war ethic. There is a realization, I think—and I don't know how well this can be brought out really—that it's not just an intellectual game of weighing things like a pharmacist filling a prescription, that to be a Christian is to be involved in a very mysterious vocation that takes many forms. Nobody can say what is *the* Christian vocation—and yet it is nonetheless a continually demanding and exhausting and renewing experience; it's all kinds of things. It is something, though, which is constantly sucking up all that is inside of you; in regard to war it is possible that we Christians have a much more profound demand on us than whether or not to take part in just wars.

The works of mercy and the works of war are opposites. They are polarities. Christians are *specifically* summoned into the world to carry out in various ways the spiritual and corporal works of mercy, as we call them in our catechism, and that there simply has got to be a confrontation with the fact, What is it to be a Christian? What does it mean? What does it mean to be a leaven, to be a light, to be the salt of the earth, and so on? What is unique and important in whatever it is that we've been put on this planet for? Is it to get involved in the casuistry of modern war, or is it to undertake some vocation which we may not even understand? We don't understand how the works of mercy relate to the political order of things. We don't expect everybody to be taken up in them. We do them because somehow or other we have to and we leave the result in hands that are not our own.

James Forest, Tom Cornell and David Miller

MILLER: We do the best we can and, doing what I can, what I'm most qualified to do, is to refuse military service and to absent myself from the Selective Service System, from all military endeavors.

FINN: You adopt your own position of pacifism, of radical nonviolence, with the realization that this is a minor tradition within the Church, one which is not going to gain much support from the established figures within the Church?

MILLER: Well, established means, effectively, that they go along with some of the worst in the tradition of the Catholic Church in relation to acquiescence in government. Let me say, though, that I really have great faith in the ability of numbers of people to grow and to come out of nooks and crannies, from places you would least expect, into good, solid radicals.

FOREST: I don't think we should get involved in any kind of fatalism—that because in World War II, say, in Germany, or here in the United States during the war in Vietnam, the Church failed to really become a prophetic witness or to become an outspoken voice in the name of justice, or whatever it should be, that this is prevented from occurring in some future time. I think that there's something going on inside the Church that has *not* happened before. I think that it can be sensed, and I think that it can be gauged, and where it's going to go remains to be seen.

CORNELL: Although I agree with *everything* you said, Jim, still I think that we are going to be a minority witness in the Church until the second coming, really. Because no matter how many conscientious objectors occur or arise from just-war thinking, from natural ethics and from the insights that they get from the Gospels, still I must admit to the presumptuous position that the fullness of nonviolence, its real applicability, its fundamental philosophical and theological correctness, is not going to be seen by a majority of people at any time.

FOREST: I think it's extremely important that I know of nobody who is devoting himself or herself to work in the Catholic peace movement, or whatever you want to call it, that is engaged in this work because of any expectation of success or, for that matter, of any expectation of failure.

It *does not* have anything to do, in the last analysis, with any expectation that it's going to work, and that the whole Church is going to become a pacifist Church, a nonviolent Church, a servant Church, a witness Church, a Church that would sooner die than shed blood. It may be that our vision of the Church is not really the best possible vision, but it's the vision that we've been given to work with for a particular reason that we don't know about.

FINN: Dave, you mentioned among the things which influenced you, a number of people. I'm not sure whether you mentioned Pope John and the Council and the Encyclicals and the whole new spirit which seems to be abroad in the Church.

MILLER: I think that's the experience and the thought that led to the movement, as we said before, of the out-of-proportion growth of young Catholics in the radical movement right now. I was very much impressed with and studied, not in great detail I must say, the encyclicals of Pope John. Just his person himself inspired me and enabled me to think along the lines of peace on earth and justice for all peoples in the world. I think this has had a great effect in my life, and is the main thought and probably the real inspiration behind these radical Catholics.

PACIFIST

A. J. MUSTE

Is the peace movement then reduced to a desperate struggle to maintain an extremely limited degree of pressure . . . to act as a tiny inhibiting factor on the larger processes of unchecked violence—is it even reduced to the position of constant and hopeless witness against the inevitable? Or is there perhaps still some unexplored approach which could lead us out of this paralysing calculus of evils?*

To a person previously unacquainted with the peace movement and the pacifist organizations, the first introduction is likely to be bewildering—and with reason. For what might appear to the outside observer as an amorphous, shapeless but somehow united mass is, in fact, a large number of organizations and people with differentiated views, attitudes and positions. Periodically able to unite in public statements, in demonstrations, in protest marches, they are also capable of sustained principled debate with a refinement of analysis that the less dedicated would regard as byzantine. Like a party long out of power and with no single, accepted spokesman, they can indulge in the luxury of factions and splinter groups. And within these groups there are positions, terms, events, persons which have become invested with meaning and charged with emotion for the initiate.

Many self-critical pacifists have been aware that this luxury is a weakness, an obstacle to concerted, meaningful action, but they regard the present time as both an opportunity for the peace

* Adrian Cunningham in *Peace on Earth: The Way Ahead,* Walter Stein, ed. (London, Sheed and Ward, 1966).

movement and a time of testing. One of these is a man who has been described as America's No. 1 pacifist, A. J. Muste. The personal history of A. J. Muste is in good part the history of pacifism in twentieth-century America.* He has commented that "anyone is on very dangerous ground when he suggests there is something I haven't joined at one time or another." And the record bears him out. He is, at the time of the interview, still active in many of the most active pacifist organizations.

A. J. Muste was born in a small town in the Netherlands in 1885. His family traveled steerage to the U.S. in 1891 and settled in the Midwest. He went to Hope College in Holland, Michigan and then to the Theological Seminary of the Dutch Reformed Church in Brunswick, New Jersey. While there he also took courses in philosophy at New York University and Columbia, hearing William James lecture on pragmatism and becoming a good friend of John Dewey. Ordained to the ministry in 1909, he became the first minister of Fort Washington Collegiate Church on Washington Heights. Reacting against what he regarded as narrow and confining religious strictures, he accepted a ministry in the Congregational Church in Boston in 1914. It was there that he became a pacifist, resolving long uneasiness, for he determined to make "recalcitrant reality conform to the high ethical demand" of Scripture, reversing what he observed to be the usual practice. However difficult the situation of someone who adopts this position today, it is better than it was at a time when Theodore Roosevelt could say, "The clergyman who does not put the flag above the Church had better close his church and keep it closed."

Muste left his pacifism for a period when he came to believe that it was only half-way to a proper revolutionary position. In 1936, after much effective work on behalf of labor and deep immersion in Marxist-Leninist theory, he returned to the pacifism he still espouses. Within the Christian community he and Reinhold Niebuhr, who broke with the FOR on the question of pacifism, have long represented polar positions. "I told Muste in 1936," says Niebuhr, "after he had been a pacifist, then a

* This history is related by Nat Hentoff in *Peace Agitator: The Story of A. J. Muste* (New York, Macmillan, 1963), to which these initial paragraphs are indebted.

revolutionary, and a pacifist once again, that he had traveled the circle and hadn't learned anything on the way."

More recently, Muste has commented on what he regards as Niebuhr's failure to learn: "Niebuhr's philosophy was too one-sided and schematic to be truly 'realistic' and now, in the field of the nuclear power struggle, it is irrelevant. It may, indeed, even contribute to the tragic denouement of Western civilization, or simply civilization, which political realism sought to avoid."

When I visit A. J. Muste he has only recently returned from Saigon where he and five other pacifists had gone on a peace mission.* At eighty-one, he gives the appearance, as one might expect, of a frail, old man. He is thin, has white, wispy hair thinning on top and heavy dark-rimmed bifocals. When he gestures his hands, like those of many older people, seem loosely attached at the wrists, but when he speaks his voice is strong and clear, and he enunciates more clearly than most of us. He speaks slowly but without hesitation and with a good deal of expression, and he listens as carefully as he speaks.

FINN: Mr. Muste, a number of people commenting on the present historical situation have suggested that it has strengthened the position of pacifists, since modern weapons systems have made more apparent the damage of war and the possible advantages of nonviolent action. Would you agree with this analysis?

MUSTE: Yes. Basically I do. I think that the objective situation now, both technological and political, poses a threat of great and expanding violence. There is, of course, the possibility of nuclear war; and then there is the possibility of an *outbreak*

---

* In addition to A. J. Muste, the members of the group that went to Saigon the third week of April 1966 included: Bradford Lyttle of CNVA; Karl Meyer, associate editor of the *Catholic Worker* in Chicago; William Davidon, professor at Haverford College; Barbara Deming, an editor of *Liberation*; and Sherry Thurber, a college student.

After his return from Saigon Bradford Lyttle said that, "The project to Saigon began a number of months ago when Premier Ky passed a law in South Vietnam saying that anyone publicly advocating peace would be liable to summary execution. A number of us noted this in the New York *Times* and it seemed to us that this created a situation in which one could carry out a very effective non-violent action project for peace in Saigon." (*Liberation,* May–June 1966, p. 11.)

of violence at a good many points, such as in the liberation movements in various countries.

On the other hand, present conditions are forcing the nations, and forcing society in general, into situations which demonstrate the limitations, if not the futility, of violence. And I think we have a prime illustration of this fact—that, in relation to war, the objective conditions now force certain decisions on nations —in the situation which the United States confronts at this very moment in Vietnam.

FINN: Can you say how you think the United States is forced to act in Vietnam in a way that is different than it would act without this enormous nuclear weapons system?

MUSTE: Well, it's now clear that the possession of nuclear weapons does not allow a great nation to have its way in the political situation, even on a strictly military basis. Here's the United States with all the power in the world, but from every point of view it's having an extremely difficult time in Vietnam.

You have also an illustration of the impasse in which I think society, civilization, finds itself at the present time in the struggle of people of Africa, of Asia, of Latin America to become a part of the modern age, to achieve self-determination and important social changes, which is so powerful a force that the United States is now in no position to deal with it effectively. It gets involved in a war of several years at tremendous expense, at increasing cost in human lives, and with no *apparent* solution along the conventional lines.

Muste then proceeded to give a fairly close analysis of the situation in Saigon at the time. Washington's claim that it wants to negotiate is laughable, Muste says, when it continues to support in every way a leader who insists on continuing the war. "There's something to be said, as the world goes, for supporting a weak man who is just and compassionate. There's also something to be said for supporting a strong man who can really govern if he is ruthless. But to support somebody who is both impotent and base is absurd." President Johnson is not in the ordinary sense of the word a warmonger, Muste says, but he is unable to follow a policy that is in the interests of the Vietnamese people or American values without withdrawing support from the present regime. And that would involve reorientation

A. J. Muste

of how the U.S., as a great power, can best operate in Asia and other continents.

The question of what kind of regime can come into existence "after all these years of civil war" is a great problem, but there are a number of things which now unite different factions, for example, Buddhists and Catholics. Both very much want peace. And Muste mentions the letter smuggled out of the country by a group of Catholic priests.* But in the event there was set up another regime which included participation by the NLF, would there not be, I ask, danger to people who are presently fighting in support of the Saigon government?

MUSTE: That is a point which, of course, Americans always raise when we come to discuss the matter. And our Vietnamese

* The letter to which Muste refers was widely printed abroad. It was published in this country in *Viet Report* and in *Commonweal* (April 1, 1966) over the signature of eleven Catholic priests. The letter reads in part:

"In their march toward victory by force of arms, both the North and South are progressively giving up more and more of our country's autonomy, thereby leading the Vietnamese problem into more and more of an impasse, where its solution is no longer the free decision of the Vietnamese People. . . .

"We cannot accept the fact that the objective of unifying the country, or of building some better future, can serve as a pretext for continuing this fratricidal war.

"That is why we urgently implore the authorities of the North and South to take all appropriate steps to bring the war to an end immediately. . . .

"Let these authorities renounce the claim that they seek through armed victory a guarantee for negotiations and the ending of hostilities —let them also renounce their ambitions of implanting or suppressing ideologies through subversion and bombardment, for that can only lead to genocide and prolong the tragedy of underdevelopment and the country's alienation."

The NCWC news service distributed to the Catholic press a story written by Father Patrick O'Connor, a long-time correspondent in the area, commenting both on the visit of the American pacifists and on the letter. O'Connor wrote that the letter "aroused strong adverse criticism from the Vietnamese clergy and laity. This correspondent heard the eleven signers—out of 1,500 Vietnamese priests—described as 'naive,' 'far from the realities' and 'in the clouds.' "

He also wrote that "some Saigon priests report that members or collaborators of the U.S. pacifists visited working-class districts in Saigon, putting the question: 'Do you want peace? Do you want war?' Since nobody in Vietnam or elsewhere wants war and everybody peace, the results of such a simplified poll are easy to forecast."

contacts had a number of very important things to say. I think it's worth repeating them because they have a bearing upon this whole question of war and violence in the modern context.

One of them pointed out that we do live in the kind of world where these things take place, purges and so on, and they pointed out that in Indonesia, for example, where there was a coup which resulted in a defeat for the Communist Party, three hundred thousand Communists have been murdered.

The next thing that our consultants said was, "Let's suppose for the sake of the argument that this is the case. If we have a coalition, the Communists will take over by some kind of force and there will be a purge of some kind. Now why do you think that you Americans are the people to decide whether we're going to run that risk or not? And why do you think that if you and the present regime continue to kill more non-Communists in order to protect them from the Communists that's going to make us love you?"

The next thing they said was that if you got a coalition as a result of having American support withdrawn from the Ky regime—and therefore a possibility of the Buddhists, the Catholics, the peasants and the intellectuals setting up some kind of an interim regime in Saigon which would sit down with the NLF —in such a coalition the non-Communists, the Buddhists and so on, *would* carry great weight because it would have been *they* who played a decisive part in bringing about peace and in getting American troops out of the country—something which the Vietcong by purely military means cannot accomplish. And that, furthermore, the Vietcong themselves were well aware of this.

FINN: I wonder if we could move away from Vietnam slightly. I have read a statement in which you commented about the American peace movement and the controversy that revolves around the collaboration of pacifist and nonpacifist organizations.

MUSTE: Yes, it does present a problem for pacifists and also for nonpacifists in the peace movement. So far as pacifists are concerned, of course, it presents a basic philosophical or ethical problem since we do reject *all* war and organized violence, regardless of who or what nation or movement resorts to it. So that we certainly do not distinguish, let's say, between Soviet and American H-bombs, and we do not accept and condone violence on the part of any people, any group. This raises a ques-

A. J. Muste

tion for us because if you engage in any kind of peace activity you will be involved with people who may tolerate or in part justify, acquiesce in, the American resort to violence. Or, let's say, the Russian. Or the Vietnamese. We constantly have to consider the question of whether, when we take part in joint action with people who would not call for the immediate cessation of United States military action in Vietnam, we are compromising our own position. My own position is that we have to answer that question in each concrete situation.

We are also presented with that problem when we engage in joint protests against the American role in Vietnam today with people who not only are *not* committed to a pacifist position but who, as for example the people in Youth Against War and Fascism, think that you should be for a military victory of the Vietcong and of North Vietnam and that you actually betray the revolutionary cause if you do not take that position. Now it happens that at the present time the people who take my position are subject to criticism from both sides. When we associate with YAWF in demonstrations we are accused of obscuring our pacifism and even, by some, of betraying it. On the other hand, I am frequently criticized by YAWF and other organizations on the ground that, after all, I am a pacifist, I present a pacifist point of view, and that any truly revolutionary and honest person ought to be for a victory of the Vietcong.

FINN: Can you be both revolutionary and nonviolent in Vietnam?

MUSTE: Yes. Our position is that you can, and my friend Dave Dellinger a few years ago put it this way: in the world as it is today you cannot be truly nonviolent if you are not revolutionary. Because if you are not revolutionary you're condoning the present setup, which is basically one of exploitation and violence and militarism. And secondly, that you cannot be truly revolutionary if you are not nonviolent because if you resort to violence you run into the kind of development that took place in the Soviet Union, for example, which began with revolution and ended up with a vast military establishment and is, along with the United States, one of the great nuclear powers today.

FINN: I still feel there's some problem here. In the world as it exists today, to be on the side of revolution, without qualification, is to be frequently on the side of those who are going to attain revolutionary success *by* violent means.

MUSTE: Yes. I think that is true as a matter of fact, and I think therefore that honest and let's say politically sophisticated pacifists have to make a distinction between the violence of liberation movements (of people who, in a situation where they have no real possibility of democratic means, resort to violence) and the violence imposed upon these countries by the imperialist powers, for example, the violence which the United States is carrying out in Vietnam at the present time. And I do constantly make a very definite distinction between the two.

This distinction has served to divide elements of the peace movement. For if one does not condemn equally all planned mass violence, then political distinctions are in order. And since, in itself, pacifism does not provide criteria for political discrimination, those criteria must be found elsewhere. In their search for sound criteria not all pacifists mine the same political quarry.

FINN: So then you're saying that there *is* violence in the world and that some violence is much worse than others.

MUSTE: Yes. Yes. I think if you deal with it on the political level, you *have to* say that, and I do say it. I think, furthermore, that at the present stage the United States, especially in the kind of role that it plays in Vietnam, is, politically speaking, the main obstacle to peace and to human development, and that accordingly, the greatest contribution that Americans—whether as pacifists or as revolutionists—can make today to peace and to human development, is to oppose to the utmost American military and foreign policy. For that reason I feel closer today to those who radically combat American military policy, the American role in the Vietnam war—even if for different reasons than mine— than I do to people who, perhaps from the best of motives, including pacifist motives, condone, or go along with, or fail to clog with all their weight the machinery of present American military policy.

FINN: This analysis and the distinctions you make would allow the pacifist to support some who are engaged in violent action because they are in the morally superior position.

MUSTE: Yes, I think that's basically what it comes to. I once phrased it this way: that I think you have to be for the defeat

A. J. Muste

of the United States in this war. I just don't see how anybody can be for anything except withdrawal or defeat.

FINN: In discussing Vietnam and writing about it, you use the phrase "American corrupt foreign policy." Would you limit the application of that phrase to Vietnam or do you mean that the foreign policy has generally been corrupted?

MUSTE: Yes, I think generally it has been, and that the Vietnam situation is vivid evidence of what our basic foreign policy ends up in. Both the absurdity of the position in which we are at the present time and its immorality seem to me to result from, for one thing, the fact that we have essentially—without it being a part of the American ethos—we've essentially drifted into the role of empire in the world. Going into the First World War, experiencing a revulsion and getting into the second one, ending up there with a vast army of occupation left in Europe.

Now you can produce rationalizations or justifications. But the fact is that you are taking on the role of empire. Then you produce the A-bomb and the H-bomb, you use them in Japan by a unilateral decision, you have your submarines and your planes all over the world, you have bases surrounding China in Japan, Okinawa, Taiwan, Philippines, so on, and then you actually go in for playing a military role on the continent of Asia in Vietnam.

And all of this with the idea that you have no expansionist or imperialist designs. It's always other people who are making the trouble and the United States has to go in there and set things right—the kind of arrogance that Senator Fulbright referred to recently. Now all of this, especially in the nuclear age and with a nuclear military establishment, constitutes in my opinion an irrational and a profoundly evil and harmful role in the world.

Muste is not the only person to refer with approval to Senator Fulbright's comments on arrogance and the dangers of power. On April 28, 1966 the Senator said in a prepared speech that "America is showing signs of that fatal presumption, that overextension of power and mission, which brought ruin to ancient Athens, to Napoleonic France and to Nazi Germany." On May 5, in an address at the Johns Hopkins University he said, "The question that I find intriguing is whether a nation so extraordinarily endowed as the United States can overcome that arrogance of power which has afflicted, weakened and, in some cases, destroyed great nations in the past." And he supplied an answer, "Gradually but unmistakably we are succumbing to the arrogance of power."

Shortly after my conversation with Mr. Muste, Senator Fulbright publicly regretted that he had charged that "we had succumbed" because it lent itself "to interpretations I did not intend."

This retraction, or modification, would not, I believe, have troubled A. J. Muste. His own opinions are quite firm. And probably the most important question to raise, at least the first question, is not whether or to what degree the Senator is correct, but on what basis one can make judgments of such a high order. Muste cites the army of occupation left in Europe after World War II (and he could have referred to the vast amount of economic aid the United States extended to the Allied powers and late enemies) as the beginning of an empire. But was such military, technological and economic aid undesirable or evil? And if not, at what point does the extension of America's vast and unprecedented power become presumptuous, overextended and arrogant?

The kind of facts which Mr. Muste cites are necessary for an adequate answer, but they do not provide it. The answer any thoughtful person offers will be shaped primarily by what he thinks the foreign policy of a great nation can and should be. We are unlikely to find a consensus among the "experts" at this level of response.

FINN: Mr. Muste, how would you regard the position of those people who are today not pacifists but who are taking a selective CO position on Vietnam?

MUSTE: I think that the government, if it is going to make provision for conscientious objection at all, ought by all means to put on an equal basis those who are opposed to all war and the young people who today are opposed to this war in Vietnam. There can't be any question that these people can be just as sincere in their opposition to this particular war as people who are on religious grounds opposed to all war. It is utterly illogical to make a distinction.

Historically, a Roman Catholic can be a pacifist or an objector to war only on two grounds: either because he feels that he has a special vocation to live as a pacifist the way others have to live as members of a monastic order, or that he regards a particular war as unjust, because theologically the Roman Catholic Church still holds the doctrine of the just war. After Pope John, the Church is very near the position of saying that under modern conditions there can be no just war. Incidentally that is another proof, from my point of view, of my contention that the whole issue of war and violence has to be faced in a new way under modern conditions, and therefore you need a new climate of opinion, a new concept of values, and to that I think the encyclical *Pacem in Terris* has made a tremendous contribution.

FINN: Do you think that the churches generally—and I mean the synagogues and churches and religious communities—are moving in this direction today?

MUSTE: Yes. I think in general they are, although what you have now in Protestantism is somewhat reverse to what you have in Catholicism, I think. In the Catholic Church there is now a very definite tendency to abandon the concept of the just war and to take what is close to a traditional pacifist position. In the Protestant communities there is some growth of pacifism, but basically there is a revulsion among nonpacifists, on what you might call the traditional just-war grounds, against this particular war. And this selective judgment is much stronger today in the Protestant communions than it has ever been before.

FINN: Do you think that the domestic scene and the undeniable effectiveness of a nonviolent approach in terms of civil rights has had a large impact here?

MUSTE: Yes, the civil rights movement that's been nonviolent has made a very considerable impression. Although the answer that you get to that, from those who take the basic Leninist or Maoist line, is that naturally the movement has to be nonviolent here in the United States. Practically it couldn't be anything else, but that's because it's still in the backward stage. And other conditions could dictate other courses.

FINN: Do you generally favor people who have been active in civil rights movements—Martin Luther King I suppose is an outstanding example—making statements about Vietnam and condemning our policy there?

MUSTE: Yes. I do very definitely. And at the present moment I think that all of the civil rights people and organizations ought to line up in thoroughgoing opposition to the Johnson policy.

FINN: You speak with some degree of optimism about the conditions of the world today. I wonder if you would, reflecting on your years of activity as a pacifist, tell me whether you have any hope that pacifism will be of increasing importance. You yourself have seen many ups and downs, you've suffered many disappointments and frustrations in your work. I think your judgment at this point would probably be tempered by a great deal of realism.

MUSTE: Yes. And I do believe there is a possibility that in our time—I guess I mean by that the generation that comes after me—an essentially warless world will be achieved. Now, for one thing, my basic personal attitude on the issue of violence is fully as strong as it has ever been.

FINN: Has it weakened at times in the course of years?

MUSTE: Well, I had a period when I definitely adopted pretty much of a Marxist-Leninist philosophy and believed that it was only by violent change of power that basic social change could be achieved. I abandoned that position both on the basis of what you might call a religious reconversion but also on the basis of my philosophical, political analysis of what was happening.

We have now the kind of crisis that I talked about a few minutes ago. I think society as a whole, mankind as a whole, is up against the problem of the role of violence in a *new way;* you have the kind of situation where people have to get off the fence. We came up against that a few years ago here in the United States in relation to civil rights when even a man like Lyndon Johnson had to come down on one side of the fence or the other. Well, he came down on the side against segregation at that point. And I think the whole world is up against that kind of a problem or will shortly be. What's happened to the United States in Vietnam is an illustration of it. Now it also is developing in the Communist world.

Both in the Soviet Union and the West, the validity of the military approach, of military coalitions, blocs and so on, is being questioned. The old setup is falling apart. The conflict which now emerges is, in my opinion, the basic question of our time:

A. J. Muste

namely, whether you have to abandon the military, the violent approach in a much more radical way and find another one.

FINN: And you are optimistic that we'll live through this threat of nuclear destruction?

MUSTE: I believe basically that we will live through it and that the right decision—if that's the term for it—may be made. I think we are, however, often on the edge of a precipice.

After his trip to Saigon, A. J. Muste decided that he was not going to make any more trips. But he went once again to Vietnam, this time to Hanoi, where he and two other clergymen had an audience with Ho Chi Minh. He returned to this country, resumed his activities and planned to help launch a Spring Mobilization Committee to End the War in Vietnam. This was the last project to engage his attention, for he died on February 11, 1967, in the middle of a conversation with a pacifist friend.

DAVID MC REYNOLDS

One of the ventures in which A. J. Muste was involved was *Liberation,* an independent monthly, on which he served as chairman of the editorial board. To anyone acquainted with the literature of the peace movement the other names on that board would be instantly familiar: Sidney Lens, Paul Goodman, Barbara Deming and Dave Dellinger, editor. In the early months of 1966, the associate editors listed were Kay Boyle, Nat Hentoff, Staughton Lynd, David McReynolds, Bayard Rustin and Mulford Sibley.

In its ten years of existence *Liberation* has accepted into its pages highly independent and disparate views. Many of the serious differences that divide the peace movement also divide contributors to the journal, including the editors themselves. One of the serious differences, which shows no sign of disappearing, runs through the entire peace movement. For many people the lines were drawn and alliances severed in April 1965, during the planning stages of the March on Washington to End the War in Vietnam.

There are a number of versions of the planning sessions, but the main outlines are clear. The groups supporting the March included CNVA (Committee for Nonviolent Action), WRL (War Resisters League), SPU (Student Peace Union), WSP (Women Strike for Peace), WILPF (Women's International League for Peace and Freedom), SDS (Students for a Democratic Society), YPSL (Young People's Socialist League), and the Committee on Christian Concerns of the National Student Christian Federation.

David McReynolds

But in line with a nonexclusion policy of SDS, the March included as supporters and participants the DuBois clubs, the May 2nd Movement and YAWF (Youth Against War and Fascism). A March in San Francisco was planned for the same day by SDS and with some of the same sponsors. According to Dellinger, both Rustin and Robert Gilmore believed that these three groups would not have endorsed the March "if it had criticized the policies of Hanoi, Peking, and Moscow as strongly as it criticized American politics." To those who objected to communist-dominated or communist-oriented groups, the issue was one which had been raised and settled in the thirties and forties.

After much debate, on April 16, the eve of the March, several leaders of the peace movement issued a carefully worded statement whose intent was clear. The March should not, they cautioned, be turned into an anti-American rally. There is a need for a peace movement but one that is "not committed to any form of totalitarianism or drawing inspiration from the foreign policy of any government." The statement was signed by A.J. Muste (who supported the March), Norman Thomas, H. Stuart Hughes and Bayard Rustin. On the West Coast a similar but more explicit caution was issued by Robert Pickus, a regional director of TTP (Turn Toward Peace) of which Gilmore is director.

Following that dispute both Dave Dellinger and Staughton Lynd strongly criticized Rustin, and an entire "moderate," "elitist" position which they thought he represented, in the pages of *Liberation*. Rustin subsequently resigned from *Liberation,* saying that his "involvement in the civil rights movement does not give me time to struggle for the point of view I hold on a number of matters, that really differs with the other Editors."

I speak with David McReynolds, one of *Liberation*'s associate editors and field secretary of the War Resisters League, not long after Rustin had resigned from the journal. McReynolds had some months earlier registered his own disagreements with what he called the "Dellinger-Lynd line." As a disciple of Muste he had said: "I would not be his true disciple if I had not learned to think on my own. The only good Musteite is a non-Musteite."

Born in 1929, McReynolds is too old to be part of the New Left generation and too young to have gone through the experiences of the Old Left that attempted, with great effort, to establish a democratic left independent of, indeed hostile to, communism. But like a number of people of his age he has assimilated the history of the latter group. He moves knowingly and easily within their historical framework.

He is an impressively articulate speaker, almost never pausing in search of the right word. Listening to him I receive the full impact of an anecdote I had heard about him earlier. Speaking at a rally he was asked by someone in the crowd to go slower. Pausing only for a second he replied, "Listen faster."

I begin by asking him how he came to his position as a pacifist.

MC REYNOLDS: I think it came about through a combination of three factors. One was the fact that I had a religious background, the Baptist Church, which I took fairly seriously. The contradictions in the teachings of the Church in the face of the reality of the world tended to drive me toward political approaches. It left me at that time, which was 1947 and '48 and '49, extremely hostile to the American government, which I largely blamed for the beginning of the cold war.

FINN: You did then or you still do?

MC REYNOLDS: I did *then*. I think it was somewhat unfair. I think now the responsibility was more evenly divided between the two powers. But at the time I took, I think, a rather procommunist position which, in fact, was based on a religious background.

When the draft came up there was a concrete question of how I was going to relate to the draft and the question of supporting the American side in the Greek Civil War and Chiang Kai-shek in China, all the rest of this. And on those two issues, the Greek Civil War and the Chinese Civil War, I was strongly against the American position and tended from that to move toward a pacifist position.

I think it probably was also a degree of rebellion against my father who was a lieutenant colonel in the Air Force at the time, and I wouldn't rule out that psychological motivation as being one of the things which pushed me toward a pacifist position. I didn't really become a pacifist until 1949, at which time I

David McReynolds

abandoned my pro-communist orientation and in a sense returned to a religious orientation.

FINN: When you did become a pacifist, who were the people that most influenced you or the political events that helped determine the development of your thinking?

MC REYNOLDS: Well, there were two major events. One of them was the draft itself which is a matter of personal decision. The other event was meeting Bayard Rustin and talking with Bayard—or hearing Bayard talk, more accurately—and hearing him put the pacifist position in the context of resistance and of struggle as opposed to passivity. He made it possible to see a social revolutionary outlook in nonviolent terms.

FINN: Have events since '49 at all troubled or disturbed your pacifist position, or have they tended to confirm it?

MC REYNOLDS: Well, they've confirmed it but they've also troubled it. In terms of a long-range analysis, I think that the pacifist position in a nuclear world is a position of overwhelming logical and moral strength—more so now than in 1947 and infinitely more so now than in 1937 or '27 and so on. But in terms of the short-range analysis, I think we're caught—I feel caught— in a problem. First of all the CO position itself has no longer any relationship to stopping war—or almost no relationship. Wars are not fought on the basis of mass armies, they're fought on the basis of technological skills. Second, we find that morality does not have any immediate impact against the state, that normally a state would have collapsed—as this government probably would have collapsed, in other periods—if it had tried to wage a war in face of the kind of opposition that it now has. It doesn't seem to stop the war, have any real effect on Johnson. And therefore the act of individual, moral decision, while extremely important in terms of laying the basis for political position, is *not* a political position. Of course it never *was,* but I think that wasn't quite clear to us before. And in that sense the pacifist approach *must* change radically from what it was in the 1940's or what it was in World War I.

Now that's one point. The second point would be that the problem of how you deal with or engage in a revolution is one that I don't really have an answer to. I think there may have been no nonviolent solution for the Cubans. I think that a violent revolution may have been better for the Cubans than not *having* a revolution, but I think there would not have been a nonviolent revolution.

FINN: Would that probably apply to some other countries?

MC REYNOLDS: It would probably apply to Vietnam, it would apply to parts of Africa, it would apply to Latin America today. And here the tragedy is that I see the nature of the West, which is profoundly reactionary—so is the East but in a different way —so profoundly reactionary and corrupting that it makes it almost inevitable that the struggles, when they occur, will be violent struggles.

FINN: Well, are the pacifists and pacifist sympathizers being effective in the peace movement today? It does seem to be taking on proportions that may have *some* political relevance. . . .

MC REYNOLDS: Yes, but it's not a *pacifist* movement. It's a movement composed of people who are opposed to the war in Vietnam *per se,* but not opposed to all war. And I think the pacifist movement is not really much larger than it was ten years ago—somewhat but not much larger. I think it is as far as it was ten years ago from developing a politics of pacifism, if that's even possible, and I think the peace movement is a reflection not of the increase of the pacifist movement but of the increase of a general realization that war is suicidal and that in the immediate situation in Vietnam the war is criminal. And you have a great many people who are veterans, who fought in one war, might fight in another, you see, who are moving into the peace movement.

That really raises for me the whole question of whether or not absolute pacifism is not a mistake. It's heresy for a pacifist to raise this, but are there times when the moral position may not in fact be a violent position? Or to put it another way because I'm not trying to write an apologia for violence, is it really morally proper to take an absolute position in regard to a *technique?* My answer would be no. The confusion here, you know, is a reflection of my own confusion, I would think.

I think there's an arrogance on the part of the pacifist in saying that never, under any circumstances, would he use violence. I think that he may find that in the reality of the instant that that may be what he will do, whether it's right or wrong.

David McReynolds

FINN: But that may be a failure to live up to the principle rather than a failure of the principle—or is that an unrealistic distinction?

MC REYNOLDS: I think probably it would be, because the West is in a sense not really cut out to be pacifist on an absolute basis. The West is terribly attached to the world. I think this is not a bad thing; I'm not against this approach by the West, because to be attached to the world is not only to be attached to television sets, it's also to be attached to people. I'm not sure that the East is superior by being unattached to people. But if you're going to be attached to people, which is a terrible kind of attachment, you may end up doing violence to some in order not to do violence to others.

This is a familiar note sounded in a less familiar key. I recall my discussion with John Bennett in which he said that one had responsibility to his close neighbors but that it did not cancel out the responsibility we have toward our other neighbors —who may even be our enemies. Attachment to life can be the other side of a regard for life, for everyone's life. It can be the basis for violence, but it can also inhibit such violence.

FINN: Does it represent any kind of a danger to the pacifist that the peace movement is not being led by pacifists? Does he think that he has more power or influence or following today? Or are most pacifists fairly clear that they are still in a minority even in the peace movement?

MC REYNOLDS: If you're talking about the people who are more or less leaders of the movement, I think all of them would be fairly clear that they are a minority. But within the peace movement the pacifists have always had the decisive role because they have thought more clearly, to be honest, than any other single group.

I mean it's taken SANE some years to move to the realization that the government has been lying steadily about Vietnam. Now they do take this position—not in such harsh terms, but they do take it—and I think in a sense that they're more outraged than we are because it comes as a revelation to them. ADA has finally moved to the position that Johnson has been lying about Vietnam. I think this hurts them; it leaves them very bitter about the whole business. But it took ADA about five years to come to that realization, which means that the decisive voice in the peace movement, prior to that time, was not ADA's position but our own. So I think we have somewhat more influence in the movement than we have numbers, but I don't think we're under any delusions we're running the movement, 'cause were not.

FINN: Do you think it is possible to develop a politics of pacifism? You used the phrase tentatively. Is there something that one could anticipate or at least realistically work for?

MC REYNOLDS: I don't have any idea what the politics of pacifism would look like. I think that pacifists get drawn off into rather secondary issues; the politics of pacifism becomes work camps or it becomes Danilo Dolce's work in Sicily. And all these are very good things, but I don't think it's politics in a fundamental sense.

I think that if you're going to have a politics which makes pacifism possible it would have to be a revolutionary politics. That is, the only thing which would make possible a nonviolent revolution in South Vietnam would be the ending of the situation where the government is backed by the armed forces of the Americans. Because the problem in Vietnam has not been the weight of *Chinese* arms; it's been the weight of American arms.

What would have made possible a nonviolent revolution in other areas—and Latin America is very difficult in this case— would again not be the withdrawal of Chinese and Russian arms, of which there are very, very few in Latin America; it would be the withdrawal of American arms. But the precondition for withdrawing American arms, which would create a different political reality and therefore make nonviolence a practical option, the precondition for that is a revolutionary policy in terms of America's own status quo and how it deals with its investments in Latin America and so on, which means that the politics that makes pacifism possible is some kind of socialist politics in my view. But the other problem is that there is nothing essentially pacifist about socialist politics.

Another problem is whether the nature of society has not changed so radically in the last ten and fifteen, twenty, years in the West that perhaps none of us understands what politics is about anymore at all. In a period of technological revolution and population growth, in a period of world turmoil, whether

David McReynolds

socialist politics as such are not completely out of date. I only pose the question. I'm not bright enough to work through the theoretical implications. I think we need someone like Karl Marx at the present time to apply himself creatively to where we go from here. The catch is we're going so fast, so *much* faster than we did in Marx's time, that by the time you got a Karl Marx to work out the implications I'm afraid you would need another Karl Marx to catch up.

FINN: Can the pacifists have a program which would be politically effective and which would modify to some significant degree the policy of the government or its course of action?

MC REYNOLDS: I don't really know. Look, the pacifist position has two problems: One is that it's an ideal which is a great deal larger than the movement and a very great deal larger than the people who are running it. It's an idea which is both a moral imperative, which it has been from the beginning, and an historical imperative which it is at the present time. In my view, it's imperative for man's survival. I don't expect man to *survive,* but if he does I think it will be because he's turned to pacifism, to nonviolence of some kind.

The difficulty, however, is that this historically imperative idea which needs political force if it is to be effective is contained by a movement which thinks very much in individual terms. McReynolds suggests an historical comparison with the socialist movement before Marx. He describes it as primarily "a series of very creative, individual Christian experiments," and it needed Marx to transform these individual perceptions into a political force. But it is exactly the ability of people to make individual judgments that pacifism demands. That cannot be given up, but it mitigates against pacifism becoming an effective political force. "I don't see where we go. I'm very much baffled."

FINN: You yourself have differed in print with Dellinger and Lynd on aspects of the peace movement. And you questioned some of the attitudes of people associated with the New Left.

MC REYNOLDS: To deal with the dispute that involved Dellinger and Lynd and myself and some others in *Liberation*—I think to some extent that there has been a romantic view of violence because of Castro. There's nothing more romantic than the story of Castro with twelve men taking over Cuba from the United States government and then throwing off an invasion planned by the CIA. It's incredible, the story, a marvelous romantic tale. The same cult of violence surrounds the National Liberation Front, and I think it has threatened the absolute pacifism of people like Dellinger. Lynd was never an absolute pacifist in this sense, but Dave was. And I would have said probably six months ago that Dellinger had moved because of things like Cuba away from absolute pacifism.*

I think I might now include myself in the category of those who moved away from absolute pacifism. At the other end of the extreme, the other person involved in the dispute—Robert Pickus —has, I think, clearly moved away from absolute pacifism, but in both cases they wouldn't admit it, or are not necessarily *aware* of it. I think Pickus, because of the attempt to defend what he calls American values and to see a peace movement that is not subversive, has become so wary of attacking the American role in Vietnam in clear terms, that whether he could be called a pacifist in the classical sense is now open to question. Both of these guys go at it from different standpoints. Pickus is overwhelmingly aware of the danger of Soviet totalitarianism as a world reality. Dellinger is overwhelmingly aware of the extraordinary immorality of the American role.†

FINN: And your own position?

MC REYNOLDS: I would tend now more to side with Dave than I did at the time. I would have a number of disputes still, but I think I would tend more to say that as we build toward a pacifist politics we must be less judgmental about those who are not following the pacifist position. We must accept the fact that there may be times and places when what is for us a personal

* Dave Dellinger has written: "Those of us who believe in the revolutionary potential of non-violence should become more actively revolutionary, and in the process of becoming so, have a great deal to learn from heroic forces like the Cuban Fidelistas and the Viet Cong, even though we are saddened by, and must speak out against, bloodletting, intolerance, and all failures to recognize the fact that our worst enemies are still human beings, not too different from ourselves." (*Liberation,* May 1965, p. 31.)

† Robert Pickus has elaborated his position in a number of essays. One, dealing specifically with Dave Dellinger, is "Political Integrity and Its Critics," *Liberation,* June–July 1965. The World Without War Council has published a useful pamphlet he wrote with Carl Landaver entitled "Peace, the New Politics, and the Pity of It All."

imperative may not be for them a personal imperative and also may not be a political reality. And in that sense we would not be absolute pacifists.

FINN: It seems to me that you're suggesting that the pacifist movement includes people who were but are no longer absolute pacifists. There are people who are *reluctant* to describe themselves as pacifists who nevertheless have great sympathy with the movement and support it and work with it and condemn with equal strength the U.S. participation in Vietnam. Does this represent a middle ground between absolute pacifists and non-pacifists? Are there a large number of people occupying that middle area or moving toward it?

McReynolds points out that Gandhi never called himself a pacifist and did on occasion support military action. He could readily have made a list of noted people who did call themselves pacifists even as they supported some military ventures. But there is a spectrum of pacifism, with absolute pacifism defining one of the limits.

MC REYNOLDS: I think one of the problems is that many of us, for personal reasons, or psychological reasons or religious insight—for whatever reasons you want to give—are not likely to use violence and in that sense probably are absolute pacifists. And probably I'm an absolute pacifist in this sense, although personally I really do think I could kill somebody given the provocation and the occasion. Nevertheless I think that in terms of premeditation that I probably am an absolute pacifist.

But I think we've got to be more charitable and instead of saying, "Our job is to attack the National Liberation Front because they're using violence," or "We have to equate them with the Americans because they're both using violence and both sides are killing children"—which is absolutely true—instead of making that kind of statement (which is fundamentally a stupid one which morally equates two sides that are not morally equatable either in terms of the terror which they are inflicting or the *reasons* why the terror is being inflicted) we ought to say "We don't *have* a nonviolent answer at the present time for South Vietnam. We are not going to use violence if we are in South Vietnam. We are not condoning the terrorism of the National Liberation Front, but neither do we feel free to make an absolute judgment on it." Our job is to probe as pacifists for where creative nonviolent solutions can be found and *not* to try to be judgmental about everything. That's an ambiguous position, but I think life is an ambiguous proposition.

FINN: Given this position and the difficulties which you said are inevitably there, how would you judge the effectiveness of pacifists, from the First World War until today, in probing the situation and finding where its creativity and imagination *can* play a part, and establishing the conditions out of which something better can grow?

MC REYNOLDS: If you're talking about individual pacifists, I think they've been extremely helpful. If you're talking about A. J. Muste or Bayard Rustin or Danilo Dolce or a number of other people, then I think you're talking about people who have been *extremely* creative in their society and who have played an enormously significant role in social change. But if you're talking about the pacifist movement as a movement, I think it's been a failure for fifty years. I think it's had no relevance to stopping war, no relevance to changing society. I think the best we can say is that it can benefit the individual or provide a platform for individuals or maintain a standard or intellectual position that others can examine and be drawn to. And I think this is, by the way, true also of the Church. If you were to ask what really the Catholic Church had done in the last two thousand years, I would say, not a damn thing that was progressive or positive. If you were to ask what individual Catholics have done, then I think you'd have a very different proposition. Or Protestants. Or Jews. The success of these things doesn't, I think, rest in terms of what the movement succeeded in doing, but what individuals coming out of it did.

FINN: This does raise the questions of what positive things organizations can do, what the sense of tradition can do for the individual who belongs to an organization that continues over a period of time.

MC REYNOLDS: But that's not a direct contribution by the organization, that's an indirect contribution. The power of Christianity was not that it ever saved society but that it saved individuals out of societies that were falling to pieces and made it possible for each new society to be renewed spiritually because this force remained. And it wouldn't have remained if there

David McReynolds

hadn't been an organization. But that's a kind of negative victory, it seems to me.

FINN: Let me ask you a couple of direct questions that either have simple answers or maybe no answers—I mean on your own part. I presume you would make a judgment that the *use* of the nuclear weapons system we have would be immoral. What follows from that in your own thinking? Is it immoral for the United States to possess these weapons, or for any nation state to possess these weapons?

MC REYNOLDS: I think it's terribly immoral to possess them, yes, for any nation to possess them.

FINN: What political course of action follows from this? Would you, as a pacifist, suggest—even if you thought it a course that wouldn't be followed—unilateral disarmament?

MC REYNOLDS: Sure. I would suggest it. It's not a political course, but that doesn't relieve any of us of the responsibility of suggesting it.

FINN: Without expecting that unilateral disarmament would follow, is there room here for pacifists to think creatively and make suggestions that the government *might* follow which otherwise would not have been presented to them?

MC REYNOLDS: I think that there *is*. I think I begin with the assumption that the possession of nuclear weapons by any power is evidence either of collective insanity or is evidence of the childlike state of man in terms of his civilization. I think it's deplorable. The fact that the rest of us permit this to happen is, I think, childlike on our part. But for Kennedy, for Khrushchev, for Mao to authorize production of these weapons is an act of insanity, in my view. Now I think that if you're dealing with a society which has collectively gone mad—it is madness to talk about defending yourself with these weapons—then part of the pacifist's job is not only to say that this is madness, that it's alienating and dehumanizing and wrong, and ought not to be done. Having said that he has another obligation, which is to say "Let us look at the situation, and taking into account the fact that functionally you're mad, what can we *do* that will create a situation where you can become more rational and be more aware of the madness which is implied by the *manufacture* of a weapon that can kill an entire city."

Now this means that the pacifist must provide some first steps without abandoning his statements, without saying that it is an absolute moral judgment that *must* be passed. We can't rest there. Can we get a test-ban treaty? Can we get agreement on inspection? Can we in some way de-tense the human relationships by getting Americans to go to Russia and Russians to come here? Can we get out material on China, that gets at the American psychosis about people who are yellow-skinned? Can we reach the Chinese in some way to try to deal with their psychosis about people with white skin?

What can we do on the individual level, on the cultural level, and on the political level to create preconditions which will make it possible one day for Mao, for his successors, to wake up and say "My God, I've got these weapons. What in the world did I ever do this for? I must get rid of them at once. Whether Russia has 'em or America has 'em or not is irrelevant." Or even more—because governments never wake up—where *people* will say, "What are we doing at the present to have these weapons? It's insanity. Why didn't we see this fifty years ago or twenty or five years ago? We must demand the weapons be abandoned." And that is more likely to happen.

FINN: Do you think it *is* likely to happen? You didn't speak as if you anticipated an end to war or that these weapons would never be used.

MC REYNOLDS: I anticipate probably an end to mankind, not an end to war—although that would effectively end war too. If one works on the basis that people who build these weapons are insane—the scientists who put their minds to work on them, the governments that authorize them, the people that justify them, the intellectuals who apologize for them, Sidney Hook right on down—are in some very definite sense mad, I think there's really little basis for hope. And that I think that the pacifist movement, the whole peace movement, works in a desperate situation where there's always hope that as long as we're alive people are going to mature or begin to have second thoughts and so on. But I think the assumption that fundamentally we're going to be rational in using these weapons is irrational.

FINN: Do you think Kennedy and Khrushchev did respond irrationally at the time of the Cuban missile crisis?

David McReynolds

MC REYNOLDS: Cuba was, I think, a rational response but *proved* the irrationality of the basic situation. I think we're very lucky to have had a rational response. Analysis of the Cuban missile crisis indicates the irrational *pressures* on Kennedy. But the frightening thing was, first of all, that Khrushchev *put* the missiles there. I didn't believe he'd done this, because I know enough about politics to know that the placing of missiles in Cuba would have meant war. Therefore when people told me the missiles were there I said this was a lie. Can't be there. Khrushchev was politically a sane person; he was not going to put missiles in Cuba.

FINN: That goes beyond just a faulty judgment that the United States would put up with this?

MC REYNOLDS: The risks of the gamble were so incredible that you see . . . my response to the Cuban crisis was "Good God in Heaven!" You know, for a whole week *every*body was disenfranchised in the whole world. There wasn't anything anybody could do but Khrushchev and Kennedy. And to call this confrontation an example of the sanity of the nuclear build-up is evidence of really mass psychosis; a week of world insanity, where everybody's lives depend on two guys where one of them has already behaved completely irrationally and taken risks that are incredible, the other one taking counter-risks that are incredible, playing it very cool.

To call this evidence of the stability of nuclear terrorism, I just think justifies my basic assumption that we're in a very sick situation, and it left my basic pacifist analysis much more confirmed than before. It was one thing to have the weapons and not really to threaten to use them. I thought it was insane to have them, but as long as Russia kept them over there, we had them here—all right. For Russia to *do* this and for Kennedy to counter-threat, you know, left me paralyzed for a week.*

* This is a reaction which many shared, but it was not the only and maybe not the most common reaction. For example, Bernard Brodie, a senior staff member at the RAND Corporation who has written extensively on war and modern weapons, wrote of this episode:
"When the crisis broke, I personally lost no sleep over it. I felt utterly confident that this crisis would not deteriorate into war. This confidence separated me from some of my friends, and I am sure it annoyed them. I felt this confidence simply because I had information which convinced me that we were enormously superior in every important branch of arms to the Russians, and that *they knew* it. . . . I was sure that when they

PROTEST: PACIFISM AND POLITICS

We had discussed some of the possibilities open to the peace movement, and some of the limitations. I recall that he had expressed strong reservations about the tactics of some peace leaders. How did he judge the various demonstrations, such as the marches on Washington, burning of draft cards and so forth? Were they effective either in terms of the influence on the government or in terms of the society at large?

MC REYNOLDS: There you're dealing with the practical question and you have to talk about *which* demonstration and *which* tactics. I'd say overwhelmingly that I thought they were good, but that they had bad aspects to them or there are dangers in all things. Let me transfer this to the civil rights struggle for a moment, where I can get a clearer comparison. I think there's no reason in the world, except moral reasons, pacifist reasons, why Negroes in South Africa shouldn't kill all the whites. I would be appalled at this, but I can't think of any *tactical* reason why they shouldn't. They're a majority; given a violent confrontation, they eventually would win.

In America they are only ten percent of the population. Therefore while the killing of a white person is as immoral in the one case as it is in the other, in this case it becomes suicidal, technically, because I think in this country whites would, without hesitation if they had to, resort to genocide against the Negroes if the confrontation were violent. I really have no illusions about what the police would do, what middle-class society would permit them to do—to Harlem and to Watts—if you begin to get more Molotov cocktails tossed at businessmen's cars or snipers firing at random in the Wall Street area.

Now this doesn't mean the Negro community shouldn't protest. It just dictates that the protest ought to be one which doesn't expose the community to the kind of counter-pressures that the whites might tend to use otherwise. In this sense I think there's no question that nonviolent protests are imperative to Negroes.

Now, I think if you have a peace movement that represents ten percent of the public, which is all it represents, it had better

realized we meant what we said, they would yield. They would and could take no other course." ("Morals and Strategy," *Worldview,* September 1964, p. 7.)

It is, of course, public information that those who actually made the decision shared neither McReynolds' paralysis nor Brodie's total confidence in the rationality of the other decision makers.

David McReynolds

be terribly cautious about how it presents its case. It was a very big mistake in the Fifth Avenue parade to march with an American flag with skull and crossbones in place of the stars. Not because I care two cents for the flag. I don't. I'm not attached to anybody's flag. I think this is a very unhappy concept, to substitute loyalty to the state for loyalty to God—which is what this really is. But *politically* most people respond in a certain way to the flag and unless I want to wage several battles at the same time I ought not to carry that particular kind of symbol. But the overall Fifth Avenue parade was a *very* important event, the one last year.

I think that the demonstrations, to the degree that they make it possible for the average person to see that there are in fact thousands of people opposed to the war, are very important. To the degree that they make it possible for the *Daily News,* for example, to say, "These people are disloyal" or are "obnoxious people," then I think it may be a mistake. Now I think to some extent the burning of the draft cards, which I took part in in November—the second burning, the first was Dave Miller's— is in a hesitant category between the two, because the *Daily News* and everybody else jumped on us for burning the cards. But I would stand by the decision to burn my draft card and I would do it again on the grounds that we carried it off in such a way—in terms of being well dressed, with ties and everything else—that we did what we really had tried to do, which was not, on that issue, to reach the general public but to reach our compatriots—people at *Commonweal, The Nation, New Republic*—and to try to explain that this thing bothered us this much. We were not going to immolate ourselves, but we were going to take a step which was a drastic one and do it respectfully. Now I think that had quite an impact on those we were aiming at. It had a very negative impact on the public as a whole, and I'm aware of that. But those demonstrations are not a moral issue, they're a tactical political issue.

While it was clear from the beginning that McReynolds had strong, well-defined positions, I could not fail to notice the number of times he qualified his statement with "I think." He wished to make clear that he is speaking for himself and not an organization, but the frequent interjection also indicated a degree of openness, of flexibility, a suggestion that he may, upon further reflection, modify his position.

Because of this quality of openness, and because of his evident discrimination in distinguishing between different tactics, I was surprised to read some time later an open letter by Dave McReynolds entitled "Impeach Johnson." In the course of the letter McReynolds writes that for some time he had considered the tactic of raising such a slogan and thought it unpolitical.

"I think now, however, that it is important to raise the slogan because it personalizes the political debate. Johnson has sought to silence and to intimidate us with charges of being 'nervous Nellies.' He has sought to equate dissent with treason. Shrewd politician that he is, he has sought to make US the issue, rather than to debate or discuss the actual Vietnam policies.

"It is time for us to make JOHNSON the issue. It would give the anti-war movement a focus. We would no longer be immobilized behind our buttons, tripping out in despair. . . .

"The immunity of Johnson from direct political attack is incredible. He is perhaps the most dishonest man ever elected President and there is no excuse for anyone believing a word he says. Let us remove his immunity. Let us demand the impeachment of a President who has lied to us so massively that we do not trust him to make the peace he claims to seek and which we so urgently demand."

McReynolds does not, of course, expect that Johnson would actually be impeached. What he does expect is that a movement to impeach him would educate the public and honor the dissenters. In terms of the peace movement, can this be considered sound tactics? Or is it simply another indication of the frustration suffered by those with strong principles and no instrument of power to implement them?

STAUGHTON LYND

The name of Staughton Lynd threaded its way through a number of conversations I had with critics of Vietnam policy. The one thing they all agreed on was the open, gentle, disarming quality of the man himself.

Lynd is the son of famous parents, Robert and Helen Lynd, the authors of *Middletown,* a sociological study that has maintained its value over the years. He was educated at Ethical Culture schools and at Harvard, where he was a member of the John Reed Society. He and his wife have lived in cooperative communities, he has taught at a Negro women's college in Atlanta, at the Mississippi Summer Project, and at Yale where he is currently an assistant professor of history.* None of these or other related activities would have brought him to national attention.

The attention which is thrust upon him now is a result of the position of leadership he has in the peace movement, or, more accurately, that segment of the movement associated with the new, radical left. In his mid-thirties, he is accepted by younger people as one who expresses their view and attitudes. He was chairman and a principal speaker at the April 1965 March on

* On leave from Yale University, Mr. Lynd was appointed to the history department of Chicago State College for the academic year 1967–68. In spite of the fact that the appointment had the unanimous recommendation of the faculty, the college's administration and the chairman of the Board of Governors of State Colleges and Universities, the Board by a five-to-one vote refused to approve the appointment. The Board made it clear that they did not question Lynd's competence and that they rejected him because his actions in the peace movement go "beyond mere dissent."

Washington and at the mass teach-in at Berkeley, California, in
May. He was an organizer of the Assembly of Unrepresented
People of August 1965, and in the same year he made a Christmas trip to Hanoi with Herbert Aptheker, a Communist theorist,
and Tom Hayden, founding president of SDS.

Our first meeting in New York is too brief for a satisfactory
exchange, so I visit him in his home in New Haven. As he comes
to greet me it is clear that I have interrupted some work. He
is quite tall, with strong square shoulders, strong jaw and brown
tousled hair. But most noticeable are his eyes and his voice. He
speaks very quietly and slowly, pausing frequently for second
thoughts before expressing the first, and his gaze is direct and
steady; the effect is as though veils which are ordinarily drawn
between new acquaintances and which screen their words have
somehow been drawn aside. As he pours coffee for us I ask him
about the background of his own pacifism.

LYND: Well, as a youngster I went to schools run by the
Ethical Culture Society, which is an outgrowth of Reformed
Judaism, and I don't *clearly* remember any discussion of pacifism at school or at home—although I'm sure there was some.
I had an older cousin who was a Quaker and a pacifist, and I
remember feeling that he was the first pacifist I had ever met.
But it was not in fact 'til after I was married, and I suppose until
after the draft question was about to present itself, that I thought
seriously of the possibility of becoming a conscientious objector.

FINN: What did this lead you to do? To investigate the moral
and intellectual bases of such a position?

LYND: Right. Investigate maybe is somewhat too pretentious
a term. I'd certainly thought about it a good deal. And in the
end, since I had a problem with the legal requirement that a
person profess belief in a Supreme Being—this being fifteen
years before the Seeger decision—I finally took a stand based
on Schweitzer's "reverence for life," saying that I regarded this
as a supreme reality. And I also took a somewhat qualified position, since I didn't really feel pacifism as a command from a
God who addressed me personally with this instruction. Perhaps it was for this reason, perhaps I would have felt it anyway—but the fact is that I was very conscious of young men
of my age who were being killed, some of whom I thought had

Staughton Lynd

probably gone into the Army without ever having heard of the possibility of being a conscientious objector. And to make a long story short, I applied not for the absolute conscientious objection classification but for noncombatant service in the Army.

FINN: Since you came to that position, have you ever been tempted to doubt its validity? Has your allegiance to it been weakened on any occasion?

LYND: No. On the other hand, I find myself still thinking about it a lot because I think that many pacifists make a number of assumptions about pacifism which, as a historian and newspaper reader, I must say I don't believe. I don't believe that in any conflict situation both sides are equally responsible in all instances, and I don't believe that violence never accomplishes anything good. And *not* believing those two things, I'm forced to imagine (even supposing that Vietnam didn't provide such a situation) armed conflict where it seems that the right is overwhelmingly on one side rather than the other, and where the victory of that side as opposed to a battlefield truce, would be a good thing.

I would prefer not an NLF victory but a coalition between them and neutralist elements in the area presently controlled by Saigon. It seems to me that in the war in Vietnam the United States has done a number of things which violate traditional criteria for a just war to a far greater extent than the other side. Although I may be a *personal* pacifist, I am by no means of the opinion that both sides are equally guilty or that it is a matter of indifference how the struggle ends. The way I feel now is that if the political unit to which I belonged, of which I was a citizen, were engaged in a war that I thought just, then I would participate as a noncombatant.

FINN: Which is what you did do.

LYND: Which is what I did do. In fact, I did *not* participate in any war as a noncombatant, but I was in the Army as a noncombatant just after the end of the Korean war, 1953 to '54. On the other hand, if my country were engaged in a war that I thought unjust, then I would take the absolute pacifist position.*

* Lynd here is using the term "absolute" in a way which varies from common use by pacifists. He means, clearly, that in a war which he regarded as unjust he would not serve even as a noncombatant.

FINN: Did you develop your pacifist position before you developed what is really a radical analysis of our present society?

LYND: It actually was more the other way around. I grew up in a certain well-known subculture of the 1930's, where there was a good deal of admiration for the Soviet Union, a good deal of sympathy for the organization of the CIO and so forth. And the framework of ideas was much more Marxist or quasi-Marxist than religious. So I think my experience was in that sense *a*typical; that it was the whole religious dimension of things which I stumbled on as an adult. I didn't read the New Testament until I was nineteen or twenty.

FINN: Well, being both a pacifist and a political radical you've had to face the problem, maybe doubly, of how to make your own minority views and attitudes felt in society, *if* you are going to be politically involved or committed. I presume the choice is either withdrawal or some kind of engagement. Did you feel the choice as a problem when you adopted your radical attitudes and your pacifist attitudes or beliefs?

LYND: Sure. And it was evident, for example, in my situation in the Army. I had been interviewed by the FBI, as most CO applicants are, prior to my draft board hearing. But they were also interested, this being the height of the McCarthy period, in various things that I had done or hadn't done, college organizations I'd belonged to, and so forth. And I told them— which I think I would not do in a similar situation now—that I would tell them everything they wanted to know, except I wouldn't refer to anybody else. And the reason I wouldn't make such an offer again is that it's awfully difficult, in fact, to make that distinction.

But in any case, I gave them beer from my icebox. I was in my undershirt painting a mural on the wall when they arrived. And we had a very cosy time. So they knew all about me—what there was to be known, which wasn't that much. And then I got drafted as a noncombatant. At that time medics were not trained separately, so what happened was that you had basic training with a rifle company and spent most of the time peeling potatoes while the other fellows were having weapons practice. I did this for about six months and completed basic training, and then I got an undesirable discharge from the Army because of these various political associations that the Army had in fact known about before my induction. About a hundred persons,

Staughton Lynd

as I understand it, were given undesirable discharges. One was sent a list of allegations. One of those in my case was that my mother. . . . "It is alleged that your mother is a hyper-modern educator." And failing to answer these satisfactorily, I guess, I was discharged. And one of the chaps took it to the Supreme Court, and later on we were all given honorable discharges and I got G.I. Bill benefits and I went to graduate school.

But I had *always* felt, I suppose, because I was something of a second generation radical and I inherited a certain sense of alienation from my folks, I'd always felt a certain distance from society. No point in describing that in great detail, but I certainly did feel it more keenly after this experience that I've just mentioned. And it was just after that that my wife and I in effect *did* withdraw for four years, living in a cooperative community in the South. I was to a very modest extent involved in the beginning of civil rights activity. The Montgomery bus boycott occurred while we were in the South. But on the whole we were just way, way, *way* off in the hills. I liked it fine.

FINN: Why, if you liked it fine, did you leave it and get involved in the hurly-burly?

LYND: I was beginning to chafe because of the community's isolation from the larger society. But another and more immediate reason was that all the members of the community except myself decided to join another more explicitly Christian and fundamentalist group.

Part of the hurly-burly to which Lynd has descended from the hills is the peace movement, its radical potentialities, and its sharp divisions. He has come to be an articulate representative for one definable position as Bayard Rustin is of another and differing position.

Lynd and Rustin are both pacifists, both opposed to the war in Vietnam, and both are described by themselves and others as radicals. Both see in the Movement (of civil rights and peace advocates) the basis for revolutionary social change. But they differ sharply, in theoretical and practical terms, about the political course that should now be pursued.

Rustin, a leading tactician of the civil rights movement, organized the massive March on Washington that preceded the Civil Rights Act of 1964. With the passing of that act, Rustin believes, one phase of the civil rights movement came to an end and began to give way to another. "The civil rights movement is evolving from a protest movement into a full-fledged *social movement*." This social movement is revolutionary because it links "Negro demands to broader pressures for radical revision of existing policies." The radical objectives posited by the movement can only be realized, however, by political power.

From these propositions Rustin draws the conclusion that "the future of the Negro struggle depends on whether the contradictions of this society can be resolved by a coalition of progressive forces which becomes the *effective* political majority in the United States. I speak of the coalition which staged the March on Washington, passed the Civil Rights Act, and laid the basis for the Johnson landslide—Negroes, trade unionists, liberals, and religious groups." What determines the nature of that coalition, as Rustin sees it, is the political objectives they share. Since there will also be objectives they do not share, compromise is inevitable. But "the leader who shrinks from this task reveals not his purity but his lack of political sense."

The article from which these quotations are drawn is entitled "From Protest to Politics." It formed one of a series of three actions by Rustin that Staughton Lynd criticized in an article entitled "Coalition Politics or Nonviolent Revolution."* The three actions Lynd criticized were Rustin's attempt to have the Mississippi Freedom Democratic Party delegates accept token seating at the Democratic convention in August 1964; the article; and Rustin's "efforts to undermine and stop the March on Washington against the war in Vietnam."

Lynd's most basic criticisms of Rustin are therefore: "(1) The coalition he advocates turns out to mean implicit acceptance of Administration foreign policy, to be coalition with the marines; (2) The style of politics he advocates turns out to mean a kind of elitism which Bayard has been fighting all his life, in which rank-and-file persons would cease to act on their own behalf and be . . . 'merely represented.' "

With the acknowledgment, on my part and Lynd's, that we

* Rustin's article appeared in *Commentary*, February 1964. Lynd's, which was one of several to criticize it, appeared in *Liberation*, June–July 1965.

Staughton Lynd

invoke Bayard Rustin's name only to facilitate our discussion of the general position he enunciated but shares with many others, I ask Lynd about the problem of coalition.

LYND: Well, I think actually there are two kinds of coalitions at issue: in practical terms, I think the first amounts to working with the organized trade-union movement and with that portion of the Democratic Party close to the trade-union movement. But the other question is coalition with groups to the far Left.

FINN: The problem for both you and Rustin is, I presume, how do you make your attitudes and views most felt in society? To make it more particular: taking for granted that you and Bayard Rustin are both opposed to Administration policy in Vietnam, and both concerned with the actual devastation and killing of people in Vietnam, the question posed is how to bring that conflict most quickly to an end. Would that be a fair way to state the issue?

LYND: I . . . don't . . . think . . . so. Because one of the subsidiary points, on which I have differed with Bayard and on which many people in the peace movement have differed, is whether to couch one's demands on the United States Government in terms of the quickest possible end to hostilities—which would presumably be some kind of cease-fire and stand-fast—or whether to insist on American withdrawal. I don't mean physical withdrawal prior to negotiations, but withdrawal as part of an ultimate solution agreed on in advance. This is an important issue in the peace movement and one on which Bayard and I happen to disagree, at least as of the letter which he and others wrote to the *New York Review of Books* about last November.*

* The letter to which Lynd refers appeared in the *New York Review of Books* of November 25, 1965. Entitled "The Vietnam Protest," it contained the following proposals as "a basis for common action":

    a) We urge the U.S. immediately to cease bombing North Vietnam;

    b) We urge the U.S. to declare its readiness to negotiate with the NLF, the political arm of the Viet Cong;

    c) We urge the U.S. to propose to Hanoi and the Viet Cong an immediate cease-fire as a preliminary to negotiations;

    d) We urge that the U.S. recognize the rights of the South Vietnamese freely to determine their own future, whatever it may be, without interference from foreign troops, and possibly under United Nations supervision.

The letter also stated that a prerequisite for a significant protest movement "is that it clearly indicate that its purpose is to end a cruel and

Because I feel that the American presence in Vietnam is illegitimate, that even if I did not feel that, the people that we are fighting *do,* and that no solution to the war is possible which doesn't include an American decision to withdraw. I think this is one of a series of issues—perhaps a third issue—on which not just Bayard and myself but two whole groups of people have tended to disagree.

FINN: Well, you didn't really mean to say there was no *solution* possible here. You mean there would be no *good* solution.

LYND: Right. It's *partly* a feeling on my part that it would be unjust for us to insist on the retention of military enclaves. But it's also a feeling—I felt this before I went to Vietnam and I feel it more strongly now—that the people on the other side, unless I am utterly deceived, are really more determined *not* to permit us to stay there than we are to stay there. I mean it's a much more intimate issue for them; it's their country. Therefore I think it is not only a morally insensitive but in fact an impractical line to suggest that the war be ended by a simple cease-fire or a stand-fast, because I don't think the other side will ever accept that.

FINN: To return to the division within the peace movement, how would you yourself define the principles which divide the two groups? Is part of it that one group hopes to be more *immediately* effective than the other, and therefore engages in political compromise?

LYND: I think that's part of it, but I also think that part of it is that. . . . Trying to look at it as a historian, which it is difficult for me to do because I'm involved in it, but nevertheless: I think that Bayard must have felt, in 1963 and '64, that the civil rights movement was on the verge of—but he said as much, of course, and continues to say in various most thoughtful statements—that now is a time when the civil rights movement needs to move from protest to politics, from direct action taken

futile war, not to give explicit or covert support to the Viet Cong. This is both a tactical necessity and a moral obligation, since any ambiguity on this score makes impossible, as well as undeserved, the support of large numbers of the American people."

In addition to Rustin, those who signed this letter were Irving Howe, Michael Harrington, Lewis Coser, and Penn Kemble.

On the basis of this letter there was an exchange between Lynd and Howe in the issue of December 23, 1965.

Staughton Lynd

by Negroes alone to a kind of coalition politics directed toward legislative goals which Negroes alone are not strong enough to obtain. I think he must have felt that the civil rights movement in the country as a whole was on the verge of a whole new period in American domestic politics, in which the Republican Party was, at least for the immediate future, out of the picture after the '64 election, and there would be a division within the Democratic Party, and Negroes as they became voters could tip the balance within the Party in the direction of its left wing, and so forth. All of which is very understandable and has its parallels, it seems to me, in the development of the Labor movement in the late 1930's.

Now then, the war came crashing in on them. And I think—leave Bayard as a personality out of it—I think many people in a sense still treat the war as a kind of automobile accident. You know, you were just on your way to something that you very much wanted to do and that you were very close to being able to do, and then suddenly came this annoying and really unexpected eventuality. But the inclination is still to treat it as a kind of detour or postponement.

FINN: It's really an aberration from the normal course of. . . .

LYND: An aberration. Aberration is just the right word: something that is exceptional and to be endured or eliminated as quickly as possible so that one can get back to one's proper business. Although it seems to me the escalation in February '65 was done in an extremely heavy-handed way, nevertheless American policy in Vietnam is consistent with other aspects of its foreign policy since 1945, and in some respects before that.

FINN: Well, you'd have people like Secretary of State Rusk to support that statement, I would think.

LYND: Well. . . . Yes, perhaps so . . . [laugh] He would want to make it consistent with 1939 and 1941, of course. I have some different analogies in mind. But be that as it may. If to begin with one feels that the war will be long . . . I confess I had that feeling right from February '65 on, that there were going to be hundreds of thousands of American troops there and that they would be there for years.

O.K., so we have this problem apparently with us for some time, but beyond that we have a pattern of foreign policy in which the United States is not the protector of freedom around the world, but rather a not too unconventional imperialist power. And therefore the problem arises as to what the attitude of the person desiring domestic reforms will be toward a state which, if for the moment you grant my premise, will for the foreseeable future be pursuing a more or less abhorrent foreign policy. I think that what happened in the spring of '65 was that you had a division between one group of people who felt that opposition to the war should not be their main concern, that in fact it was almost a distraction to make that a kind of emergency attitude, to make that the main concern rather than the slow building of a domestic movement.

That attitude in itself doesn't define Bayard, since a lot of SDS people felt that, but I think in addition that Bayard must have felt that it was better to cooperate with the Administration, at least in the form of relative silence in the area of foreign policy, in the interest of building a domestic coalition which, among other things, would sooner or later produce a better foreign policy. The parting of the ways, as you know, came on the question of cooperating with groups that were felt to be Communist or Marxist or extreme.

FINN: This is the second point you mentioned when we were initially talking about coalitions.

LYND: That's right. Yes. I suppose it seemed that not only were there bitter experiences from the thirties about cooperation with left-wing groups or communist-oriented groups, and not only did one *personally* find this distasteful, but in addition there was the sense that this would be fatal for the building of the domestic coalition. Why in the world sacrifice a whole spectrum of liberal allies whom it might be possible to win if one kept clear of left-wing groups who were in any case small and uninfluential?

Whereas to others of us, you see, the exclusion of these groups from concerted activity where possible was of a piece with the whole iniquitous nature of American foreign policy since 1945. And one had to confront the question of working with Communists domestically if only for the sake of fighting the whole cold-war atmosphere that has enveloped this society.

I'm sorry I've spoken so diffusely but it's a complex thing and I'm involved in it and I probably don't see it with complete clarity. But it seems to me that there are three issues: first, whether one's emphasis, as far as the war is concerned, is on negotiation and cease-fire, or on American withdrawal; the second, the question of the degree to which one emphasizes foreign policy and breaks with the Administration on the one hand, or deemphasizes foreign policy for the sake of working with more middle-of-the-road elements on domestic issues; and third, the question of working with domestic Communists and left-wing groups.

The question of working with communist and left-wing groups has a tortuous history in America. I ask Lynd if his analysis of communist activities in the thirties and forties would differ significantly from that of Social Democrats such as Rustin and Irving Howe. There would be, he says, "a *certain* difference." He recalls that years ago, when he made a brief venture into the organized Left, he became a Trotskyite rather than a Communist because he insisted that the Soviet Union was a deformed bureaucracy with slave labor camps. On the other hand, he adds, he has *never* had the attitude of many in the Socialist Party "that if it came to a choice, the United States with all its faults was a superior or more hopeful platform for social change than the Communist world with all *its* faults." But neither would he choose to maintain the reverse of that proposition.

FINN: How influential do you think those who share your opinions are, say, simply within the peace movement, and how much influence do they have on the direction of American foreign policy?

LYND: Well, you see part of what is perplexing to me, and a real burden to me actually, is that I am not a strategist or an organization builder or a kind of spider spinning a web of intrigue. I became involved in all of this quite accidentally. After the escalation in February '65 I was asked to speak at a rally here at Yale. I did. I read the Declaration of Conscience which I had just signed. Then I was asked to chair a meeting in New York City. Then I was asked to speak at the SDS March on Washington in April. It was all quite pragmatic. And *then* I had one apocalyptic and sectarian adventure. I felt after the SDS March—there was a follow-up meeting that very night in Washington of people who were interested and then several meetings in succeeding weeks—and I had just a strong sense in say May—

June '65 that a kind of dangerous thing was happening; that the war was expanding very rapidly but that the peace movement had in a sense shot its bolt.

And the one web I did weave or ball I did start rolling was to ask a number of people from a number of organizations to get together in Washington in June of that year to talk about what could be done during the summer just to keep protest alive. And out of that grew the demonstration in August in which several hundred people were arrested, and the formation of the national committee which sponsored the October and March Days of Protest last winter.* And since that time what I've done is on the one hand go to Hanoi, and on the other hand I have just written with Carl Oglesby a kind of statement which we are inviting others to sign with us, whereby persons who are not young men of draft age can identify themselves publicly with a whole series of nonviolent, opposition actions including draft refusal and the sending of medical aid to all combatants and so forth.

The point I'm trying to make therefore is that I haven't been trying to organize a faction. At the same time, it's perfectly true that I feel very strongly about the question of passing by on the other side of the war because of the concern for domestic reforms which, in absolute human terms, just seem to me less important. And I also have a concern with a certain style of social action which continues to emphasize what it seems to me were the essential characteristics of the civil rights movement; that is to say, individual people taking what seemed to them appropriate actions, not without calculation as to consequences, but in a certain sense with the feeling that one couldn't calculate consequences.

I think a *great* deal of what happened in the South simply involved the assertion of human dignity without terribly finespun theories as to what sitting-in at the restaurant would make possible or what one could do once one had the vote and so forth. Now I feel, you know, that this was a kind of gift of God to a society that morally had lost its way, and it's just *terribly* important that . . . we not too casually and too quickly say "Well, that was fine and that's over with and now we can go back to organizing that new group of voters into a conventional electoral coalition." I've just *begun* to say something that concerns me there, but I want to indicate that it is perfectly true

* This is a reference to the National Coordinating Committee to End the War in Vietnam.

Staughton Lynd

that in that sense I have a position which I feel passionately about and which I hope to persuade people is valid, at least in part.

FINN: You put it in terms of persuading people. But you're not interested simply in persuading people, I presume, except for the purpose of changing and improving. And this is the whole problem that faces every minority group that thinks that the majority is off on the wrong tack.

LYND: I would say, first of all, that I believe that extreme protest against war has, up to this point at least, stimulated moderate protest rather than the reverse. You can never rerun it a second time, and I am conscious of the familiar argument about civil disobedience, that too reckless an attitude toward the law invites a time of lawbreaking, invites fascism. But my feeling is that on the whole those extreme acts, acts of personal witness, that people have taken in response to the Vietnam war, have stimulated protest in other forms. And I think that we come to a very interesting time when rather respectable organizations such as the ACLU and the AFSC and significant articles in journals like *Commonweal* and *The Christian Century*. . . . How do I want to say this? I think that many more groups and individuals are coming now to the position that this is an important, perhaps an indispensable kind of response to this sort of situation.

I think that the argument between so-called moral action and so-called political action has gotten very murky, because I think very few people take "moral" actions without the hope that their action will somehow encourage and stimulate and inspire others. My own feeling is that it's not so much a distinction between people who care about affecting the situation and people who only want to stand against the skyline as romantic heroes, but between people who feel led in two different ways to try to influence a situation.

FINN: How do you regard the interaction of moral and political evaluation? There are a number of political realists, among whom would be included Kennan and Acheson and Morgenthau. I recall Morgenthau writing some years ago that insofar as a person is true to Christian principles he must be a poor politician. And the reverse is true because Christianity says you should love your neighbor as yourself and the cardinal principle of political action is that you should use your neighbor as the means to the end of your own power.* Well, he sees there an almost necessary opposition, and there are other analysts who make this distinction, so that one doesn't easily make moral judgments of political actions. Does this kind of framework have any validity for you?

LYND: I'm sure it does have some validity. To put the case in what I would regard as its strongest possible terms: in the interest of compassion, in the interest of concern for one's fellow men, doesn't one need to act by a special set of rules in politics which are effective, which will in fact help them, rather than naïvely applying a personal style of morality—which may be gratifying to oneself but doesn't benefit anyone else?

Now I find it a difficult question to answer because all of my life, all of my experience, despite the fact that I did not have a conventional religious upbringing, has been concerned with— if I use words like "childlike" and "naïve," then the newspaper the next morning says "Mr. Lynd himself conceded that he was childlike and naïve"—so I don't know quite what words to use any longer. All I can say is that where I went to school, in this rather religiously diluted atmosphere of the Ethical Culture Society, there was written up over the platform of our assembly hall, "The place where men meet to seek the highest is holy ground." And it has always seemed to me that however lacking in faith I might be, at least I had the responsibility to seek the highest of which I was aware. And it has never occurred to me that life could be anything else than an attempt to follow one's highest insights. That is so much the definition for me of what life ought to be about that it's very hard for me to shift into

* Mr. Morgenthau had begun an article with the statement that "An unbridgeable gulf separates the demands of Christian ethics from the way man is compelled by his natural aspirations to act." And in the course of developing this idea, he wrote:

". . . For the natural aspirations proper to the political sphere—and there is no difference in kind between domestic and international politics —contravene by definition the demands of Christian ethics. No compromise is possible between the great commandment of Christian ethics, 'Love Thy Neighbor As Thyself,' and the great commandment of politics, 'Use Thy Neighbor As a Means To The Ends of Thy Power.' It is a priori impossible for political man to be at the same time a good politician—complying with the rules of political conduct—and to be a good Christian—complying with the demands of Christian ethics. In the measure that he tries to be the one he must cease to be the other." ("The Demands of Prudence," Worldview, June 1960, p. 6.)

Staughton Lynd

the terms of reference which your quotations from Morgenthau and Acheson suggest.

There are really two problems. The first is a question of goals. I have quite a different sense of what society ought to be and how men ought to live than persons who write in the language of political pluralism, who take a competitive economy based on private property for granted. And I would be inclined to describe what seems to me an ideal society much more in religious terms, I think, than in the language of socialism, which seems to me after all a question of means. The important thing is that men love one another, which it seems to me they *can* do and *have* done at any level of material abundance—even though abundance creates possibilities just as it creates temptations.

But leaving aside the question of goals and the quality of life that one is aiming at, and coming just to the question of effectiveness at a certain limited task such as stopping a particularly hideous war or achieving minimal civil rights for an excluded portion of the population, I can only say that it's been my *experience* that people who feel and act in a way that I feel drawn to—roughly speaking, the mystical- romantic- adventurous- sectarian putchist way—are not ineffective. I mean it may very well be that both kinds of persons are needed, and Thomas More is needed both in the King's Government and out of it so to speak. But I have a feeling that both kinds of action are effective.

I think one of the reasons that I and others involved in the New Left develop a certain passion about this is that we associate the radicals of the thirties with a style of calculation which, paradoxically enough, is not very different from that of many liberals who are fervently anti-Communist. Let me try to explain what I mean. That anti-Communist liberal who is putting together his coalition to get through a certain kind of legislation— let us say a minimum wage bill—in fact performs operations rather similar to that Communist putting together his united front coalition to stop fascism or protect the Soviet Union or whatever it is.

And in each case, I think what I and many of the young people involved in the movement feel, is that there's a quality here of acting, a kind of acting in which a person doesn't put his whole personality into his acts. And because of that, in my experience, Communists tend to be politically ineffective—not all Communists, but most Communists I've known. Not because they were too radical; most of them were trying to be very moderate. But because they were so busy trying to be that kind of person they thought would have an effect on people quite different from themselves, they didn't speak as human beings, they didn't speak with a natural tone of voice. (You've obviously asked the right question, because this is very much at the heart of what I feel about all these things.) It seems to me that in any kind of action where one does involve the whole of oneself, the element of unpredictability or lack of control over the whole situation is very much a part of the nature of such action. And *something* like that, I think, is intended by the language of the New Testament about losing one's life to find it.

Well enough! I just wonder whether there isn't a certain inherent tension, permanent tension, between two kinds of action which it would oversimplify to describe as a contrast between effective and ineffective action or action concerned for results and action concerned only for moral integrity or something of that kind.*

FINN: Another issue about which you've written is the problem of the elite, of elitism. But this seems to pose a problem *also* for people who are in a minority group. There's a danger that they will regard themselves not only as a minority but, being correct while the majority in this case is wrong, as the elite. And it seemed to me that in the ending of the article you wrote on "Coalition Politics or Nonviolent Revolution," where in fairly grand terms you talked about the March going on and into the Capitol and possibly occupying the offices, however briefly—that you left yourself open to that charge.†

* What Lynd has here posited as a permanent tension seems very close to the distinction between an "ethic of responsibility" and an "ethic of ultimate ends" which Max Weber developed in his classic essay, "Politics as a Vocation." Weber stated that these two codes of behavior are "fundamentally differing and irreconcilably opposed." Much of the dissension in the peace movement can be analyzed in these terms. And I would add, without applying the judgment to Staughton Lynd, that much of the dissension flows from a too simple application of the distinction to international affairs.

† "At the April 17th march in Washington it was unbearably moving to watch the sea of banners and signs move out from the Sylvan Theater toward the Capitol as Joan Baez, Judy Collins and others sang 'We Shall Overcome.' Still more poignant was the perception—and I checked my reaction with many many others who felt as I did—that as the crowd moved down the Mall toward the seat of government, its path delimited on each side by rows of chartered buses so that there was no-

LYND: Seemingly so. Well, to begin with, if one wants to speak of classical democratic theory, there was nothing more clear in the political philosophy of the eighteenth century than that a legislature did not have the right to surrender those powers of which they were trustees for the people to the Executive, no matter if they did it unanimously. Whether the United States Congress could give the President the right to make war whenever he chose to—by any number of Tonkin Bay Resolutions—is, therefore, a *very* real question from the standpoint of precisely that majoritarian, democratic political theory which is appealed to in this instance.

And I find the same thing when, in that *New York Review of Books* letter, it is said that blocking troop trains is a different kind of action than conscientious objection because it not merely withdraws one individual's energy from a collective enterprise but attempts to obstruct the rule of the majority. Well, I just think that those who argue that the decision to escalate the war in Vietnam was made democratically are on very tenuous ground. The mandate at the polls in 1964 would indicate the opposite. And therefore it seems to me that the whole problem just can't be simplified as if we were dealing with a Rivers and Harbors Bill in a sort of quiet backwater of conventional politics. It seems to me that the American state is operating in a kind of twilight zone between what have conventionally, classically been considered democratic procedures and what have conventionally and classically been considered something quite different.

Our situation, it seems to me, has to be recognized for what it is: that the people did not, in any very meaningful sense, decide upon our present Vietnam policy; that in no very meaningful sense do they have an opportunity to decide until at least the next Presidential election—and probably the one after that; and that in the meantime we have a very frightening situ-

---

where to go but forward, toward the waiting policemen, it seemed that the great mass of people would simply flow on through and over the marble buildings, that our forward movement was irresistibly strong, that even had some been shot or arrested nothing could have stopped that crowd from taking possession of its government. Perhaps next time we should keep going, occupying for a time the rooms from which orders issue and sending to the people of Vietnam and the Dominican Republic the profound apologies which are due; or quietly waiting on the Capitol steps until those who make policy for us, and who like ourselves are trapped by fear and pride, consent to enter into dialogue with us and with mankind." (*Liberation*, June–July 1965, p. 21.)

ation, not only morally in that we are inadvertent accomplices, but politically in that we are relatively helpless as citizens. And it seems to me that a responsible discussion of our situation has to begin with the sense of dilemma, and those that begin a discussion from the premise that somehow a conventional decision has been made and a handful of putschists are adventurously disregarding it or are no more in contact with reality than those they condemn.

When the voters chose between Johnson and Goldwater in 1964 they did so on the basis of a large complex of things, and to many citizens Vietnam did not seem the great issue it has since become. I ask Lynd whether he thinks the American people would support or dissent from present policy in Vietnam if there were a direct vote. He answers that they would probably support it, but he makes several "basic points."

First, Samuel Lubell and other analysts suggest that the most important issue in the '64 presidential election was not a verdict about Vietnam but a sense that Johnson was "reliable when it came to issues of war and peace and that his opponent was reckless and adventurous." Johnson's statements that the U.S. would not go North, would not engage in a land war in Asia, helped define that sense. He also points out, quite accurately, that the ambiguity of the polls on Vietnam reflects the ambiguity of the American people. They can be interpreted to make the majority seem more dove than hawk, or the reverse. And there was a time, Lynd recalls, "when we scornfully contrasted what we regarded as a real democracy with what we called the plebiscitory democracy of powerful heads of states who made decisions and then had them ratified by public opinion polls." Whether a decision is democratic is not resolved by public opinion polls.

LYND: But let us suppose that it were possible to resolve that question. I don't think that whether or not a majority of the American people support the war has anything to do with whether the war is immoral; has anything to do with whether the war is unjust; and only in part has to do with whether the war is illegal, because the United States Constitution is not the only relevant body of law. It *does* have to do with whether the

Staughton Lynd

war is undemocratic in the sense of truly expressing the will of the American people. But if the United States Congress were to declare war tomorrow, it wouldn't affect my feeling about the war or response to the war at all. That's a strong statement. But I mean the fundamental considerations which lead me to oppose the war are *not* those having to do with whether or not Congress gave the President the proper mandate and so forth.

FINN: I would presume this would be the case. But it does raise a problem of how the minority reacts in a society such as ours when it is in disagreement with, presumably, a significant majority.

LYND: Right. Well, I think that nonviolent civil disobedience is a legitimate kind of action, and in times like our own, when national states have such enormous power, should probably be a routine form of democratic dialogue. And in saying that I recognize there is a price, and the price is in creating generalized disrespect for law. But on the other hand I think it's completely inappropriate to make no distinction between, let us say, shooting a civil-rights worker in the back with a shotgun and nonviolently disobeying the laws as a form of conscientious protest. And I feel that this applies just as much to the white Southerner, who might wish to disobey a Federal civil rights law in a way that would at least immediately harm no one else, as to me when I object to the policy in Vietnam. I feel that he might be calling to my attention, by the degree of inconvenience to which he was subjecting himself, some negative aspect in a law which I had, up to that point, regarded altogether positively. In other words, I don't think I'm trying to make out a special case for the particular kind of minority to which I belong.

Now, how would I feel about his temporarily occupying Congress? Our plan, actually, in August 1965, was to assemble on the steps of the Capitol building and solemnly to declare that as far as we personally were concerned, we were not at war with the people of Vietnam. Well, let me just say that I think the particular expression in the last paragraph of that article is more open to question than a general defense of the practice of conscientious civil disobedience. The same kind of problem is involved as is involved in the troop trains. That is, it's not simply a personal withdrawal, it involves the obstruction of activities which the majority is carrying on.

The position Lynd presents here is one which is accepted by many people who would regard themselves as a part of the New Left. It is opposed not only to prevailing opinion but, as he says, to the opinion of other groups on the Left, specifically those groups represented by the signers of the letter he mentions.* It is a deep and principled difference not readily resolved.

We turn to an earlier point. If both sides in a conflict engage in vicious practices, say gross individual torture, are they to be equally condemned for such practices, even though the cause of one side is thought to be more just than the other?

LYND: I think so. It's a bit of a hypothetical situation for me, but if I were confronted with, let us say, torture by the National Liberation Front, certainly my *hope* would be that I would react to it *exactly* as to torture by the other side.

FINN: So that there are some things, some means, even in justified conflict, that should simply not be allowed. There are limits beyond which no one should transgress, no matter what the cause. I would think this might be one of the instances where you could make a decision apart from calculating consequences.

LYND: Yes. Well insofar as I can imagine the situation, that would be my reaction.

* The signers of that letter reject the analogy Lynd posits between civil disobedience in the civil rights struggle and stopping troop trains to protest the war.
"The situation of the Vietnam protest movement is somewhat different. Thus far, it has by and large been able to express its dissent openly and publicly, through the usual channels open to members of a democratic society—and this fact would seriously call into question any effort to employ civil disobedience as a political tactic by an organized movement. We question the rightness, for example, of recent efforts to stop troop trains in California: they involve an action by a small minority to revoke through its own decision the policy of a democratically elected government—which is something very different indeed from public protest against that government's decision or efforts to pressure it into changes of policy. Tactically, it might be added, such attempts at 'symbolic' interference with the war effort are self-defeating, since they merely result in a display of impotence and alienate people who might be persuaded to join in political protest against the Johnson policy. A 'revolutionary' tactic in a decidedly non-revolutionary situation is likely to do little more than increase the isolation of those who undertake it."

Staughton Lynd

FINN: Wasn't a question like this involved in the dispute between Sartre and Camus? The question which was raised then is one which will probably be around to plague people for a long time. It's a real problem for at least some people in the peace movement that I've talked with.

LYND: But, what I was fumbling to say a moment ago was not that I thought a double standard should be applied to some people's torture or some people's terror. To use the Sartre-Camus example—and I don't know as much about their differences as I would like to—it has always seemed to me that the strongest argument for the proponents of Sartre was Camus' lack apparently of clear-cut opposition to the Algerian war. So what I'm trying to say is that were I in Vietnam, were I on the National Liberation Front side of the lines—and, by the way, I'm not at all sure that I *would* be; I think I might be an anguished neutralist Buddhist someplace—but in any case were I on the NLF side of the lines, and were I conscious of torture going on, I *hope* that I would not merely refuse to do it but that I would try to block the troop trains, so to speak, or occupy the halls of Congress. I would really try to stop it. But, you know, I say that with some consciousness of *not* being in Vietnam.

The friendship of Jean-Paul Sartre and Albert Camus was severely strained by more than one issue. Some people in the peace movement have attempted to read their own differences in terms of these issues and, according to their own lights, side with one or the other of these French moralists. I introduce their names into my conversation with Lynd intending to refer to an early dispute that became public in 1952.

Using the literary device of replying to someone who had criticized one of his novels, Camus accused Sartre of becoming an apologist for the Communist State, of refusing to acknowledge, for example, the existence of the Russian labor camps. In a fierce direct reply Sartre controverted both the alleged facts and the consequent argument of Camus. Yes, he found the camps inadmissible, Sartre replied, but equally inadmissible is the exploitation of these camps by the bourgeois press—and by Camus.

Another issue which divided the two was the Algerian war. On this war, which put to the test the moral and political al-

legiances of a divided France, Camus was silent, Sartre his usual,
voluble critical self. Addressing Europeans generally he wrote,
"You condemn this war but do not yet dare to declare your-
selves to be on the side of the Algerian fighters; never fear, you
can count on the settlers and the hired soldiers; they'll make you
take the plunge."

It is, of course, this issue that Lynd refers to here. He had, in
fact, commented precisely on this statement of Sartre's in a
guest editorial in the *National Guardian* at the end of 1965:
"This is the winter when American opponents of the war [in
Vietnam] will have to confront Jean-Paul Sartre."

The example of Algeria serves admirably well for a dis-
quisition on torture, for in the Algerian war torture and terrorism of a most vicious and degrading nature were practiced
by both sides. And Lynd had editorialized, with the experience
of the Algerian revolutionaries in mind, that in his opinion "no
one who has not passed through that battle of conscience personally should either absolutely condemn *or* absolutely support
revolutionary terror."

His present comments about judging torture seem to be not
in complete accord with that statement, but the stress—which
is crucial here—on the importance of being *in* the situation is
the same. I ask him if he means the decision made in abstraction is different from one made in the actual context.

LYND: That's right. And one of the reasons that I think it is
difficult to be absolutely clear-cut, unambiguous, in responding
to such matters as those about which we have been speaking is
that, in addition to the situation that confronts one, there are
all the situations which are on the other side of the world, that
are at a distance from oneself, about which one is not doing
anything.

You know I find myself constantly talking pacifism to Marxists and Marxism to pacifists just because of the inherent complexity, it seems to me, of the problem.

I ask from which of the two groups he gets the best response,
but at his pause for amused reflection, I ask him to recall a
story about Niemöller that he had earlier mentioned.*

* We did not explore the difficulties of discussing pacifism with
Marxists or Marxism with pacifists, but Lynd has mentioned some of

Staughton Lynd

LYND: Well, actually it expresses much more clearly what I have been trying to say because the question in my mind was: how could it be true on the one hand that he had organized a rather effective resistance movement among the German churches shortly after Hitler came to power, but on the other hand that he had, in a famous statement *vividly* expressed the sense of having been too late? And his explanation was that the German Christian churches responded to the situation of Jews who had been converted to Christianity but not to Jews who had not been converted.

His statement—at least as I've heard it quoted—is that "When the Communists were jailed, I was not a Communist; when the Jews were put in concentration camps, I was not a Jew; when the trade unionists were persecuted, I was not a trade unionist; and when I was imprisoned"—which I think was '36 or '37—"it was too late."

My understanding is that he felt, in retrospect, that his responsibility as a Christian concerned not merely the state's invasion of the traditional sphere of the Church, but what the state was doing in the state's own sphere, which was after all also God's concern. I think this has relevance to the immediate situation.

---

these difficulties in his writing. He mentions the problem as it initially presented itself to him:

"For me, and I believe for many others, the years of coming-to-maturity after World War II involved a continuing dialogue between the hard-boiled centralizer and the sensitive anarchist, the Commissar and the Yogi, the Marxist and the pacifist, a dialogue which (at least in my own case) expressed itself in a most erratic sequence of personal actions. Books such as Silone's *Bread and Wine* which seemed to achieve some synthesis between the two viewpoints became treasured talismans. In such an atmosphere of schizophrenia on the Left, it was easier for defenders of the Establishment to come on stage as champions of freedom and the individual." ("Socialism, the Forbidden Word," *Studies on the Left*, 1963, Vol. 3, no. 3, pp. 18–19.)

JACK BOLLENS

While factionalism is endemic in the peace movement, so is the effort to find a center, a core, some central thrust that will unite the movement. One of the organizations that is trying to overcome this factionalism, to coordinate many of the separate unrelated activities is Turn Toward Peace. TTP is, in fact, less an organization than a cooperative venture which has brought together more than sixty national organizations in a search for ways to avoid war without surrendering democratic values. Norman Thomas and E. Raymond Wilson are co-chairmen of TTP; Robert Gilmore is executive director; Robert Pickus, Western area director; and Jack Bollens, Midwest area director.*

Jack Bollens was born in Detroit, Michigan in 1928. He attended public school there and in Amherst, Ohio. He graduated from Heidelberg College, Ohio and Eden Theological Seminary, Webster Groves, Missouri, and has done graduate study in the social sciences at Washington University and the University of Cincinnati. He has served as youth director of an interracial community center in a slum area of Cincinnati and minister of the United Church of Christ in Dayton, Ohio.

Along with Erich Fromm and David Riesman he was a founder of the Council for Correspondence, a small group of academic and professional peace workers who shared a common interest in the exploration of ideas about war and peace.

* As if to underscore the factionalism I have noted, Turn Toward Peace was reorganized in 1967 under a new name, World Without War Council of the United States. The emphasis is on religious, economic and cultural organizations; some peace groups previously associated with TTP have gone their own way or have moved over to the New Left.

Jack Bollens

He is a member of the executive body of the AFSC (American Friends Service Committee), the National Advisory Committee of the WRL (War Resisters League) and CNVA (Committee for Nonviolent Action). He says that he has had experience at every level of work in peace education, from running a mimeograph machine to developing alternative positions to present national policies.

We have tried a number of times to meet for an interview, and we finally get together in my office between a meeting Bollens has just attended and his plane back to Chicago. Bollens is tall and trim with an open face, good strong features and an equally strong and pleasant voice. His speech tends to be a steady, even, but expressive flow of words interrupted occasionally with a burst of laughter. Because I know he has been involved in many aspects of the peace movement, I ask him to describe his present position.

BOLLENS: My *specific* job title is senior associate with the Center for War/Peace Studies, which is a new organization attempting to develop materials for nongovernmental organizations that wish to enter the war/peace field. We have a body of associates who essentially are consultants, people across the country who work with some of the major organizations—churches, synagogues, organizations dealing with public affairs, human relations, labor—on how you can grab hold of this, what obstacles you have to overcome.

FINN: Obstacles toward what?

BOLLENS: Toward coming to grips with what I would call the war/peace question: how to get engaged in learning something about, thinking through, discussing, debating and taking political stands on foreign policy issues. And then helping groups to develop a program to do this. That's what my *specific* occupation is. I'm putting equal energy in an organizational complex called Turn Toward Peace, which is made up of the key leaders, nationally and on a number of regional levels, of these very organizations, along with some of the peace organizations, in an effort to have some connection and communication between these groups and get some community visibility. This complex has, in fact, quite a different political outlook and context than some of the present peace activities that are taking place.

And I do that as the executive vice president of TTP in Chicago. It has fifty-five people on it, most of whom are the key staff or board members—either the chairman of the board or the executive director—of some forty major organizations in the Chicago area.

FINN: What kind of organizations?

BOLLENS: The Catholic Adult Education Center, Church Federation of Greater Chicago, Union of American Hebrew Congregations, Chicago Board of Rabbis, YMCA, American Jewish Congress, and also the Committee for a Sane Nuclear Policy, the Fellowship of Reconciliation and American Friends Service Committee, to name three peace organizations.

FINN: You said that you brought together discussants to consider foreign policy issues. But you said earlier that it was in terms of war/peace, so you're not going to be confused with the Foreign Policy Association or something which is concerned with everything that comes under the rubric of foreign policy.

BOLLENS: Right. Ours *is* a fairly wide and complex definition of peace, or that area of foreign policy which is crucial to peace. But unlike the Foreign Policy Association and the Council on Foreign Relations, we have made some value judgments that are explicitly stated to begin with. We're not just a grouping of organizations or people that discuss the state of the world as it is so we can *know it* better. There are some judgments in terms of the kind of a world we want to see, and the areas in which we need change to move toward these goals.

FINN: Could you state some of the shared values or goals that these groups do have, that allow them to work together?

BOLLENS: Our goal is a disarmed world, under law, in which free societies can grow. We share recognition that fundamental changes of our understanding and our policy have to take place in this country and other countries of the world, including the communist countries, if we're going to have any chance of achieving this goal. We share a recognition that in order to achieve that goal we need to search for ideas and policies and implementation in six or seven areas. So there isn't any agreement on, you know, the *specific* program or policy or way to implement it, but there is agreement on movement in these specific directions.

Jack Bollens

One is toward disarmament. The recognition of disarmament alone, however, isn't really an answer; it's not enough. You also have to have movement toward the expansion of international institutions and growth toward at least minimal law. Along with that recognition comes the recognition that law doesn't function unless it's undergirded and supported by some sense of international community; that you have to knit together a whole fabric of relationships, of communication and so forth, or law just isn't going to function even on a minimal level. And then there's also our recognition of how you get law; we're not just interested in blueprints being drawn up. You get law step by step as nations interact, as policies are accepted, as agreements are made and acted upon. Law is pretty much the codification of existing practices and relationships—although it helps to have a blueprint or an idea that can win acceptance.

Fourth, you come to the fact that two thirds of human beings on the face of the earth really don't want law and stability, if by that you mean things as they are; they are the basis for profound revolution. They want *change,* and somehow we in the West have to respond *adequately* to that gap between the developed world and the underdeveloped world. And that's a whole other area that's directly connected to population, to economic expansion, to the whole political, psychological development over centuries of colonialism and so on.

A fifth area is this area of international crises and immediate situations where political settlements are needed. All of the first four things I've talked about are really long-term propositions, although again we agree and disagree. Within this are our very immediate issues. We are, for example, in the business of creating discussion and dialogue on immediate issues such as Vietnam. Again, there's no agreement on a policy, but there's agreement that it's important to get political settlements in those kinds of areas—in Berlin, in Vietnam, in the Congo—or you have no chance in the long run.

And finally we agree on this whole area of nonviolence, nonviolent ways of prosecuting conflicts and forcing the needed social change and defending values that you hold. And again, there's only agreement that there may be a germ here that ought to be explored and people encouraged to explore it. And part of this comes from the common outlook that we have on the role conflict plays and the nature of law and the theological and ethical assumptions underlying this. And unlike some *parts* of the pacifist tradition, in which conflict is something that is to be solved, reconciled, done away with, so that men can be as they're meant to be, our assumption is that conflict is real, that men are going to continue to mistreat their wives and beat the kids, kick the dog and cat and grab for power and manipulate and misuse other people. There are real conflicts of value, conflicts of power.

FINN: And there will have to be some means to *order* that conflict in the society?

BOLLENS: There has to be a means to *order* it with your institutions and law; there also have to be means for *change* that's needed when people conflict and want a change. And unless you go the military road—which has been the pattern of two thousand years—it seems you ought to at least take a look at nonviolent action, Gandhian thought.

FINN: To consider conflict in domestic society. Is there any agreement or understanding that we'd need some kind of policing force that would try to resolve conflicts when the two contending parties cannot do it peacefully?

BOLLENS: I think there would be widespread agreement that we want institutions and want enforcement of *law*. To what degree you need a police force, to what degree that police force needs a concentration of military power, there's wide disagreement. I think inherent in our agreement that we want *law* and *order* is some functional mechanism to make it work.

But if you take this country with something of a moral, ethical consensus on one issue, the civil rights issue, you've still got a situation in which, unless you want to break the thing wide open, polarize it and use mass organized violence, you need nonviolent techniques of forcing change. And it's this idea of nonviolence, coupled with law, institutions, that seems to at least bear investigation on an international scale. Our agreement here is that we're open to it and we're looking at it.

FINN: Well, you mentioned among the organizations that are grouped together here some which are historically for nonviolent, pacifist means. And there are some that I would presume are *not*.

BOLLENS: The vast majority are not.

FINN: So although you suggest these as goals that bring you together, they're really goals that you hope to see shared by large numbers of the people.

BOLLENS: Right.

FINN: It would be very easy to find people in our government, for example, who are executing United States policy in Vietnam right now, who could agree with the goals you stated. I forget what the slogan of the Air Force is—"Peace is our Profession"? Nevertheless, the ways of getting to this goal of peace are what tend to separate people fairly early.

BOLLENS: It's that, but it's something else too, Jim. You *measure* any policy in terms of this one overall goal and within the areas I mentioned. You have to ask if this is a step toward the goal of peace. That makes *all* the difference in the world.

FINN: I would assume that any group which today has under its general umbrella pacifists and nonpacifists will find itself in sharp disagreement on particular issues. I mean, they will share the disagreements that exist in society. And since we have today different positions on the validity and viability, the moral acceptability of deterrent systems, of our action in Vietnam, I should think that these questions would not shatter but disrupt what might otherwise be peaceful discussions.

BOLLENS: They aren't always peaceful, but I don't think particular issues even have to shatter them. I think what is shattering is the attempt to force people to take positions—to get unanimous positions.

If you work a position out so that it's acceptable to everybody, it's the lowest common denominator and completely meaningless. That's why we attempt here to set a different context, get people searching, thinking, talking, and acting—expressing their positions with agreement to disagree. And Turn Toward Peace does not take any one foreign policy position itself. We never make a statement.

It seems to me what's needed is dialogue, and debate between the pacifists and nonpacifists is *desperately* needed. Let me start with the pacifists because I consider myself a pacifist, a person who has said, "No, I'm not going to participate in organized mass violence and the use of military power by my

nation." And each of us is required to face that question: are
we or aren't we? That's one personal responsibility. It seems to
me that we have another responsibility, and that is to say what
alternate policies are possible, to make judgments and to make
recommendations. And I think this has been a tragic failure
of the pacifists, not to apply that body of pacifist thought, that
tradition, to international politics today and the policy of this
country. Many pacifists still duck the hard questions completely,
like the pacifists in the thirties who just said, "Don't get involved
in war; it's evil and I don't want to participate in violence." But
they never had any answer to what you do with the other guys
that want to use violence, and then they never even *considered*
how you stop the spread of Nazi power.

FINN: The experience of the thirties, I take it, is, in terms of
the pacifists in this country, not one of their shining moments.

BOLLENS: It sure isn't. Trouble is some of them, you know,
still live in the thirties. They ought to be forced by the nonpacifists to grapple with this. On the other hand, what the pacifist has to offer, and what the nonpacifists ought to grapple with,
is a statement of the problem. The problem is war. The problem
is getting rid of war by major technologically developed nations
and finding alternate ways for nations to relate and to conflict
and compete. That involves institutions, understanding. It also
involves one of the pacifist insights which, if they're not interpreted so much in psychological terms but in political terms, *can*
become meaningful: this whole concept of initiatives.

When Charles Osgood—who's a psychologist—dealt with it,
he dealt with psychological terms—you back off a step from
the teeter-totter and automatically the other guy's gonna back
off too. That's part of the truth. You know, a lot of international
relations are based on misunderstandings and hatred and fear
that generates a reciprocal response from the other guy, and if
you take a step backward, it's going to affect him; he's going to
see you more clearly and act a little better. But it's only *half* the
truth. A lot of the conflict isn't from misunderstanding.

FINN: It's real?

BOLLENS: Yes, you need pressure, you need coercion, and
initiatives to change the understandings of the other guy. (And
we can try to apply this to Vietnam.) You know, what fifteen or
twenty steps can be taken to really try to change the context

Jack Bollens

and come out of it with some possibility to put together a fractured community? to begin to have a supranational presence, even if it just acts as a trip wire? Down roads that can begin economic development if necessary, so that there will be an alternative to the Communists on the one hand and a man like Diem or Ky on the other, neither of whom met the economic, psychological, political needs of the people. Well, it's that *kind* of discussion and debate that I'm looking for.

A number of pacifists have said that they are not listened to; and their opposites in political debate usually reply that they have nothing to say. Paul Peachey, I recall, pointed out that John Bennett had not included pacifists in his symposium on morality and nuclear weapons. Can the pacifist enter into political debate with the same appreciation of the political realities as the nonpacifist? Does he, in fact, do so? Or should he? Are the "political realities," viewed from widely divergent viewpoints, so different that discussion between pacifists and nonpacifists becomes meaningless?

Will the pacifist be regarded much as a vegetarian who will try to pass judgment on rare roast beef when in fact what he's objecting to, or what he himself will not do, is eat any kind of meat? His particular judgment on the rareness of the roast beef may not be very useful.

BOLLENS: Well, it may or it may not be. If the person lets his vegetarianism really poison his objectivity—and none of us can be completely objective—then it ought to be known. On the other hand, when a person looking at a vegetarian's analysis of the meat doesn't listen to what he's saying because he knows he's a vegetarian, that person usually feels justified. Which, in fact, is *exactly* where the peace movement, particularly in the churches, *is;* the past history of pacifism invites skepticism that pacifists, in a sense, justly deserve. As I said, the pacifists of the thirties—not all, but the majority—only asked half the question; they didn't ask the other half, what do you do about Nazi power? So there came an issue like the repeal of the arms embargo legislation; the pacifists obviously don't want those arms shipped because they think it's going to result in more people getting killed. So they're on a platform where the whole thrust is just "Don't repeal the arms embargo legislation." And

along comes another even more sizeable group, the isolationists
—Colonel McCormick and William Randolph Hearst and so
forth—who for quite different reasons say "Don't repeal the
arms embargo. Europe's none of our business." They're quite
willing to use violence; "Fortress America" was the slogan.
There's no distinction made, and these two groups are marching,
putting out petitions, standing on the same platform with the
same public speakers.

Then there's a third group. Some of the isolationists, in fact,
slid over to this group—they're the group of pro-Nazis, the
German-American Bund, Father Coughlin, Gerald L. K. Smith
—all of them were against America repealing the arms embargo
for their reasons: they wanted to see Nazi power spread. And
then there's a fourth group, which, in fact, was the largest group
in this country at that time, an *ad hoc political* group working
in this country, the League Against War and Fascism which was
dominated by the Communists.

Well, it's that *kind* of heritage which in one sense justified
nonpacifists ignoring the pacifist and deciding instead that this
guy's just a vegetarian, so don't listen to anything he has to say
about meat.

It seems to me we *have* reached a point now where dialogue
can take place and *should*. But then you get into the tragic situation: where is the peace movement, including many of the
pacifist groups, going? You get almost the same choice developing in this country, as I see it, in the overall political choices.
One is in confidence in the continued development and use of
military power. And the other choice is now and has been taking
on for the last few years isolationist overtones. This time it's not
the conservative isolationists, it's the liberal radicals who are
now moving in an isolationist direction. It's exacerbated greatly
by Vietnam.

It seems to me very clear that the United States and the West
have to remain in Asia. It's *desperately needed* that we have influence and weight, that there's communication and a sense
of community, that there's major help in a capital way and technical way, or you're not going to have the sense of community,
you're not going to respond to the economic and population
problems that are needed.

What you have developing politically in the country is a new
isolationism which this country isn't going to buy. It's been
through that. Then come the elements or the remnants of the

old political Left in this country, various Communists and pro-
communist groups. One thing ought to be clear: organized,
disciplined communist activity in this country is almost nonexistent. I'm pretty well convinced from people I've talked to,
whose judgment I trust, that there are as many FBI members
in the Communist Party as there are CP members, or close to it.
Well, it seems to me it's a grouping of those three forces:
isolationist trends in the liberal community; the remnants of
left-wing Marxist political activity, which are now coming to the
fore in many different ways; and *some* pacifists and pacifist
groups I think are making the wrong case and just becoming
an opposite pole to the dominant advocates of power policy.
And the country is going with the latter. It's certainly not going
to go with the isolationist-Marxist-pacifist combine. Now there
are some pacifists and some pacifist groups that are aware of
this and are not going along.

FINN: I'm not sure from your tone how optimistic you are
about how this should be overcome, or how these very real
problems can be resolved.

BOLLENS: Well, it's not that the isolationist-neo-Marxist-
pacifist combine, or parts of those elements, is a threat in this
country. The country isn't going to go that way.

FINN: No, I mean how this affects the possibility of finding
new alternatives.

BOLLENS: I'm very worried; I think the odds are that we're
probably not really going to get the country or the major organizations or the churches, the thoughtful leadership in this country,
searching in that third area. And I'm very worried. If I was doing
what I'm doing because of the odds, I wouldn't be doing it. I'm
doing it because I think it's possible, but mainly because it's
needed and my values just require of me that I try.

Bollens has mentioned his pacifism only in terms of international affairs. When I ask him if he applied the concepts of
nonviolence to all areas of life, he says that he might well resort
to personal violence in some instances, but he also adds with
a smile that he thinks in most instances it's self-defeating. He
had come to his pacifism with some slight help from his father,
but mostly through a personal struggle in which the aids were

books, discussion and debate. For him "the central question is how do you prosecute conflict in a way that builds community."

His pacifism is more than just a personal moral decision. "It takes political forms, it takes institutional forms, it takes social forms in communication and discourse." The inspiration is Christian but is informed equally by the thought and practice of Gandhi. He had resolved the major difficulties before induction and completed two years alternative service just as the Korean War broke out.

BOLLENS: And with the recognition I had then and have even more strongly now, that in fact communist power and the use of violence and the expansion of that political philosophy is wrong and it has to be met, I was a CO still for one reason. It seems to me the central problem facing us and is going to face us over the next twenty or thirty or forty years, or we're not going to be around, is how do you find nonviolent ways of prosecuting that conflict? And in a world where violence in fact is accepted, to go along with that pattern is to follow the path of cruel desperation.

DAVID REED

My introduction to David Reed was a news report which the New York *Herald Tribune* of April 1, 1966 headlined "Boston Crowd Bloodies Four Card Burners." It reported that "the crowd of about 75 knocked the four youths to the ground and beat them with fists and feet until they were bloodied yesterday."

David Reed was one of those four. It was almost two months after that beating that I visited him in the CNVA house which was, at that time, in South Boston. When I later wrote to ask for some additional biographical information, he included with it the following statement that he had drawn up for his own benefit but which he placed at my disposal. It is reproduced with only a few minor deletions.

THE DEVELOPMENT OF MY THOUGHT AND ACTIONS WITH REGARD TO MILITARY SERVICE

by David Allen Reed

On February 25, 1966, and again on March 31, I intentionally destroyed draft cards that were issued to me by the Selective Service System. On May 25, I openly disobeyed an official order to report for induction into the armed forces of the United States. I now face several years in Federal prison for these actions. But I do not repent of my "crimes," for I feel that they were not crimes, but, rather, morally correct acts. When a government undertakes crimes against humanity, it is the duty of its citizens to refuse to cooperate—more than that, it is their duty to try to obstruct the commission of the crimes.

Would that more Germans had shared these views, rather than cling to the notions of majority rule and blind obedience to authority that gave Hitler millions of willing servants.

The leaders of our government have not been cremating people in death chambers, but they have been pouring flaming napalm over people's homes. They have not tried to expand their borders, but they have committed naked military aggression against the people of the Dominican Republic. They have sent over a quarter of a million troops to fight against a popular revolution in Vietnam. Our nation's leaders have also covered the globe with the instruments of American military power and have placed the threat of nuclear annihilation over the heads of millions of people.

I cannot cooperate with these things. My criticism of the Germans who "obeyed orders" would be hypocrisy if I were to help carry out these policies of my government.

In order to be a law-abiding American, I would have to pay for the napalm and the bullets and the bombs. I would have to cooperate with the military system that trains people to kill, to bomb, and to destroy. Rather, I have chosen to noncooperate and to try to obstruct the war machine.

During my seventeenth year, I began to think seriously about my position with regard to military service. I was aware of American military actions in Southeast Asia and Latin America, and I opposed them. But there seemed to be little likelihood that I would ever be ordered to participate as a soldier in such actions, since only a small part of the U.S. armed forces was then involved.

However, there was a real possibility that I would, sometime, be called to bear arms in a war. Thus, I did face the question of whether or not I would kill a foreign soldier in battle—since once one is in the armed forces one is expected to obey orders. I realized that the foreign soldier was probably a person very much like me—just obeying the orders of his government— and I felt that I had no wish to hurt him. I thought a lot about these matters, but I always looked at them as questions that could be answered later.

In February of 1964, I wrote to the Massachusetts Selective Service headquarters in Boston and requested information on

David Reed

student deferment and peacetime conscientious objection. Soon thereafter, I was accepted at Harvard with a National Merit scholarship. Since I was not sure about all of my attitudes toward war, and knew that they might change during college years, I decided to apply for a student deferment with the intention of applying for conscientious objector status when through with college and graduate school.

On June 5, 1964, I turned eighteen and registered with Local Board No. 125 in Milton, Massachusetts. I spent the summer teaching mathematics in a National Science Foundation program at Thayer Academy and Tufts University. When I entered Harvard in the fall, I filed Selective Service Form 109 (Student Certificate).

At Harvard, I worked with Students for a Democratic Society in its anti-war activities. I leafleted and participated in demonstrations in Cambridge and Boston against the war in Vietnam. I also participated in anti-war vigils on the Boston Common sponsored by the Quakers. On April 17, 1965, I was SDS coordinator for a bus bringing people to the March on Washington to End the War in Vietnam. I found myself devoting more and more time to anti-war activity as the war went on and escalated.

During the summer, I read the *New York Times* in detail and thought a lot about the war and my responsibilities. In August of 1965, I went to Washington to participate in the Assembly of Unrepresented People—several days of meetings and demonstrations called by pacifist groups and leading individuals in the peace movement. In the evening of August 7, I joined an unplanned sit-in at one of the main gates of the White House. Later, all of the gates were blocked in spite of police warnings that we would all be arrested. I stayed at the gates all night and about thirty-five of us were arrested the next morning when police cleared all of the gates. I was released on $10.00 collateral that afternoon after those outside the jail raised money.

On the next day was the planned march of 2,000 on the Capitol to declare peace between the unrepresented people of the United States and the people of Vietnam. The police announced that anyone who crossed First Street would be arrested. I crossed with about three hundred others. A couple hundred police in military formation blocked the entrance to the Capitol grounds. When we reached the police line, the leaders were arrested and the rest sat down to avoid a violent pushing and shoving contest with the police. We read several statements on the war and then began to rise, a few at a time, and walk toward the police who were blocking the entrance. The police renewed arrests, and after about an hour arrested about three hundred of us.

I was sentenced to $25.00 or three days. I refused to pay the fine because I am opposed to a system in which the rich can buy freedom and the poor must go to jail. I was carried out of the jail when a friend paid the fine against my wishes on the second day.

The August experience was important in radicalizing my thinking and behavior.

During the summer, I read various news reports about draft refusers and began to think about my cooperation with the Selective Service System, which chose to give me a privileged, exempt status. I did not want to apply for recognition as a conscientious objector for several reasons. I could not have said truthfully at that time that I would not participate in any war— there seemed to be no alternative when faced with a Hitler. Moreover, I did not think it was right for me to apply to the government for a license not to kill people. By presenting my background and beliefs for examination by the government, I would be tacitly acknowledging the right of the government to draft those who lack special religious training and belief or who are not as articulate as myself.

For several weeks, I was seriously considering not filing a Selective Service Student Certificate in the fall. In exploring this possibility, I wrote letters to the Central Committee for Conscientious Objectors and to the War Resisters League, of which excerpts follow.

I plan to refuse military service as long as our armed forces remain other than a purely defensive force. I will not be a party to American aggression against Vietnam, Cuba, the Dominican Republic or any other nation. Nor will I serve with the American forces which cover the globe in an attempt to intimidate all nations. Nor will I cooperate with preparations to annihilate millions of human beings in a nuclear attack, whether offensive or "retaliatory."

During the past year, I have been classified 2-S by the Selective Service. I will be a student at Harvard for at least three more years, and I could continue my student deferment. However, I have strong moral objections to my being listed by the Selective Service as a spare part for the war machine. I would like to disassociate myself from the Selective Service System— to refuse to file a Student Certificate or other classification form, to refuse to submit to physical examination to determine my fitness for service, to refuse to report for induction. I would deliver the statement of the above paragraph to the draft board as my reason for disassociation.

Could you send me information on the legal consequences of such action . . .

I am beginning to fear that it may be unfair, cowardly, and dishonest for me to hide behind a student deferment.

During these weeks, the question of my own relation to the military caused me to do a lot of thinking about war in general. I was not studying or working, so I had plenty of time to think. I was still reading everything in the *New York Times* about the war in Vietnam, and I was also reading *The Rise and Fall of the Third Reich*. The following excerpt from a letter I wrote to a friend on September 8 sheds light on my thinking at that time.

I appreciate your paternalistic advice on the Selective Service System. At the present time, I think that I will file my Student Certificate in October, although I plan definitely to refuse if called for a physical or mental exam or for induction. Avoiding the moral compromise involved with filing the Certificate is probably not worth a five-year prison sentence in view of present circumstances: the value of a formal education and the necessity of working against the war before it grows into a larger conflict.

You mention that you do not know the nature of my objection to military service, i.e. political or conscientious. Here is a brief explanation: I do not object to the use of limited violence to stop the crimes of gangsters or madmen, when all possible nonviolent means have failed. This applies both to individual gangsters and madmen who attack people on the streets and to organized gangsters and madmen (like the Nazis) who torture and kill on a larger scale. My mention above of "limited violence" means that we must never resort to a cure that is worse than the disease. A nuclear attack on Nazi-occupied Europe could be an example of such a "cure."

If the people of an invaded nation can be mobilized to fight, then it should also be possible to mobilize them to resist non-violently and to engage in a campaign of noncooperation with the invaders. If the people do not cooperate, then the invader has not conquered, even if his armies march across the length and breadth of the country.

I would like to see the United States unilaterally abolish its entire armed forces and adopt the following system of defense: full participatory democracy. Every apartment house and every city block should have an organization to which every resident belongs and which handles all of the affairs of the apartment house or neighborhood. (Students for a Democratic Society is working to establish such community action structures in Boston, Chicago, and other U.S. cities.) Then, in case of invasion, the replacement of the present government by a foreign power will have little effect on the people. If they are prepared to govern themselves, then they can ignore the forces of occupation and continue to conduct their own affairs. They can greet foreign troops without a shot and invite them to stay for a while as guests.

Of course, when the invading government discovers that its troops have successfully "invaded" without firing a shot and that the "captive" people continue to govern themselves, frustration may cause it to order its troops to kill those who refuse to cooperate with its orders. If the people continue to resist nonviolently, and if the soldiers obey orders to attack nonviolent men and women, then certainly many will die. But if the people are sufficiently well trained in the theory and practice of nonviolence, they will continue to resist. The invasion force, if it is composed of human beings, will *not* continue to slaughter the population. Probably thousands will be killed in the first cities captured, but the men in uniform will not continue to march across the country, killing everyone. After they have occupied a few cities and discovered that they cannot control the people, they will withdraw—probably after much hesitation and many confused efforts to conquer the people.

Of course, this method of nonviolent defense will involve the deaths of many thousands of the "defenseless" people. But there will not be as many casualties as in a nuclear conflict.

Nor will there be as many casualties as would result from a conventional war (think of the millions who died in World War II).

But could the American social structure be reorganized into a participatory democracy where nonviolent defense would be possible? Perhaps, if the $50,000,000,000 "defense" budget could be diverted into a program in which our million-man army would be replaced by a million SDS-type community organizers and apostles of nonviolence.

Even after this letter I continued to undergo internal conflict over the question of filing a Student Certificate. I sent the following letter to Local Board No. 125 to be sure that I was not being deferred under false pretenses—i.e., to make it clear that I was not asking to have military service postponed until later.

(September 26, 1965)

You have me listed under Selective Service number 19-125-46-130. However, I wish to make it clear to you that I am not prepared to commit murder for the United States government or anyone else. Nor will I be a party to American aggression against the people of Vietnam, the Dominican Republic, Cuba, or any other nation. Nor will I participate in our government's preparations to annihilate millions of human beings in a nuclear attack, whether offensive or "retaliatory."

Thus I state my refusal to serve in the armed forces of the United States.

On September 30, I filed a Student Certificate but wrote a statement similar to the above in the box labeled "Remarks."

At Harvard, I continued working against the war through SDS. I was on the mailing list of the Committee for Nonviolent Action (CNVA) since August, and I helped organize and participated in a CNVA demonstration for peace at Fort Devens on Veterans Day. A soldier from the base joined our demonstration and was taken into custody by military officials. The vigil line was attacked several times by people who tore up signs and hit demonstrators.

At about this time, I had an opportunity to speak on a Boston radio program on the draft, in which I stated that I would refuse to serve if drafted. Sit-ins at draft boards were receiving much publicity and some of those who sat in were reclassified

1-A. General Hershey, Director of the Selective Service System, stated that young men who publicly state their refusal to serve would be declared "delinquent" and would be drafted. It was announced that students would soon be subject to the draft and tested to see who would serve. I felt I would not cooperate with the test. As a result of all these things, I feared that I might soon face the draft and have to go to prison.

I did not want to spend several years in prison, so I decided to leave the country. After making housing arrangements with European peace groups, I flew to Luxembourg after finishing my first semester exams and formally withdrawing from Harvard. I went to Germany from there and stayed with a worker for the *Verband der Kriegsdienstverweigerer* (Organization of War Service Refusers). I soon began to feel that I was running away from my responsibility to stay in the United States and oppose the government's policy even if it involved major risks to my own personal security. I felt I would always wish that *someone* had stood up against the war and regret that I had run away.

So I came back after just a few days. I was in time to go back to school, but I decided not to. I wanted to devote my full time and effort to working against the war in Vietnam. Two days after returning to this country, I went to the New England CNVA headquarters on a farm in Voluntown, Connecticut, to work with that organization. Immediately, I became involved in the Peace Caravan: I traveled around New England distributing literature and speaking to groups. I discovered that I was rather good at speaking to groups and felt that I could work against the war effectively in CNVA.

I wrote the draft board a letter telling them where I could be found. On February 25, while at the Farm, I received a new draft classification card—2-S. Instead of cutting it out and putting it in my wallet, I tore it up. I certainly did not think that I would accomplish a great feat by doing this. Whether or not I had that piece of paper in my pocket was a matter of very little consequence. The destruction of the draft card, then, was a symbolic act—it indicated my open refusal to cooperate with the military organization.

I thought it was silly to be very concerned about destroying a draft card, but, obviously, the government thinks otherwise—it has made it a "crime" punishable by as much as five years in Federal prison.

I thought of mailing the fragments back to Local Board No. 125 but decided, in the end, to return them in person. I wrote a letter to Local Board No. 125 announcing and explaining my actions and mailed out a few hundred copies, together with a call to demonstrate on March 8 at my draft board, to CNVA supporters and to members of the press. This is a copy of the letter.

SAY *NO* TO THE SELECTIVE
SERVICE SYSTEM

R. F. D. #1   Box 197B
Voluntown, Connecticut
February 25, 1966

Local Board No. 125
Norfolk County
60 Adams Street
Milton, Mass. 02187

Gentleman:

On June 5, 1964, I was registered for the draft under the Selective Service System. Since that time, I have seen the government of the United States rain bombs upon the people of Vietnam. I have seen American soldiers burn the homes of Vietnamese peasants with cigarette lighters, with flame-throwers, and with napalm bombs. I have seen the government of the United States lie to the American people and invade the Dominican Republic. I have seen thousands of American troops enter battle against the people of the Dominican Republic on behalf of their oppressors. Moreover, I have repeatedly heard spokesmen of our government threaten to wage total war—nuclear war—against the people of the Soviet Union and China.

These actions of our government are crimes under the Constitution of the United States; they are crimes under the Charter of the United Nations, and under international law; and, most importantly, they are crimes against humanity. In attempting to act as the world's policeman, this country has made itself an outlaw.

I refuse to participate in these crimes, and I declare my intention to do all that I can, as one citizen, to stop my government from behaving in this manner.

Thus, I have chosen to discontinue my participation in the Selective Service System, an essential part of this nation's war machine. I have destroyed the draft card that I received in the mail today and have also destroyed the Registration Certificate and the Notice of Classification that you sent me previously. No longer will I cooperate with the Selective Service System or any other part of the military apparatus. I choose this course of action because I think it is the duty of every American to say "NO" to the government and to face jail rather than fight in a brutal war of aggression against the people of Vietnam, the Dominican Republic, or any other nation.

Sincerely,
David Allen Reed

On March 4, 1966, special agents of the F.B.I., Edgar C. Forest and Thomas M. Murphey, came to the Farm and spoke with me for three quarters of an hour. I showed them the fragments of the draft cards that I intended to return to Local Board No. 125.

On March 8, I returned the cards. About thirty people joined my vigil outside the draft board. The press was out in force; television cameras were even waiting behind the desk in the draft board office.

On March 25, I participated in civil disobedience at the Boston Army Base and was arrested with ten others. While being dragged off military property by two Defense Department Security Police officers, my friend David Benson tore up his draft card. Then, on March 29, two days before our scheduled appearance in South Boston District Court for the Army Base charges, Benson and I received new draft classification cards, both 1-A, in the mail. We decided to destroy these publicly on the steps of the courthouse before trial. Our friends John Phillips and David O'Brien decided to burn draft cards of their own at the same time.

We announced to the press that this would take place. To our surprise, when we showed up at the courthouse, a large crowd had gathered. We made our way up the steps through a throng of reporters, then turned to face the street and burned our draft cards. While we were burning the cards, I was shoved down the steps twice from behind. After the cards were burned, we began to answer reporters' questions. A state representative

David Reed

from South Boston interrupted with a loud denunciation of us. Immediately, the crowd surged around us and individuals began to shove and hit us. We made our way as best we could up the steps and into the courthouse, but two of my friends were pulled down and beaten by the mob before they could get in.

There was a brief pause during which all was calm, but then the mob poured through the front entrance to the courthouse. About fifty people approached us in the lobby, and some of them attacked a Harvard student who was one of those facing trial for civil disobedience. He was surrounded and beaten. Then some policemen appeared and cleared the crowd from the courthouse.

In the trial, I represented myself and openly admitted violating the law. I told the court that I felt it my duty to violate laws, if necessary, in an attempt to obstruct, nonviolently, the military acts of our government. The judge then spoke at length about his nephew in Vietnam, found me guilty, and sentenced me to pay a fine of $20.00. He changed this to twenty days in jail when I refused to pay the fine.

I was held in the Suffolk County Jail until April 19. During that time I received in the mail an order to report to Local Board No. 125 for a physical examination on April 25. On April 16, I learned from reading a newspaper that I had been indicted on the previous day by a Federal Grand Jury for destroying my draft card on March 31.

I did not report for the physical examination on April 25, and I received a delinquency notice in the mail on the next day. I did not report to the draft board as ordered in the delinquency notice. On May 6, I received a notice to report for induction into the armed forces of the United States. I was to fill out a questionnaire and report with it to Local Board No. 125 on May 25. After a few days, I wrote a letter to the draft board. . . . [The letter summarized, for the draft board, the reasons for Reed's refusal to report for induction. J. F.]

On May 23, I was arraigned before Judge Caffrey in the Federal District Court in Boston on the card-burning charge contained in the Grand Jury indictment. I represented myself in court and explained that I felt I had acted properly in destroying my draft card and did not wish to enter a formal plea. Judge Caffrey entered a plea of "not guilty" on my behalf, and I was released on $1000 bond, without surety, to await trial.

Two days later, I appeared outside Local Board No. 125 at the time when I was ordered to report for induction. I vigiled for an hour, accompanied by about twenty-five friends and supporters.

David Reed established his vigil on the day I have an appointment to visit the CNVA house at One Dewey Street in South Boston. After instructing me how to get there from the center of Boston, a friendly conductor adds, "Keep your hand on your wallet." With such cautionary advice I find my way to South Boston and to One Dewey Street.

Following the directions affixed to the door I enter what seems to be an empty house. I pass by what obviously serves as an office, through a living room in which the broken windows are partially covered by widely spaced slats, into what had served as a kitchen and small bathroom but which seems to have been visited by an only slightly domesticated hurricane. I return to the "office," glance at the clippings on the wall, note the posters of Pete Seeger and SNCC, the battered furniture and what appears to be the work of an arsonist with rather meager talents.

I am there only a few minutes when David Reed, a sturdy, good-looking young man of medium height, comes in from the street and asks if he can be of help. He is dressed in light levis, a dark shirt and has noticeably long, thick hair parted neatly and brushed to one side. As he talks to me he notes and obviously dismisses the charred evidence of an unsuccessful fire. (I learn later that the kids of the neighborhood are intrigued and puzzled by the members of the house and apparently attempt to push them into a display of violence.)

As I talk with Dave Reed I am unaware of the history he is to set down in the document I later receive. And I try to find out what were the choices, the path, that led him to his present position as a staff member for the Committee for Nonviolent Action. He speaks at first almost shyly in the presence of a tape recorder, but he has a good resonant voice which gains strength

David Reed

as he becomes increasingly articulate in expressing his convictions.

REED: SDS at Harvard disappointed me largely because of the nature of the organization—not its aims, but the fact that it did very little and the fact that the students were, as far as I'm concerned, quite conservative. They were interested in maintaining their privileged position in this society and weren't willing to take any radical action that might endanger it.

FINN: That's not true of SDS though across the country, is it?

REED: I think largely it is. I think the student organizations are made up of people who are protesting against various things but meanwhile are clinging quite tightly to their own middle-class positions and their own futures in the top positions in this society. And I think that radical opposition to aspects of this society and trying to attain a high position in this society are incompatible. I think that a lot of the students are just being bought off by the lures of a rich society.

FINN: I take it you think that many of the people who are in SDS are not going to maintain what they regard as radical positions?

REED: Well, the thing is that, for example, students will say "The draft is wrong," and "We shouldn't be fighting in Vietnam." And they'll say this to other young people who are eligible for the draft while they themselves are taking full advantage of their position as students. They're avoiding the draft, dodging the draft. And the main reason for this is their own intellectual ability and the money that their families have that allow them to stay in college. I don't think that they can really do this without being hypocritical to a large degree.

FINN: Well, is there any moral way for these people to resolve this problem, aside from getting out of school?

REED: Well, I think they can stay in school but I don't think they should be taking advantage of this privileged position to set themselves up above other people.

FINN: I take it that you found some of these organizations, and specifically SDS, less than perfect. You might not even say CNVA is perfect, but it's more appropriate to the needs of society and to your own thinking?

REED: Well, the position of CNVA is quite definite, whereas, for example, SDS is a New Left organization and it comes out in an opposition to the imperialistic wars that are being carried on by this country; but it doesn't have a very strong position on things like World War II or World War I. SDS is basically a *political* organization, whereas CNVA is a *pacifist* organization. They're really different in nature.

FINN: When, hopefully, the war in Vietnam comes to an end, war itself will still be a major problem that you would concern yourself with?

REED: Yes. I expect to see more Vietnams in Latin America and other parts of Asia. In opposing all of these wars in a pacifist organization we don't neglect the social aspects of the war: we point out the reasons why you have these revolutions, the reasons why the United States becomes involved in supporting oligarchies and aristocracies. We go into the same things that SDS goes into, but we also go farther by opposing the methods of violence altogether.

FINN: And methods of violence used by both sides?

REED: That's right. We condemn violence on the part of the Vietcong as well as we do on the part of the United States and the Saigon government. But we also will say that although war itself is unjust, there can be a just side in a war. In Vietnam the people who are fighting against us are justified in doing so. I wish that they used nonviolence as they did in the beginning before they were repressed by Diem's secret police, but I can understand their use of violence and I see the right of people to revolt, violently if necessary, against oppression.

FINN: Although you yourself would be opposed to this.

REED: Well, I would recommend as strongly as I could to these people that they should use nonviolence to obtain freedom.

FINN: One of the problems that I presume is posed to every pacifist is the idea of developing a politics of pacifism. Do you see a viable politics coming out of pacifist groups or movements or being developed by individual pacifists?

REED: Yes. I'm not sure if there's really much hope of this taking root at present. I have very little faith in conventional American politics. I've seen people like Fulbright get up and

David Reed

speak against the war quite strongly, condemn almost every aspect of the war, and then vote in favor of the appropriation so that they can maintain their Senate seats. What I'm interested in primarily as far as politics is concerned is the participatory democracy that's been advocated by SDS and Student Nonviolent Coordinating Committee; [the] actions by people themselves, direct action, going into the streets, nonviolently, to try to influence their own affairs. I think that the tendency to leave things up to City Hall will always lead to a form of tyranny, even if we call it democracy. As long as you go to the polls once a year and vote in a man who says he's going to do a good thing, you're just asking to have other things done instead.*

"Participatory democracy" is a phrase that is central to discussions of and by the New Left. Seemingly self-explanatory, a developed statement of what it means that invites general agreement is apparently difficult to formulate. As a result the phrase seems open to more definition than it has yet received. David Reed suggests what it means to him; he would find some supporters among the New Left, but also some critics.

As we talk it becomes increasingly clear that Reed sees as a possibility for modern society the vision conjured up by Orwell's *1984* and he wants to set other goals. What he sees as the path that will lead us to those goals is less clear. We turn to a discussion of one of the channels that are open for the direct expression of nonconformist opinion—the demonstration. Reed says that each demonstration has its own purpose. I ask him about the demonstration, which had attracted national attention, in which he and others had been beaten up by high school students. What had Reed and the others hoped to accomplish?

REED: I think most people just don't see any alternative to the draft. They grow up and they know that when they turn eighteen they have to register and soon after just go into the Army and they don't even know that the conscientious objector status is available to non-Quakers. And they don't even think of the possibility of just refusing. And what I'm trying to do—I don't know how many people are actually convinced—but at

* David Reed said this with a laugh and his comment recalls the story of the old man who, when asked what candidate he was going to vote for replied, "I *never* vote; it only encourages them." But Reed is serious.

least I'm trying to put this alternative before them. I didn't think I could maintain my own self-respect if I cooperated with the Selective Service system. But then I had the additional motive of trying to convince other people to look at it the same way, and that's why I did this publicly.

FINN: Do you have any idea of why people in the crowd *did* react violently? Do you speculate about their motivations?

REED: Well, I think largely their violent reaction is caused by fear and fear of facing up to what we were saying. Rather than listen to us they wanted to just shut us up by striking at us. I'm not sure exactly how these thoughts hit them. But they were shouting things such as "Kill them," "Destroy them," as they attacked us.

FINN: How would you judge the effectiveness of that demonstration? Did it accomplish what you intended?

REED: Well, what I intended was to place the alternative to obeying the military service laws before as many people as possible, and I think that *was* done. I would much rather have avoided the violence that took place, however. But I think that this violence did cause a lot of people to think about things they wouldn't have thought about otherwise.

FINN: One of the references that I ran across commented that you and the people with you—Vietniks, as you were referred to—picked the wrong place to stage a protest, that in South Boston the inhabitants, to quote *Time*, "take most unkindly to unpatriotic displays." Do you have any reaction to comments like that?

REED: Well, I think it's a mistaken notion to believe that patriotism consists of blind obedience to the government. I think that patriotism is trying to save the better values of the country rather than just blindly obeying the government. I don't think I would call a German unpatriotic because he was opposed to Hitler and disobeyed the orders of that government.

FINN: What kind of reaction did you get from your own family and friends as you were developing your own ideas about nonviolence, and therefore necessarily placing yourself in a minority group?

David Reed

REED: Well, my friends and family have generally disagreed with the views that I've held, but they've always acknowledged my right to hold these views. It's only since I began acting unconventionally and violating laws that people have really started condemning what I've been doing. Many of my friends and family have been saying that I'm throwing my life away by leaving college and giving up the National Merit Scholarship; they say that I'm destroying my future. But they don't seem to understand that it's not material things that are important to me, not the career as a government major at Harvard, but certain values that are more important to me than that. I've had difficulty convincing them that I'm not actually throwing my life away.

FINN: Dave, I wonder if you'd tell me a little bit more about the background out of which you developed your ideas of nonviolence. Was there anything specifically religious involved? Did you get these from *a* church or from Christianity or anything you'd recognize as religious?

REED: Well, I was brought up in the Unitarian Church and part of the educational program I attended involved discussion of religious principles of many different religions, so I encountered the ideas of the Quaker Church, the Buddhists, the Catholics, and I did some reading of the Bible. Although I rejected the theological aspects of the Bible and Christianity, I found that I accepted basically the moral teachings. The reasons for this I suppose are many. I'm not sure if I could actually analyze it myself.

FINN: What is your family's attitude toward the war in Vietnam? Do they tend to support the government?

REED: No. Some members of my family agree with my position that this particular war is wrong and that most wars are wrong. Other members of my family feel that this war is correct and that it should be pursued more vigorously. However all of them are agreed in opposing the actions that I've taken in the past few months.

FINN: Would you regard yourself—I mean the CNVA— as part of what people call the "peace movement" today?

REED: Yes, definitely, but I think the nonviolent section of the peace movement is a small minority even among the peace

movement. Most of the people connected with the peace movement are opposed to this particular war and don't concern
themselves too much with other issues.

FINN: Given the ideas you are now developing, do you think
that you can work in a political way with the people in the other
groups who do not accept pacifism?

REED: Well, an awful lot of our activities *are* combined. We
have various area committees composed of several different
organizations. There are many things that I cannot go along
with. The other groups will often ask for police protection, depend upon certain methods of violence that I don't think I should
depend upon. Some of the other groups are interested in conventional politics, which I'm not interested in at all. SANE has
recently had its Voters Pledge campaign, which I don't think
worth working on. I think that the so-called peace candidates are
really a farce. I'm interested primarily in nonviolent, direct-
action programs and direct educational programs.

FINN: How much support do you think the direct-action,
nonviolent groups have today?

REED: Well, support in numbers is small compared to the
other elements in the peace movement. I think it's growing, and
I think it's. . . . Well they'll dispute it. The nonviolent peace
movement is the most active and most prominent as far as the
public is concerned. They tend now to call almost all peace
demonstrators pacifists because [laugh] they've seen us in
headlines. I think that we should put our trust in civil disobedience and direct action on the individual level. The Committee
for Nonviolent Action is a radical pacifist organization. Just
about everyone in the Committee who's male has served a Federal prison term for draft refusal and even the most respected
members—the eighty-one-year-old A. J. Muste—is constantly
being arrested.

FINN: How do you get enough money to put out the pamphlets and do the other things that you do?

REED: Some of us have part-time jobs, but we get most of
our financial resources from contributors. There are several
hundred people who contribute anything between a dollar and
a thousand dollars. And of course since we live in voluntary
poverty we devote almost all of the money to the program rather

David Reed

than to living expenses. Staff members like myself get room and board plus a dollar a week, and this board is as inexpensive as possible. We buy surplus food and big sacks of powdered milk, for example.

FINN: Are you finding you get more or less support for your activities as the war in Vietnam goes on?

REED: I find that we're getting a lot of more active support and at the same time we're getting more active and determined opposition. I think what we see is a polarization of opinion. It hasn't diminished our support at all, but it's increased the opposition.

FINN: The incident that we mentioned was not the first time you were attacked when you were in a demonstration?

REED: No. In fact recently almost every demonstration is attacked violently. We had a meeting at the Arlington Street Church in Boston on March 26 which was attacked by a mob of several hundred people who broke through police lines and attacked the church.

FINN: Are these just ordinary citizens who do this?

REED: Well, they seemed to be ordinary citizens. They just formed a crowd across the street from the church and they threw hundreds of eggs at the church. The front of the church was completely covered with eggs. And at a few points they surged forward and broke through the line of about fifty Boston policemen. Eventually the mounted police in Boston were called out to disperse the mob. On this occasion I was part of the nonviolent defense squad that put itself in between the attackers and the church.

FINN: Who gets chosen, or volunteers, to be part of this squad? I presume it can put you in pretty uncomfortable positions at times.

REED: Well, it's people who have had some experience in nonviolence, and of course some people get their experience by being in the defense squad [laugh]—people who are willing to be slugged on the head and promise not to strike back.

FINN: And this, I presume, has been your experience.

REED: Yes, I've encountered violence both from counter-demonstrators and from police on several different occasions.

FINN: Why do the police have to act violently, or feel that they have to?

REED: Well, recently when I was arrested in Durham, New Hampshire for marching in violation of parade permit, I felt that my rights were being violated so I didn't cooperate with the police at all. They had to carry me around. And they forcibly fingerprinted me. These were the New Hampshire State Police, and I was ordered to sign the fingerprint cards and I refused to sign my name to them. And when this took place one of the state troopers put me in a wristlock and applied pressure on my wrist and ordered me to sign the paper, and another one pulled my hair, and they tried to get me to sign the paper by violence. And on another occasion in Washington, D.C., several demonstrators and myself were in a paddy wagon after being arrested outside the White House for blocking the gates, and once the police got us inside the basement parking area they inserted some gas pellets in the vents of the paddy wagon and kept us locked up for a half an hour in a condition where it was very difficult to breathe.

FINN: What kind of gas? Like tear gas?

REED: Well, the police called it tear gas. Some of the people inside claimed that they thought it smelled like ammonia. I'm not sure exactly what it was, but it did produce tears and it made it very difficult to breathe.

FINN: So this is the kind of thing that you can expect with some regularity if you're going to be part of demonstrations, I suppose?

REED: Most police forces that I've encountered have been gentle and have behaved without any unnecessary violence, but occasionally we run into violence from the police. More and more we're running into violence from opposition. People are showing up at almost every demonstration now and pelting us with eggs and rocks and fists.

FINN: Do you take this as a sign of success for your efforts, that you're getting this attention?

REED: No, I think this is unrelated to our efforts. I think it's a product of the war hysteria. Fulbright said "war breeds war fever," and that's what's happening.

David Reed

FINN: Well, how would you judge your own effectiveness in trying to combat this war fever? If the war fever is growing do you get discouraged at the apparent ineffectiveness of your actions?

REED: Well, no. I don't think it really has much to do with the effectiveness of what we're trying to do. It's basically a small group of people who resort to this kind of mob violence.

FINN: I presume under such conditions that your life isn't always an easy one, and even though you participate in these demonstrations you don't look forward to the possibility of getting beat up.

REED: No, not at all. In fact, I'm usually petrified when I encounter a hostile mob like that, but this is the situation that we're running into. We often find that we're being watched by the FBI or by hecklers, or someone, during a large part of our time, even when we're not involved in peace activities.

I left Dave Reed talking with the other staff members about the conditions of prison life, which they knew they might have to face, but determined to carry on in their activities until that time. That evening the front page of the *Boston Traveler* combined in one news story three different threads of the Vietnam war. Over three separate photographs was the caption: "He Died . . . They'll Serve . . . He Refuses." The first picture was that of the funeral of a Roxbury soldier killed in Vietnam; the second, that of a group of new inductees; the third, that of David Reed, described as a "self-proclaimed pacifist."

In addition, the *Boston Traveler* carried other stories concerned with domestic reactions to Vietnam. There was to be a one-hundred-mile Teamster march to support President Johnson and, in the words of the ex-Marine who was to lead it, "to protest against the dope fiends, beatniks and Communists who are trying to destroy our country with their actions." General Maxwell Taylor explained in an article that the issues were "simple, clear and readily explained." He ended his article by saying that, "We are engaged in a test of our national character. If we fail this test, we will soon face harder ones with greater [sic] diminished chance of success and at greatly increased cost." That day psychiatrists had testified before Congressional committees.

According to Jerome Frank, Vietnam had turned into an ideological war and was losing whatever basis of rationality it had.

That evening I walked in Park Square reviewing my own day's activities. It was a pleasant evening, the air was soft and warm and filled with the fragrance of the flower gardens, the fresh cut grass and all the sappy bite of spring. It was an evening to make one feel keenly that it was good to be alive and free. And I thought then—as I do now—that if David Reed and others like him are imprisoned for years because of their opposition to the war in Vietnam, they are as surely casualties as those who are struck down in combat.

On November 21, 1966 David Reed was sentenced by the U.S. District Court in Boston to three years' imprisonment, which he is currently serving in the Federal Reformatory of Petersburg, Virginia.

POLITICAL

JACK NEWFIELD

In addition to those whose protest against the war in Vietnam is informed by a religious/pacifist tradition are those whose protest is primarily political (although parapolitical might better describe some of their activities). And in the political spectrum these protesters are found principally on the Left. The story of the radical movement in this country during the forties and fifties is not, on the whole, inspiriting, probably least of all for the radical. The thirties, which were years of high accomplishment and higher hope, remained for long the principal point of reference, for it was in that decade that major social issues were defined and the major organizations fought out their theoretical and practical positions. But the experiences of the thirties gradually became dimmer in the succeeding decades and their relevance to the immediate scene less apparent. The distinctions between the various Communist-front groups and the Trotskyite, socialist and other anti-Stalinist organizations now have, for most younger radicals, all the flavor of dry-as-dust history.

The strong civil rights movement gave more life and vitality to the Left than it had felt for some years. As Bayard Rustin wrote, the movement seemed to be evolving into a "full-fledged social movement." And many people thought that the U.S. and Russia had reached, after the Cuban missile crisis, a stage of mutual understanding that would allow each to attend to internal domestic problems. While some intellectuals, themselves ex-Socialists, were remarking at length on "the end of ideology," members of the Left thought they saw new levers for policy and action. And although the generation of radicals that should have been produced in the fifties seemed to be missing, it also seemed as if the gap between the older and the younger radicals would be bridged in the "movement" of the sixties.

But with the sixties a new and unexpected phenomenon appeared: there *was* a new surge of interest in radical thought and action among the young—but high on their list of targets was the tradition of the Left in this country, particularly as it had been maintained by the anti-Communist, democratic Socialists. This is the phenomenon that was soon known as the New Left.

The New Left is too ill-defined in actuality to be well-defined in description. After acknowledging the real difficulties of attempting such a description and making sound disclaimers that his comments did not apply to all young radicals, nor all of his comments to any of them, Irving Howe, one of the members of the suddenly "Old" Left, elaborated in an extended article some of the characteristics of the New Leftists: They manifest, he says,

"An extreme, sometimes unwarranted, hostility toward liberalism.

"An impatience with the problems that concerned an older generation of radicals.

"A vicarious indulgence in violence, often merely theoretic and thereby all the more irresponsible.

"An unconsidered enmity toward something vaguely called the Establishment.

"An equally unreflective belief in 'the decline of the West.'

"A crude, unqualified anti-Americanism, drawing from every possible source. . . .

"An increasing identification with that sector of the 'third world' in which 'radical' nationalism and Communist authoritarianism merge." *

* *Dissent,* Summer, 1965. Since this article there have appeared several books on the New Left. The *New Radicals,* edited by Paul Jacobs and Saul Landau, is a comment with documents. *The New Student Left,* edited by Mitchell Cohen and Dennis Hale, two members of the student Left, limits itself to major issues of domestic policy. David Esmond's article on "The New Left and Foreign Policy" appears in the November, 1965 issue of *The Activist,* a "student journal of politics and opinion."

This is the expression of a view that finds much support, although different points would be emphasized by different critics. And some social critics, like Jack Newfield, express quite different judgments.

Jack Newfield is twenty-eight. After being graduated from Hunter College in 1961, he spent a year in which his time was divided among a number of diverse activities which included working with SDS, with Michael Harrington and with Mark Lane. After some months as a reporter on the New York *Post,* he became in 1964 assistant editor of the *Village Voice.* His informed and perceptive political reports and a strong individual style have earned for him a growing reputation.

The highly contemporary character of his mind and of his interests is indicated by his comment that the major influences on his thinking have been Albert Camus and Michael Harrington; on his writing, Norman Mailer and Murray Kempton; and that listening to the records of Bob Dylan is one of his few leisure activities.

He has written for the *Nation* and *Commonweal,* for *Monocle* and *Playboy.* He has just completed *A Prophetic Minority,* his description and analysis of the new radicals, and is anticipating the publication date. Since one of the problems that invades every discussion of the New Left is one of identification, I ask Newfield who and what he would shelter under the term.

NEWFIELD: I think it would represent a generational cluster of organizations and movements. I would say the most visible of these are SNCC, SDS, the Free Speech Movement, Vietnam Day Committee, the Southern Student Organizing Committee, organizationally. Then there are publications like *Liberation* and *Studies on the Left*; and there are the new institutions like the Mississippi Freedom Democratic Party, the Institute for Policy Studies; and then a group of people—for example, Tom Hayden, Bob Harris, Staughton Lynd; and then a cluster of stray indigenous insurgent movements like the Grape Strike, the Lowndes County Freedom Organization, the Bob Scheer campaign for Congress. All exist under the umbrella of the New Left in a very chaotic, disorganized fashion.

FINN: But these people and organizations would probably recognize each other as belonging to the same complex?

NEWFIELD: Yes, they share a common ethos and a common style rather than a program or ideology.

FINN: You mentioned the term "generational," and "Don't trust anyone over thirty," is a New Left statement, but obviously to take one example, *Liberation* doesn't represent a new generation.

NEWFIELD: Yes. A. J. Muste is like eighty-two, I think. He's in many ways the dean of the New Left. The New Left is a state of mind rather than anything to do with calendars. I think probably what defines the New Left is its half-assimilated pot of a variety of political and philosophical traditions which have never been mixed up together before. I think this would include pacifism, anarchism, transcendentalism, socialism, black nationalism and romanticism. And these are taken as stances toward the world rather than coherent programs or ideologies.

FINN: Do these various aspects come from traditions with which these people would identify?

NEWFIELD: I think they would identify with the Wobblies, for example. And the American Revolution of Paine and Jefferson. Or with the Whitman-Emerson transcendentalists. And some would even identify with certain mystical literary traditions, but that would be a very sophisticated fringe. I think they *would* feel close to Bill Haywood or John Brown, rather than Marx, Lenin or Trotsky. And Camus, Paul Goodman. The more contemporary kind of people they would identify with. Mills, Fanon, Dylan, Castro.

FINN: Well, the debate between Camus and Sartre divides some of the people in this group, doesn't it?

NEWFIELD: I think they're not that aware of it. I think there is, among the negative things about the New Left, a kind of anti-intellectualism which is almost anti-rationalism. They feel an emotional empathy with Camus, but haven't read his debates with Sartre.

FINN: Yet, you brought together a number of things which suggest, initially, a degree of intellectual awareness here.

NEWFIELD: There's an awareness, but I think there's also a hostility to scholarship and to serious reading in these traditions, which is mitigated against by the extreme, almost manic activism. And they may be aware of Thoreau's essay on Civil Disobedience and maybe they've read something Kropotkin wrote, but not much more than that. Except for the leaders—who are brilliant—I don't think many of the kids have read Weber or Stuart Mill or Tocqueville.

FINN: You're a charter member of SDS, so you've been able to follow it from its beginnings, not too long ago. Has SDS undergone a kind of change which would allow you to infer or at least speculate about the future of SDS and other organizations in the New Left?

NEWFIELD: I think I could try. I think each organization has its own fate and its own sort of trajectory across the horizon of history. Whereas I think SNCC has peaked and is now sort of flaming out, I think SDS has not yet peaked. And again, I would emphasize, as one of the strongest trends in the movement, the growth of local movements unaffiliated with national organizations—movements like the Mississippi Freedom Democratic Party, the Black Panther Party in Lowndes County, the Grape Strike, the anti-draft movement, political campaigns like the Scheer campaign and other peace candidacies. I think this is the strongest trend, the grass-roots, decentralized local movements around the country.

FINN: So any kind of success or failure these local operations would have would somehow influence the entire movement.

NEWFIELD: Right. I think one of the disturbing qualities of the New Left has been a faddish orientation which allows it to leap from one issue to another—beginning in '62 being very much involved in the peace question and then losing interest in that quickly after the [H. Stuart] Hughes' campaign failed and the peace movement was so impotent at the Bay of Pigs; then getting very much involved in the poverty question in '63 when Harrington's book [*The Other America*] came out and Rustin spoke to the SNCC convention about organizing poor whites. And they were very much involved in problems of poverty, but then Mississippi came along and they all went back to the South. Then there was the Berkeley outburst and university reform became the big issue. Then Vietnam came up and there was a massive switch back to the peace question. And I think this kind of helter skelter, fireman kind of action—rushing to wherever the new fire is and quickly forgetting about the last one—characterizes the movement.

FINN: So you're suggesting a lot of activity without much direction?

NEWFIELD: Yes. The New Left has no underlying ideology or philosophy.

FINN: You didn't answer specifically the question about SDS.

NEWFIELD: I would think SDS has the most hopeful future, partly because it is basically a white, middle-class organization and doesn't suffer the physical and psychic damage that SNCC does in the South—functioning in crisis and tension all the time. And the SNCC guys really pay the mental and psychic price, and a lot of them are quite crazy. Whereas I think SDS is in a way buffered and protected by being largely in the campuses, and having a lot of stable graduate students and young professors in the organization.

FINN: You said that SNCC was in a sense flaming out. I wonder if you would elaborate. It's clearly getting as much attention as it ever did. And the effects are difficult presently to assess.

NEWFIELD: Well, SNCC keeps changing. It's like the writings of Norman Mailer or the songs of Bob Dylan, or Picasso's painting; SNCC keeps going through different periods very quickly. It began in '60 with the sit-in movement being religious and quite middle-class; the kids who would sit-in would wear suits and ties and they would read the Bible or some philosophy textbook when they were sitting in. And then in '61 and '62 they went off the campuses into the communities, and went into a populist period. And then by '64, when they had been battered and bruised very badly and when Bob Moses was the major intellectual force in SNCC, it went into a kind of existentialist period; they were very pessimistic and very bruised, and they felt the act of rebellion itself was the only valid thing they could do. And now they're into a fourth period which is openly revolutionary and very much concerned with the problem of négritude, and I think this comes from a tremendous pessimism about the whole civil rights movement being in decline since Selma. And since all the strategies seem equally doomed, SNCC has now chosen the most revolutionary path.

Jack Newfield

FINN: Well these changes *could* be interpreted as a sign of strength, in the sense that they are changing responses to changing judgments about the situation.

NEWFIELD: And that's how SNCC perceives the situation: it's that they've tried integration and it doesn't work, and now they're mostly concerned with the black psyche.

FINN: But your own implied judgment is that this is not a sign of strength.

NEWFIELD: I think on some things SNCC is really probably right: on the emphasis on dignity, and black self-image, and on black psyche I think they're right, and even on the question of self-defense I'm persuaded that they're right. But I think that the idea of going it alone and of forming alliances primarily with the Muslims and politicians like Adam Clayton Powell are tactical errors which will isolate SNCC. And I think SNCC has a very simple-minded view of the "third world" and see themselves now as part of the "third world," the South as sort of a colonial enclave within the United States and themselves as anti-colonial revolutionaries.

FINN: So they find it very easy to identify with those people who are oppressed by whatever major powers, or . . .

NEWFIELD: I think SNCC primarily identifies with those oppressed by what they see as Western imperialism. I think that they would make a mistake in trying to use people like Nkrumah or Nasser or Sukarno as any kind of model. Castroism is very different from Arab nationalism or Pan Africanism. But Stokely [Carmichael] sounded frighteningly like Nasser when I heard him in Jackson at the end of the Meredith march. You just had to close your eyes and you got "Black Power, Black Power." Said with Carmichael's accent, it's frightening.

FINN: You suggested, however, in one of the things you wrote about that speech, that he didn't get the response from the crowd that he really wanted and that King came through with greater strength.

NEWFIELD: Right. I think King can strike the deepest chord in the Southern Negro because he is a Southern Negro; the legend of King has grown up since Montgomery.

FINN: Do you think there is a proper role for SNCC and CORE and other civil rights organizations in foreign policy issues? Should they, if they are to be as effective as they can, make statements about United States foreign policy?

NEWFIELD: For SNCC and the other groups like it, one of the basic criticisms of big politics in America is the divorcement of ethics from politics. And they will not compromise about the war in Vietnam; they're going to say that even though they know it's going to cost them financial support and sympathy in the liberal community. But when SNCC and CORE first came out against the war in Vietnam they were pacifist organizations. I think it's very logical for a pacifist organization like the SCLC to come out against the war in Vietnam. But since both of them have abandoned nonviolence as a principle, I think it opens up a much more tangled box about the "third world" and about the three power blocs. And I think both SNCC and CORE need more sophistication in dealing with the "third world," which is not black and white—and is not even an entity—but a whole lot of things which they don't distinguish. It's just oppressed non-white people to them.

FINN: But they can point to some of the effects of discrimination in this country when they point out the greater percentage of Negroes who are in the Armed Forces in Vietnam and within the Armed Forces the higher percentage of Negro casualties.*

NEWFIELD: And also our national budget, X number of dollars which should be funding antipoverty and welfare programs are going to subsidize the Vietnam war.

FINN: And this is *an* approach for these organizations.

NEWFIELD: It's a wholistic approach of revolutionaries who are wholly alienated from the mainstream of society, even from the liberal Left.

FINN: Would that apply to most of the New Left, the statement you just made?

NEWFIELD: I think it applies to SNCC and to a good segment of SDS, and to most of the indigenous movements. I think the New Left is largely trying to polarize the country between the

* According to the Department of Defense, Negroes constituted 9.1 percent of the total active Armed Forces of the United States as of December 31, 1966. In the period from 1961 to 1967, 16 percent of the American forces killed in Vietnam were Negroes.

Jack Newfield

Movement and the Great Society, and making liberals and moderate Socialists choose. They can do this because I think they're not concerned with immediate goals. They have a utopian and visionary view of another society, of a counter-society.

FINN: And it's clear that the word compromise is, in their terms, a very bad word indeed. And that's why they criticize people in the Old Left who see some need for compromise and some need to work with a power base in this country, which is composed of liberals, trade union leaders, religious leaders and so on.

NEWFIELD: Well, I think that there are some people within the New Left who accept the notion of a coalition. But I think they would argue that their own base has to be stronger before they enter a coalition, so they won't be absorbed. And they would argue about who should be in that coalition. There is a group now, the National Conference on Politics, sort of put together by Arthur Waskow, which Stokeley belongs to. And I think that coalition includes the New Left, Reformed Democratic politicians, the churches, but consciously excludes the labor movement. The New Left says the labor movement is hopeless; it cannot be reformed. It is absolutely part of the power elite now, as much as the arms industry. And they can list all of the crimes of the labor movement, from not endorsing the [April] March on Washington after Cardinal Spellman endorsed it, to supporting Balaguer in the Dominican Republic against Juan Bosch. And on that score they're probably right. The Old Left has a hangover of Marxism and believes the working class is the agency of history and the labor unions are the expression of the working class; they have a somewhat mechanical faith in the labor movement. The New Left, however, which derives a lot of ideas from Mills' criticism of the labor movement, writes the labor movement off *ab*solutely as an agency of progressive change.

FINN: A number of the people in the New Left not only refuse to identify themselves as anti-communists; they say they are a-communist. But they make the charge that older leftists —to put this in generational terms—are obsessed with this, and therefore misinterpret present-day history.

NEWFIELD: And I think the criticism, especially that made by Howe and Rustin, has been misstated. I mean it's basically been in terms of communism and infiltration and domination, whereas I think the real flaws of the New Left are on the questions of irrationality and romanticism, psychological things rather than the question of communism. To phrase it in the context of communism or fuzziness about authoritarianism is wrong, and just enrages the New Left.

FINN: Do these attitudes strongly influence the judgments that the New Left makes about what would be a desirable outcome in Vietnam?

NEWFIELD: I'd say they don't have a horror of communism. They haven't lived through the Stalinization of Eastern Europe or even Hungary, and it is not a tragic option that Vietnam fall under the leadership of Ho Chi Minh, and I think it would really be a tragedy to Irving Howe if Vietnam went communist, even in an election. I think the New Left sees communism as something they're not attracted to but something they're not psychologically troubled about; they can treat the Communist Party the way they treat the Republican Party. And they just say that Communists are bureaucratic, they're elitist, they're puritanical, they're square, they're not democratic, but it's not a deep, traumatic emotional question. The Social Democrats have a long tradition that's bitterly antagonistic to and entangled with the Stalinist tradition. Social Democrats can still tell you the names of the Social Democrats Stalin shot in Poland in 1939.

FINN: The Social Democrats, along with many other people, would also point out the very real possibility, maybe likelihood, of great purges if there were a Communist takeover in South Vietnam. Which these people don't regard as much of a likelihood.

NEWFIELD: That's true. I think the kids have seen Communists only as victims and never as executioners. They've seen them denied burial in Arlington Cemetery, they've seen them banned from the campuses, they've seen them pilloried before the HUAC, they've seen them driven from jobs. They haven't seen the Russian tanks go into Budapest, they haven't seen the Stalin purges, and since 1960 an almost-legitimate case can be made that the Soviet Union has been more peace-loving than the United States. And these kids, if they don't read and are anti-

Jack Newfield

historical and have no scholarship, judge everything starting from the Bay of Pigs.

FINN: A short history.

NEWFIELD: That's right. And in terms of the Bay of Pigs or the Dominican Republic or Vietnam, I think America does have a shoddier record in foreign affairs than does the Soviet Union.

FINN: And they can read statements by J. Edgar Hoover, suggesting that Communists are going to infiltrate civil rights movements, New Left organizations, with the suggestion not only that they're going to be there but they're going to direct and control.

NEWFIELD: And the kids can't conceive of a progressive anti-communism. I mean the only anti-Communists they know are the people who red-baited the Free Speech Movement or SNCC or SDS, and unfortunately they don't understand that there are progressive anti-Communists. And equally unfortunately I think there are members of the Old Left who have not been as outspoken as they should be, on issues like Vietnam or poverty. Part of the problem is that the sharpest, most strident critics of the New Left *have* been members of the Old Left: people like John Roche and Sidney Hook and Howe. And in the vote at Berkeley, when it came to support the FSM or not, the sharpest critics of the FSM were Old Left professors at Berkeley, like Lipset and Feuer, and not the run-of-the-mill professor, you know.

FINN: Do you see any possibilities for some kind of reconciliation between Old and New Left? Are you willing to look say five years into the future?

NEWFIELD: Well, I think there are three problems which the New Left must deal with, two of which are beyond their control. One is the war in Vietnam. I think if the war goes on and it continues to escalate and the 400,000 troops in Vietnam now grows to 550,000 by next year, I think it's going to begin to close the country down the way France closed down during the Algerian war. I think what Senator Fulbright called a war psychology will develop in the country, and there will be a general clamping down on dissent. I think the New Left would be a victim of that, a victim of events in Hanoi and Washington, in Moscow and Peking, events beyond their control.

FINN: You mean their dissent would really be washed out, or damped down to such a degree that . . .

NEWFIELD: I think there would be a kind of a return of McCarthyism in this country. I think there are already certain signs of this: the Julian Bond thing in Atlanta, where Julian's seat was denied him; the Justice Department investigating SDS; and that shooting of the Trotskyite in Detroit a few months ago; the recurrent violence in the South. I think there's always been a nascent anti-intellectualism in the country which can become a new McCarthyism if the war endures and the country becomes frustrated.

The second problem which the New Left faces is its own internal weaknesses: a romanticism, anti-intellectualism, unfocused freneticism, a desperate militancy which is sometimes unthinking. And a third problem is the culture's genius in absorbing every dissenter and turning him into a vaudevillian or a celebrity so you end up like Mailer or LeRoi Jones. To be a radical now is like trying to punch your way out of a marshmallow cage. But I think those are the three problems facing the movement. But I think that the things that have caused the New Left, the problems in this society—racism, poverty, militarism, moral decay, bureaucracy—as long as they endure then the New Left will endure in very chaotic, decentralized forms.

FINN: One of the elements that's very strong in the whole movement we were talking about is the issue of peace, but you've also pointed up that it tends to have a crisis quality. Do you think that there will be some concentrated or continuing discussion of peace as an issue if the New Left develops as you suggested it might? Will there be something that might even be called a continuing peace movement?

NEWFIELD: I would hope so, but I doubt it. I think the New Left continues to counter-punch the world; the Bay of Pigs excited them, the missile crisis excited them, and now Vietnam is exciting them. But I think the New Left is not, at its soul, internationalist yet. I think it is still basically energized by the domestic questions of poverty, segregation and bureaucracy.

FINN: So their participation—calling for Marches on Washington, protesting the war in Vietnam—is primarily a political protest addressed to domestic affairs?

Jack Newfield

NEWFIELD: I think it's deeper. I think it's fueled by hysteria and desperation. I mean they're just incredibly disgusted in their bowels by what's going on in Vietnam and want to stop the war —without any sophisticated political program or without much thought. They're just ethically disgusted.

JULIAN BOND

When I first spoke with Julian Bond he was public information director of the Student Nonviolent Coordinating Committee. I had wanted particularly to ask him about changes in SNCC's attitude toward nonviolence since the group was formed in 1960 and about the SNCC statement opposing the war in Vietnam.* (Because of his support of that statement the Georgia House of Representatives had refused to seat Bond, although he had won the seat by polling 82 percent of the votes cast in Atlanta's 136th district.)

Since its inception SNCC had adhered to principles of non-violence, although the "Snick kids," operating on the cutting edge of the civil rights movement, had been harassed, beaten,

---

* The SNCC statement opposing the war in Vietnam said in part: "We believe the United States government has been deceptive in its claims of concern for the freedom of the Vietnamese people, just as the government has been deceptive in claiming concern for the freedom of colored people in such other countries as the Dominican Republic, the Congo, South Africa, Rhodesia, and in the United States itself. . . .

"We have been involved in the black people's struggle for liberation and self-determination in this country for the past five years. Our work, particularly in the South, has taught us that the United States government has never guaranteed the freedom of oppressed citizens, and is not yet truly determined to end the rule of terror and oppression within its own borders. . . .

"We are in sympathy with, and support, the men in this country who are unwilling to respond to a military draft which would compel them to contribute their lives to United States aggression in Vietnam in the name of 'freedom' we find so false in this country. . . .

"We take note of the fact that 16 percent of the draftees from this country are Negroes called on to stifle the liberation of Vietnam, to preserve a 'democracy' which does not exist for them at home. We ask, where is the draft for the freedom fight in the United States?"

Julian Bond

bloodied and killed. But about a month before I visited their new headquarters on Nelson Street in Atlanta, SNCC had held a staff retreat near Nashville which was to change the character and tone, the leadership and strategy of the organization. Stokely Carmichael replaced John Lewis as chairman and "black power" replaced the concept of the "beloved community" of blacks and whites. And once again the meaning and value of nonviolence for the movement was thrown up for analysis and evaluation.

It was not, of course, only people in SNCC who questioned the continuing relevance of nonviolence. Shortly before my visit with Bond, James Meredith, on his march through Mississippi, had been shot down from ambush. For Meredith, and for others, this could only strengthen what he had said shortly before he was shot: "The time has come when Negroes have got to work for their rights and perhaps even fight for their rights. Nonviolence is not in the American tradition. The American tradition is to get out and work for what you want, to fight for what you want." *

Nothing I had heard about SNCC quite prepared me for what I experienced as I waited in their offices for Julian Bond to arrive. Their lack of organization was fabled, and many people have said that they were frequently indifferent and sometimes hostile to Northern reporters and observers. But I found the entire operation not only more extensive than I had expected, but neat and well ordered. And far from being hostile the people I talked with were abundantly helpful and pleasant.

I have seen pictures of Bond and know he is young. (He was

---

* I was interested in reading, some weeks later, a comment which related "black power" and nonviolence. In a letter to the *New York Times,* Monroe H. Freedman, Professor of Law at George Washington University, wrote: " 'Black power' and rejection of nonviolence are essentially distinct issues. Yet both involve the question of whether American Negroes are prepared to accept American political and moral ideology. Black power is nothing more or less than bloc power. . . .

"The doctrine of nonviolence in the face of physical attack is foreign to American law and morality. Its rejection by Negroes is long overdue. The vast majority of Americans have consistently recognized the moral imperative of self-defense, both in international relations and in private action." The *New York Times,* July 24, 1966.

In the summer of 1967, H. Rap Brown, who replaced Carmichael as chairman of SNCC, said, "Violence is as American as cherry pie."

born in January 1940.) But nevertheless I am suprised, when he comes in, to see just how boyish and attractive a person he is. By himself he should be enough to shatter any stereotype of the SNCC worker. None of the many struggles in which he has been involved have left any external marks. He looks much more like the journalist and spare-time poet he says he would like to be. It was easier to think of him tossing off the two lines,

> Look at that gal shake that thing
> We can't all be Martin Luther King

than it was to see him as the organizer and leader of militant attacks on segregation, or as the man who left school a semester away from graduation in order to work with SNCC or as the man who had been elected to, and rejected by, the Georgia Legislature—but he was all of these things.

I recall the statement of purpose SNCC initially adopted, which said in part: "We affirm the philosophical or religious ideal of nonviolence as the foundation of our purpose, the presupposition of our faith, and the manner of our action. Nonviolence as it grows from Judaic-Christian traditions seeks a social order of justice permeated by love. . . ." I ask Bond if he subscribed to this credo when it was adopted.

BOND: Yes. I was at the meeting in Raleigh on Easter weekend in 1960 where that statement was adopted, and it was adopted, as I recall, without much discussion. The membership of SNCC has changed a great deal since then. I should say we're not a membership organization, and when I speak of membership I mean basically the employees. In 1960 we had no employees; we were a coordinating agency; we were sort of a tremendously large board of directors and nothing more.

And almost all of the people who were involved in what was then simply a student movement were southern Negro college students who came, most of them, from lower-middle-class homes, from religious backgrounds. There were a great many divinity students or pre-divinity students, a great many young ministers, a great many young men who were seniors in college who had already been ordained. And there was a great deal of reliance then, I think, on Dr. King and his ideas about nonviolence. Not much of Gandhi or Thoreau or anything else.

Julian Bond

Those people, including myself, drew our ideas about non-violence from Dr. King.

Now, six years later, that make-up has changed and the majority of the people who are in the civil rights movement—in SNCC at any rate—are not the same sorts of people. They're urban, northern Negroes, a few southern Negroes, and northern white people for whom nonviolence is largely a technique and not a way of life—as I think it was for most of the people who agreed with our original statement. It's not that people's ideas have changed, but that the membership of this body has changed. Those people who believe in nonviolence as a philosophy were in the majority in 1960, and they're in a minority now—not because they have dropped away but because newer people have come into the movement, people who didn't come out of the same sort of background. The whole idea of nonviolence as a force to do *any*thing was new to most people in the civil rights movement; they'd heard about the Montgomery bus boycott in '56 and they had an idea that nonviolence meant if someone hit you and you were on a picket line that you didn't hit back. And there were only a few people, I think, who knew anything at all, however limited, *more* than just that. And I was probably one of those few. I happened to go to a Quaker school where I first heard about nonviolence. I must say I never thought about applying it to anything. It was just a concept; this was the way some people believe in doing things, and other people believe in doing things in other ways. It had no reality to me then, but I had *heard* of the idea and heard of the concept before SNCC was set up.

FINN: And what have the intervening years done? It's six years since that statement was written. Have your own ideas developed or changed or have they simply become confirmed by your experience?

BOND: Well, I tend to be a pessimist about most things, and I have to say I'm just pessimistic about nonviolence being a successful force for the sort of social change I want to see. Not that I don't think nonviolence will work, but I just don't think people will use it. I don't think that people against the sort of change I'm interested in are going to give it a chance to work, and I don't think the people *for* the sort of change that I'm interested in are going to give it a chance to work. So if anything, I've become *pessimistic* since 1960. In 1960 things were relatively simple. I mean, here was a lunch counter that was segregated, here were people who were willing to undergo some slight, and in some cases very heavy, brutality to prove the point that they had a right to that lunch counter. It was a black and white issue—not in terms of race but in terms of goodness and badness. Here were students protesting in a nonviolent manner; they were good. Here were the store owners whose *ideas* were bad. And these two forces met and goodness prevailed.

Now it's much, much more complicated. The issues have become who controls what, in what manner, and how do you take that control from him and give it to those who need it, and so on. It's a much more difficult matter. And then I think that frustrations that have built up over the past six years—or probably have been building over the last four hundred years—are just so great that an idea like nonviolence . . . I'm *sure* it doesn't have the same appeal, to young people especially, that it had in 1960. And it doesn't have the same appeal to older people.

FINN: But you still retain it as a personal concept even though you think it may be less effective than means that other people follow.

BOND: Well, I don't really know if the means they use are completely effective. Certainly if Negroes in the United States were able to rise up tomorrow and arm themselves, they'd probably be put down. But they might be able to make some really significant inroads in the forces that are arrayed against them. But even if they're successful, it just becomes a reversal of the thing that we've been fighting against.

FINN: One of the reasons that a number of people, certainly outside of Georgia, first heard of you was not only because of your election but because of your support of the draft-card burners, people who decided they were going to opt out of this war in Vietnam because they said it was not a just war. Does your own concept about the use of nonviolence play a strong role in your judgment of the war in Vietnam? You criticize U.S. policy in Vietnam, but is this a particular critical judgment or does it follow from a general condemnation of war?

BOND: Well, it's both things. This *particular* war is just so reprehensible. As far as I'm concerned, it's a blatant attempt by the United States to frustrate what appear to me to be the desires of the people of Vietnam to govern themselves; that we're intervening in what was, at its beginning, a civil war against a despotic government. I think this particular war is *particularly* indefensible.

FINN: So this is the kind of judgment you could and would make even if you did not hold a nonviolent position.

BOND: Right. I heard something recently that I don't know anything about, about a Catholic idea of just and unjust wars, and that's the sort of thing I'm thinking about here. First, I don't think there can be just wars, but I can very easily see how people might make the distinction.

FINN: As a matter of fact, that distinction troubles a number of people I've talked to who *would* like to adopt a pacifist position, absolute radical pacifism, but know that this would keep them from supporting strong revolutionary forces such as those in South Africa or a number of countries in Latin America, or even Southeast Asia. So they're torn between the desire to adopt this position and the desire to see radical changes come about in the social development of these countries. And that's an unresolved question for them. I presume you don't feel the same tensions.

BOND: Well I *feel* them, but not. . . . On one hand I'd love to see people in South Africa get the sort of things I think they need—the ability to participate in their government, which would mean, in fact, running the government, since they're in the majority there. But it seems to me the only way they would be able to do it would be through some sort of armed conflict. I mean certainly the white South Africans are not sensitive to nonviolent protest. It seems the only *resolution* of that situation can come about through armed conflict. If it were to begin I'd feel enormous sympathy for the South Africans and would want to do something, if I could, to help them in some way and still rectify that with my own feeling about nonviolence. So I *do* feel that tension.

FINN: How would you describe your own basic beliefs? They apparently are very strong and resist what would pull you in the direction of supporting violent action.

BOND: I believe that violence, whether it's between two men or two nations or two groups of people, is an immoral way of settling differences, and it leads, I believe, to further differences and to further wrongs. The tension arises when you realize, as I think I do, that in some cases violence is really inevitable. I can see no solution to the conflict in South Africa, again, except violence.

FINN: And the outcome, at least as far as one can readily observe, might seem to be an improvement. When you say that violence doesn't lead to success or improvement, that's really a matter of faith and hard to substantiate historically, isn't it?

BOND: I imagine so, but suppose there were an overnight successful revolution in South Africa, which would have to involve some sort of bloodletting and some sort of violence. I'd . . . I was about to say I'd rather they achieved their freedom through nonviolent means, which might mean another hundred, two hundred, three hundred years of the sort of conditions there, but I don't know if I'm willing to impose those sorts of conditions on them. (I'm not able, of course, to impose any conditions on them.)

Another feeling I have about my nonviolence is that it is a personal thing with me, that it applies to *me*, and that I realize that other people don't have the same ideas about *hundreds* of things—baseball and the weather and automobiles—and I don't expect them to have the same ideas about nonviolence that I do. I wish everyone did. If everyone did then this would be a. . . .

FINN: It would be a different world.

BOND: Right. We'd have a different world. But everyone doesn't. In fact, very few other people do.

FINN: You spoke earlier of your pessimism. You don't *expect* that there will be a number of conversions to nonviolence because the achievements of the civil rights movement were won partly at least through nonviolent means?

BOND: Well, the difficulty with that situation is that the civil rights movement has won successes, partly *I* think, because of violence, because of the potential of violence inherent in the civil rights movement. The uproar in Birmingham, the killing of those four little girls, the murders of Mickey and Jimmy and

Andy in Mississippi, and all of the other acts of violence* I think contributed *far* more heavily to that sort of legislation.

FINN: Those were acts of violence perpetrated *upon* the people in the movement. . . .

BOND: Right. But it was violence nonetheless. What I'm saying is that violence caused the passage of the Civil Rights bill, no matter who caused the violence. This country, unfortunately, reacts to violence. Look at what happened the day before yesterday with Meredith. Everyone is in an uproar now that he's been shot, but they didn't care the day before whether he marched all over Mississippi.

We come back in our conversation, to the relation between the individual and the nation state. Does he think it possible to make moral judgments of the nation state? If so, by what standards?

BOND: Well, when I think about Vietnam, when I think about American involvement in South Africa or in Latin America and the Dominican Republic, I guess I have a tendency to make moral judgments of the state. But I'd never thought about it in that light. I'd always thought that Vietnam was something President Johnson was doing—not because he is an evil man or a dishonest man—but it was something he was doing rather than America. But in fact I *don't* really think that. I think it's something the country does; the country allows it to happen and the country is bigger than Johnson.

When Secretary McNamara orders bombing in North Vietnam you know, the first thing you ask is, "Why is McNamara doing that?" But I like to think that instead of saying that, you say, "Why does the country let McNamara do that?" Rusk and McNamara and Johnson and Goldberg—and all those who have the responsibility for doing these things—why are they allowed to do them? And I transfer blame, if blame is to be given, not

---

* In September 1963, four Negro children were killed in Birmingham when the Sixteenth Street Baptist Church was dynamited. In June 1964, Michael Schwerner, James Chaney, and Andrew Goodman, all from SNCC, were murdered, it is charged, by Mississippi law-enforcement officers. Their bodies, bearing evidence of great torture, were uncovered only after a large-scale search.

to the men who push the buttons but to the society which lets the man get in a position to push that sort of button.

FINN: And what kind of answer do you get when you ask yourself why the society allows this?

BOND: I think this is basically a brutal society; it's a brutal society, it's a racist society. It doesn't thrive on brutality and racism but it either enjoys them or just doesn't care. It's sort of a care-*less* society. It places the same value, I think, on the people who are napalmed in Vietnam as it does—did—on the Negroes who were lynched in the period after the Civil War, and as it sometimes does today on Negroes who are shot down in Mississippi or the South. Meredith was the exception; he was a famous man. Andy Goodman and Mickey Schwerner were the exceptions; they were white. If James Chaney had been by himself he would have been no more than an object like objects in Vietnam. They're not people any more; they're just little objects; they're figures on a chess board.

FINN: Are you suggesting that there is some racist element in U.S. policy, racist in the sense that it considers people in Vietnam less important than the white members of this society —or maybe even white *and* black members of this society?

BOND: Well first, *I* think the country as a whole figures they're less important than white *and* black members of this society, and secondly the country as a whole thinks that white people are more important than non-white people. President Johnson's famous quote about if we don't stand off communism we'll open ourselves to every little yellow devil with a pocket knife*—I mean that's a racist slur. And a couple of weeks ago I was at a peace rally where one of the United States Senators who's very strongly against the Administration's position in Vietnam was talking about the Red Chinese. He was trying to downgrade their Navy and he said, "They're nothing but a lot of Chinks with junks." And you know, that's another racist slur. I

---

* This statement of President Johnson's was unfamiliar to me at the time I talked with Mr. Bond. I subsequently found it quoted in *Mission to Hanoi*, Herbert Aptheker's account of the trip he, Lynd and Hayden made to Hanoi. There the then Congressman Johnson is quoted as saying on the floor of the House on March 15, 1948: "No matter what else we have of offensive or defensive weapons, without superior air power America is a bound and throttled giant; impotent and an easy prey to any yellow dwarf with a pocket knife."

just think that with Orientals and even with Latin Americans and with Africans this country as a whole thinks they are lesser beings; they haven't reached our level of civilization; they're not as clever or as astute as we are.

FINN: Do you think that if race relations in this country were improved to a point where you could describe our society as relatively non-racist, that this would be some kind of help in the way we regard other peoples in the world?

BOND: Oh, I think so. A great many people who concern themselves with foreign policy of this country—a great many Negroes I know—are convinced one of the reasons we're not taking a hard line against Rhodesia is because it's a white *minority* government—had it been a Negro majority being brutal to a white minority, then we certainly would have intervened. We're quick to enter into the Congo and bomb civilians and so on, but we don't do the same sorts of things in Rhodesia. I guess we could say the situation is different: there's no insurgency, you know, there's no armed uprising. But it's the same sort of thing to me.

FINN: You would support—at least have some sympathy with—people who make that judgment?

BOND: Oh yes. Yes. I think the United States made a racial judgment. I think England did. I mean Harold Wilson talks about fighting our kith and kin in Rhodesia. Those people are not the kith and kin of people in England, they're rebels, they're traitors.

FINN: Is there any kind of a process of political education— I don't mean simply face-to-face confrontation but political education—that society can provide for people to reveal to themselves racist judgments they have hidden or have failed to perceive?

BOND: I don't know. I don't know how you educate people to what I consider a proper position. You know, I was in Guinea in West Africa last in 1964, and some of the employees of the American Embassy there were very decent, very nice, and very kind, but some of them just had this strange stereotyped view of Africans. And, you know, I just thought it made them unfit for their jobs. *Unless* their job was to further that policy of our government which assumes that colored peoples, no matter where they are, are childlike and simplistic—then they were *supremely* fit for their jobs.

FINN: Let me ask again about the relation between civil rights organizations and our foreign policy—particularly SNCC, but others if you want to mention them. In his book on SNCC, Howard Zinn said "Whether SNCC will continue as a vital force in American life will depend on whether it thrusts and points beyond race, probing the entire fabric of society." Well, one of the ways in which some of these organizations are questioning much in our society is by direct criticism of our foreign policy. Some of this criticism, as you yourself have suggested, is made in terms of race. There are two questions here. What effect do you think this is having on the organizations themselves? And second, what do you think it is doing or can do in terms of our foreign policy?

BOND: Well, it's interesting. I've been doing a lot of reading about civil rights organizations taking foreign policy positions. You know, when SNCC first took its position there was a great hue and cry; this was something that had never been done before. Well, it's been done since almost 1910. The NAACP has *always* taken positions on foreign policy questions, particularly those that relate to Africa, and it's often taken positions at variance with the prevailing Administration position. More recently, NAACP was very critical of the Administration's position on Rhodesia and South Africa. Since SNCC issued its statement on Vietnam the Southern Christian Leadership Conference has issued one, the Southern Conference Educational Fund has issued one, the Congress on Racial Equality chapter in New York City has issued one, and it's very likely that CORE will issue the statement that they tabled last summer when they have their next convention this summer.*

Secondly, I think that a great many people in the movement see things in racial terms. They're made to see things in racial terms by this country; the country makes them race conscious. In all the news stories about James Meredith he's not James Meredith, he's "Negro James Meredith." I remember—when he was at the University of Mississippi—he made, at a press conference at the beginning of his second semester, the announcement that "the Negro will not return to Ole Miss," and a lot of

* Under the leadership of Floyd McKissick, CORE has become a strong critic of the war in Vietnam.

people applauded. And then he said, "But James Meredith will be back." And I think it was an attempt by him not to say "I'm not a Negro," or "I'm ashamed of being a Negro," but "I just resent being called 'Negro James Meredith.'" It's not his name, you know. His name is James Meredith. Or Jackie Robinson. He's "Negro baseball star Jackie Robinson." Paul Robeson's a "Negro singer," and Robert Weaver is "the first Negro to do this."

You know, it's sort of irritating and it's difficult to talk about because Negroes will say, "Well, you're ashamed of being a Negro." And white people say the same sort of things: "Don't you have any racial pride?" But it's not that at all, it's just that the country continually tells you that you are a Negro, and being a Negro in this country means to be unfortunate. It means probably to be poor, probably to be uneducated, and it means that the country continually reminds you of your status as a second-class citizen in the midst of what they call the affluent society. And you begin to forget that there are white people who are in generally the same sort of circumstances, and your whole attitude toward the world—not just the country but toward the world—is a racial attitude.

When I read a newspaper I don't look at the sports or the comic strips or anything. I look for what they call the race stories. And if I do read the sports, I want to see what whatsis name, Hank Aaron, did; you know, I don't care what Ted Williams does. I want to see what Hank Aaron did; he's a Negro. I think the fact that CORE or SNCC or SCEF, and to some degree SCLC, couch their criticism of the war in Vietnam in racial terms is an indication of what the country has done to them and what it's doing to Negroes in this country. And that's the way we're *conditioned* to react, and that's the way we *do* react.

Finally, there *is* a racial connection, we think, between Mississippi and Vietnam, between, as some used to say alliteratively, between Angola and Alabama, South Africa and South Carolina, Mississippi and Madagascar—not Madagascar anymore. But, you know, the same sorts of things go on in both places; a nonwhite group of people is set upon or put upon by a white group of people in a great many instances.

FINN: You said earlier that the NAACP for one had ventured into foreign policy judgments and criticism. How were the judgments and criticisms received, 'cause you're quite right, I think that when SNCC ventured into foreign policy people began to be disturbed.

BOND: I don't know. I imagine it was the same sort of re-action, that some members of the NAACP have towards SNCC's position on Vietnam: that this is an issue that we, as civil rights people, don't need to involve ourselves in. The most discourag-ing criticism I heard came from Roy Wilkins who said that peo-ple in the civil rights movement don't know enough about Vietnam to have a point of view about it. And then he said he fully supported the Administration's position in Vietnam.

FINN: Meaning presumably he knew enough to support it. . . .

BOND: Right, or else that he didn't *have* to know anything about it but could support it anyway. So either one of those is very disturbing: that he knows enough and the rest of us don't, or that he knows just as little as we do but can support it any-way.

FINN: What kind of division does exist on Vietnam among people who are very active in the civil rights movement?

BOND: Well, there are two sorts of divisions: There's one group of people who think it's unwise practically for civil rights people to involve themselves in what they think is another issue, that of foreign policy. Then there are those who think that if a position is taken that does not agree with theirs, then that is unwise as well.

FINN: Do you think there is a danger that this element of race consciousness may be exaggerated in actually arriving at foreign policy decisions? Maybe you could explain how the de-cision to condemn the war was arrived at in SNCC.

BOND: Well, it was made over a period of almost six months, and then in the summer of 1965 we first began to think about saying it. The anti-war movement in the U.S. was beginning to build larger and larger, and individual people who worked for SNCC would go to an anti-Vietnam war rally and say "This is what *I* think about the war in Vietnam." And people would say "Well, what does SNCC think?" And they'd say, "SNCC doesn't think anything at all about it. We're not for it or against it." And they began to get tired of disassociating themselves from

Julian Bond

their organization, and we began to consider taking an organizational position on the war. There were one or two members of the staff who said "Don't do it. It will hurt us financially"—as it has done. "It'll lose us friends, it'll lose us support," and so on. But the general feeling was that we should do it.

As time passed the urgency of it just became greater and greater and greater. The war really loomed over us, first because so many of the people who work for SNCC are young males out of college who certainly don't have jobs that can defer them from the service. And because a great many of them think that the work they're doing here is five thousand times more important than fighting in Vietnam. For a lot of different reasons the urgency of it just became greater and greater.

FINN: And when it came to the test, I take it that the majority support was overwhelming?

BOND: Oh, *really* overwhelming. I mean out of say, two hundred and twenty members we have on our staff I doubt if more than five were against it—or even that many. And even they were not against the statement. They were against having a position. And Lewis says—he was the chairman then—that if we have to die for standing up, that is, if the organization has to die because it loses financial support if we take a principled position, then that's the best way for us to die.

FINN: Has SNCC's position influenced other organizations?

BOND: Well, I think our position has helped a lot of people to come to a position. I think one of the reasons CORE tabled their resolution is because of Farmer's *real* concern that taking a position on the war in Vietnam would have hurt CORE a great deal. And Farmer's position against the war is quite well known; he's very strongly against it and he's made speeches to that effect. But he wanted to keep separate what he considered separate issues. Now I think the SNCC position has helped a great many people to come to an anti-war position, particularly people in the civil rights movement. I think it helped SCLC to come to their position, I think it helped SCEF to come to their position, I think it's gonna help CORE come to their position.

I think the *tragedy* among Negroes in particular and people in this country in general is that they don't have *any* position on Vietnam. Unless they've got a son or a brother or a father or an uncle over there, it's just not going on as far as they're concerned. They just don't care about it. That's particularly true with Negroes, I think. They're just completely divorced from considerations of foreign policy. And if they do have a position it's likely to be a sort of conservative one.

FINN: Why would you say that Negroes particularly are less concerned?

BOND: Well, first, because they've begun to believe that it's really none of their business what happens in Vietnam. They had nothing to do with making the decision about fighting there— and it's not their business in that sense. And then they tend, I think, to take a conservative position for the reason that you stated earlier, that minority groups tend to be superpatriots and super-Americans, with the Italian-Americans very proud of their service in the Second World War in Italy and Japanese-Americans very proud of their all-Japanese-American battalions that fought in the Pacific, and so on.

FINN: Have people in SNCC gotten involved in some of the almost intramural controversies that have taken place about moving too close to the centers of power, being too persuaded, in terms of tactics at least, by people who are responsible for the governmental decisions?

BOND: Our feeling is that when you get too close to the centers of power, when you get inside the structure, then you're treading on dangerous ground.

FINN: There was a question I wanted to ask earlier when we were talking about how SNCC arrived at its position on Vietnam, and it refers to Wilkins' statement. How highly informed did people in SNCC think they had to be before they could arrive at a responsible position?

BOND: Well first, I think we wanted to be as informed as possible; the people who really took the lead in drafting statements started to read all sorts of things. For instance, the *New York Times,* which you seldom see down here, and other publications—especially anti-war publications—to find out things they could about the war in Vietnam. But I don't think there was a feeling that we had to be experts; what we were saying basically is that we thought the war was wrong, and we thought it was wrong from what we could gather simply from a reading of the American press. You didn't have to go to specialized sources to find out the wrongness of it. It was just there.

FINN: I think you'd have support from a number of people on this. There's enough information available for people to form sound opinions. And President Johnson, in the *New York Times* for today, came out once again for the right to dissent, only he said that people who dissented should be informed, know what they're dissenting against and have some alternatives to offer him.

BOND: Right. Well, I'd agree that it's nice to be informed, but I don't agree that you have to offer an alternative. If you see a man beating someone, what he should do is stop. You don't have to suggest that he beat a dog or beat a horse instead. He should just stop beating. And I think that's what the SNCC statement on Vietnam said: Stop beating the Vietnamese people. And we didn't say withdraw through free elections *and* they should be supervised by the Geneva Conference as opposed to U.N. observers, or live up to this agreement that was signed then, but simply that what you're doing is wrong. We want you to stop it. And we would hope that Dean Rusk and President Johnson, Secretary McNamara, are capable enough to devise a solution that would be satisfactory to us and satisfactory to them. Now probably that's contradictory. It can't be both satisfactory to them and us, but I think they could do it if they wanted to.

FINN: I wonder if you would speculate about the effect your rejection by the Georgia Legislature has on the people who pay enough attention to it to know exactly what you said. I mean particularly the people in Georgia. Do you think that it was a politically educative act?

BOND: I think so, but the difficulty is that not a great many people to this day know what SNCC said or what I said. Just last night I was talking to the man who's going to run against me this fall and who ran against me last year as a Republican —he's now a Democrat—and I beat him then. He charged that I wouldn't fight for my country and implied that I was a coward, that no one should live in this country and benefit from its greatness and not be prepared to defend it. And I told him I thought the best defense was in making the country stronger. I said if he's worried about the Chinese marching through Honolulu then he should make sure that things are all right in Honolulu, and I thought that's what the civil rights movement was doing —trying to make America, American democracy, safe for Americans, before we tried exporting the sort of democracy that we have here. I think the difficulty is that the SNCC position was never *really* made clear. The Atlanta newspapers began to say that we urged all American young men to burn their draft cards—which is not exactly what we said. We said we had sympathy with those young men who could not respond to the military draft, and that included those young men who burned their draft cards. We sympathized with them, we understood why they did it, and appreciated the act for what it was. We considered it a real and a meaningful protest against induction, against the war in Vietnam.

FINN: One of the problems that concerns some people who are involved in the peace movement is that it brings together people who are objecting to the war in Vietnam for widely diverse reasons. There are some people who are pacifists and think that their position is somehow in danger of being diluted or contaminated by people who are not pacifists but who object to this particular war, or by those who are using this war as a political protest against Johnson or the Administration for a variety of reasons. Do you feel that there is danger to civil rights organizations when they participate in large-scale protests with people who have different goals, different motives?

BOND: No, no. I think one of the hopeful signs about the *peace* movement is that all of the different groups that have different reasons why they're opposed to the war in Vietnam seem at times, not always, but at times to be coming closer and closer together. Not that their ideas are becoming the same, but they're willing to agree on, say, a large demonstration that involves different groups with differing ideas—you know, pacifists, people who want the National Liberation Front to win, people who don't want the National Liberation Front to win but want to see a stable, democratically elected government in North and South Vietnam. People who have all these different points of views seem to come together much more than *I* can remember them coming together in the past. And I think it's a good thing to have happened.

* * *

On December 5, 1966, the Supreme Court ruled that Julian Bond was legally entitled to his seat in the Georgia Legislature,

Julian Bond

and he has subsequently remarked on the good relations that obtain between him and the other representatives.

I talked with Bond very briefly after the extensive summer riots in 1967. He no longer described himself as a pacifist and he said that violence might be necessary if the Negro is to be treated justly in this country. He spoke of his changed attitude only in personal terms and was unwilling to generalize. But as recent events in our country make clear, there is a declining faith in the efficacy of nonviolence to break down racial barriers, and SNCC leaders now speak in extremely violent terms.

JOHN LEWIS

Almost immediately after speaking with Julian Bond I spoke with John Lewis. The contrast in appearance was marked. Where Bond has light skin, the clean-cut features of a model (which he very briefly was), an easy and confident manner, and speaks in distinct and cultivated tones, Lewis is stocky, very dark, with the broad features that racists choose to caricature, a shy, gentle, almost diffident manner and a voice which carries the accent and rhythm of the Deep South. But that rhythm is controlled and shaped by the intense moral pressure which pulses under everything he says.

Except for that moral intensity, it is difficult for me to bring this person into focus with what I know about him. In August 1963, Lewis, then twenty-three, was one of the civil rights leaders who addressed over 200,000 people who gathered for the historic March on Washington. Born on an Alabama farm, he had come to that position by way of a Nashville seminary, workshops in the study of nonviolence, the Nashville sit-ins, freedom rides, jails and beatings. When he entered the movement, he wrote to his mother "I have acted according to my convictions and according to my Christian conscience. . . . My soul will not be satisfied until freedom, justice and fair play become a reality for all people." *

And a little more than a year before I sat with him in his office, Lewis had led a march that was to go from Selma to Montgomery to protest discrimination in Alabama. Just outside of Selma they were stopped by state troopers and posse men,

* Quoted in Zinn, p. 19.

clubbed and gassed. Lewis was hospitalized with a fractured skull.

It is clear, as I talk with him, that the brutality to which he has been subjected has not shaken his commitment to nonviolence; if anything, his commitment has been strengthened. Now the task is to find the "means, the methods, the tactics" that will be "radical enough to meet the feelings and demands of people in the movement." The framework of the whole nonviolent movement, Lewis believes, provides means and methods "to solve some of the basic problems of American society." Those involved in the struggle to change and improve our basic social, economic and political structure must be convinced that "we cannot separate the means from the end." The end that Lewis has in mind is "a community of love, the beloved community." But Lewis, firmly committed to this belief, says he does "not have a plan, a blueprint, a road map" to bring about the needed changes.

He acknowledges that his view is that of a minority in SNCC, and that there are many within the whole movement who question the efficacy of nonviolence. Nevertheless Lewis adheres to his belief that nonviolence remains the best way to combat, not people, but a system that is corrupt, a system that victimizes both white and black. Like others I have talked with, he believes that violence engenders more problems than it solves. And nonviolence will be most effective, truly effective, when it is accepted as a way of life, not as a technique that "can be turned on and off like a faucet."

And as he talks Lewis makes clear that he applies these concepts to both the civil rights movement and the peace movement —that, indeed, he finds the distinction unhelpful.

LEWIS: I've said on many occasions that there's no sense in any of us in the so-called civil rights movement talking about civil rights when civil rights are based on laws and on court decrees and legislation. More and more I think we have to talk about human rights and the rights of all of the people, not just people in America and not just Negro people. Somehow we have to look at the movement that we are involved in as part of a world-wide movement wherever people are oppressed. And as long as there is violence and suffering and conflict in *any* part of the world, I think we all have to be involved in that, trying to bring the end to it. There's no sense in talking about civil rights today and tomorrow, if there's no civilization. *I'm* convinced that the civil rights movement and the peace movement in a sense are inseparable. I think we have to look at it as a larger movement.

When I point out that violence *does* seem to have gained some victories, both domestically and internationally, Lewis agrees.

LEWIS: Well, I would be the last person to deny that there have been victories and a certain amount of progress through the use of violence. On the other hand I think this type of victory is very temporary. In America, and not just in America, but in the world, I'm still convinced that if we want to build a world community at peace with itself then I think we have to recognize —now maybe this has something to do with my commitment to the philosophy of nonviolence—that man himself is important. And I hate to use a religious term, but I consider that man is sacred, that life is sacred and something very particular, something very special, and that none of us has the right to destroy another man or take another person's life. It may happen that mankind will never accept nonviolence until it is seen as the most practical thing to do. Maybe they have to have shock treatment, see so much terror and so much suffering and so much violence that they come to that point where they say "We've had enough."

FINN: Do you think that the possibility of all-out nuclear warfare is so terrifying, that for some people this is a kind of shock treatment and leads them to question the value of war in a way they never did before?

LEWIS: I do think it is. To begin to think about and imagine the effects of an all-out nuclear war, I think, is setting into motion a great many people who would never before discuss the whole idea of nonviolence, the whole idea of non-war, an end to war, no war. I think it is in a sense getting more and more people at least to the point of discussion of the whole idea of peace.

FINN: You said a minute ago you hated to use a religious term, that life was "sacred." Why do you say that?

John Lewis

LEWIS: Because I think for many people a certain term will build up a wall, a sense of resistance. It's not necessarily religious; I still think that life itself is sacred.

FINN: Well, I was asking whether this reflected a judgment about religious groups in this country, about how effective or ineffective they've been in changing the social order.

LEWIS: Well, as I've said so many times—and in spite of my growing up in a church and all that—I still consider organized religion in America as being behind. Even before Dr. King said it I think Bishop James Pike said that organized religion was a taillight rather than a headlight when it comes to certain basic changes. And I think it is true that even now within the whole movement, the peace movement and the civil rights movement in America, that the church is far, far behind. And the church should be, organized religion should be, taking the lead. For the basic principles of the Judeo-Christian heritage, to the best of my knowledge, should be what we are following.

Like many who share the view of "the Movement" as not divisible into civil rights and peace movements and who believe that it is an entire system that they attack, Lewis is critical of the expansionist quality of U.S. foreign policy, at least as it is expressed in military terms. In his own terms he makes judgments similar to those expressed by, for example, Reston in his comments on the "Rusk Doctrine," Fulbright in his address on "The Fatal Arrogance of Power," and Morgenthau in his article entitled "Globalism, Johnson's Moral Crusade." *

LEWIS: I think there's a myth, some type of fever or something, that's running wild on the American scene that gives us the idea that we are so right, and that we are so powerful that we should emerge as the keeper of the world's record, as the big cop. We are more and more going to different places around the world, and we're going in the name of peace, and to stop the spread of communism. We're going to the Congo and to the Dominican Republic and Vietnam, and after Vietnam no doubt

* These comments are, respectively, in the *New York Times,* February 20, 1966; *New York Times Magazine,* May 15, 1966; and the *New Republic,* July 3, 1965.

we'll be someplace else, saying that this is part of a peace-keeping effort.

And one of the real problems is that our whole economy in
this country in my own estimation is built around war and conflict. We have a war economy and we hate to do any serious
thinking or contemplation about peacetime economy. When
people raise questions about planning the economy they're accused of being a Socialist or a Communist or something worse.
And somehow the American people must force the government
to do some serious thinking, some serious planning, about a
peacetime economy and of absorbing the millions of men that
we have in uniform into our economy.

FINN: Presuming that we do presently have a war economy,
is this the result of external objective facts which the United
States government feels it has to meet and can only meet by
large armaments?

LEWIS: No, I don't think it's just that. I think it has to do with
something else also. I think that the American business community, particularly big business, has a great deal of influence
on our foreign policy in suggesting and in a sense putting pressure on the President of the United States, to move in to certain
areas and move in certain directions. And not just with the
President but with different agencies within the government.*

* The kind of criticism Lewis makes here, and which he elaborated,
was developed at greater length by Carl Oglesby, then president of SDS,
at the November 27, 1965 March on Washington sponsored by SANE.
A few paragraphs from the entire address may be sufficient to indicate
the nature and depth of the charge:

"In 1954 the democratically elected Arbenz of Guatemala wanted to
nationalize a portion of United Fruit Company's plantations in his country, land he needed badly for a modest program of agrarian reform. His
government was overthrown in a CIA-supported right-wing coup. The
following year, General Walter Bedell Smith, director of the CIA when
the Guatemala venture was being planned, joined the board of directors
of the United Fruit Company.

"Comes 1965. The Dominican Republic. Rebellion in the streets. We
scurry to the spot with twenty thousand neutral Marines and our neutral
peacemakers—like Ellsworth Bunker, Jr., Ambassador to the Organization of American States. Most of us know that our neutral Marines
fought openly on the side of the junta, a fact that the Administration
still denies. But how many also know that what was at stake was our
new Caribbean sugar bowl? That this same neutral peacemaking Bunker
is a board member and stock owner of the National Sugar Refining
Company, a firm his father founded in the good old days, and one
which has a major interest in maintaining the status quo in the Domini-

John Lewis

In Vietnam we have United States forces now. And to see
our own government saying that we're fighting to give people an opportunity to engage in free and open elections, to stop
the spread of communism in Asia; and to see us go and burn
villages, and bomb and kill innocent people, and kill I guess both
innocent and guilty—but about being guilty I don't know—it's
something that I just cannot digest. And if there was a war and
violence in the Congo or in South Africa, in Rhodesia, or in
Mississippi or in Alabama, again I could not digest it. And I
just *do not* like violence. I do not like war. I have a hatred and
a dislike for it all.

FINN: So that your dislike is so intense that even where it
would seem to many people to be the *only* way to *reverse* a
grave disorder, you would reject it?

LEWIS: I would have to take that position; it's my basic
makeup. If there must be a struggle, let it be peaceful, nonviolent
struggle. I cannot accept the whole idea, the whole position of
Gandhi saying that people must struggle. I think he said in
effect if he had to choose between no struggle and a violent
struggle then there'd be a violent struggle.

FINN: And you'd part company with Gandhi here?

LEWIS: Right. I have to make a decision for myself. As an
individual I cannot decide for people in SNCC, for the people
that we work with or for other people. But I have to be consistent with what I believe is right.

---

can Republic? Or that the President's close personal friend and advisor,
our new Supreme Court Justice Abe Fortas, has sat for the past nineteen
years on the board of the Sucrest Company, which imports black strap
molasses from the Dominican Republic? Or that the rhetorician of
corporate liberalism and the late President Kennedy's close friend, Adolf
Berle, was chairman of that same board? Or that our roving ambassador
Averell Harriman's brother Roland is on the board of National Sugar?
Or that our former Ambassador to the Dominican Republic, Joseph
Farland, is a board member of the South Puerto Rico Sugar Company,
which owns 275,000 acres of rich land in the Dominican Republic and
is the largest employer on the island—at about one dollar a day?
"Neutralists! God save the hungry people of the world from such
neutralists!
"We do not say these men are evil. We say, rather, that good men
can be divided from their compassion by the institutional system that
inherits us all."

FINN: Does this pose for you and others who have your position a problem when there are demonstrations criticizing policy in Vietnam? And some of them have your position; some, although they would accept some wars as just and have even fought in them, would reject this war as unjust; and some think this reflects the kind of built-in racism that our society has within it and which flows into our foreign policy as well; and others think it's a political tactic they would like to use to criticize the present Administration. All of these in one big movement. Now you have to do what you say is necessary to preserve your integrity, but you're involved in this movement with people who have quite different approaches.

LEWIS: I think it *is* a problem in the movement, because at least some people may be forced to give up something at a particular time in the name of unity or for the sake of cooperation. But we have to work and continue to work in those areas where we agree, and at the same time we continue discussion and dialogue in those areas where there's some disagreement.

FINN: You said earlier that the thing to do, at least what you thought the proper attempt, was to criticize not people but the system in which people were caught up. What about the businessmen you referred to earlier; are they caught in the same system?

LEWIS: Well, I think they're more or less in charge of the system, they control it. I think the whole operation is controlled *by* and for a few people. In a sense the whole nature of our government. That's why people must be willing to force not just the national government, but the state and local governments, to become responsive to their own needs and to their own demands. What we've had so long in this country is the politicians' politics. We must have what we like to call a peoples' politics where the people would lead—where a so-called political leader would emerge from them and be responsive to their needs and their demands. It will be from the bottom up rather than from the top down.

FINN: A number of our political leaders, like President Johnson, have emerged from the bottom. How optimistic are you about those leaders who emerge from the bottom once they attain this prominence?

John Lewis

LEWIS: Well I think the political leader that emerges from the bottom to the top, who emerges as a spokesman for a group of people, must forever be conscious of the people that he is supposed to serve. A politician or so-called politician must be one of what people have described as the good people. I like to think of all people as being good, but I think there are certain obviously good people.

FINN: All are good and some better than others.

LEWIS: Somehow some of the morality and some of the ethics that have been projected in the so-called civil rights movement, in the peace movement, must be projected in the political arena. The people who are involved in the movement must get involved in the political arena.

I think there can be an attempt on the part of the newcomers to the political arena, particularly the young people, because I still believe there's primarily three communities that offer hope in America. There's an element within the peace movement, an element within religion—and this element is rebelling against organized religion—and there's an element within the civil rights movement. They can bring something different and something new that would be consistent with what is right and what they feel is true. And they will not be willing to engage in petty politics. Then the political community will not become the realm for the few, a place where a few people get on top and the masses continue to suffer. But I think these people would help to make the whole political arena an instrument for basic social changes in our society.

FINN: I take it from what you said earlier, that you would like to see other civil rights groups make statements on foreign policy.

LEWIS: I think it is a tragedy that the so-called responsible, well-established civil rights organizations, the so-called responsible leaders and Negro leaders and civil rights leaders in general, have not taken a position on the war in Vietnam. It is so inconsistent for us in America to talk about love and nonviolence —and even today people preparing to march from Memphis to Jackson, Mississippi in a nonviolent and a peaceful and a very orderly fashion—and at the same time not have the courage to take a position there. I think other organizations, civil rights organizations, should speak out against the war, pointing out the billions of dollars that we are spending in Vietnam that could be used to do away with the ghettoes and the slums in this country. That the war won't be in Vietnam if we continue the way we are going; it will be here in the urban centers of the United States—in the Watts, in the Harlems, in Chicago, in Philadelphia, in Washington, Detroit.*

FINN: Well, why do you think that some of the leaders you refer to have *not* talked out against the war?

LEWIS: Well, I don't know the particular reasons of people like Farmer or Wilkins or Whitney Young. On the one hand I do have a feeling that some of the people cannot understand, or just refuse to understand, that what is going on in Vietnam or in Africa or in Latin America, or in Europe, is part of a much larger struggle; that in a sense what we're doing is part of that whole struggle, a world-wide struggle on the part of people, and that somehow we must be in tune with the mood of the people. And on the other hand I think that some people, some of the so-called Negro leaders in particular, are involved in the whole political game; they're getting involved in things with President Johnson.

They want to get something for keeping silence, for not getting involved. They want to support the Administration. You hear certain so-called Negro civil rights leaders say that "We do not know enough about the war to take a position, and we should support the President." And right then the person making that statement *is* taking a position. In a real sense I think people many times are doing the *whole* movement a disservice by refusing to link up the struggle of poor people in this country —white and black, the American Indians or the Puerto Ricans, the poor whites of Mississippi and Alabama, and the Negroes whether they're in Watts or in Georgia—with the struggle of people around the world.

* It may be well to recall that these remarks preceded the extensive urban riots of 1967.

ROBERT SPECK

Students for a Democratic Society (SDS) is a protean organization and, as Jack Newfield rightly said, many of its manifestations are ephemeral. Serious basic differences exist among the members, but they are united in their basic criticisms of our society and in the way they regard the potential role of "man in society." As one of its prominent members stated, "At our best, I think we are SNCC translated to the North and trained on a somewhat different and broader set of issues."

After an almost aborted delivery from the League for Industrial Democracy, SDS was really established in the summer of 1962. General guidelines for SDS had been formulated only weeks earlier at the 1962 student convention in Port Huron, Michigan. Their examination of our society led them to conclude that "although mankind needs revolutionary leadership, America rests in national stalemate, its goals ambiguous and tradition-bound instead of informed and clear, its democratic system apathetic and manipulated rather than 'of, by, and for the people.' " The basic values upon which SDS drew were a belief that men are "infinitely precious and possessed of unfulfilled capacities for reason, freedom and love." The goals of man and of society should be personal individualism and fraternal interdependence. "As a social system we seek the establishment of a democracy of individual participation, governed by two central aims: that the individual share in those social decisions determining the quality and direction of his life; that society be organized to encourage independence in men and provide the media for their common participation." Violence was "abhorrent" because it turned the person or community under attack into an object. Ways must be found, the document said, to "encourage non-violence as a condition of conflict."

SDS encountered some of the classic social and political problems, and in a paper written for the 1965 convention Dick Flacks pointed out some of the dangers for an organization that emphasized simultaneously the development of the person and the restructuring of social institutions:

"The obvious difficulty with trying to encompass both existential humanism and radical politics is that they are not only plausibly independent, but sometimes incompatible. Thus the effort to be politically effective can involve one in efforts at manipulation and compromise. The effort to be morally consistent can radically separate one from effective communication with others. The virtue of SDS and SNCC, it seems to me, is that they have so far done a pretty good job of maintaining the necessary tension between these two orientations."

In their efforts to be politically effective, members of the SDS have actively opposed the war in Vietnam, planned the effective April 1965 March on Washington and participated in many others, carried on an anti-draft campaign and have sold many thousands of copies of a guide on how to claim conscientious objector status in the draft. Not surprisingly, it has been attacked by the natural opposition, for example Senators Thomas J. Dodd and Strom Thurmond. But it has also been criticized by Senators Mansfield and Kuchel, Attorney General Katzenbach and has come under investigation by the FBI. In mid '66 one FBI agent, denying that the organization was being investigated, said that there was only an inquiry into "possible infiltration of [an] SDS chapter by Communist influence." SDS found it difficult to regard this and other inquiries as acts of disinterested sympathy. Paul Booth, national secretary of the organization, had already spelled out the position of SDS on the issue of Vietnam at a 1965 Washington press conference:

"The commitment of SDS, and of the whole generation we represent, is clear: we are anxious to build villages; we refuse to burn them. We are anxious to help and change our country; we refuse to destroy someone else's country. We are anxious to

Robert Speck

advance the cause of democracy; we do not believe that cause can be advanced by torture and terror. . . .

"Our generation is not afraid of service for long years and low pay: SDS has been working for years in the slums of America at $10 a week to build a movement for democracy there. We are not afraid to risk our lives—we have been risking our lives in Alabama and Mississippi, and some of us died there. But we will not bomb the people, the women and children, of another country."

When I visited the national SDS offices they were only a few blocks south of the University of Chicago, but the spiritual difference would be hard to measure. The area has been decaying for years, and the SDS offices, generally grimy and unpainted, were redeemed mostly by evidence of continual activity and the many familiar posters and cartoons.

Paul Booth, just returning from a New York meeting of the National Conference for New Politics, had been delayed and I talk with Robert Speck, twenty-three years old, a high school dropout and presently acting assistant national secretary, editor of *New Left News,* and membership chairman. When I ask if he will give, in addition to his own views, those of the organization, he insists that he can give only what he *"thinks* to be the attitudes prevalent within SDS." We agree on that and I ask him first if the members of SDS are united in their opposition to the war in Vietnam. What are the issues on which they are divided? Our conversation is punctuated regularly, frequently and noisily by the passage of the Sixty-third Street El passing just outside the window.

SPECK: There's a division on how we should react to U.S. policy. It's almost unanimous that we oppose the war in Vietnam. But ideas of what we should do to get out of Vietnam range from support of the Vietcong on the ultra left, to a call for cease-fire and negotiations; the same positions that, you know, exist within the peace movement. The differences of opinion are political, depending on how you see the Vietcong and their relation to Vietnam; how you see the U.S. and its relation to Vietnam; what role in decision-making the Army and the Pentagon play in the war in Vietnam. There are a lot of tactical differences also—like how we apply our opposition to the American populace in such a way that we get a favorable reaction.

FINN: Are there people in the SDS who, while opposing U.S. policy in Vietnam, would nevertheless allow themselves to be drafted and participate in the war?

SPECK: I have been opposed to U.S. foreign policy since 1959, and I joined the Navy in 1961. I spent three years with them. I'm the only one I know of who has the theory that men should join the Services so as to bring dissent into the Services. But there are others who, rather than go to jail, will allow themselves to be inducted or will join.

FINN: The particular criticism that SDS makes of the Vietnamese war derives from, is a logical inference from, a general criticism of U.S. foreign policy?

SPECK: I would say so. I would say that within SDS Vietnam is considered a typical example of what we can expect if U.S. foreign policy continues along its present lines. That's the overriding viewpoint of the National Council and the leaders, you might say, of SDS. A lot of our members, our newer members —we have something like three thousand people that are new to us, that joined this year—came in because they opposed the war in Vietnam—for moral reasons, for political reasons, for conscientious reasons. They don't all have that same critique. One of the jobs of this office, I suspect, is internal education of the membership, to try to solidify the multi-issue approach that we used to take; so that people who came into SDS on the issue of Vietnam start to apply that issue to other lines of thinking throughout the society.

FINN: The multi-issue approach you used to take means that you would bring up various social and political issues and attempt to relate them. You still do this, don't you?

SPECK: We certainly do. But we've not been effective with it recently. Because Vietnam is an overriding consideration of the majority of the membership.

FINN: You said many of the new members were opposed to the war in Vietnam for political, social, moral reasons. Do the new members of SDS see the political criticism of our war in

Robert Speck

Vietnam also as a moral criticism—not accidentally, but inevitably?

SPECK: A significant proportion believe that the political considerations are also moral considerations, and a significant number aren't concerned with the morality of the issues, because they believe morality is something which is very ill-defined and depends on emotionalism more than anything else. These groups have their continual fights.

FINN: Are some of their differences resolved on the basis of the effectiveness of some particular action? For instance, the March on Washington?

SPECK: A large number of people contended at the time of the March on Washington that we sponsored, that that was a political action designed to mobilize people around an emotional issue. They were right. Many of those very same people now oppose more Marches on Washington, any more International Days of Protest. They say such marches are no longer political actions since they can't mobilize new untouched segments of the population in significant numbers. And what is necessary at this point, they say, is community organization against the war, organization against U.S. domestic policy, and the application of the multi-issue approach; in other words, linking domestic policy with foreign policy. That's the only way, this group says, you're going to increase significantly the base of protest against the war, and to go out and march and demonstrate just makes the faithful feel better, more than anything else. Then there's the other group within SDS, of which I'm not a member, which feels that the moral thing to do, or even the political thing to do, is to show that you yourself are opposed to the war by a dramatic method, and that that converts people.

Remarking that many people still fail to see strong links between domestic and foreign policy, I ask Speck what he understands that relation to be.

SPECK: Well, in my mind that comes down to who I believe controls the American society. I believe that four percent of the owners of capital, who own something like ninety percent of the capital within this country, control our foreign policy.

Those are major stockholders of A.T. and T., DuPont, Ford, General Motors, U.S. Steel, so on and so forth. And when they're threatened abroad, then they bring the entire propaganda apparatus of the country to bear on whatever is most effective in determining what our foreign policy is in relation to whatever it is that threatens them.

Speck applies this concept, as he understands it to operate, to the Congo, Cuba, the Dominican Republic and Vietnam.* He also says that the nature of the exchange between our country and those less developed has introduced unconsciously an element of racism into our foreign policy. And when we turn to the U.S. he says that he believes "we are fast approaching, if not already in, a period of revolutionary change." When he says that the direction that change takes depends on "what kinds of things we do," I ask whom he includes in that "we."

SPECK: The kids in SDS, the Old Left, the New Left, the liberals who are sympathetic, the conservatives who understand full well that the state is an enemy of theirs, you know. One of the things I've noticed is that both the New Left and the New Right, or whatever it is, have very much the same attitude toward the institutions of the state. They break down attitudes of property rights as compared to human rights. And there're a helluva lot of people that can go either way in that. They can either assume that property is king or that mankind is king. And so what *we* do, I think, will determine which direction the country takes.

FINN: How would you assess the attitude of most people in SDS in terms of the analysis you just gave? Is there much agreement there?

SPECK: I would doubt that there would be. Oh, I don't know, we might find twenty-five percent of the SDS members that would agree with that.

FINN: What kind of responsibility does the organization feel for presenting alternative courses of action for present U.S. policy?

* A sophisticated version of this argument, "American Imperialism and the Peace Movement" by Robert Wolfe, appears in *Studies on the Left* (Vol. 6, No. 3, 1966).

Robert Speck

SPECK: There are differences of opinion within SDS about that. I personally do not feel that it is my obligation to provide an out for the government. There are other people within SDS, however, who see things like McNamara's speech in Montreal as going in the positive direction—which we have been advocating. Often the alternatives we pose are not alternatives for the government to follow, but alternatives for people to follow; we don't conceive of ourselves as being an influence upon government, and in many cases our membership doesn't *care* to be an influence upon the course of the government. They contend that the government in any of its forms right now is not something we wish to have. And only at the point that we radically change it, and there's a new power structure, would we be interested in posing alternatives for a government.

The alternative which we propose through community projects, which is the only alternative we have ever posed and actually worked on, is an alternative which says that the least government possible at the lowest level possible with maximum control by those it affects, is the kind of new power structure we want to see.

FINN: There is a problem that all radical organizations have when they operate politically. In order to be politically effective in this society, it's often argued, they must compromise with elements that have power at their command; in order to gain something you have to give something.

SPECK: Within SDS the dominant thought is that that's not necessary. We say that because we can see what other organizations have accomplished in the last twenty years while they've been compromising. They've compromised themselves right out of their radical rhetoric. They've compromised everything and achieved nothing. They didn't even get the half loaf. They get, you know, like the crumbs that are left over if they get that, and they go right on compromising.

FINN: SDS has been criticized for not being sophisticated about or critical of Communists, individual Communists and Communist groups in this society. . . .

SPECK: Personally I view American Communists as a bunch of very ineffectual middle-class people. In the world international scene, I see them very often as sell-out artists first class. I see them as people who will accept all kinds of atrocities. But

I don't feel that I should waste my time, as I have seen the Old Left waste its time, fighting about the Communists and the Communist question. That question is not a question that is meaningful to the American working class and it's not going to be meaningful in achieving a change in this country. But I don't want to have to say I'm an anti-Communist every time I open my yap. The Old Left has people who do that.

FINN: That's not really true, is it, of people in the LID and the SP?

SPECK: Of course it is. Every other pamphlet they put out deals with "The Nature of Communists" by Irving Howe, or "Why We Didn't Ally with the Communists," or whatever. I mean, what the hell does that have to do with changing the U.S.? And the SP's politics and the CP's politics are so close together at this point that I don't know what the difference is.

FINN: But there are differences and they do have some effect, say, on Vietnam. The people in the LID and the SP with the viewpoint you're describing don't, for example, argue for or think it would be desirable to have a Vietcong victory in Vietnam.

SPECK: Who else are they going to have victorious? It's either going to be the Vietcong or the United States. I don't see that it's my position to decide it's going to be the United States. I do not see the United States as the lesser of two evils in that case. They may be Vietnamese Communists, but they're Vietnamese, whereas we're American anti-Communists in Vietnam. And the victory will be decided by Vietnamese Communists versus American anti-Communists.

FINN: So the differences between SDS and the older Socialists really do lead to different political decisions.

SPECK: Very often. Especially in the case of Vietnam. In the case of the United States, we often agree with the Old Left, except we don't agree on whether we should shout "anti-communist." The anti-communism issue has been forced on us by the McCarthyites, and I should bow down to them and let them decide what I'm going to be? And decide what kind of politics I have to have? No, I can't do that. And that's the attitude of a helluva lot of members at SDS.

We say that we want a change in this country. We want that

change to be based on humane values rather than property values. We say that that change is obtainable. We say that that change can only come about by looking toward the kind of society you want to see, and then using the methods that you would use *in* that kind of society. In other words, the ends are determined by the means. We intend to make our means humane means. We intend to be concerned with alienation now as well as tomorrow. The revolution does not decide that in order to further the cause of the revolution we have to go out and do things which are dirty, sneaky, trick things. If we do that then the society that we're going to achieve is not going to be any different than the kind of society we're in now. Those are the main things which tie us in SDS together.

FINN: How does this set of values help people in SDS to approach one of the things that certainly determines a good part of our social existence—the nuclear weapons system?

SPECK: I don't believe the question's ever been really discussed, except in the Port Huron statement when we say that we're opposed to nuclear weapons. But we see that getting rid of nuclear weapons is not an end in and of itself. It cannot be done unless you change the society, so we don't even bother worrying about that for the time being. If they explode the bombs over our heads tomorrow, then we're dead. If they don't, they don't. In the meantime we work, but not to remove those bombs as an end, because that's not going to resolve the problems. It's like trying to end the war in Vietnam. The way you work to end the war in Vietnam is to work to change the social structure in this society which allowed that war to happen.

BAYARD RUSTIN

In the course of the colloquium held to celebrate the twenty-fifth anniversary of *Christianity and Crisis,* Bayard Rustin said that "nothing that is good, personal or social, can begin to occur so long as there is any effort to pursue security." This is not a new idea. It could even be read as a variant of the biblical "He that loses his life shall find it." But the concept is revivified, is weighted with renewed meaning when it is enunciated and developed by someone who has given to it more than rational assent, whose own mature life can be read in the light of that concept. And Bayard Rustin is such a person.

Mr. Rustin was born in West Chester, Pennsylvania in 1910. He went to high school there and then to Wilberforce University, Cheyney State Teachers College in Pennsylvania, and to the City College of New York. In his twenties he was in the Communist movement and for about four years was an organizer for the Young Communist League. He broke with the Communists "over the question of violence in 1941," and since that time he has developed "a totally different attitude toward the use of violence." After leaving the YCL he joined the Fellowship of Reconciliation as race relations secretary and also worked as youth organizer for A. Philip Randolph's famous and successful March on Washington. When CORE grew up within the FOR in 1941—though it consciously dissociated itself from the religious orientation of the Fellowship—Rustin became the first field secretary. In 1943 he was interned in a Federal prison for three years as a conscientious objector.

When the war ended and he was released, Rustin traveled

Bayard Rustin

and worked in countries around the world: in India, several times as a guest of the Congress Party; in West Africa to work with Nkrumah; in England to help organize the first Aldermaston Peace March; in Addis Ababa for the All African People's Congress. During these years he was developing and attempting to apply his very early ideas of general social reform. He was also engaging in "subversive" activities that were to land him in jail a score of times. In 1947 he went on the first freedom ride— called the "Journey of Reconciliation"—to test the application of the 1946 Morgan case outlawing discrimination in interstate travel. The trip led Rustin to thirty days on a chain gang in North Carolina, and his journalistic account of those thirty days led to the abolition of the chain gang system in that state. He worked with A. Philip Randolph on the Committee to End Discrimination in the Armed Forces (ended by executive order of Harry Truman in 1948), with Martin Luther King in organizing the Montgomery bus boycott and in setting up the Southern Christian Leadership Conference. In 1963 he was deputy director of the March on Washington.

During these years, in which he fought against injustice, racism and poverty, he insisted that the problems were interrelated, that they could not be solved separately, and that their solution depended upon a general social reform with a strong economic base. When I speak with him he is, as executive director of the A. Philip Randolph Institute, working on *A "Freedom Budget" for All Americans*. In the introduction to the Freedom Budget it is stated that *"We propose and insist that poverty in America can and therefore must be abolished within ten years."* And there is an explicit and strong rejection of the argument that "the termination of the Vietnam conflict is the prerequisite for acceleration of domestic social programs."

My talk with Rustin is actually in two sessions separated by some months. The first time we get together the heat of New York's brutal summer takes its impartial toll and we both sit dabbing at ourselves with handkerchiefs to keep from being drenched with sweat. At my next visit, in the A. Philip Randolph Institute at 217 West 125th Street, the weather is cooler and Rustin, dressed in a light-colored suit, is soon to leave for a speaking engagement at a midtown hotel. In both instances he is able to shift his attention from whatever he is doing and to focus sharply and directly on the issues we discuss. He is a large man with a settling athletic build, an attractive and expressive face, and a distinctive, cultured voice that I would have difficulty assigning to any geographical area. He gives the impression of being more fully alert and alive at every instant than are most "lively" people and it is partly this that makes him appear many years younger than he is.

We discuss some of the various factions within the peace movement and the issues on which it does, to some degree, fragment. There is, for example, the fact that some of the people associated with *Liberation* magazine, from whose editorial board he has just resigned, are sharply critical of his own position.

RUSTIN: I believe that the great majority of the American people may well want to get out of Vietnam. The question, therefore, for them is: *How* do we get out? And it's not enough to just keep saying, "Get out." I think that many groups in the peace movement fail to provide a step-by-step method by which the U.S. can get out and still have any national pride. Now it may be that they are right and I am wrong, that there is no way to gradually educate people for a way out. I happen to believe, however, that there is, and therefore I call for negotiations. I call for sitting down with everybody involved. I call for the United States taking unilateral steps, to stop bombing in the North. Now if the nation does all that and the other side still rejects it, my next step may be to take the Muste position. But I am not prepared to do that yet, because we have not moved and I still believe that people can be educated to a next step. Now I don't want to contend with anybody about this. I just want to make my own position clear.

FINN: You're saying it's a matter of judgment, of which yours is one that's yet to be tested.

RUSTIN: Because I take this position, some people have called me "forerunner of the Marines" and "social fascist," and one thing and another. I want you to take notice, I have not made any moral judgment on them because they differ with me.

FINN: What are the most formative influences on your own thinking about nonviolence?

Bayard Rustin

RUSTIN: I think the formidable influences on my thinking were the Quakers; A. J. Muste, to whom I owe a great deal although we differ considerably on the Vietnam question; my years of working in *Liberation*; my years of working in the civil rights movement in which I saw how destructive violence can be to everybody.

FINN: You have described yourself as a "post-Niebuhrian, post-Gandhian pacifist." I wonder if you could say how Niebuhr and Gandhi complement each other—if they do.

RUSTIN: Gandhi emphasized the goodness of man. Niebuhr emphasized the depravity of man. And I believe if one does not both believe in the goodness of man, while realistically evaluating the depravity which is in all of us, then it is not really possible to be a pacifist. Because one must love oneself to love others. And one must therefore see in himself his own depravity in order to understand the depravity of others. And that is the reason I call myself a "post-Niebuhr, post-Gandhi" pacifist.

FINN: Do you think that many people can learn something from the use of nonviolence in civil rights, something which they could apply to other areas of life in our society?

RUSTIN: I think this is true and I think that is the reason a great number of the youngsters in SNCC and CORE, who came into the civil rights struggle to win their rights and who adopted nonviolence merely as a tactic, have since become real pacifists who apply the principles of nonviolence to all things. I think that this is an indication of the fact that one grows and that what one learns in one sphere of life, if one is well-rounded, will be applied in others. Because you tend to carry from one situation to another what is of value.

FINN: How would you evaluate those people on the radical left or in SNCC or SDS who think that nonviolence has reached a limit of its value and argue that they should at least keep open a possibility of violence?

RUSTIN: In my discussions with these people they have never been able to make clear to me in any way how violence could at all be applied in the internal situation in the United States to bring about any progress. I think that they talk this way because they need an emotional possibility for it. But when you say to them, "All right, now how would you apply it? What would the results be?" etc., they chicken out. That's my experience.

FINN: In the *Christianity and Crisis* colloquium you said, "Nothing that is good, personal or social, can begin to occur so long as there is any effort to pursue security." Many people would find that a meaningful statement in terms of the person, but would find it very difficult to apply to the nation state which must have, as one of its conditions for existence, the maintenance of security.

RUSTIN: Well, of course that is precisely the reason the nation-state idea is an anachronism, because the nature of modern weapons, which is a basis of that security, is itself suicidal today. Therefore the argument logically ought to be that the concept of nation state is no longer a real one. Now this is true economically, it is true socially, it is true even politically. All along the line.

Things should be produced not because we have in our nation, for example, people who want to produce china now. The likelihood is that we ought to select the place in the world where people can best produce china most cheaply and let them produce it. Now I think this is the future. And the real security, therefore, for the present is not armaments and that kind of security. It is the giving up of things. It is the voluntary acceptance momentarily of insecurity.

FINN: Given your argument, we are existing in an interim period. What will it take before there's a general realization that the present order is an anachronism and another form of international order has to be formed?

RUSTIN: Well, all good institutions for the future are going to grow out of institutions which we now have. That's number one. Number two, I feel that our obligation is not to think in terms or to work for that which is now feasible. That is dead too. What one works for and strives for is that which is essential, relevant and necessary. It is necessary, over and above how feasible it is at the moment, that I want to put my weight not to building General Motors or to making money or to selling stock, but to proclaiming the prophetic message as it were, the good news, that something new is needed. Now the people will say to me, "You are unrealistic," and I will say, "Depending." And they will say, "This is radical," and I will say, "Depending."

Bayard Rustin

For, leaving all of these halitosis terms aside, it is essential for the future. And there are times in a revolutionary situation where anything that is proposed that appears feasible is already useless, and that anything which is useful has to appear as if it is not feasible.

FINN: Many people understand that the security of the United States today is guarded by our nuclear weapons systems. As I understand what you said before, you would be in favor of working, by some planned steps, toward unilateral disarmament.

RUSTIN: Well, I would feel that it is imperative to get rid of these arms, and I don't believe you can get rid of them by agreement. Some nation has to say, "I will not truck with this thing; I will not have to do with it." When we had the A-bomb, Russia then had to get it; then we had to get a hydrogen bomb; then they had to have it. What we are in fact doing is arming each other. Now if the process of arming each other can go on, then I am convinced the process of *disarming* each other can go on; and that if one powerful nation would give it up, other nations might well look for an opportunity to do the same.

FINN: Let me relate this to Lord Acton's statement. If people don't know anything else about him they know he said that "Power tends to corrupt and absolute power corrupts absolutely." Would you think that his statement has a general validity?

RUSTIN: I think the United States is one of the most powerful nations on earth, not because we sought it but because the objective situation pushed us into it. And I believe that to accept Lord Acton's statement would mean we might just as well all commit suicide, because there is always going to be somebody more powerful than others. And there *is* a certain corruption to power. But in a democracy people are capable of creating the kinds of political coalitions to change things—as the British did. When Britain walked into Suez, the British people rose up in arms and the government changed its policy. I think it is absolutely essential to believe this.

FINN: Well, to relate this to the first question I asked: If the United States were to engage in some kind of unilateral disarmament, or take steps in that direction, it would leave other nations possibly more powerful—nations in which the people probably have less influence in determining government policy than they do even in America.

RUSTIN: Yes, but there's another side to this question. The higher the pile of armaments gets, the deeper is the inner fear and insecurity of people. The real problem which has got to be explored, which nonviolence hasn't explored at this point, is whether people are prepared to revolt out of the poverty of plenty. We know that people will revolt out of other forms of poverty. And we must explore this. I have no answer to this.

FINN: Let me ask you to comment briefly on something I read recently. Joost A. M. Meerloo wrote, "Before we investigate the positive actions we can take against the atomic peril and atomic fear, we have to be deeply aware of man's contrasting attitudes toward danger and catastrophe. There's a tragic side to our personalities which accounts for our unconscious readiness to engage in war. Consciously, and truthfully, we say we hate war, we hate death and destruction, but deeply rooted in each of us is a primitive urge, a submerged personality level, that finds satisfaction in war's terrible destruction. Indeed, it craves such a nemesis." *

RUSTIN: I would put this quite in a different fashion. What I have observed is that when people think about nuclear war, which is total, and you say to them "What can you do about it?" they do not see how they can be related to it, and this creates in them a recklessness similar to that which one found in Britain just prior to World War II, when people were saying, "Well, maybe we're not going to be able to stop a war. Let it come, we're ready. Come on." Now I do think that there is something to what he's saying here; and we have to come to grips with that. We have to come to grips with a great deal more than that, though. Many, many people crave a unity with their society which *is* meaningful. They can observe this unity in wartime and we give them so few opportunities to experience it in peacetime. That is what made the civil rights movement such a blessing. People felt a great moral crusade; they could readily join something which was not destructive. I think our object ought not to be to talk about man's subconsciousness, but to substitute for that a conscious moral crusade in terms of the war against

* "Can War Be Cured?" *Breakthrough to Peace* (New York, New Directions, 1962), p. 198.

segregation, the war against poverty, the war against ill housing —and *that* can be learned.

FINN: So however one would analyze the human person, there would need to be, in William James' phrase, "a moral equivalent to war."

RUSTIN: Right. Yes, I agree thoroughly with this.

FINN: I have talked to some people who thought that there was in U.S. foreign policy an unconscious element of racism. Because of the kind of society the United States is, it can formulate and carry out actions, say in Vietnam, that it could not in other parts of the world. And it's partly on that basis that they would criticize U.S. policy. Does that have any kind of validity?

RUSTIN: I suppose that after three hundred years of the kind of history we have had, it would be very difficult for our nation to do anything that didn't have some racial overtones. But basically, the history of America is a history of America fighting whoever got in its way and seemed to impinge on its national interest— the French, the British, the Spanish. Therefore I think a basic aspect of foreign policy here is that of power, and that if in Vietnam the people were green or white or anything else, but were Communist, we would be fighting them.

I think it is easier for Americans to see and hear that Americans are burning the huts of colored people than it would be if they were doing this in England or France or Germany. I think it is easier to hear that people are being burned by our napalm bombs in Vietnam.

The reason it is easier, Rustin stresses, is that the Vietnamese have no constituency in the U.S. Most American citizens trace their ancestry back to some European country and, even when tenuous, that relation has emotional resonance. "If this is what people talk about as a subconscious racist aspect, then I agree," but many people seem to mean something less palatable.

FINN: There seems to be for many people who are pacifists, who advocate nonviolence, a theoretical and real problem about how to cope with the conditions in various parts of the world. In some countries in Asia, Latin America, Africa, there is an established disorder which many of these pacifists think can only be overcome by some kind of violence. They don't want to advocate violence, but neither do they want to support that condition.

RUSTIN: Let me say this: if I had been in Algeria I would have supported the revolution, but I would not have carried a gun. I would have been a medical officer in the hills with the rebels. If I had been in Cuba at the time, I would have been in the hills with Castro, but I would have been a medical officer. Now here again there are plenty of arguments that people can give me as to the inconsistencies in this position. I know them better than they do. But if one is going to struggle for justice by violence or nonviolence, he will face equal numbers of inconsistencies on both sides. Now this is what I think we have to see, and this is what maintains the humanity and the relevance of the peace position: that we are not arrogant, that we are not holier than thou, that we know our own position, which we feel is socially right, may have consequences which are very difficult. And I think all we can do is have certain standards and pray to God that we can live up to them.

FINN: You've said that we must strive for what is relevant and necessary rather than what seems to be feasible and practical. Nevertheless I'd like to ask you to make a judgment on how likely you think your views are either to prevail or to be effective.

RUSTIN: Depending on how I do it. Let me give you an illustration. I do not believe that Negroes in Harlem cleaning up the streets, making vest-pocket parks, getting rid of rats and roaches, and all the things that they are so deeply involved in now, are terribly important. They are certainly at the moment relevant to them. To be without a few more roaches and rats is important. Therefore I work with many people who are dealing with these day-to-day, immediately relevant problems. But only where, while working with them, I can use that situation and its limitations to educate them to the more profound needs for basic social change, for redefinition of work, for guaranteed income, for public works. I think the true strategist attempts to sell ultimate ideals which are relevant and necessary while working through that which is now feasible as an educational method. I don't think people can listen to you if you're not saying something which they understand. I think this is what's wrong with

Bayard Rustin

a great deal of the peace education today; they are not attempting to make this marriage between that which seems relevant to people plus educating for the long term.

FINN: In talking with people who have been engaged in the peace movement, I find that almost all of them have been what would be described as "on the Left"—either the Radical Left, Democratic Liberal, or whatever—and very few are on the Right. Why is there this apparent convergence of interests?

RUSTIN: Well, I think the Right almost always means conservative, people who have a stake in the present condition and who want to maintain it, to hold on to it. Now these people never really understand the relationship between law and order and justice. They never understand the relationship between peace and justice. They never understand that the good life proceeds from the broadest possibility of justice for all. Therefore, why should they be interested in other viewpoints? Why should they be interested in public works? Why should they be interested in whether or not the Puerto Ricans are properly housed? Why should they be interested in peace? Because they have what they want to hold on to; it's their preoccupation. Now the interesting thing is there's an ambivalency here; revolutionary education almost always proceeds from the children of conservatives who have broken away.

FINN: I wanted to ask about the peace movement as it exists in the country today—although peace *movements* might be more accurate. I find it hard to judge what it has accomplished, but one of the things it has not done is to change perceptibly U.S. policy in Vietnam. Does this mean that it is ineffective?

RUSTIN: No. For one thing, that policy might be much worse without it; the escalation might be much higher if the peace movement was not active. But secondly, even if the peace movement were not able to change a single policy, everyone would have to admit that *having* that kind of voice in this kind of atmosphere is a moral necessity.

FINN: What would you think are the most important manifestations of the peace movement today? Which of the things people are doing seem to be most useful or helpful?

RUSTIN: Well, I think the emergence of a great number of young men as conscientious objectors to war is very good for the society. It holds up a moral standard to which we ought all repair. I think propagandizing the kinds of things which normal Americans are forced to do in this dirty kind of war is important; it is a judgment on this society.

When I was in jail during World War II, practically all of us were opposed to all war. Today the greatest upsurge is among young people who do not say they are opposed to all war but are opposed to *this particular war*. And I believe that there are elements of this particular war, where people are required to put flame throwers on homes where there are women and children, scorching the earth, destroying vegetation, that are new factors; and I welcome this kind of conscientious objection.

FINN: Some people attempt to distinguish in this group you just mentioned between those who regard themselves as objectors on a moral basis and those who say they're doing it out of political judgments. Are those properly distinguishable?

RUSTIN: I don't believe that anyone is prepared to face five years in jail and a great fine for any reason that is not deeply moral. I think that words are not particularly meaningful. Because most of these young people, when you pin them down as to what they mean, will tell you there are just certain types of things they are not going to do to people in this context. And when a man says, "What does this do to me? What does this do to society? What does this do to other people?" he is really raising a moral question as well as a political one.

FINN: Do you think there's a kind of timidity or reluctance among these people to say they are adopting moral positions? Or do they think it's somehow more realistic to say it's hard and political?

RUSTIN: Young people have seen so much immorality on the part of the religious people of this country while they proclaim that they are moral that I think there is a tendency on their part to want to do away with the term "moral," and they are therefore putting it in political and economic and social terms. This doesn't disturb me one bit.

FINN: What effect do you think the war in Vietnam has on this country?

RUSTIN: Well, I think the effect on this country is devastating, for we are in a situation where we should be wiping poverty off the face of this earth. Poverty in India is a tragedy. Poverty in China is a tragedy. And it is very difficult for the Chinese and Indian governments really to deal with poverty. But in the United States, poverty which we have the funds to deal with is not just a tragedy—it is criminal. Now many people argue that you can have both guns and butter, and economically this is possible. Psychologically it is quite *im*possible. And therefore *perhaps* the greatest danger of the war in Vietnam—over and above that it lays waste to Vietnam—is that it is destroying us inwardly. It is destroying our spirit, it is destroying our imagination, it is destroying our ability to deal with domestic problems, and it is leading to rioting in our streets by frustrated poor people (who happen to be Negro) because they are in motion. To me this is one of the greatest tragedies of all. Furthermore, it tends to give strength to all of the rightist, negative, conservative forces in this country. And it will create, before this war is over, a neo-McCarthyism. War has its own logic. It makes important everything that is ugly and destroys everything that is beautiful.

FINN: So when people talk about this as a limited war, they're talking about it in very limited terms, I take it.

RUSTIN: Yes, I think so. And nothing which does the kind of thing which is being done in Vietnam—by *all* sides—could be termed "limited." There is no limit on the spirit of man and no limit therefore on what can happen and how that spirit can be destroyed.

FINN: In practical terms, how do you think the war in Vietnam affects the plans that you're engaged in now with the Freedom Budget?

RUSTIN: Well, I think that one cannot take the view that we must wait until the war is over before we can have a Freedom Budget. We have to go out and propagandize and work for it in the same way one works for peace in the midst of war. But I know that it is going to be very difficult to get the Freedom Budget for the psychological reasons which I mentioned earlier.

FINN: To pick up something we mentioned before. You said the times today *are* different than they were in the past, and you indicated that one of the differences was the number of particular-war objectors. We also have the other phenomenon which people have grouped loosely under "the New Left." These people also say that times are different and they attempt to formulate some different patterns of action, "participatory democracy," for example. I wonder if you could comment on the whole phenomenon.

RUSTIN: Well, I think the real phenomenon is that great numbers of young people are alienated. They do not really believe that a society which engages in the kind of war in Vietnam, a society which leaves so many millions of people poor, a society which will not give true equality to Negroes and other minorities, a society which will not make it possible for all people who want work to have it, they cannot *believe* in that society, and naturally they cannot engage in wars which that society carries on. Now in their effort to reject the society, they must put something in its place, and they reject democracy as we know it and are making experiments in democracy, participatory democracy—meaning get people involved, get people talking, get people trying to make their own decisions. Now I think this is a good move. I don't necessarily come out where they come out because I think in large groups you cannot really make decisions in this manner. But that's not the important thing. The important thing is that these young people are probing. I welcome that probing.

FINN: But you don't see participatory democracy as developing into a whole theory and way of acting which will replace the tradition we have in this country?

RUSTIN: I don't, simply because I don't know how you can get a thousand people in a room and have them talk until a decision is reached.

FINN: There are going to be some few people who are going to assume positions of responsibility and obligation.

RUSTIN: That is true. And very often that small group ends up having more power in that confused situation than when there is a referendum and you count heads.

FINN: Do you think that the direction of the war in Vietnam is heavily influenced by a very small minority of people, or does it grow out of the conditions of society, which means that in order to have the change you mentioned there has to be a real reordering in society, not just a change of a few individuals here and there?

Bayard Rustin

RUSTIN: I believe that it is *absolutely* imperative to go very deep. I do not accept the theory that a few people have dragged us into the war. I believe that our whole way of life has dragged us into the war.

ARNOLD S. KAUFMAN

> Men who rule are forced to place values such as order and justice ahead of truth and communication. Spiritual pre-eminence can rarely if ever be sustained in positions of political power. (Glenn Tinder, *The Crisis of Political Imagination*)

> One group of critics of President Johnson's policy in Vietnam . . . need not be taken too seriously. It includes many of the poets, pediatricians, novelists, painters, and professors who have been making so much noise during the last few months. Most of them are deeply humane people who loathe war and wish it would go away. In a rather vague fashion they feel that the way to avoid a fight is to drop your gun and back off—forgetting the disastrous results of these tactics in Ethiopia (1935), Spain (1936), and Munich (1938). (John Fischer, *Harpers*)

The intellectual and artistic communities in this country came belatedly to their intense involvement in the war in Vietnam. With a number of important exceptions, the poets, painters, novelists and professors responded to President Johnson's interpretation of America's increasing presence in Vietnam as trustingly as any political leader could have wished. But as Administration rhetoric seemed to grow increasingly distant from reality, as the military and political estimates of the probable cost and extent of U.S. efforts in Vietnam seemed to develop a pattern of remarkable inaccuracy, a sense of uneasiness and skepticism grew up within the intellectual community. Among this community some few worked to forge from their sense of skepticism and their own academic disciplines an instrument of reasoned investigation.

The instrument this group fashioned became known as the

Arnold S. Kaufman

teach-in. The first teach-in took place at the University of Michigan on March 24, 1965, was picked up the following day at Columbia University and then radiated to campuses across the country. The teach-ins varied in size, intensity, organization, purpose and accomplishment. But since they were initially conceived to present a side that had not yet been developed in the feeble national debate, the main thrust was critical of the government. In the praise and criticism of the teach-ins this point was often overlooked. The normally imperturbable Dean Rusk was moved to say, "I sometimes wonder at the gullibility of educated men and the stubborn disregard of plain facts by men who are supposed to be helping our young to learn—especially to learn how to think."

In spite of such criticism the movement gained strength, and in less than two months the organizing group, by then known as the Inter-University Committee for a Public Hearing on Vietnam, arranged a national teach-in in Washington, D. C. When Presidential Assistant McGeorge Bundy agreed to participate and present the views of the Administration, the status of the teach-in was established. Although he was unable to attend (because, as it was later learned, his attentions were secretly diverted to the Dominican Republic) the list of participants on both sides of the debate carried distinguished names.* The teach-in lasted approximately fifteen and a half hours, was attended by approximately 5,000 people and, by way of special radio hookups, was heard by more than 100,000 other people on over one hundred campuses. Although it drew some sharp criticism, Max Frankel's comment in the *New York Times* the next morning probably best expressed the general reaction: "The teach-in attained tenure here this weekend. It became respectable, accountable and probably permanent."

Arnold S. Kaufman is one of the small group that initiated the teach-in. He was born in Hartford, Connecticut in 1927. He was graduated from the City College of New York and received his Ph.D. in philosophy from Columbia University. In 1953–54

* Among those who supported government policy were: Arthur Schlesinger, Jr., Zbygniew Brzezinski, Wesley R. Fishel, Robert A. Scalapino, P. J. Honey, Leo Cherne, John Huizinga. Among those who were critical: Hans J. Morgenthau, Stanley Millet, William A. Williams, Bernard Fall, Robert Scheer.

he attended the London School of Economics on a Fulbright scholarship and the following year studied at Oxford. Since 1955 he has been on the faculty of the University of Michigan where he is an Associate Professor in the Department of Philosophy. He was at the Center for Advanced Study in Behavioral Sciences in 1962–63 and he was an Exchange Professor at the Tuskegee Institute in Alabama in 1965–66.

Mr. Kaufman says that his main interests in philosophy are in social and political philosophy, ethics, and the philosophy of social sciences, and that his main aim in life is to close the gap between the rhetoric and the practice of American liberalism. These combined interests and aims are apparent both in his scholarly and journalistic articles. When I spoke with him he had just completed for *Dissent* (September-October 1966) a book-length discussion of contemporary American politics entitled "Where Shall Liberals Go?" * His own not wholly irreverent reply to the question could well be read as an implicit response to Dean Rusk's comment on the teach-ins, for it is an exercise in thinking through some hard political problems, both long-standing and current, with the help of some "plain facts."

When I ask Kaufman if the impulse to develop a new forum to debate the war in Vietnam came from accumulating dissatisfaction with Administration pronouncements or whether it was sparked by some particular incident, he said it was both. The particular incident was the first bombing of North Vietnam by U.S. planes in February 1965.

KAUFMAN: A number of us got together to talk about what we should do about it. And we divided into two groups: one felt that some militant action was required, the other that some more conventional and modest expression of opposition was in order. At the time a lot of us didn't have settled convictions about what was appropriate. I was in the more moderate group at the very outset. But then the other group got together and decided to call for a work moratorium for a day in the University, and to use that day to conduct informal seminars off campus to go into the whole business in detail.

The general feeling that we all had shared was that the

* An extended version of this essay has recently been published as *The Radical Liberal* (New York, Atherton Press, 1967).

Arnold S. Kaufman

escalation hadn't been well justified by the Administration, that the Administration had been less than candid about its decisions and reasons for its decisions, and that whatever the justification of the policy might be, the manner in which the decisions were made and presented to the American people was completely inconsistent with our notion of how these things ought to be done in a democracy. Now when the other group announced the work moratorium, there immediately followed an enormous amount of flac from state officials, University officials and so on. Immediately after this developed I and others who had been dubious about the particular tactic adopted did succeed in having it somewhat modified. As I recall, the main issue was to make it very clear that we weren't abdicating our teaching responsibilities but, from our point of view, actually fulfilling them more responsibly. This was in direct answer to the charge that Governor Romney made that we were being irresponsible.

FINN: Did that work moratorium actually take place?

KAUFMAN: No, it didn't because then the flac really went up, and everybody began to talk about the formal responsibilities of the teacher. This seemed to a number of us to be a very bad thing because we wanted to focus attention on the issue of Vietnam and instead, all of the attention was focused on the responsibilities of teachers. And while we all felt that we weren't being irresponsible, a number of us did decide that this was tactically wrong, that we were harming rather than helping our main aim, which was to focus attention on Vietnam policy and to get some debate on it.

You see, not only did we feel that the Administration was being disingenuous—the so-called White Paper they issued was a scholarly monstrosity which, in effect, the State Department has since conceded. In private conversation even some of the people who participated in the writing of it have told us that they recognize it as a blunder. And, indeed, Arthur Schlesinger, Jr., who was recommended by McGeorge Bundy to give the Administration position as an Administration sympathizer for the National Teach-In, began his speech there by wondering how gullible a Secretary of State could be who would have released such a document.

But since the work moratorium idea was taking attention away from the main issue, we began looking for an effective means of opening up debate and of protesting to some extent

the actual policy, the escalation. But many of us, even at that
point in history, were concerned to an even greater extent by the
bad faith of the Administration. Well, six of us got together,
and it was at that meeting that Marshall Sahlins in effect invented the concept of the teach-in. He proposed it, and we
worked out a plan which we presented to the large group of fifty
the next evening. And we used the word "teach-in" for the first
time on that occasion. This was accepted by the larger group
and the first teach-in was held at Michigan about a week after
that.

We weren't sure how many people would show up. In trying
to estimate how large the crowd would be, we figured that we'd
be lucky if we had eight hundred. Well, in the event, over three
thousand people showed up. It was an enormous success. It
lasted all night. And a number of us got on the phone—principally again Marshall Sahlins—and began to call friends at
other universities to tell them about the idea and to encourage
them to do the same. Well, the rest is history. You know that it
spread like a brushfire all over the country and they're still
going on.

Our next step was to see how we could exploit what we'd
achieved in a way that would give us greater national visibility.
And the National Teach-In idea emerged from a number of meetings we had. At first we were dubious about it, but we decided
to go ahead. The first one, you had only people who were opposed to the policy to speak. And our reason for this was not
that we didn't want to encourage debate, but many of us felt that
the Administration hadn't, so to speak, been excluded from the
mass media in presenting its side of the case, and we wanted to
have opportunities to somehow correct the balance of debate.
But at the National Teach-In, we decided to have *both* sides
represented in order to have a direct confrontation between the
critics, who by this time had become prominent as a result of
the many teach-ins that were occurring over the country, and
the Administration.

FINN: Do the teach-ins remain true to their purpose as it was
initially conceived? You said first that they were really to examine the kind of statements the Administration was putting out
because they seemed to lack integrity.

KAUFMAN: Well, I think like all devices the teach-ins became
a tactic which was used in various ways by various people, de-

Arnold S. Kaufman

pending on their purposes. There was no organized teach-in movement that could impose a discipline. And also, as we began to get more deeply into the issue, a lot of us became more convinced than we were at the outset that the policy was wrong. So obviously we sought other outlets for this. Sometimes the outlets sought were called teach-ins, but they were teach-ins in name only.

FINN: How would you assess the effect of the teach-ins, particularly the ones you participated in, but all that you know about?

KAUFMAN: Well, it's very hard. Nobody has the precise information about the impact of the teach-ins one would like to have. What seems clear is that they filled a vacuum, a great need that existed, because lots of people—either passionately opposed to U.S. policy or just terribly anxious about it, not knowing whether it was right or wrong—who felt very sure that they hadn't been given sufficient information or reasoning from the Administration on the basis of which to make a judgment. So that there was a tremendous enthusiasm for the idea, especially after the National Teach-In, because it filled the vacuum that had been left by the virtual abdication of the Congress in this matter. It all happened without Congressional debate, and that's a very important part of it.

James Reston, who was quite skeptical about the thing at the outset, wrote after the National Teach-In that "the importance of this weekend's debate in Washington is that at least a means has been found to discuss these realities, to move from protest against the effects of world disorder to analysis of causes to a choice of hard options. The Inter-University Committee, which was responsible for the Washington teach-in, should be continued and supported financially. It started at the University of Michigan as a protesting movement against the Government's Vietnamese policy."—I was never able to convince Reston that it wasn't just a protest for a lot of people—"Threatening an academic strike"—it was a moratorium, it wasn't a strike—"it has now developed into a form of national debate which could be of fundamental importance to the nation." So he changed completely in a couple of weeks. I know he changed because I talked to him by phone after his first articles, which were quite uncomplimentary.

FINN: Well, that's a pretty good testimony to their effectiveness.

KAUFMAN: The point is that they served the need. Now that some of the debate at least has gotten into the Congress, the meaningfulness of such a movement is diminished, though I do think the Congress is sort of focused almost exclusively on the arguments that go to whether or not the national interest is being served, not enough on other matters which I think are of quite fundamental importance in Vietnam.

FINN: You said one of the things that happened initially was that when you and other faculty members once started exploring the credibility of the Administration statements you began to question more intensively the actual policy.

KAUFMAN: Yes, our initial feelings about the policy were increasingly confirmed, and everything that's happened since has only served to confirm them more. We began to understand, for example, that the Administration spokesmen, those who had been willing to make predictions about the war, had been consistently wrong in their predictions.*

* Kaufman then listed a number of predictions that have been faulty. In his article, "Where Shall Liberals Go?" he presents this orderly account: "Consider the following record. On February 25, 1963, Senator Mansfield, after a fact-finding trip to Vietnam reported to President Kennedy that, 'Those who bear responsibility for directing operations under the new strategy are optimistic over prospects for success. Indeed, success was predicted to the group (of senators) almost without exception, by responsible Americans and Vietnamese, in terms of a year or two hence.' In a footnote, Senator Mansfield added that Admiral Harry Felt more cautiously predicted that it might take three years. Three years later, almost to the day, President Johnson ordered the bombing of North Vietnam. Four years later, there are over 280,000 men in South Vietnam, and at least 400,000 will be there by the end of this year. In May 1963, Secretary of Defense McNamara announced that we had turned the corner in Vietnam. On October 2, 1963, he and General Taylor reported to President Kennedy that in 'their judgment the major part of the U.S. military task can be completed by the end of 1965.' On February 18, 1964, Secretary McNamara predicted, in testimony before the Congress, that the 'bulk' of U.S. forces could be expected to leave by 1965.

"After the war's escalation in February 1965, the Administration justified its course in terms of the following considerations:

"i. Air strikes would stem the flow of men and materials from North Vietnam into the South.
"ii. The show of force would weaken our adversaries' will to fight.

Arnold S. Kaufman

If you're a rational man and you're continually wrong in the predictions that you make, then it's either because you don't have access to the facts or the basic assumptions in terms of which you interpret the facts are wrong. Now we believe that the Administration has access to as many facts, more facts than we do, so the only alternative explanation of this absolutely terrific record of wrong prediction is that their basic assumptions are wrong. We began to focus attention on those. Of course this general skepticism was reinforced by what happened after the escalation. They claimed among other things that it would weaken the will of the North Vietnamese to fight, that it would move them to the negotiating table more readily. (Of course at the time we didn't have all the facts. We didn't know that the North Vietnamese *had* tried to move the thing to the negotiating table in '64—I'm referring among other things to the approach made to U Thant and the stuff reported in Sevareid's article.*)

Most of us are convinced that the national interest, far from being served by our present policy, is being impaired; that the policy we're pursuing does far more to jeopardize world peace than to preserve it. But even if one grants that there's a kind of stand-off in argument on these two points, I think the third point—that we have a moral obligation to be there based on our commitments to the Diem regime initially and our concern to stop the forces of darkest evil from destroying the liberty and the democracy in Vietnam—precisely for that reason, becomes decisive: namely, we think that the present policy is a moral outrage. It seems to me that here is precisely the sort of situation in which morality gets its grip in foreign policy; where at *best* the Administration can argue that it has some plausible reason to believe what it believes, but nothing decisive. And no rational man could believe it has.

"iii. Air strikes would hearten our allies and dismay Peking.

"iv. The air strikes would diminish the need to send large numbers of conventional forces.

"v. Escalation would stabilize the political situation in the South.

"A year later, not one of these predictions has been proved accurate."

* The fullest account to date of U Thant's efforts is a detailed article by Mario Rossi, former Special Correspondent of the *Christian Science Monitor*. Entitled "U Thant and Vietnam: The Untold Story," it appeared in the *New York Review of Books,* November 17, 1966. In a special supplement to the May 4, 1967, issue of the same journal, Theodore Draper places the negotiating efforts in a large historical context.

FINN: Just one thing. You didn't mean to say that *no* rational man could accept that evidence as decisive, because there are apparently people in the Administration who do.

KAUFMAN: I would say that they're flying in the face of the evidence that's as plain as a light in a dark night and are not being rational. I can see how they'd accept it, but not that they have an iron-clad or convincing case. So in this situation, in which no clear case can be made that what we're doing is either in the national interest or essential to world peace, and a pretty strong case can be made on the other side—at least as plausible a case as the Administration's, and I put it as modestly as possible—then you have to ask yourself especially about the morality of the means which you're employing in pursuing this policy.

And it seems very clear that what we're doing is engaging in an indiscriminate form of warfare, careful as we try to be. And you have to have a fairly good reason to believe that what you're doing is right before you put lives in jeopardy, either the lives of your own combatants, the lives of innocent civilians, or the lives of the other combatants.

FINN: Of course our Government insists upon their continuing efforts to discriminate.

KAUFMAN: Oh, I'm sure that they're making efforts. But they're not making the kind of effort that is required; they're using weapons that are indiscriminate in their physical impact on people—napalm, and bombs that explode and scatter in every direction. I think even people sympathetic to the Government policy, those who are objective at all, will admit that the kill ratio of civilians to combatants is in the neighborhood of four to one; and the estimates are varying from anywhere from four to one to twelve to one; nobody really knows. These are figures which both *Newsweek* and Bernard Fall had estimated on the basis of their battlefield investigations.

In addition, rather than having succeeded in building up the political integrity, the freedom and the democracy of the South Vietnamese people, we've consistently eroded those institutions and now, as Senator Mansfield said in his most recent report to President Johnson, so far as the political, economic and social efforts that we're making in Vietnam are concerned, we're still at the beginning of a beginning—those are his words—

Arnold S. Kaufman

just as we were in 1955 when we first got in there. So that there's been *no* progress in all these areas.

Now you could say, "But the adversaries are committing terror and doing terrible things," and no doubt that's true. At least people like myself have no desire to justify the Vietcong or to defend the Vietcong or the North Vietnamese. That isn't the issue. Let's say they're sinful. The question is whether we're justified in stamping out sin there, given the balance of argument so far as the national interest and world peace are concerned. And it seems to me that the sins that have to be committed to stamp out their sins are substantially greater. In any event, we can't possibly morally justify what we're doing in Vietnam now.

FINN: Now these are really conclusions you've reached, not positions you had at the start of the teach-ins.

KAUFMAN: That's right. My initial motivation was due more to the sense that I'd been used as a citizen, manipulated and treated with great contempt by the Administration; that there was no effort being made by the Administration at that time to level with the American people, to tell them the truth as they knew it.

FINN: Do you think there is any more of an effort?

KAUFMAN: Only what's coerced through this dissent.

Although Kaufman had said that the effects of the teach-ins were difficult to assess, I ask if he can say something about their effect on the students, some of whom have to face the draft. In reply he points out that unlike any other movement of social protest that has taken place in recent years, the teach-ins were "initiated, organized and carried through by faculty members, with increasing help from students." And one could make three comments about their effect on the student body.

First, because students saw the faculty express their concern in a socially and politically responsible way, some of the deep distrust between faculty and students was diminished. And Kaufman compared the cooperative effort at Michigan favorably with the situation at Berkeley where the alienation of student body from faculty and administration for long plagued the school. Second, the teach-ins channeled energies into constructive programs. Third, and "perhaps most important in the long run," more people, including those who support government policy, "have been moved to study this as well as other relevant foreign-policy matters much more carefully and intensively than before." The teach-ins have helped to develop a more intelligent and critical citizen, one prepared to make independent judgments instead of "giving it all over to the experts or the mysteries of foreign-policy decision making."

Kaufman expressed deep reservations about some of the protests made by both student and faculty. The International Days of Protest against the War in Vietnam he termed a "strategic disaster," doing incalculably more harm than good to the effort they purported to serve. Nothing, he said, could have been more convenient for proponents of the Administration's views than the "weekend of draft-card burnings, marches on Selective Service boards and attempts to impose civilian arrests on military personnel." He rejects the attempt to apply techniques that have proved effective in the civil rights struggle to U.S. policy in Vietnam. And he is critical of what he calls "the unrestrained impulse to moral integrity."

I point out that a number of people have questioned the competence of many who participate not only in the teach-ins but in the protest movement. The critics emphasize what is undeniably true, that the number of political scientists involved in the movement is very small, and they cite this fact as a very telling and incisive criticism of the protest movement.

KAUFMAN: First, that isn't quite true; quite a few of the most distinguished political scientists in the country sponsored the National Teach-In. But it is true that the political scientists have not flocked to the cause with any passion. But I think there are good epistemological reasons for this. Political scientists are involved in a discipline which focuses on power and the manipulations of power. More than most scholars, they're inclined to be rather indifferent to or even contemptuous of moral considerations because they tend to view the whole political process primarily in terms of the confrontation and management of power. They tend to dismiss lots of the considerations that weigh very strongly with people like myself. It simply means that they are different kinds of persons, not that

Arnold S. Kaufman

they have hold of more facts.* If you start from fundamentally
different human premises, you're bound to come up with
fundamentally different policy conclusions. Also, they engage
in what I call role playing: that is, they're always trying to
view things from the perspective of the people *making* the decision. They want to act as if they were President or Congressmen, and so on. Whereas, from my point of view, I'm trying
to play a role as a citizen in a very large and complex process,
and trying to play that role as decisively as possible and trying
to advance the things I believe in. And so I think it's a fundamentally bad tactical error to always put yourself in the place
of the men in power. I remember in the Fulbright-Rusk exchange
during the Foreign Relations Committee Hearings, Rusk at one

* Other people have given different responses to this particular charge.
Hans Morgenthau, for example, has written that "large segments of the
intellectual world have indeed been silenced or corrupted. This is
especially true of those segments which are professionally concerned with
the activities of government. If one examines, for instance, the lists of
intellectuals who have gone on record against the war in Vietnam, one is
struck by the relative paucity of political scientists. One is also struck
by the frequency with which those who remain silent in public express
their opposition in private. It must also be noted that some intellectuals
have attacked their dissenting colleagues with unaccustomed violence
and with arguments so tortuous and inconsistent as to be inexplicable
on purely intellectual grounds while, unknown to the public, they were
working for the government part-time or accepted a government position
shortly afterwards. Finally there is the type of intellectual who habitually
moves from the intellectual into the political sphere and back again and
whose overt political views change with these movements and with
changes in the climate of political opinion." ("Truth and Power: Intellectuals and the Johnson Administration," *New Republic,* November
26, 1966, p. 12.) In the *New Republic* of December 17, Melvin Urofsky,
an historian at Ohio State University, wrote a strong rejoinder to Morgenthau.
    Another example might well be cited. On June 8, 1966 a group of
Princeton historians responded, in a letter to the *New York Times,* to a
previous news article by John Pomfret, who, they thought, misrepre-
sented both the "amount and identity of the opposition."
    "The article reinforces the Administration's apparent belief that most
of its professorial critics are poets, philosophers, or psychologists, and
that social scientists and historians, being better informed, appreciate the
necessity of action.
    "This letter is addressed to that belief. It is, in effect, a poll of the
Princeton History Department. All 33 full-time members of the department not away on leave were invited to sign it. Twenty-one of them
did so. They speak, of course, neither for their department nor for the
university, but they are not a fringe group.
    "We did not like the President's Princeton speech, as Mr. Pomfret

point said he urges every American to put himself in the place of the President and ask himself what he would do if he were President. And I think in this statement more than any other in the whole Hearings, Rusk—and Johnson *has* said things like that—displays a *profoundly* defective conception of what the democratic process is or should be all about.

---

says most professors did, but found its arguments confused and repellent. We are not, as Mr. Pomfret suggests, merely a little unhappy or a bit irritated by the President's handling of the Vietnamese problem, but opposed to it. . . .

"On the two basic policy questions—the deterrence of Chinese aggression and the protection of the people of South Vietnam—we believe that American actions in the last year have done more harm than good. . . .

"However interest, power and danger may be reckoned for Asia and elsewhere (and we do not all make the same reckoning), we believe that this war is costing the United States more than can be gained from it. We believe, in short, that future historians will judge the President and his chief advisers not as leaders who bore the tragic burden of power and responsibility with strength and wisdom, but as shortsighted, self-deceived, often willful men."

STANLEY MILLET

In his "Nervous Nellies" speech President Johnson urged voters to "read carefully the statements of every public official and every candidate for every office" in order to note those "ready to turn on their own leaders, their own country and their own fighting men." The men that President Johnson was referring to were otherwise known as "peace candidates" in the 1966 elections. As the elections turned out, the President could have spared the country this unpalatable admonition and himself the concern that must have prompted it.

Of the approximately eighty nonincumbent peace candidates, none—if we except Oregon's Mark Hatfield as a special case—gained office and few survived the primaries. Most of these were single-issue candidates who in varying degrees stressed the responsibility of the U.S. to provide the initiatives for a peaceful termination of the war in Vietnam. The elections showed that, at least in '66, the issue of peace in these terms was insufficient to propel into office the unfamiliar amateur, for most of the candidates were academics, professional men and housewives who had not previously run for office and who ran without much organizational support. The closest significant races were run in California where Bob Scheer, Ed Keating and Stanley Sheinbaum, all associated with *Ramparts* magazine, received substantial support. The question for anyone in the peace movement, of course, concerns the significance not only of the outcome of the election but the emergence of so many peace candidates.

Stanley Millet, who ran from the Third Congressional District in Nassau County, New York, is one of the defeated candidates. One of his campaign brochures reads in large block letters "Use Your Ballot to End the War Now," and in smaller type:

"This open-ended conflict which threatens to erupt into World War III is against the best interests of every American. In addition to the brutal and cruel destruction of Vietnam, the war is

- Killing our sons
- Sapping our economic strength
- Curtailing the progress of the Negro people towards full equality
- Preventing us from dealing realistically with pressing domestic programs."

Stanley Millet was born in New York in 1917. After serving for four years in the U.S. Army Air Force he continued his academic career. He has held various positions in the political science departments of Hobart College, New School for Social Research, Briarcliff College, Bard College and Adelphi University, where he is now Professor and Chairman of the Department of Political Science. In 1961–62 he was Smith-Mundt Visiting Professor in the Faculty of Law at the University of Saigon, Vietnam.

He is an advisory editor for *Viet Report* and a member of the National Board of the Inter-University Committee for the Debate of Foreign Policy. He spoke at forums and teach-ins on Vietnam at over twenty universities and at the National Teach-In in Washington in May 1965. He has written articles on Vietnam for *Harper's, War/Peace Report, New Magazine* and *Viet Report*.

We do not immediately discuss peace candidates but, more generally, the peace movement and its leadership. Millet tells me of a meeting in Cleveland that was held in early September. It was initiated, he thinks, by a group within the Inter-University Committee, and was initially interpreted by the National Coordinating Committee (NCC)—which tries to coordinate activities of hundreds of local *ad hoc* community organizations—as a challenge to its authority. Nevertheless, representatives of many organizations came, ranging from SANE and the Amer-

Stanley Millet

ican Friends Service Committee to Youth Against War and Fascism and Young Socialist Alliance.

MILLET: My own feeling is that when you add it all up it was an interesting and important meeting. As they said in the course of the discussion, there was never such unity within the peace movement before: a great number of groups were at the meeting; a small number of people—about one hundred and ten people—but a spread of groups. And they did resolve on a common action. But what seemed clear to me was that it's the weakness of the peace movement that accounts for both the unity and the presence of so many groups. The convincing argument to anybody, at any time there was a dispute, was, "If you insist on your position, regardless of what it is, you'll break the unity, and we need the unity." If the peace movement had been stronger, the need for unity would not have been felt so strongly. So I see it as an indication of the weakness of the movement and what I myself interpret as a series of defeats for the peace movement during last spring and this summer [of 1966].

The movement is by no means dead, because it rests on a current of hostility to the war and other things, but it's not a movement that will grow in size, find new channels to manifest itself in. It has, in many senses, no way to turn at the moment. So I think that unless the political situation changes—and that's a long-term thing—it's reached the peak of its popular support. Other things will have to come into play, like a much clearer and stronger impact of inflation and a greater casualty rate, or something of that kind. But whoever is going to get caught up in the Vietnam issue, and for whatever reasons, has been caught up by now. And in terms of a movement that conceives of itself as having a certain goal, that's just not enough. It's not enough. And looked at most realistically—that is, considering all possible things from the most far-out kind of demonstrations to teach-ins and political candidacy—the power has been exhausted; the roads to influence and power are not available any longer to this movement. And I think that there are real reasons why that's so.

Millet then makes an assessment that a number of the people I had talked to were unable to make—or had consciously rejected. One of the "real fascinations of the Vietnam question is," Millet says, "how much light it throws on our politics. American politics, like most politics, is *basically* group politics. And the Vietnam question belongs to no group." There are, he points out, no ethnic groups, no economic groups, no religious or racial groups with a real investment in Vietnam. The closest thing to effective groups with vested interests are the government agencies and political and military leaders who have acquired a stake by virtue of past policies and decisions. Granting that this is a correct reading, what are the groups, I ask, and who are the people who are included, not always appropriately, in the peace movement?

MILLET: Look at the kinds of groups. When you want to talk about who's who in the peace movement, again you turn to A. J. Muste. Now if ever there was a marginal political figure in American life, it would be A. J. Muste, in spite of his life-long involvement in political movements. He's a man who has stood for things that have found very, very small audiences. And so have the Catholic Workers and the FOR. They're enjoying a tremendous renaissance because most of them have been peace people for years and years and years. And now they have this tremendous audience to talk to. Then there are things like SANE, or Women Strike for Peace, or Women's International League for Peace and Freedom, who represent a general tendency—quasi-liberal, quasi-leftist. They have been around for some time, but when the Vietnam movement came they were not really the dynamic elements. Then there's the New Left kids, like SDS or the NCC offshoot, or the DuBois Club, which is Communist but I think a new breed and restive with the old leadership, and a body like the IUC which is impossible to define in any strict sense.

What interests me most of all in the New Left is the fact that a great deal of the youth protest is intrinsically moral, which again separates it from interest-group politics, and that's a problem of both the civil rights movement and the peace movement. The peace movement is, from this point of view, exactly as the civil rights movement would be if there were very few Negroes. All the arguments and all the views which underwrite the civil rights movement, the theoretical structure, are just as relevant to, say, Mexicans or Indians, but there is no strong movement pressing for their rights because there is no large vested group there. Now many of the kids, the students especially, are caught up in the movement in terms of moral considerations. It's often a very simplistic and very old-fashioned morality, but it's powerful because it is the foundation for their actions. What's made the civil rights movement a real political force is the fact that there is a real Negro population. But that's missing in Vietnam. We don't have enough Vietnamese in the country or a single, strong committed interest group.

FINN: Before the elections, the National Committee for an Effective Congress published a number of things, all calling for support of moderate candidates. And one of the pieces said— this was for the Senators McCarthy and McGovern Special Fund—"It depends upon whether enough citizens like you realize that the moderate response to the Vietnam war will collapse if world-minded candidates are overwhelmed by extremists at the polls." In these terms, the peace candidates are clearly extremists.

MILLET: I'm an extremist on this question. I accept that description with pride. I think that there is much to be said about what moderation and extremism can mean in this situation.

When I suggest that many political leaders interpreted the defeat of the peace candidates as support for present U.S. policy in Vietnam, Millet agrees but he does not think that their election would have significantly affected that policy.

MILLET: For example, the most important escalation that the United States made in the war was the involvement of our own troops in massive quantity in the summer of '65. Now that move was taken at a time when the peace movement was far, far stronger than it is even at the moment and there were strong pressures against escalation. And I think that even if peace candidates had shown extremely well, that it would not have militated against any serious policy change that the Administration really wished to undertake. And I think that this is so for the very reason that I gave before: a contrary opinion in American politics is only important if it represents a serious *group*. And a widespread, diffuse demonstration—including, say, even ten congressmen—wouldn't be *tremendous,* wouldn't signify anything from the point of view of political inhibitions. Men like

Fulbright, Morse, Gruening or Hartke, who represent a mitigating effect upon policy, will weather this setback in the peace movement and will be there playing a role. So I don't think Congressional elections will produce, one way or another, significant changes in policy. I don't think it's important what ordinary people think about the war in Vietnam at this time, because it cannot be converted into political power. What difference does it make?

When I ask Millet why he campaigned as a peace candidate if the outcome made no difference, he gives several reasons. First, he was in a "position of maximum frustration"; there was nothing else to do that made any sense. Second, there was a possibility that his opponent might be forced to shift his position at least slightly. Third, as the campaign developed, there was a possibility that he might win and for a political newcomer to win as a peace candidate would have real significance, "although I would hardly justify it in terms of a real change in policy."

FINN: Would you be willing to speculate about the effect of the peace candidates across the country?

MILLET: Take the strongest case that one can make: Bob Scheer's campaign in Oakland, California. What'd he get? Forty-seven percent of the vote. Something like that. Those are significant votes. And I think that all one can say is that those votes, statistically significant, have turned out to be politically without significance. Suppose all peace candidates throughout the country had gotten between forty and forty-nine percent of the vote; I think it would still be politically meaningless within the framework of the American system.

FINN: If it had an impact, would it have to be in the way in which you described it: by forcing the candidate who did win to acknowledge that there were many people in his district who dissented?

MILLET: No. No, it's more complex than that, because Vietnam policy—and I think that this is a *tremendously* important point—Vietnam policy is not controlled by Congress. And as a matter of fact, Congress has very little impact on Vietnam policy. Vietnam policy is Executive. For most foreign policy issues now, the role of the Congress is relatively weak.

Stanley Millet

FINN: Without disagreeing with that, I would presume that the President and others would be sensitive to a large body of public opinion that was opposed to the war in Vietnam, and would feel it at least as an inhibition on a harder approach.

MILLET: That seems like the most evident inference to make from the way our political system works. But it hasn't worked that way. The men in Congress who have been critical of our policy have been influential without a demonstrated popular opinion to ride on. And these men are there and functioning regardless of what happens to peace candidates, but they cannot change our present Vietnam policy. If the President comes to the position that the war requires the bombardment of Haiphong, then we will have it, just as we have the increasing investment of American troops.

FINN: Do you think Congressional critics act as an inhibition at all?

MILLET: Yes. Yes, and I think this is another one of the places at which one gets profound insight into our political system. Because the real alternatives in the war, as they're debated in Washington, are, within the military framework, very extreme positions. There are many influential men who are not taken over by extreme military positions. But the crucial moment has always occurred when actual military requirements are demonstrated; that demonstration overrides the resistance. And then we get the bombardment of North Vietnam or the investment with American troops or perhaps the blockade of Haiphong Harbor, or maybe even—if the requirements should push us that way—the invasion of the North, which is one of the alternatives in the discussion now. But that's another political process, and it's quite unrelated, or not clearly and directly related, to the political process that has to do with candidates, elections, public opinion in a general sense.

Millet adds that if Bob Scheer, for example, had defeated Cohelan, who is also a critic of our Vietnam policy, "it would have been tremendously heartening to the peace movement," but it would have had little political impact. And again he stresses that since sometime after World War II many foreign policy issues are under Executive control and are not affected by Congressional elections. But many who parade, march on

Washington or sign protest statements do not make the same political distinctions. Their actions would suggest that they expect to influence foreign policy decisions in much the same way they would influence domestic policy—by bringing pressure on their congressional representatives. I ask Millet if the poor showing of the "peace candidates" will cause such activist critics of U.S. policy to correct what he would regard as faulty political analysis.

MILLET: I think that the consequences for people in the peace movement are already fairly evident. The tendency to turn toward more militant forms of action, away from what have been traditionally considered the channels for political influence in the United States, becomes more appealing. This tendency accounts for what happened to SNCC, and it partly manifests itself in the split in the IUC. It will leave the more moderate groupings and the older organizations to longer-range things. And they're already talking in these terms. "Our task," say people from Women Strike or SANE, "is long-term education. We mustn't look to something that will bring policy change now; we've got to engage in educational work." This means that in effect they recognize that political influence is denied to them at the moment. Whereas those who say, "What we have to do is get out and burn down the Pentagon," want to have political influence now, but they turn to extra-parliamentary techniques.

FINN: In at least partial support, I think, of what you're saying, let me read to you a section in an article that Staughton Lynd wrote.* This was in April of '66. "To those now throwing themselves into Congressional campaigns and talking about a new people's party. Please don't turn your backs on the movement and condemn the rock from which you were hewn. I have seen too many pamphlets which in one form or another strike the note, 'Tired of demonstrations? Why not do something real? Join the campaign of —— for Congress!'" And Lynd asks, "Do you really imagine that you can resist the inertial drift of all politics toward compromise without some of us—call us rearguard if you like—who stand outside politics and say things politicians cannot say, and so make it possible for politicians

* "Radical Politics and Nonviolent Revolution," *Liberation,* April 1966, p. 14.

to say them?" It's clear that Lynd is in the group that you've suggested wants immediate effective action.

MILLET: Yes, and I think this is characteristic of Staughton's positions all along.

FINN: Well, is the group that he represents, and those who would agree with him, a group *more* likely to be isolated by present events, by the weakening of the peace movement? If the peace movement *is* weakening, are the people who are looking for long-range effects more likely to survive this and carry on?

MILLET: Oh, I don't know. I think Staughton's going to come out a historic figure, like Thoreau, and he'll be a guy we'll read about in books someday. He is a real spokesman for the New Youth—they call him "the saint." His authority is tremendous because he expresses many of their attitudes, including those about participatory democracy, and I think really gives a big insight into what they're all about. But I don't think these ideas play a role on foreign policy issues really. I think their concepts of participatory democray will play a role in American life for a very long time, because they're the kind of ideas to which people who are profoundly disenchanted with the organized society in which we live, who are casting around for some form of group living which is different, turn to. But these ideas have to have a field to operate in, and that means that they will always be operating, by the very nature of things, within the framework of small local community actions. And so they'll turn up over and over again in connection with some local poverty program or some local housing issue. Perhaps they'll turn up in the trade union movement in a very small sphere, spotted here and there; on the universities because those notions have *tremendous* appeal to this new generation of kids—for a *reason*. I mean, I think I understand why. But again, I don't think they can play any effective political role in foreign policy because foreign policy issues are always issues that belong to the state. They don't belong to a little group in Passaic, New Jersey.

FINN: But you said that you thought Staughton Lynd would emerge as an historic figure even though the direction which he has taken here, as a spokesman for groups who want to participate *in* foreign policy judgments, is clearly off on a wrong tack.

MILLET: Wrong in the sense of pragmatic politics. Thoreau didn't play a role either in this sense. And *he's* an historic figure. And I think that in this period, because of the sentiments that Staughton gives voice to, that he will be historically a personage of that character.

FINN: But if he doesn't have political effectiveness, how would you measure his effectiveness'

MILLET: How would you measure Thoreau's?

FINN: I'd say that Thoreau has voiced ideas and principles which people continue to find illuminating in their own lives and activities—not always leading to particular political action.

MILLET: Well, I think that this is the sense in which Staughton will emerge as a figure who manifests some form of highly prized American thought, a way of thinking about things, the same reasons for which men praise Thoreau in every classroom that I know. But nobody behaves like Thoreau, least of all myself. These men express what in another context I would call the poetic manifestations of political life. They're the men who many others see as the embodiment of what one ought to be. But they're very difficult when you confront them face to face in immediate life. Unlike the guy from time past, the guy from now confronts you with a real alternative. When you meet Staughton Lynd, or when he's there, you have to say I am with you or I am not with you. Whereas Thoreau is beautiful. He imposes no burdens on me. And I don't mean to do anything more than to describe what I think is the case. I think the kids are right: Staughton *is* a type of the saint. I think every one of us will admit, saintly figures met face to face are extraordinarily difficult and not to be followed

FINN: Often admired but not so often emulated.

We shift the topic back to Vietnam and Millet's own passionate involvement. He says that before he went to Vietnam he had no strong position, but developed it while he was there. In order to make the significance of such a shift more evident Millet offers a thumbnail political autobiography,

MILLET: When I was a kid before the war, I had the vague liberal-left tendencies of students in New York City, with nothing specific other than the characteristics of the time. I was a City College kid in the thirties and a member of no organizations, but leftist in tendency and in temperament. As we went into World War II, my responses again were typical for the time. I became involved in World War II, and I wouldn't pin it on anything higher than the response of a Jewish kid from New York City involved in the issues of the day, with no great theoretical rationale. I came out of the war really fairly shocked by the character and extent of the war, and I actually went into political science in a very naïve way at that time, wishing to understand how wars came into being and how they could be avoided. And I formulated my political ideas actually in graduate school. Partly because of the graduate school I went to, partly because of the times, I was myself a very doctrinaire anti-communist and anti-leftist in the fifties, and developed a reaction against those tendencies because of the McCarthy period—which outraged simple notions of decency. And in the meantime I was becoming more and more caught up with just academic political science, with no political overtones. I was a member of nothing and couldn't care less. I was happy and content in my academic life.

When, in 1961, I went to Vietnam I scarcely knew anything of the Vietnam issue. I wasn't concerned with the confrontation with communism, particularly in that area. I'd spent a lot of time in the study of Soviet things because I was interested in the Soviet Union. When I went to Vietnam I had a very academic notion about things, thinking, yes, there was a revolution going on in Vietnam, and I would see what one was really like— thinking of revolution largely in terms of the winds of change, rising economic expectations, and a leading role being played by the Communist Party. When I was in Vietnam—and I think that for guys like me this is always there—when I was in Vietnam I actually came face to face with the simplest kind of moral judgments. You know, one can have all kinds of theoretical and analytic discussions of moral things, but there is a bedrock of morality in men like us which makes it impossible for me to steal your money or you to steal my money. There's nothing to discuss, no matter how ranging our discussion is; there are very simple things that one can't do. And I was literally shocked by the bedrock of dishonesty in the Vietnam thing, the simple kind of lie that in this very literal, old-fashioned sense sticks in your mouth; you can't say it.

FINN: And who was telling the lies?

MILLET: Our government, and all the people who were involved in it. For example, the first thing that caught me up was the problem of Vietcong terrorism. The Vietcong was pointed to as a terrorist agency, commanding peasants through acts of terror. This was literally and patently not true.

FINN: But there *were* acts of terrorism, weren't there?

MILLET: Not really. And certainly not at that time. And certainly not of the character described by the prevailing thesis. It was quite the other way around. To the extent that there were—without getting into the really sophisticated question of terror—to the extent that there were in a simple sense terrorist acts, men scaring the hell out of other men by acts of wanton brutality or deliberate brutality, they were on the government side.

FINN: I've read and heard people like George Tanham, George Carver, and Douglas Pike, who say there are such acts of terrorism by the Vietcong clearly planned to remove and kill those people who have or are likely to assume positions of leadership in the community within South Vietnam.

MILLET: What I'm talking about comes down to things as simple as who cut who's throat. Who are people actually afraid of? And if you go into the villages, when do the villagers tremble and when do they not tremble? Simple as that. Now it turned out it was *our* side that was making the villagers tremble, and not the VC side at all. You talked with ordinary Vietnamese and you'd say, "Have you been to your village lately?" "Yes, I was down there last weekend." "How are things down there?" "Not bad. Peaceful and quiet." "Who's in control down there?" "Oh, the VC is in control." "How are things in your village?" "Oh it's terrible. The army passed through." Yes, the army of Saigon.

FINN: Do you accept as true the statement that many thousands of South Vietnamese local officials were killed by the Vietcong as part of a deliberate plan?

MILLET: Oh, certainly. But then if we were to get involved in a more sophisticated discussion, we would have to discuss not what does killing men consist in, but what does terror consist in and what's the political meaning of who gets killed. Within

Stanley Millet

the framework of political morality, what is the moral meaning of who gets killed, and how did these assassinations come to take place?* And I wouldn't be talking biographically, but I'd be doing something else.

But I began to try to learn as much as I could about what was going on in the country while I was there, and I formed a picture of what was going on in Vietnam that was vastly at variance with the established American view. This led next to the question of Vietnam within the structure of American foreign policy, the strategic implications and the like. My views have gone much further than that, and they made kind of a problem for me while I was a peace candidate. It seems to me *now*—and my own position on the question reflects this—that there are things which are beyond politics, and things that men cannot do no matter what the political justification may be. Political justification only takes you so far, and the Vietnam war has exactly this character; it's the kind of thing that decent men can't do.

FINN: What is the kind of thing that they can't do? Are there things that particular individuals cannot do, shouldn't bring themselves to do, for political effect? Or is it that the government, the entire apparatus, the whole system, is. . . .

MILLET: Both, because when men do these things it calls into question the character of the entire system. For example, the men who sit in the embassy in Saigon, or the men who sit in the Department of State, are men who are neither more decent nor less decent than I. They're guys just like me in many, many ways.

But, Millet continues, the "guys like you and me" are engaged in a war which is based upon the "very careful physical annihilation of the population of the other side." Given this kind of conflict, "you don't have an organized cohesive state whose will to fight you have to break." Instead one is forced "to break the popular morale or the guerrilla's will to fight. And this leaves little choice but to kill until the guerrilla forces disappear."

I question whether the difference is really that posited by Millet. Doesn't the same principle operate in every war, that one

* These questions are discussed in the growing literature on the war in Vietnam. Especially helpful are Malcolm W. Browne, *The New Face of War* (New York: Bobbs-Merrill, 1965) and Douglas Pike, *Vietcong* (Cambridge, Mass: M.I.T. Press, 1966).

does what is necessary in order to reduce the enemy to a condition in which it cannot fight effectively? Millet does not accept this and gives historical examples to counter it. We agree on the examples and agree further to continue the discussion in terms of modern war.

MILLET: But modern war takes us pretty far, takes us, in fact, to the point where we are in Vietnam. In World War I, the closest that one could come to present conceptions of total war was the economic blockade. But you were still not killing civilians. They tightened up their belts. In World War II, we developed the theory of strategic bombing, which took us a step further along this road. In strategic bombing you attacked the morale of the population by a devastating blow physically upon the population. This is, in the history of modern warfare, a relatively novel notion, and it's again one of those things which is intrinsically not justifiable. That is, there cannot be a political end so overweening that it requires a tactic of this kind. Now, the next step is not a logical one really, because nobody anticipated guerrilla warfare. But it develops in the guerrilla warfare of Vietnam that the physical annihilation of the other guy's army becomes the precise tactic. Not to defeat his army, but to annihilate physically. It doesn't matter if you win a battle in Vietnam —and the newspapers show you this—it doesn't matter if you win a campaign. What matters, from our side, is the number of VC we can say are killed.

FINN: Well, I agree with that, but the *nature* of this kind of conflict is determined, in this case, by the guerrillas themselves. And it seems to me if there's going to be a criticism directed in *military* terms it's that we are trying to find ways to respond, and the only way that we have found is as you described it.

MILLET: But I'm not posing this as a military problem. The military comes to us and says, "Yes, we can win this war if we poison all the wells. We can win it." Now it's up to us to make the decision whether that is within the range of the permissible. In effect, to say or not to say to the military, "Yes, do it." Now, strategic bombardment and anti-guerrilla warfare, as it's carried on in Vietnam, seem to me—and the anti-guerrilla warfare in Vietnam much more so than the strategic bombardment, incidentally—seem to me to go beyond that which is permissible for men to do for political ends.

FINN: We're getting a little bit away from the biographical, but I'd like to pursue this. Does it follow from what you say that we either have to say we cannot fight against guerrillas successfully, or we have to find a more limited, measured way of conquering guerrillas?

MILLET: Let's raise the question in the broadest sense: is it the case that the techniques we use are *always*—grant me that they are immoral for the moment and I'll cast the argument against myself as hard as I can—are they always impermissible? Or is there not a situation in which men are justified in doing these things if it is necessary to win? The answer is that I'm not any longer certain whether political ends—as a matter of fact I'm fairly certain that they're not—that political ends are the highest ends. I think that there are standards which overreach the political, and that it's very difficult to hypothecate the situation in which the political end can run over all considerations. *But* let's assume that it does, which is the harder argument. Then at least this must be said: if you must overreach fairly simple moral standards for political ends, you have to be awfully damned careful that the end is essential in the immediate case. And if you cannot make an overweening argument that in this instance defeat would be the end of all that is politically desirable, then it seems to me to be unjustifiable.

Now that argument cannot be made in the Vietnam case, because the political justifications are very weak ones. They're very questionable ones which are, with the best will in the world, difficult to accept.

FINN: Do you think that the United States is capable of successfully fighting a guerrilla war in a way which you think would be morally acceptable?

MILLET: One of the baffling things about the Vietnam case is that the achievement of the basic policy goals of the United States was there to be grasped, and with magnificent success, had the actual techniques that we use in Vietnam not been used. Everyone says it's a history of mistakes, and then brushes that history off. But it's really instructive what the mistakes were and what their consequences were. Because it's hard to argue, as it always is for the past, that the men involved should have seen it. But a real understanding of Vietnamese life would see Diem as a mistake. The conquest of the sects, a mistake. The consumption of the political parties of Vietnam, a mistake. The way in which the war was prosecuted, a great mistake. The attack on the Buddhists was a mistake, because if the United States had wished to secure Vietnam, even as late as last year, the Buddhists were a road. The extreme gentility with which we handled the Diem regime was a *terrible* mistake, because you could have taken the Diem regime and done what any great power has done up and down the line, a thousand times before. You're supporting the goddamned guy, he does what you tell him to do! We have sufficient skill, sufficient knowledge and sufficient resources; we could have brought about economic reform in that country in '56, '57, '58, if only we had put the screws on Diem. And putting the screws on Diem is far less problematic than putting the screws on the peasants of Vietnam.

FINN: To return to the war itself. People have called it illegal, immoral, unjustified. I don't know whether you'd accept any or all of these terms.

MILLET: Oh, all of those. The only characterization that fits now, from my point of view, is the contemptible war. I believe that it is a contemptible war.

FINN: How do you distribute the responsibility for the war in terms of the statesmen who make the policy, the military who carry it out and the citizens who to a large degree support it? Is it possible to make an assessment that goes from the immorality of the war to the moral responsibility of these people? Can one transfer moral judgments of political actions to . . .

MILLET: . . . moral judgments of the men involved? No, I don't think so, I think that one of the problems of a man like Johnson, confronted with the opposition, is that by this time he sees the war as a moral act. McNamara is troubled; he has made these troubled speeches. And I don't think that either McNamara or Johnson or certainly John Kennedy—*certainly* Eisenhower, who was simplistic—that any of these men were immoral men. But I think that their morality is defective. They intend to be moral men, they intend to do moral things. They do not see what are to me the overpowering consequences of the acts they do, and they don't see the gulf between what they intend to do and what they really do. And I think this is true for the people as a whole.

I think that there is a problem of perception, ideology, and political history involved. I think that if I had to give an account-

Stanley Millet

ing of how the hell Johnson takes these damn decisions and what does he really see, I'd say that Johnson partly is a product of pre-World War II and the Munich argument is very persuasive to this man; that's exactly what he sees. He doesn't see the problem of defeating communism like an extreme right-wing guy, but in a way in which most people saw it fifteen years ago. And Rusk is *exactly* that kind of man. I think John Kennedy is a lot more complex. But I think that, for the really responsible men who make policy, there are moral blindnesses involved plus overriding doctrine—not immorality. I don't think that they are immoral men. I think the war is immoral, even contemptible, but these men don't see that.

DOROTHY DAY

The Catholic Worker movement has had an influence in this country far in excess of its size and material resources. A social history of contemporary American life that failed to consider the contribution it has made would be lacking, and a history of American Catholicism that omitted such a consideration would be simply inadequate.

The Catholic Worker is a movement that has sheltered people with many diverse viewpoints, although they would probably all be united in their urge to improve the social order. The *Catholic Worker* is a paper that was initiated in May 1933 with a first issue of 2,500 copies, a run that peaked to 150,000 by 1936. From the first issue to the present, the price has remained the same—one cent a copy. The movement and the paper are still imbued with the pacifist-anarchist sentiment with which the organization was launched by Dorothy Day and Peter Maurin, the French peasant, now dead, whom Miss Day continually credits as the source and inspiration for many of the ideas and principles which underlie the Catholic Worker.

Dorothy Day has told, in *The Long Loneliness,* the story of much of her life. The early years lend themselves to glamorous summary. She spent her childhood in Brooklyn, where she was born in 1897, in California and in Chicago. As a result of winning an examination sponsored by the Hearst paper in Chicago, she won a scholarship that allowed her to go to the University of Illinois. When she returned to New York she began to work on radical publications and to develop her concern for and attachment to the poor. Then, as she traveled to Europe and

Dorothy Day

worked in different parts of the United States, there moved through her life people whose names summon up entire attitudes and feelings: Eugene O'Neill, Mike Gold, Max Eastman, Trotsky, Ben Hecht and Charles MacArthur, Malcolm Cowley, Allen Tate and Hart Crane. And there was work on radical journals such as *The Call* and *The Masses;* a novel that was sold to Hollywood; occasional journalistic assignments (she worked, for example, as a taxi dancer in a cheap New Orleans dance hall in order to write a series of articles about the lives of the girls); harsh and humiliating periods in jail because of her radical activities; love, a common-law marriage and a daughter; and conversion to Catholicism.

Dorothy Day's life changed when she became a Catholic and, not long after, started the Catholic Worker, but her concern for the poor and underprivileged deepened. Her life since then has been one of devotion to them and their interests. For many people, Catholics as well as others, the Catholic Worker was the first and sometimes the only indication that the Church was concerned with the destitute. Since those early days many people have had their lives touched if not transformed by the Catholic Worker. The movement's influence continues, as Tom Cornell and David Miller have testified in this book.

There is a temptation to speak of someone who has been such a strong influence for so many years as an institution, worse yet, a monument. But the actual presence of Dorothy Day dissolves all such temptation. I visit her in her small apartment on the Lower East Side when New York is drooping under an unrelenting summer sun. Even on such a day my first impression is of a person of both great strength and beauty. Miss Day has still a sturdy figure, strong handsome features and a mass of neat, pulled-back white hair, but the impression of strength comes less from her physical appearance than from the spirit of her movements and gestures and voice. She is slightly weary from a visit with some young girls who wanted to run through, once again, the catechism of, "Isn't force *ever* justified? Wouldn't you defend yourself if you were being attacked?" But a passing visit from a neighbor stimulates Miss Day to make a lively and eloquent comment which, in brief, reveals the passion of her whole life. Her neighbor is a woman who is exploited by everyone in the neighborhood because she responds to every call for assistance. But it is even worse, Miss Day breaks out, when people from the Bowery are called upon to do some odd job and then given just enough to buy another bottle of wine. "That's when I become violent; I'm a regular Carrie Nation." And when a chair I am sitting on creaks ominously as if about to give way, she remarks ironically, "Looks as if it's about time to give that chair to the poor," a remark that passes sure judgment on many of the "gifts" which the poor are supposed gratefully to receive.

I visit Dorothy Day again at the Worker farm in Tivoli, New York, within sight of the Hudson River. The grounds seem extensive and there are a number of large buildings which, Miss Day says, will for years provide work for the people on the farm. We are joined, in our conversation, by Marty Corbin. It is difficult to say that any one person is typical of the people at the Catholic Worker, but to say that Marty Corbin is not untypical may be sufficiently ambiguous to be accurate. He was born in New York City in 1926, received a degree in English literature and philosophy from Fordham University in 1945, served in the Army Air Force, and returned to New York, where he was a social worker in the Welfare Department for five years. For eight years he lived in a community in Glen Gardner, New Jersey, where he worked as a compositor and editor for the Liberation Press. In 1964 he moved, with his wife and three children, to the farm at Tivoli, where he became editor of the *Catholic Worker* and took charge of the farm.

As we discuss the Catholic Worker movement I focus rather narrowly upon pacifism and nonviolence, but under the pressure of Dorothy Day's rich memory, easy allusions and ready reference, the conversation continually flows into broader paths. I ask, for example, if the Catholic Worker was from the beginning a pacifist organization.

DAY: The emphasis was always, from the very beginning, on the use of nonviolence as a way of changing the social order, and in that sense it could be said that it was always a pacifist group. But the objective, as Peter Maurin phrased it, was to try to work so as to bring about the kind of a society where it is easier for people to be good. And it's always remained with us as a very good expression of the ideas. I think we're primarily religious. I think we're primarily trying to live our faith and we think in terms of man's showing his faith, his love of God, by his love of his brother. We are trying to live the second commandment and to fulfill the precepts of the Gospel, not just the counsels. The precept that Christ laid down was that we should love our brother as He had loved us, and that is to the laying down of our lives. Not to the taking of lives, not to violent revolution as a means of changing the social order, but to a nonviolent process—a true revolution in which we follow the Gandhian techniques. Martin Luther King now, it seems to me, is *the* most important expression of nonviolence in the country, and of a religious position too. He said he was inspired by the Gospels and learned his techniques from Gandhi.

When I mention people I have known in the Catholic Worker movement who are not pacifists, Miss Day agrees that differences exist. Across the country the various "houses of hospitality" in the movement—houses that fed and sheltered as many of the poor as they could—did not always agree with each other.

DAY: As a matter of fact, the Los Angeles group used to take bundles of the *Catholic Worker* and burn them when they arrived during the Second World War. I said, "For goodness sake, send them back to us. Don't burn them. Or just say you don't want them." Oh, there are many groups in the Catholic Worker movement who are interested in one or another aspect of the work. But the emphasis of the Catholic Worker has been, from the beginning, in each and every war—beginning with the Chinese-Japanese War and then the Ethiopian War, and the Spanish Civil War, the Second World War and the Korean War, the Algerian War—it's been always on nonviolence. And we've always emphasized the necessity of developing a love of enemy as well as a love of brother.

I am reminded of Paul Ramsey's comment that the nonpacifist, in emphasizing the need to protect one's friends and neighbors, is likely to overlook exactly this point—the need to love one's enemy as well. Both Miss Day and Ramsey relate this need to religious categories, but I wonder if it is merely fanciful to relate their statements to Mitchell Goodman's stress on the need to feel, through an imaginative grasp of the enemy as person, compassion for that enemy; or to Arnold Kaufman's admonition that we must not be confined in our thinking by those categories that are most congenial to political scientists.

Miss Day acknowledges that the ideal of the Catholic Worker is not always met, that there have been a variety of failures, but "the emphasis has always been there: to lead by example, to lead by the emphasis on the human person rather than mob action, or mass action or legislation." I remark that part of the problem, specifically for Catholics, is education, to let them know that there is, within the Catholic tradition, room for conscientious objection. But I also add that a number of well-informed people who are not Catholics have been led to believe that absolute pacifism has long been precluded by the Church. There is, Miss Day responds, "an abysmal ignorance on the part of a great number of people in the peace movement itself of Catholic ideas and traditions." And with easy reference to the lives of the saints she moves from historical times to the present.

"We have our first draft dodger, Curé d'Ars. We can cite him as a draft dodger, *really* a draft dodger. He evaded it," she says. And Theophane Venard—one of the favorite saints of Saint Thérèse, who was herself almost sent to the Carmelite Convent in Hanoi—was martyred in what is now Vietnam. "And Saint Ignatius, on his conversion, laid down his arms and went off to work in a hospital, the works of mercy." But many people still think first in terms of the Crusades and of Joan of Arc. There is little reason for people to cling to such ideas, however. Since World War II the *Catholic Worker* has published articles such as Father John Hugo's "The Crime of Conscription" and "Catholics *Can* Be Conscientious Objectors."

DAY: When these articles first began to appear Cardinal McIntyre was a bishop in New York. He spread the *Worker* out in front of him and looked at me and said, "We never studied these things in the seminary." But he made no objections to our bringing it out in the paper. The only correction we suffered was when Bob Ludlow wrote an article advising people not to register for the draft. In a *way* I think the bishops were right when they told us that this wasn't a question of breaking a law; it was a question of the necessity to educate people so that they could make up their own minds, rather than telling them what to do. It seems to me that there has to be a good deal of preparation for a person to decide whether or not to take the consequences of not registering. I think it is probably *that* that the bishops were taking into consideration. But I didn't know what they meant when they said, "You must stand corrected." I suppose they meant some retraction was necessary, and I never made one. You were called in and you just stood corrected. That was all. I didn't know any other action was necessary. But I think they regarded it as resistance to advice on my part.

FINN: The Vatican Council and the encyclicals of Pope John have made a great impact, and the Vietnam war coming at this time has raised in the minds of Catholics, in this country certainly, a very real problem. There are undeniably more conscientious objectors among Catholics than there were in the Second World War. Do you think this indicates a profound, and not merely temporary, change?

DAY: There seems to be a great reluctance to face up to the issue in various schools I've spoken at. I'm speaking mainly of the faculty. Maybe it's the first time they've ever begun to think about it, but I feel they would like to evade the issue. They like to talk about the works of mercy and about unemployment, and the machine, and the new morality, and all the different things that they come up against through the students, and the study of all these documents coming out of the Second Vatican Council —those are all the things they want to talk about. When it comes down to talking about the issue of Vietnam they have a hard time. They'll listen and they'll be interested enough, but you feel that it's one of the first times that they've ever really started to think about it or discuss it. I find that everywhere.

FINN: Part of the difficulty may be that they would not get much support, in any critical view, from the hierarchy, and it's frequently the hierarchy in this country from whom they have taken many of their cues.

DAY: I wasn't at all enthusiastic about the statement of Cardinal Shehan of Baltimore, speaking as though we had so far used moral means; as if we must now beware not to go beyond these moral means. I felt that didn't meet the issue at all. We already had gone beyond the bounds of morality. And I'm not at all surprised that he comes out and says now that he's behind the Government in this. So there's no expression from the hierarchy. There's no real questioning of the morality of means, no questioning with even the conditions laid down by the just-war theory. It's just as though they were completely unrealistic, and *unknowing* even.

I used to think, years ago, when I worked for the FOR, that all these books giving pictures of the horrible sufferings, the deformities and the shattered limbs and the bloody heads and all that, was a very foolish way to fight war. And I'm inclined to think that emphasis on the suffering makes the most idealistic youth feel impelled to share in the suffering. Wars should, I thought, be fought more on the principled grounds rather than showing how awful it was. But I don't think that any of the bishops know what napalm is. I don't think any of them know anything about the obliteration of cities. I think that they are totally *ignorant*.

I recall a bishop I met on board ship on the way over to the Council in September of '66 and he hadn't even read over this Schema on the Church in the Modern World, which dealt with war and peace. He was totally concerned with the problem of birth control. In face-to-face conversation with the bishops, I found them in many cases evasive.

FINN: What was your reaction to the statements dealing with war that finally came out of the Council?

DAY: Well, I was not at all satisfied, of course. I thought the bishops far more ready to take a radical stand. I mean, I think there were many who were ready. I think it was the American bishops in particular who forced modifications. I think that, as Pope John said, one of the greatest evils is nationalism, and I think that we are an *American* Church and these were *American* bishops, and accustomed to think along these lines. I think one of the greatest things the Council did was to bring together these bishops from all over the world to have these head-on collisions. But a lot of them were meek and humble of heart too. They didn't want to speak out: who were they, in the face of world-wide famous theologians, you know, to be speaking out on this? And also there were some *vociferous* American bishops who were close to the Pentagon and to the government.

Dorothy Day

FINN: What do you answer to people who, when you question the government, ask "What makes you an expert? What makes you think you have enough information?" and so on.

DAY: I say my old age and experience. After all, I've lived through a lifetime of war and wars to end wars. And you get to see the insanity. Somebody once said "War is such folly and we have to match it by the folly of the Cross." That's the *only* thing strong enough. And you'd expect bishops to have some knowledge of the folly of the Cross. But bishops, unfortunately, are mortal men, and this kind of conflict's gone on in the Church from the very beginning. That's another thing that you learn in the lives of the saints: there's always been a constant criticism of the tendency to amass wealth and prestige and power. Churchmen are freer of that today than they have been for centuries. I would even say that there's great *opportunity* for them to be heard, to be listened to. The Church *is* a family—even if it's world-wide. And in a family everybody can speak out. And I think there is that in this age, which is tremendous. You know that Bishop O'Hara said to Peter Maurin once, "You lead the way and we'll follow." In other words, he felt Peter was a prophet and a leader, and he felt that it was the work of the laity to explore every field of activity and to plunge in.

FINN: Have the laity been providing most of the leadership in the peace movement? Have you over the years gotten much sustained support from bishops and cardinals?

DAY: No. I would say that we have been left to our exploration of the field, with perfect freedom to continue; not support, but great permissiveness for this anarchist society within the Church.

As we discussed other peace groups we mentioned both the Clergy Concerned about Vietnam and the National Inter-Religious Conference on Peace. Both Miss Day and Marty Corbin thought the first group was very valuable, and they were pleased that there were—largely through the efforts of Bishop Wright of Pittsburgh—many Catholics present at the Inter-Religious Conference. But they noted with misgivings that a number of Catholics who strongly supported Administration policy in Vietnam dismissed the critics with some asperity and created a charged atmosphere.

Dorothy Day regretted the relatively small number of young people present at that particular conference. They have much to offer, she says.

DAY: I think among the young people there's a real searching and inquiry. Whether they'll carry it all through, that's the point. But they are interested in the whole change in the social order. I think more things are happening now than have happened in this whole century—in this poor people's corporation, in those cooperatives down through Mississippi, in civil rights. The linking up of everything, the whole struggle. I think it's a tremendous advance.

I ask Dorothy Day the question that I had put to other pacifists who were dedicated to improving the entire social order, the political pacifists who are torn by the terms of the problems in Asia, Africa and Latin America. Must one choose between nonviolence and progressive revolution?

DAY: You never think in terms of the masses, for one thing. When I've talked, especially to faculties or clergy in regard to Latin America, I've always felt that the only hope for the Church —speaking of the Church itself—is nonviolence; that if the Church is driven into support of the status quo, the government and the rich, why, it's lost completely. It seems to me that in espousing the cause of the destitute and being with them, the Church also has to make it clear that it is nonviolent in being on their side. It also has to keep this nonviolent position in regard to the rich—with some hope that there are reformers and legislators and educators among them who are men of integrity who will be part of the pattern of a new social order.

But it seems to me that we've got to take the *nonviolent* position, and work with the hope that violent revolution can be prevented; that there will be opportunity to build another social order within the shell of the old, as Peter Maurin always said. The situation seems hopeless in Vietnam now, it seems hopeless in Latin America, but you have to "hope against hope." This is looking at it, of course, from the standpoint of the man of faith. And it seems to me that you must look at it in that way. And also you look at it in terms of God's providence, that He enters in and that leaders rise up from among the workers. I mean, who would have foretold such a prophet as Martin Luther King rising up from a ministry to be such a leader? From the act of a woman who refused to change her seat in the bus, Rosa Parks, who attended conferences like those we have here at the farm and who went back from the Highlander Folk School, a weekend conference, to take this brave action which began the explosion. Who would have known that a Chavez would rise up on the West Coast? And other people like Danilo Dolci in Italy, Vinoba Bhave in India; and, closer to home, the proposals of men like Bob Swan and A. J. Muste. These are the kinds of things that we think the Catholic Worker is for, to give knowledge of these movements to people—even though in a very inadequate way.

FINN: Much of what you say about "the whole social order being geared for the few and for profits, not for the common good" corresponds to what people in, for example, SNCC and SDS feel without putting it in religious terms. And I've talked to people who were very definite: they were not doing this in religious terms, because they thought that religion—and here they were thinking of the organized churches—had failed them and failed society. So they had to look for their own moral resources someplace else.

DAY: Of course they have lost a sacramental sense. There's a great richness in the faith, and more than ever these things are coming out. But both Mauriac and Maritain, you know—I've quoted this a number of times—said that "these men are working for Christ even though they deny Him"; they're working for justice, they're working for the common good, they're working for their brothers. Peter Maurin *always* talked in terms of the Thomistic doctrine of the common good, and of the necessity of working together and finding accordances. He *never* thought in terms of what faith a person was or whether he was without faith. He was interested in the ideas by which people could come together to work for decent social order, where people had a sufficiency and could develop what he called the synthesis of culture and cultivation.

Dorothy Day had referred to some group as "romantic." I say that a number of people who dismiss the protesters today say that those who are out demonstrating and carrying banners are moved by a sense of romanticism which will get sloughed off when the crisis passes.

DAY: I think that it's always logical to bring your protest into the streets. I used to say that if a poet wasn't being accepted he should write his poems, mimeograph them, and pass them out on street corners, you know, for people to read. Just so as to be heard. People need to be heard. No, I think that is not a romantic attitude. It's a very realistic attitude. And it always has been the technique of the labor movement: picket lines and signs and leaflets and so on. It's very effective. They're not going to have the press on their side, of course. Whenever the *New York Times* refers to me, it's as a "social worker." Pacifism and anarchism are just dismissed. As for the young people going to jail, I think that's a splendid thing to do. This summer half a dozen of the girls have gone to the Women's House of Detention, gone through all that rigmarole, and spent five days for demonstrating against the bombing of North Vietnam. And those teach-ins are very interesting. I think that is a very effective way of stimulating a really concentrated study of a situation and issue. I think now more than at any other time in our whole existence there is a steady pressure being brought by such groups. And there is a great growth, it seems to me, in various aspects of the peace movement—whether it's just this war or whether it's war in general.

CO'S AND
THE JUST WAR

ARLO TATUM

Arlo Tatum probably knows as much about the conscientious objector—his background, his problems, his prospects—as any man in the country. He is presently executive secretary of the Central Committee for Conscientious Objectors (CCCO) with headquarters at 2006 Walnut Street, Philadelphia, Pennsylvania. Since his is the office through which is channeled many of the most difficult cases, the office to which people are frequently referred by local organizations unable to cope with their difficulties, his expertise is not surprising. But Mr. Tatum was highly knowledgeable about CO's before accepting his present position, which is only one in a continuum of work, practical and theoretical, based upon a principled objection to war.

Arlo Tatum was born in 1923. As his parents were Quakers, he is, in his terms, a "birthright Friend," and was at an early age a member in the Meeting of Westbranch, Iowa, of which Herbert Hoover was a member. He attended William Penn College in Oskaloosa, Iowa, and the American Conservatory of Music in Chicago. For a number of years he sang professionally in opera, oratorio and folk singing groups. He has also worked with the American Friends Service Committee, as executive secretary of the War Resisters League, and as director of *Peace News,* a weekly newspaper published in London. As general secretary of the War Resisters International he has traveled extensively in Western Europe, Ceylon and India, and has visited Nigeria, the Middle East and East Germany.

Arlo Tatum is also co-director, with his wife, of Canonbury, a Country Center not far from Philadelphia which provides facilities for groups that wish to meet for several days. There is no group meeting when I visit Mr. Tatum, and we sit in one small corner of a room that could easily accommodate fifty people. His quiet voice seems to soften the expression of opinions that are firm and attitudes that have been strengthened over the years. His conversation is laced with laughter as he recalls amusing comments and episodes that lightened what were obviously rather grim situations.

He expressed very early his strong objection to the war and to conscription. In 1940, when he was to register for the draft, the Society of Friends, like other peace organizations, supported civilian alternative service camps, and "conscientious objectors paid thirty-five dollars a month for the privilege of serving in those forced labor camps instead of going into the military." The churches raised money for men who couldn't afford this, "parents went into debt and some Meetings mortgaged their Quaker Meeting houses." Tatum rejected this entire procedure, refused to register for the draft, and at the age of eighteen was sentenced to three and one-half years of imprisonment. (Nine years later he was imprisoned for the same offense and served most of a sentence of one and one-half years.) He has not, in the intervening years, doubted his pacifism in questions of organized violence, although in personal situations he might not respond as a pacifist, and he recalls the startled expression of the prison guard who came upon him in a fist fight during his first prison term.

I ask him what changes, if any, he has noticed in his work with CO's in the last year or two. The first thing he notes is not that the number of CO's has increased—which it obviously would in response to higher draft quotas—but that the known *percentage* of CO's has steadily risen during each of the drafts since 1940. (The percentages that are known are those for alternative service [1-O position] but do not include the noncombatant soldier [1-A-O] or noncooperator.) Second, because there is now a significant number of selective conscientious objectors, men who would accept service in some wars but not in the conflict in Vietnam, there is much more complicated legal work, education and counseling. Third, statistically the religious background of the CO's is changing. Mennonite, Church of the

Arlo Tatum

Brethren, and Quakers still contribute most of the present number of conscientious objectors. But there is a very noticeable increase, Tatum says, among the unchurched and Roman Catholics. Fourth, and related to the previous two points, "for the first time in the history of the United States conscientious objection has become a political factor precisely because many of the men who are becoming conscientious objectors now *are* concerned with the world, they *do* include politics in their objection to war or to this particular war." To stress this point Tatum recalls that when he was eighteen he "could combine being a nonregistrant with being a Republican without seeing a contradiction. This kind of naïve religiously oriented conscientious objector, as far as I can tell, is neither diminishing nor increasing in number. The tremendous increase is coming from the politically oriented."

When I ask why he thinks there is such a marked increase in the number of Catholics claiming CO exemption, his answer conforms with that of most Catholics I have talked to: "It was the direct influence of Pope John." But he makes a point I do not recall Catholics making: *"Pacem in Terris* is Pope John's expression of what I would call nonviolent attitudes in relation to the humble, the poor, the imprisoned; a kind of humility that one does not—I'm sorry, I'm not speaking as a Roman Catholic —associate with the pope but which one does associate with nonviolence. So it wasn't simply what he said but his manner. And this is being furthered, of course, by Pope Paul and the Ecumenical Council." Further, many Catholics, just as many other Americans, "fail to see a connection between the war in Vietnam and national security, national defense."

Given the fact that there is conscription, is it fairly devised and administered? Here Tatum says that he agrees with the Director of Selective Service, General Lewis Hershey, that there are inequities in the draft and there always will be.

TATUM: Of necessity, for example, any procedure is going to benefit the person who is better able to express himself. I don't think it can be avoided. One thing that could be avoided is the prohibition against having a counsel when the young man claiming exemption as a CO has his personal appearance before the local board. Here is somebody who doesn't have a *clue* about the law. He's had his claim rejected in the first instance or he wouldn't have requested the personal appearance. The local board has either said, "You are insincere," or "You are not religious." He doesn't know which.

All he's done is receive a 1-A classification. So this eighteen- or nineteen-year-old, very often a young man who doesn't know the law, goes in and is confronted by three or five men in their fifties or sixties who presumably do know the law, and he stands accused either of not qualifying or of being insincere. And he can have no one beside him to counsel and advise him in dealing with these men—which is an intimidating situation to begin with. They ask him to swear on the Bible to tell the truth, but many a local board member doesn't tell the truth—either because he doesn't know it or because he's trying to test the young man before him to see whether he's sincere.

And this is obviously an area where procedures could be more fair. And it's extraordinary, I don't know if there's any other department in the government where administratively you're prohibited from having an attorney. We bring this up in court repeatedly and always unsuccessfully, because the courts have continued to say, "The man is not accused of a crime and therefore the right to counsel doesn't exist." I maintain the man *is,* he's accused of fraud.

And how could it be a disadvantage to a local board to have someone who knows the registrant and represents his interests? If the local board isn't trying to pull anything, why should they object to having a counsel present? But this isn't, you know, a local-board decision. The law *prohibits* their admitting a counsel. So this is one area where it's grossly unfair.

FINN: What about the actual questions on the form that the draftee has to fill out, the SSS No. 150?

TATUM: Well, even courts have said they're trick questions and misleading, so you don't have to rely on my prejudice on that. You first sign a statement to the effect that you are by reason of religious training and belief opposed to—and then you have a choice of saying "combatant and noncombatant" or simply to "combatant," and to participation in war in any form. Then the next question is: "Do you believe in a Supreme Being?" This question is still there and Selective Service is technically right, I suppose. The Supreme Court didn't say it was illegal.

Arlo Tatum

But the Circuit Court in the Flemming case said that the registrant is perfectly entitled to think that this is a different question. He has just said "I am by reason of religious training and belief opposed to participation," so that "Do you believe in a Supreme Being?" must be another question and theoretically one should be able to answer it "yes" or "no." *Or* there should be some warning to the registrant, "If you are unable to answer this affirmatively, your above statement is untrue according to the Selective Service definition of religion." The next question asks the person to describe the basis of his belief—and mind you, this is not simply a belief in God, but it says "your relationship to a Supreme Being involving duties superior to those arising from any human relation." It seems to me it's getting on pretty complicated theological grounds. And if you don't bear in mind that a very high percentage of the people answering these questions are eighteen years old, I think you miss some of the point. At a recent seminar for men who want to counsel conscientious objectors, I required that each man fill out a Number 150. These men ranged in age up to about fifty-five, I would say. And they were very, very bad claims. I mean, there was only one claim that I think might be accepted by a local board. This group happened to include an Episcopal bishop and a number of ministers, but nonetheless their answers would not have been satisfactory to Selective Service. An eighteen-year-old confronted with this is very often overwhelmed and does a less good job than he's capable of doing.

But then there's the question, "Under what circumstances do you believe in the use of force?" I don't know the bureaucrat who wrote the question, and I don't know what he meant by force. Many a young man writes "None," and thinks he's put the strongest possible answer down; very often he puts it in capital letters and perhaps with an exclamation mark after it— NONE!—to show how absolutely solid and pacifistic he is. But of course any local board loves this because it's impossible to sustain.

FINN: And that's the wrong answer.

TATUM: That's the wrong answer. I don't give right answers to anybody. The right answer is what you yourself believe and can justify, defend and expand in contact with Selective Service officials, and any other answer is going to be wrong.

FINN: But, these people who write "none" think, at least for the moment, that that's what they do believe?

TATUM: Certainly. And I think they are interpreting the word "force" as meaning armed forces, but they don't say what they have in mind when they read that word "force," which is not defined by Selective Service.

Tatum mentions other instructions that are at least unclear and disconcerting. For example: "Describe those activities and actions which indicate the consistency of your beliefs." The next question asks the applicant to indicate the public expression of his stated beliefs.

TATUM: Many a shy young man has made no public expression whatsoever, but he's afraid to put "no," and he can't put "yes," and he doesn't know what to do with the question. And the worst thing probably is to leave it blank. So that by and large I would say that these are *not* good questions. And yet, again, if I were to replace General Hershey—God forbid! —and could rewrite the form, I'm not at all clear what questions I would put on it. In other words, when you're dealing with nonmaterial things, with a man's beliefs, it's very hard to probe them in a dozen questions or so and *really* have any basis for determining the nature of these beliefs and whether they're sincerely held. And, of course, part of the problem is that sincerity is a matter of degree and it's not a constant factor in one's life. My criticism of the questions is tempered by my conviction that there just *aren't* some few questions that can be asked which would with any certainty determine this.

FINN: With forms that will inevitably confuse a number of applicants, and possibly members of the local draft board, how does the prospective CO actually fare? What are his chances of gaining an exemption?

TATUM: The guidelines are certainly not clear. I would say that by and large local boards try pretty hard to be fair. I do not agree with a fairly large percentage of people in the peace movement that General Hershey or Selective Service is out to get the conscientious objector, that somehow built into the system is a prejudice against the CO, that you may get called up

Arlo Tatum

sooner or you may not get a deferment if you say you're a CO, and this kind of thing. With the thousands of cases that I've dealt with, I see no support for this attitude. And I sometimes wonder if this attitude isn't the result of a young man with a chip on his shoulder looking for trouble.

FINN: Then there aren't many people who are inducted into the Armed Services because they weren't able to satisfy both these procedures and their consciences?

TATUM: There are *some* who couldn't satisfy the procedures, although by and large if a sincere man under advice goes through the whole works and is opposed to war in any form he will be granted his classification. The percentage of those who success- fully apply for CO exemption is extremely high. I would esti- mate that eighty to eighty-five percent of those who are sincerely opposed to war in any form are given CO status. This is no pro- tection for the Vietnam war resister. I would say a lot of men are so intimidated by the procedure that they don't go through it, and go into the Armed Forces. A number of these end up in mental institutions. My father works in a veterans' mental hos- pital and both he and I are convinced that a number of the men there had just enough of the Judeo-Christian ethic, the thou shalt not kill, etc. that when they got into the situation of violat- ing the ethic they couldn't do it and cracked, or they did it and cracked. So that a number of these men who should not have gone in may not have even heard of the term "conscientious ob- jector." Others may have thought they were CO's but were afraid to apply, and some of the others, of course, are now ap- plying for discharge—but they're much less likely to get that than they would have been to get the CO classification to begin with.

FINN: Are there many people *in* the Armed Forces who be- come conscientious objectors while they're in service?

TATUM: You don't qualify under the discharge regulations unless you *did* become a conscientious objector after you en- tered. The man who applied to Selective Service beforehand, was denied, but accepted induction, I think they consider with some justification they can continue to coerce him into serving. He's agreed to violate his conscience. Now this man, of course, may end up on a psychiatric ward too.

I recall, as Tatum says this, the case of a soldier facing court martial for refusing to fight in Vietnam. Private Adam R. Weber, Jr. had warned consistently, according to his mother, from basic training through to Vietnam, that he would not kill Vietnamese, that he considered the Vietnam war morally wrong. "He is not a conscientious objector, not a pacifist, he just can't kill those people," his mother said.* Tatum knows of the case and comments.

TATUM: He just can't kill those Vietnamese. Well, you see, killing people is really contrary to human personality, human psychology—leaving morality completely to one side. Most people can't do it under ordinary circumstances: they have to be extremely agitated and stimulated in order to do it, *or* they have to do it in a group. Now this is sufficient for a lot of people to do all kinds of things that they cannot do individually. You have the same psychology working in a race riot, of people who would ordinarily be polite to Negroes but are able to lynch Negroes as a member of a group. The same psychology works in the Armed Forces. I'm not commenting about the United States. I'm commenting about the use of armed force.†

* The *New York Times,* May 22, 1966, p. 9.
† The point Mr. Tatum makes here would find some support in General S.L.A. Marshall's analysis of the American fighting man: The American ground soldier "is what his home, his religion, his schooling, and the moral code and ideals of his society have made him. The Army cannot unmake him. It must reckon with the fact that he comes from a civilization in which aggression, connected with the taking of life, is prohibited and unacceptable. The teaching and the ideals of that civilization are against killing, against taking advantage. The fear of aggression has been expressed to him so strongly and absorbed by him so deeply and pervadingly—practically with his mother's milk—that it is part of the normal man's emotional makeup. This is his great handicap when he enters combat. It stays his trigger finger even though he is hardly conscious that it is a restraint upon him. Because it is an emotional and not an intellectual handicap, it is not removable by intellectual reasoning, such as: 'Kill or be killed.'

". . . A revealing light is thrown on this subject through the studies by Medical Corps psychiatrists of the combat fatigue cases in the European Theater. They found that fear of killing, rather than fear of being killed, was the most common cause of battle failure in the individual, and that fear of failure ran a strong second.

"It is therefore reasonable to believe that the average and normally healthy individual—the man who can endure the mental and physical stresses of combat—still has such an inner and usually unrealized resist-

Arlo Tatum

It seems to me, from what I know of it, that Weber should have been given the 1-A-O, the noncombatant classification, and then he would have been all right and the Army would have had a good soldier. He would have been happy and the Army would be happy. But when you don't have access to advice, then you get in these terribly traumatic situations.

We return to the number of people who do, while in service, realize or decide that they are conscientious objectors. Tatum says there are regular procedures now to deal with such cases, but subject to vast improvement. Some soldiers are given CO status, some are not.

TATUM: The man whose application is rejected is restored to combatant service and confronted with either proceeding to be a soldier and violating his conscience or following his conscience and violating military regulations.

FINN: Are there many people who follow conscience and therefore violate the military regulations?

TATUM: There are a good number. At any one time we're involved in from a half dozen to two dozen court-martials. Again, you have the two kinds. You have Vietnam war resisters who have used this procedure to apply for discharge honestly, have not said they were opposed to war in any form knowing in advance that they would be denied discharge. You have those who simply state to their commanding officer that they will not go to Vietnam—sometimes they do it in advance, sometimes when they get the orders. So that you have a variety of resistance within the Armed Forces. I would say the most common is just doing *something* to get you in the stockade or the brig. At Fort Dix, in January of '66, there were just over a hundred men; in April '66 there were over five hundred—which is in excess of

ance toward killing a fellow man that he will not of his own volition take life if it is possible to turn away from that responsibility. Though it is improbable that he may ever analyze his own feelings so searchingly as to know what is stopping his own hand, his hand is nonetheless stopped. At the vital point, he becomes a conscientious objector, unknowing. That is something to the American credit. But it is likewise something which needs to be analyzed and understood if we are to prevail against it in the interests of battle efficiency." *Men Against Fire* (New York, Apollo Books, 1947), pp. 78–79.

capacity. And I had a conscientious objector refuse orders who couldn't be put in the stockade 'cause there wasn't any place to put him, and he was just confined to the base. Now I'm not saying that these are men opposed to the war in Vietnam on principle, and I'm certainly not saying that they're all conscientious objectors, but I am saying that this pattern, which I understand is repeated across the country, of bulging stockades and brigs, does represent an extraordinary resistance within the Armed Forces to the present engagement in Vietnam.

FINN: This kind of resistance has not gotten much public attention.

TATUM: It hasn't. But that doesn't mean that the Pentagon isn't worried about it. And I would say that one of these men is probably worth ten civilians making a CO claim from the point of view of affecting policy. I'm sure that there are men now in the Pentagon remembering that one of the principal reasons France was obliged to end its colonial rule of Algeria was that the Armed Forces became unreliable, not out of opposition to war in any form but to the French trying to run Algeria. And it's not being bought today, the plausibility or the viability or the morality of the war in Vietnam, and it's simply that most people don't realize that this also applies to a smaller but appreciable percentage of men actually in the Armed Forces.

FINN: People speak, with whatever degree of precision or accuracy, of the military mind and presume that the term is invested with some meaning. Is there such a thing as a pacifist mind?

TATUM: Well, I'm not even sure there's such a thing as a military mind, although I used the term before I started dealing with men in the Armed Forces. I can tell almost nothing about a man now by the fact that he's in uniform. I find so much difference that I no longer have this sort of faceless approach to somebody in uniform. I think a discussion of the pacifist mind would be an effort to continue the stereotype of the pacifist, just as sometimes the pacifists are rather keen to stereotype the military. I know humanitarians in the Armed Forces, I know deeply religious men, I know atheists. You can fall into a conscientious objector classification, particularly if you belong to one of the historic peace churches, without every really having thought things through. You get in on the label. You can be in-

Arlo Tatum

sensitive and insincere if you have the right label. But I think the kind of society we have is the kind that we deserve, which is a pretty severe criticism of our society.

We have a need, as a nation which consumes two thirds of the world's wealth every year and lets the rest of the world have the other third, we have a very strong need of access to raw materials and so forth. Now I'm certainly not representing the pacifist movement when I say this, but I think the principal function of the Armed Forces is to ensure that access, rather than defense. Pacifists who want to talk in terms of substituting some kind of nonviolent or unarmed body for the military just don't understand what the function of the military is. And I would become more critical and say that a good many of them would not give up the standard of living which would be involved in giving up our military.

FINN: You're suggesting if we did give up the military, or cut it back sharply, that we would simply have to pull back from some of the areas of the world where we now get materials?

TATUM: Can you think of any way that we could run the Panama Canal, except by having troops there or the threat of violence? We can't keep it away from the people whose land it is, unless we do it by force. Now a pacifist is not going to say that he wants to keep the Panama Canal, but as a member of the bourgeoisie myself, I know that a good many of them want the benefits that come from our controlling the Panama Canal. And your own prognostication that this limited war, possibly guerrilla war, is the kind of war with which the world will be faced in the foreseeable future is extremely compatible to my theories as to their function in the first place. And nuclear war *cannot* fill that function. I know that the feeling in many countries of the world is different, but I personally think that the United States will not launch a nuclear attack. I don't think any other country will either, because it doesn't meet the requirements of the situation, which are economic. You don't want any wars except little ones where you can use up a tremendous amount of materials and have a lot of things grow obsolete, and replace them and so forth, *and* serve the function of protecting our access to raw materials.

FINN: Your own pacifism is obviously part of, or has become part of, a general political orientation.

TATUM: I suppose so. Anarchists consider me to be a Socialist, and Socialists consider me to be an anarchist, and I don't know what I am. I run the gamut of having very strong pull toward some of the things that Barry Goldwater said about the freedom of the individual and some of the beautiful things that President Johnson sometimes says and sometimes means about trying to uplift society in general, even though it involves coercion on the part of the state—which all of these programs, to some extent, inevitably do.

FINN: What kind of force do you think is proper to the state in order to preserve itself?

TATUM: I differentiate between restraint on the individual when it jeopardizes other individuals and forcing an individual to do something because it's good for him individually, or because you think it is, which is obviously purely paternalistic. President Kennedy said, "Ask not what your country can do for you." If your country's not doing anything for you, I can't see any reason to have it whatsoever. The government is purely the servant of the people, the people are *not* servants of the government. I don't care how beautifully you phrase it, I cannot be convinced, and I consider it an extraordinarily dangerous concept. You see, one of the reasons that communism and capitalism are such bitter enemies is what they share in common; it isn't their differences. And they both have a distorted attitude toward the relationship of the individual and the state. If a Communist says, "Serve your government," we think it's a totalitarian concept. If we say it we think it's democratic. But it isn't. It's the same thing.

FINN: Well, have there been large societies, states, in history that have *not* established that particular relation?

TATUM: Well, it's all a matter of degree, isn't it? There are several countries that I would consider to be more democratic than the United States and that I think most sociologists would —with the possible exception of American sociologists. So that it's not a case of our having refined democracy into its highest form, which we like to think.

FINN: I find it very difficult to think of a modern, highly developed society not having a strong armed force in the world today, or getting along satisfactorily without it.

TATUM: Well, Great Britain's going the other way, would you not agree?

FINN: Oh yes. I can imagine a country getting less powerful and therefore giving up some of the trappings of power.

TATUM: Well, is that bad?

FINN: Not necessarily, no. But this was not by choice on the part of England. Would you yourself be in favor of unilateral *nuclear* disarmament at this point?

TATUM: Certainly. The greatest threat to the United States of America, from the old-fashioned point of view of defense, is the possession of nuclear weapons; and the greatest security from nuclear attack would be to get rid of the weapons. I don't think there's the *slightest* question of it. And yet, in the terms that you just expressed, this would be becoming less powerful— if one must think of power in terms of military power.

FINN: Well, that is certainly one factor in power, not the only one.

TATUM: But we'll do it when we're coerced into doing it, and we won't do it before, I imagine—and by then it may be too late. We would certainly be taking a step into the right direction.

FINN: Let me ask you to explain something. You said that your reaction here *is* related to your area of expertise.

TATUM: Well . . . yes, if I have any area of expertise it's on the draft, and the draft is the method by which the government knocks on every door in the United States of America and its colonies—there's some resistance to it in Puerto Rico— and says "We are going to take you if you have any draft-age men, for two years, and put you into this whether you like it or not." It's what the Constitution calls "involuntary service." Taking one's money is so nominal, so trivial, compared to taking one's body. I like the recent statement of the American Civil Liberties Union, which has been silent for a long time on the issue of conscription, that this is something which is only acceptable in a democratic society when there is a clear and present danger to the continuation of the society itself. And that does *not* now exist.

You know a lot of our fathers came to this country to get

out from under conscription in Europe, and they wanted to live in the kind of country that wouldn't have conscription: a better society. We call them pilgrims, but I suppose in present-day terminology we would call them draft dodgers. At least that's what we call the young men who are going to Canada to avoid conscription in the United States. This is, I think, one of the reasons I feel so strongly about conscription. There's a lot in this society, as in every society, which has *never* been right. But here is one area at least where we could say that we were better, intentionally better, than any other country in the world. It wouldn't be a case of being a country which couldn't have conscription because they couldn't enforce it, because there wasn't enough government. It would be a case of our saying in principle, "We want the kind of society where this would not exist." And we've gone back on this one thing in our tradition that really was an improvement on every society in existence in the world. It's a great pity.

FINN: I take it that you did not have a high opinion of McNamara's statement that he thought every young man should give a couple of years . . .

TATUM: Well, this is the old universal military training that General Hershey's been pushing since he was fourteen, I guess. General Hershey's also said that it's no longer experimental, so why do we have to keep renewing it every four years? The thing that fascinated me most about McNamara wasn't the fact that he put it in liberal terms and that a lot of liberals have had a very favorable reaction to it, as intended, but that he said *in the beginning* men will have a choice as to whether to go into the Peace Corps, this, that or the other, and that women would *in the beginning* be encouraged as volunteers to participate. It's the first suggestion by a high government official of ultimately introducing military conscription for women—which currently is confined to China and Israel, I think. This, if acceptable, would be a step in the direction of subservience of the individual to the state, of intentional, continuous, permanent, involuntary servitude for a given period, regardless of whether it was required or not. And I think it would be leading us in the direction of a totalitarian state. But, my, he put it beautifully, didn't he?

WILLIAM V. O'BRIEN

Anyone who finds that some wars are justified, e.g., the fight against Hitler, and some are not, e.g., the present conflict in Vietnam, has some concept of a just war. Nevertheless, the critics of the Vietnam war who are knowledgeable about traditional just-war theory and capable of employing it confidently are very few. The majority of the critics are either ignorant of the tradition, judge it unhelpful or irrelevant, or are content to borrow from the traditional theory what seems applicable within their own framework. That difficulties attend the theory will be clear from several quotations:

"From the time of Grotius to the drafting of the United Nations Charter, international lawyers have tried to distinguish between 'just wars' and 'unjust wars.' It is a difficult problem of law and an even more difficult problem of morality, but it is certainly a valid problem." J. W. Fulbright, "The Fatal Arrogance of Power," *New York Times Magazine,* May 15, 1966, p. 103.

"Just war must be made possible, and only just war should be allowed to be a possibility." Paul Ramsey, *War and the Christian Conscience* (Durham, N. C., Duke University Press, 1961), p. 311.

"Primarily its value [the traditional doctrine] resides in its capacity to set the right terms for rational debate on public policies bearing on the problem of war and peace in this age, characterized by international conflict and by advanced technology. This is no mean value, if you consider the damage that is presently being done by argument carried on in the wrong terms. . . . [The] doctrine still seeks to fulfill its triple function: to condemn war as evil, to limit the evils it entails, and to humanize its conduct as far as possible." John Courtney Murray, S.J., "Theology and Modern War," *Morality and Modern Warfare,* William J. Nagle, ed. (Baltimore, Helicon, 1960), pp. 86–87.

"The development of the Just War doctrine, under the sway of Christian moral philosophy, was able neither to discourage violence nor to mobilize the collective force of the community against the unjust breaker of the peace." Richard A. Falk, *Law, Morality and War in the Contemporary World* (New York, Praeger, 1963), p. 70.

"I see no persuasive basis for picking and choosing wars. However glorious the objective may be—to liberate Boston from the sales tax in 1776 . . . or to emancipate the Negro, or to save the world for democracy or the Jews from Hitler—every war is just as unjust as every other because it cannot be otherwise. It cannot be otherwise because it is war." Milton Mayer, "The Professor's Problem," *The Progressive,* June 1966, p. 25.

"Wars in history can be divided into two kinds, just and unjust. All progressive wars are just and all wars impeding progress are unjust. We Communists are opposed to all unjust wars that impede progress, but we are not opposed to progressive, just wars." Mao Tse-tung, *Selected Works,* Volume II (New York, International Publishers, 1954), p. 199.

"More than any other great nation, America's basic predispositions and her experience in world politics encourage the

William V. O'Brien

dissociation of power and politics. This dissociation is most marked in America's traditional conception of war and peace as diametrically opposite states of affairs, to be governed by entirely different rules and considerations without regard for the continuity of political conflict." Robert E. Osgood, *Limited War* (Chicago, University of Chicago Press, 1957), p. 29.

Some of the obstacles to a general acceptance of just-war doctrine should emerge from these comments. First, every nation participant in war feels compelled not only to explain but to justify its conduct, although, as Mao Tse-tung makes clear, the terms of the justification will vary markedly. Some dismiss the traditional terms as readily as they would Mao's. Second, since the traditional doctrine admits recourse to war but sets moral limits upon it, the doctrine is rejected both by pacifists and by those who say that war must drive unhampered to total victory. Third, in modern times even advocates of the doctrine have, with few notable exceptions, fallen silent during war and have seemed thereby to acknowledge its irrelevance.

Nevertheless, the doctrine of the just war is being re-examined by people who argue that it is both necessary and serviceable in modern war. They argue, as does John Courtney Murray, that it sets the correct terms for rational debate; it asks the right questions in a sound politico-moral framework. "Limited war," which stands as the alternative to large-scale nuclear war, seems highly amenable to analysis in just-war terms. And the case for the moral objection to specific wars—selective conscientious objection—rests almost entirely on the validity of such a concept.

Although it has its analogues within both pagan and Jewish teaching, the dominant Western tradition of just war developed within Christianity and most rigorously within Catholicism. An adequate history of the development of the doctrine would note the pacifism of the early Church and, with its desertion at the time of Constantine, the need for rules of war. These were provided by the first great articulator of the just-war doctrine, St. Augustine. The history would then examine the growth and refinement of that doctrine during the Middle Ages and Renaissance, when it received its most elaborate consideration in the works of Thomas Aquinas in the thirteenth century, Francisco de Vitoria in the sixteenth century and Francisco Suarez in the seventeenth century. It would note the relative neglect of the theory in the succeeding centuries until in our own times international relations and modern military technology made it seem, once again, a subject of practical interest.

The conditions governing a just war have been variously stated, but however stated they traditionally include the following:

1. *Legitimate authority*. War must serve public, not private, purposes, and the question of whether any particular war serves that purpose can be decided only by the highest public authority.

2. *Just cause*. The war must be waged in defense of a profound right, the chances of victory must be reasonably high, and the good consequences of the war must be judged to exceed the inevitable evil effects.

3. *Last resort*. Having made the previous calculations, the competent authority has a responsibility to explore and exhaust all peaceful remedies before resorting to war.

4. *Right intention*. The war must be directed to just goals and not allowed to exceed these, e.g., it must not become needlessly brutal or drive to an unfair settlement.

5. *Moral means*. No intrinsically immoral means may be employed. There must be due proportion between the means used and the goal of the war (principle of proportionality), and innocents or noncombatants must be immune from intended, direct attack (principle of inviolability of noncombatants).

These conditions are amenable to the highly refined development they have received. Recently, what has been most discussed and disputed is the question of moral means. For example, President Truman justified the bombing of Nagasaki and Hiroshima by the principle of proportionality, arguing that the lives lost were less than the number of American and Japanese lives that would have been lost if the war had continued by conventional means. But if noncombatants are not proper targets in war, those bombings would be judged morally unwarranted according to just-war doctrine.*

* To avoid possible confusion it may be advisable to recall the elementary distinction implied in the term "intended direct attack." A mili-

William V. O'Brien

Because the just-war doctrine provides analytical tools to discuss the war in Vietnam and because it has been invoked by some to discredit that war, I talked with two people who have attempted to apply that doctrine to contemporary warfare. Both William V. O'Brien and Paul Ramsey have, in general, found the course of U.S. policy in Southeast Asia, including the war in Vietnam, to be justifiable.

William V. O'Brien was born in Washington, D.C. in 1923 and has remained remarkably faithful to his hometown. He received his degrees in foreign service and his Ph.D. in government from Georgetown University in Washington where he is now Chairman of the Institute of World Polity and Professor of Government. He was a Fulbright Fellow at the Faculty of Law of the Sorbonne in 1951 and Visiting Professor at the Max Planck-Institut Für Ausländisches Offentliches Recht und Völkerrecht in 1963. He is now President of the Catholic Association for International Peace and Washington Consultant for the Council on Religion and International Affairs.

In addition to collaborating on a number of books concerned with international law, Christian ethics and nuclear warfare, and contributing to numerous journals and encyclopedias, Dr. O'Brien is Editor of *World Polity: A Yearbook of Studies in International Law and Organization,* and Associate Editor of *World Justice* (Louvain) and *World Affairs.* His most recent book is *Nuclear War, Deterrence and Morality.* When I speak with William O'Brien he has just been invited to help represent the Catholic Peace Movement at the Third World Congress of the Lay Apostolate in Rome late in 1967.

Dr. O'Brien is a compact bundle of directed energies. When he becomes engaged with an issue it receives the full force of his attention and he drives straight to the crux of the problem, expressing his own opinion in direct, clear terms. There is

---

tary installation or force, a dam, a bridge, etc. may be judged a proper military target and subjected to direct, intended attack. If, in the process, some noncombatant bystanders are killed, their deaths are unintended and incidental. The attack has had a double effect, one of which was intended, the other not. While this distinction is open to ready abuse, and has become a point at issue in the bombings in Vietnam, there can be no doubt that its application would have precluded the horrors of Hamburg, Dresden and Hiroshima.

rarely any doubt about where he stands on a disputed question and he becomes impatient with those who wish to run through familiar arguments unless they have something new to add. In political affairs he knows that action must be taken before all the data are in, because all the data are never in and decisions must be made. In matters of such profound importance as modern war he thinks one must speak, in his term, with "bone-dry honesty."

I ask William O'Brien why, contrary to much current opinion, he thinks the just-war doctrine has utility now, and whether the Christian community within which it developed might well attempt to refurbish it.

O'BRIEN: I think that just-war theories are still necessary because they ultimately raise the two fundamental normative questions about recourse to force. One: when, and under what justification, may a state or other international entity have recourse to force? And two: by what standard should the means employed be judged? And however one modifies just-war theories, or substitutes something else for them, these issues are perennial, it seems to me.

Everything we know about political society seems to indicate that from time to time coercion is necessary in order to protect a society against internal and external threats. This presumably would still be the case even in some kind of a world authority or world state. Now if Christians can't find it within their own traditions and standards to meet these threats, they would have to stand aside, whether it be with respect to problems of the United States or, for that matter, with respect to maintaining order in a world state that we might have in fifty years or more.

Traditional Christian teaching has been that political society is necessary for man's good on earth and a necessary and highly desirable precondition for his successful attainment of his eternal destiny. Therefore it would seem to me that since we believe that the political society is necessary and good, the necessary defense of that society is something with which the beneficiaries should be concerned.

FINN: You use the phrase "necessary defense of society." It raises the question of what is allowable and under some circumstances necessary if the state is to be defended. In your writing on the just war and in the presentation you gave to the

William V. O'Brien

Catholic Press Association recently, you suggested that it may be necessary to give up what many people consider an essential part of just-war theory: the inviolability of noncombatants. For example, to quote Father Ford in his article on the hydrogen bombing of cities, "Catholic teaching has been unanimous for long centuries in declaring that it is never permitted to kill directly noncombatants in wartime. Why? Because they are innocent of the violent and destructive action of war, or of any close participation in the violent and destructive action of war. It is such participation *alone* that would make them legitimate targets of violent repression themselves." *

O'BRIEN: Well, this is quite controversial, but I have a number of assertions to make. The first is that as far as I can find out the principle of noncombatant immunity from direct intentional attack is *not* deduced from some first principle of the natural law. The contention or the rule doesn't even appear in Saint Thomas' formulation, which is not even directly concerned with the means of war, aside from the general prescriptions which respect the right *intention*. I have reason to believe that the noncombatant immunity rule arose not out of immutable first principles but out of the practice of individuals and states in the late medieval and early Renaissance period, out of the positive emerging international law and national law of the time. By the time of writers like Vitoria and Suarez the principle of *custom* and of positive law was introduced, or was emphasized, or made more explicit in the late just-war teachings.

Secondly, this rule of immunity was possible because of the material facts of war in those times. The material facts today are such that a literal acceptance of the principle would make anything other than the most trivial and extraordinary kind of defense morally impossible, aside from some hypothetical war between representatives of different powers in the Sahara or in the Antarctic. The third reason—and there are many—is that this principle, which is *always* referred to in what little literature we have, has *hardly ever* been referred to explicitly in papal and other authoritative statements in our times. So we have the curious situation where this alleged immutable principle that Father Ford talks about is somehow escaping the popes who are writing the messages on this subject.

So, putting all these things together, I find on the one hand

* John C. Ford, S.J. "The Hydrogen Bombing of Cities," *Morality and Modern Warfare*.

insufficient authority for the contention that this *indeed* is a principle which we must accept and, on the other hand, a practical fact that if we did accept it we probably would have to opt out of the business of defense. Now if someone could prove to my satisfaction that there is indeed authority which we must accept for this principle, I would have to be the first one among those who haven't already gone out the door to abandon just defense. But I simply don't believe that this has been proven.

FINN: If we're going to talk about just defense under the conditions of modern war, the problem involves, I presume, the possibility of counter-city warfare—or at least the destruction of *some* cities in warfare. Can you anticipate a war in which some cities would be destroyed which would nevertheless be, in your terms, a just war?

O'BRIEN: I can envisage it, but I would do everything to avoid that eventuality. I think that every effort should be made to limit deterrence to the threatening of counterforce war—which is, I think, of such a magnitude that it would probably be a sufficient deterrent. I can conceive of defensible attacks on cities because of their fundamental relationship with the enemy's ability to attack with nuclear weapons, but I *certainly* could not countenance *at all* a destruction of cities that were not essential to the enemy—and by essential I mean really essential, such as a capital city or a city where the major strategic air command would be located. But just the fact that the city was important and had a relation to the overall war potential of a state would not, in my opinion, justify the wholesale slaughter which I tend increasingly to believe would be disproportionate in itself.

Now this is not anything that can be based on any solid theoretical analysis, but we do have the statements of the Council in the pastoral constitution and we have Pope Paul's statement on Hiroshima, which say that an attack on a major population center is simply wrong. And although one may not be able to explain exactly why it is wrong in the sense that the traditional theorists could explain why an intentional attack on noncombatants was, nevertheless I think that this rule is gaining increasing acceptance.

FINN: Is there an obligation for those who say the destruction of cities is wrong to explain why it's wrong, or is the obligation here reversed, for those who say it is allowable under certain circumstances to give reasons why it is allowable?

William V. O'Brien

O'BRIEN: This is a very hard question because there are legitimate arguments in both directions. From the point of view of those seeking to identify reprehensible things that ought not to be done, I think the emphasis should be simply on the fact that people of great authority and dignity *said* that these things were wrong. If, on the other hand, you take seriously the continued statements by the Council and by the popes of the right of self-defense and then ask what is necessary for defense in our time, you'd probably say, "Well, I have a right to everything that you cannot clearly prove to me is prohibited by the moral law, and the burden is on you to explain to me why this or that particular thing, which I find very necessary, is wrong." Actually, I think we're somewhat in between these positions and not too sure on any side where we stand on this right now.

FINN: Let me read to you one portion of the Constitution on the Church in the Modern World. "Any act of war aimed indiscriminately at the destruction of entire cities or extensive areas along with their population is a crime against God and man himself, and merits unequivocal and unhesitating condemnation." Does this have any direct application to our present nuclear weapons system? Is it possible to draw from this some specific inferences that would seem to outlaw the destruction of cities?

O'BRIEN: Well, that statement, in the broader context of the treatment of deterrence, leaves me in something of a dilemma because it is quite unqualified. On the other hand, we know the Council did *not* flatly condemn deterrence generally or any particular form of it, and yet we know that precisely the threat to do this kind of thing, which is "a crime," is the basis for the deterrence which the Council hesitates to condemn and in effect merely deplores. More or less in the manner of *Pacem in Terris* it says we surely must do something about this state of affairs. So a thing in the abstract is defined as a crime, but the totality of threats to do it are not condemned as a crime.

I suppose that to the pacifists this would be a disheartening failure of nerve on the part of the Council. I view it somewhat differently. I think that they realized that they hadn't worked these dilemmas out and they had better not condemn things, that would if suddenly suspended put the world in a very unstable situation, until the Church had given it more thought. I don't know whether that's satisfactory or not.

PROTEST: PACIFISM AND POLITICS

FINN: Well, you stated that there is a dilemma here and the dilemma, as I see it, is this: we have a nuclear weapons system which does not preclude counter-city warfare, and we have a statement of the Church Fathers which would seem to preclude counter-city warfare. And there seems to be no possibility of reconciling these two things. Now as I understand your own writing on just-war theory, you are attempting at least to lessen the difference, to narrow the gap.

O'BRIEN: That's right.

FINN: But you're doing it by jettisoning what some people regarded—correctly or not—as an integral part of just-war theory.

O'BRIEN: I really would have to correct you, I think, because it's highly controverted whether it's an integral part—the non-combatant immunity. As I say, it wasn't there at the outset clearly. The fact that more recent writers have often said, as Father Ford said, that it was doesn't prove that it was. I could argue if need be that it has been conspicuously and increasingly violated in wars for one hundred and fifty to two hundred years. The churches didn't find it necessary to condemn these wars, the bishops blessed the troops and sent them off. So it's a curious kind of integral principle if it is simply ignored for centuries on end.*

FINN: Let me read to you from Clausewitz a passage relevant to the terms we tend to use today in discussing escalation. Clausewitz said, "He who uses force unsparingly, without reference to the bloodshed involved, must obtain a superiority if his adversary uses less vigorous application. The former then dictates the law to the latter and both proceed to extremities in which the only limitations are those imposed by the amount of counteracting force on each side." And he adds: "To introduce into a philosophy of war a principle of moderation would be an absurdity. War is an act of violation pushed to its utmost bounds." Now of course the just-war concept does attempt to introduce into war a principle of moderation. But Clausewitz seems to have a point when he says that whoever decides to use force unsparingly must seem to have an advantage. And what the two great nuclear powers say is that they *will* prosecute to

* A scholarly discussion of this point has been written by Richard S. Hartigan. His article, "Noncombatant Immunity: Reflections on its Origins and Present Status," appears in the *Review of Politics,* April 1967.

the end a war without realizing any extreme. This would seem to bear out what Clausewitz himself said.

O'BRIEN: Well, in the first place I doubt very much that one can really make analogies from pre-nuclear wars to the situation we have in the world today. To prosecute a war unsparingly with nuclear weapons in a nuclear exchange would not seem to me the kind of approach that Clausewitz or any other sensible military man would follow.*

FINN: Well, unsparingly means until there's some victory, and this is in fact what we say we *will* do. Or at least we do not say we're going to set limits.

O'BRIEN: Well, I think it's increasingly agreed that victory is not a meaningful concept and that the only purpose of an execution of nuclear deterrent threats would relate to the limitation of damage to one's own society, to deterring further attacks. And in this sense, from the just-war point of view, a state that had suffered so badly from nuclear attacks that it had no practical prospect of winning would be quite clearly immoral by continuing to lob whatever missiles it had left at the other out of spite or revenge. This would not be meaningful. There

---

* Mr. O'Brien's knowledge in these matters is extensive, yet this judgment, if sound as a generalization, is subject to particular reservation. General S.L.A. Marshall, the noted military historian whom I have previously mentioned, has expressed views not wholly congruent with O'Brien's. Writing specifically of the impact of modern weapons, Marshall wrote:

"Whether wars between nations become total in character or are conducted on a limited scale by moderately sized military forces is not determined finally by the rapacity of either side, though it is a common illusion that such is the case. The condition is fixed by the range and the hitting power of the dominant weapons, coupled with the ability of the state and people to sustain this power. The possession of weapons which make possible direct attack upon the very heart of society during the early stages of conflict is the factor which assures the totality of wars between great states.

"The true objective not only of the atomic weapon but of rockets and modern bombing fleets is the physical destruction of a society, just as in limited war the true objective of short-range weapons was the annihilation of its military forces. This will continue to be not only the most profitable and vulnerable target but the actual object in war, and it cannot be changed by humanitarian declarations of policy or by international agreement. To suggest that these super weapons should be aimed at military installations only would be like bringing up the heavy artillery to shoot at a clay pipe; they are designed, primarily, for no such limited target." *Men Against Fire* (New York, 1947), pp. 28–29, 30–31.

are several other aspects to Clausewitz; while he has this, if you will, almost psychological element in his thinking, he also has a strongly rationalist concept of war as the continuation of politics, so presumably you use it in the limited and moderate ways when that's appropriate. And thirdly I would say that this intensity of violence which he talks about, which other German thinkers like the first von Moltke thought of, got the Germans some victories, but it also got them some rather catastrophic defeats. So I don't know whether this recommends itself too much.

FINN: To leave Clausewitz aside for the moment, the point I really would like to get at is whether there are any limitations imposed upon what might be called the necessities of state if that state is threatened, or do necessities of state override all other moral concerns? I'll quote one passage from Robert Tucker who states this problem, I think, very well. He says: "Whereas reason of state must reject the claim that there are any inherent limits on the means that may be threatened or employed to preserve the state, *bellum justum* must insist that there are such limits and that whatever the circumstances they may never be transgressed. The argument of necessity must reject the claim of inherent limits on the means of war, not because it is informed by an 'ethic of responsibility' and therefore requires the statesman to calculate and to weigh the possible consequences of alternative courses of action, but because it presupposes as an ultimate end the preservation and continuity of the state."* This allows the possibility of real confrontation between just-war theory and necessity of state, and it does seem in fact to be what many people are facing today. Now do we have to give up one or the other, or is it sensible to try to reconcile the two?

O'BRIEN: Well, I have to start by wanting to believe that they can be reconciled, otherwise I'm all the way back to where we started, talking about the early Christians and so forth. Or I'd have to say that somehow we need states and they're good but that there are no moral limits on what they can do to preserve themselves and advance their interests, which doesn't make too much sense. They're not as definite as one might like, but I think there are limits.

The first, I think, is surely in terms of the ends of defense

* Robert W. Tucker, *Just War and Vatican Council II: A Critique* (New York, Council on Religion and International Affairs, 1966), p. 21.

William V. O'Brien

and the idea of right intention. This is vague; this has to be defined. But the concept of right intention does not permit unlimited pursuit of alleged national interest, and this must be understood in the broader context of the traditional Scholastic idea of a hierarchy of values, starting with an international common good, recognition of the good of other states or, if you will, their national interest in your own. So you start out by saying there is a limit to *raison d'état*. Hard as it may be to define in the concrete, the first limit is the good of the whole world—and this is not too theoretical when you're talking about nuclear weapons. And secondly, it's the rights of the other nations who also have their right of existence. So that's one limit.

A second potential limit, with respect to means used to protect the interest of the state, would be things that would be called *malum in se,* and this is really what Tucker is talking about. And I would be delighted if I could supply a large number of things that are *malum in se,* but I can't, since I reject the noncombatant immunity principle as being self-evidently *malum in se.* And the main thing that the papal constitution refers to that is *malum in se,* genocide, is something that one would argue, just on the basis of common sense, is not a requirement of a state. As I understand genocide it is essentially superfluous to any acceptable notion of *raison d'état.*

This leaves then the principle of proportionality which Tucker finds to be excessively general and open to abuse. But this doesn't mean it's not a limitation. And it seems to me that the determinations made from time to time, either by societies or by individuals or indeed by authoritative persons in the Church, as to what in this context, in this time, is proportionate, could very well lay down meaningful limits on *raison d'état.*

FINN: Let me ask the same question in a different way and again use Tucker as the spokesman here. He also wrote that, "it is not enough to argue that one may never do evil that good may come because the good will not come (only the evil), or that the evil act will corrupt the actor and therefore defeat his ends (however desirable in themselves), or that the means cannot be separated from the ends but are themselves the ends in the very process of coming into existence." And he says, "It is not enough to argue in this manner if only for the reason that each of these familiar contentions is open to question. Whether the use of evil means will always and necessarily defeat the ends of action, if only by corrupting the actor, is not an issue that can be decided in the abstract." * Now clearly it has been, for many people, decided in the abstract. And Tucker is saying that one can only look at history to make such statements and that the statements do not find adequate support. And it's for this reason, I think, that he has a good historical basis for saying that reasons of state rather than just-war principles will be *determining* in any conflict.

O'BRIEN: What he's really saying is: are there any foreseeable occasions when the statesman will forego something or do something primarily because of a moral imperative, and not primarily because of some utilitarian concept, that may ultimately turn out to be disadvantageous or self-defeating or bad for one's own state. Well, of course it is very difficult to disentangle that because it is hard to imagine decision makers saying, "Well, everything is on one side, but solely because of some moral norm I have, I'm going to decide against all the other factors which would seem to indicate this course of action." But it is possible to imagine things that might, in some sense at least, seem to be rational options but which, by some process, one has decided were not morally permissible and that therefore one would forego these things.

FINN: Even if the viability of the state was in question.

O'BRIEN: Yes, I think so.

FINN: That's a good hard line—except it's hard to say what these things are.

O'BRIEN: Well, I think it might be increasingly easy to say what it is.

FINN: Well, we're back to where we started with Tucker. He says that reasons of state must reject the claim that there are inherent limits, and you said there are inherent limits.

O'BRIEN: Ah yes, but he means, I think, by inherent limits *specific* prescriptions which can never be violated, like the one on noncombatant immunity. I simply don't know of any in this category. But I think that the rule of proportionality is implicit to all social relations, and certainly to all coercive relations of social entities. This is inherent, but the content of it necessarily has to be worked out in specific times and specific circumstances.

* Tucker, p. 22.

William V. O'Brien

FINN: Let me ask you about one thing concerning the war in Vietnam. Although we use the terms, counterinsurgency and counterterror, men who have fought there say, "Let's be clear about it; we're using the same weapons of terror that they are," which means certain methods of torture which traditionally the Christians have not accepted as proper, just and appropriate in war. Would you think these things can be justified by certain circumstances in Vietnam or in other wars?

O'BRIEN: This is the hardest question in the whole field. It's harder even than the quantitatively more ghastly problems of nuclear war. I know that torture is a universal practice in all such wars. Everybody does it. Everybody realizes it's necessary. Even if one could eliminate ninety percent of the torture in such a war it would seem to be a hard-core requirement that X amount of torture is necessary. What form it takes would make a great deal of difference in any systematic thinking. One could probably distinguish between types of torture and constraint that were, by some formula, considered to be dehumanizing, really dehumanizing, perhaps even leaving the victim almost unrecognizable as a human being, and others which would be quite a shattering experience for him but from which he could recover. This is just a broad initial breakdown.

And after all what *is* torture? I'm not so sure that some slaps in the face or a couple of kicks constitute torture. But we know there are *ghastly* types of torture that do such serious mental and physical and moral damage that they certainly are unspeakable things, and it's pretty hard to justify these. So I would hate to be the first one to write the book on just torture, but one could probably, if he confronted the thing honestly, list some broad outlines for types of torture which in terms of the reason, the cause and the results would be considered to be, if unpleasant, morally defensible.

FINN: Well, it's clear that for many Frenchmen the kind of torture that was used by the French army in Algeria became excessive and abhorrent to such a degree that, on this basis alone, they rejected French participation in that war. I'm not sure whether there is a possibility of similar American reaction to the war in Vietnam, but torture seems to be an increasing cause of concern among people who are already critical or at least undecided about what moral stance to take in regard to Vietnam.

o'brien: I would simply say that the war in Vietnam and the kind of insurgencies we find threatened in Latin America and various other places are, presumably, exactly the kinds of wars we're going to have to live with for a long, long time. That's the first point. The second point is that certainly as far as the insurgents are concerned, torture is a standard procedure—not only just to obtain information but for outright terror, and because of their weakness very often they have to do by terror what they can't do by military efficiency and power. So that if one were to start with a flat proscription of torture in such a war, one might make a very good case that there would be very little possibility of winning the war. And therefore the conclusion might be, "Very well, we're barred, as Christians, from participation in any of these counterinsurgency things, and isn't that a pity, because there are going to be many of them—which means we better start making friends with Communists and other advocates of violent change because the future is with them." This is a point of view, but I don't think it's one that's been systematically thought through.

finn: Well, I think both the question of nuclear weapons and the question of torture, which are the extremes of modern military war, do raise questions like this in the mind of many Christians; whether indeed they can participate with the full Christian tradition behind them to support such activity.

o'brien: This may be good in a perverse sort of way, because we simply are denied the feeling of camaraderie and righteousness that people apparently got in some past wars when they marched away after having been blessed by the local bishop. War is increasingly so dirty and so unpleasant that it does have to be considered as a necessary evil and not as a source of satisfaction and glory.

PAUL RAMSEY

Paul Ramsey was born in Mendenhall, Mississippi, in 1913. He received his B.S. from Millsaps College and his B.D. and Ph.D. from Yale. He has taught at a number of schools, including Millsaps, Yale, Garrett Biblical Institute, Union Theological Seminary and the University of Chicago. He is an active member of a number of learned societies, including the American Society of Christian Ethics, of which he is a former president. He is presently Harrington Spear Paine Professor of Religion at Princeton University.

Mr. Ramsey contributes to a wide range of journals and is the author of a growing list of books; these include *Basic Christian Ethics* (1950), *War and the Christian Conscience* (1961), *Christian Ethics and the Sit-In* (1961), *Nine Modern Moralists* (1962) and *Who Speaks for the Church?* (1967).

These are only some of Paul Ramsey's academic credentials, and they fail to suggest the extent of his activities, for he is a frequent lecturer and a very prolific writer. But even a full list of his activities could not do justice to Ramsey himself. He is a large, robust, outgoing person with immense energies which he can readily focus in involved reasoning and subtle distinctions. I have seen people emerge from initial exposure to the Ramsey presence with some continuing uncertainties about natural law but with absolute certainty that they had encountered a natural force.

He is one of the few American ethicists who can move with ease between Catholic and Protestant frames of reference. As one who traverses that bridge frequently, he draws fire from critics on both sides; Protestant critics say that he too nearly approximates the legalistic and formalistic approach they associate with Catholicism, and Catholics sometimes say that he is adopting methods that advanced Catholic thinkers are discarding. But these criticisms are the reverse side of frequent commendation. And even Ramsey's critics must admit that he is one of the few ethicists who has worked hard and consistently to familiarize himself with the technical aspects of modern war so that his politico-moral judgments will be firmly grounded.

We begin our discussion with Christian pacifism. Ramsey states that there are, broadly speaking, two ways of basing pacifism upon the New Testament. The first (which was that stressed, and rejected, by John Bennett) is that of the literalist, who bases his pacifism upon an exegesis of particular teachings of Jesus. This, Ramsey says, might be called "Sermon on the Mount pacifism," and is typical of the Mennonites. The second approach recognizes that, in terms of specific things, the Church's teachings have changed over the years, and it seeks behind these various teachings for the "inner spirit or ultimate norm of Christian life." This is found to be Christian love, Christian charity. This is the approach of the Quakers, for whom the inner light, "understood at least in early Quakerism as the spirit of Christ," leads to the conclusion that one should withdraw from political life insofar as it makes use of violent force.

But, Ramsey continues, if you take the second approach— that charity is the ultimate norm—you should ask whether the passage from the "almost universal pacifism in the early Church to responsible participation in political life of the Christian empires" was a shift from that high standard to a lesser one. Was it, for example, a shift from the essence of the Christian ethic to a lower norm, a standard of justice imported from Greek or Roman stoic philosophy? To this question, which some of the pacifists I have talked with would answer affirmatively, Paul Ramsey gives a strong and definite "No."

The reasons Ramsey gives for rejecting this kind of pacifism are not wholly limited to the Christian context. For he contends that it is out of charity, out of love, that Christians, "as they grew in number and strength, felt themselves bound to take responsibility for the political life of the society in which they lived, to share in it, to defend it by use of arms"—and so it is today. This is an argument that a number of Jews and other non-Christians have developed within their own conceptual framework. And then Ramsey makes an interesting observation (similar to a point made by Paul Deats) with which many pacifists would agree. The pacifist and the nonpacifist ought, in charity, to admit that each of them probably has a blind spot. The pacifist, out of charity, emphasizes the humanity of the enemy and tries to surround his enemy neighbor "with the protections of a charitable refusal ever to take his life." He tends not to focus upon the possible victims of an aggressor's injustice. The nonpacifist, on the other hand, feels bound out of charity to help the victim, to prevent the aggressor from inflicting greater suffering. In stressing this responsibility toward the "weak of the earth, in surrounding them with the protections of a political order," the nonpacifist is probably blind to "charity's continuing obligation to the enemy."

The terms in which Ramsey states this difference seem to me to be very close to those used by many people who judge very differently the justice of the war in Vietnam. The first group, critics of U.S. policy in Vietnam but not all of whom are pacifists, stress the suffering inflicted upon the people of Vietnam, North and South, soldiers and civilians. It is undeniable—and this is the cutting edge of their argument—that the entire population of that poor country, men, women and children, must bear the brunt of the war. The second group, generally supporters of U.S. policy, admit and deplore the deaths and injuries and they sympathize with the people of Vietnam, but they say that this suffering is necessary in order to prevent the imposition of an unjust order in that area of the world. I ask Ramsey if the arguments of these two groups do not correspond roughly to the distinction he was making.

RAMSEY: Yes, I see your point. The latter group judge that the cessation of our Vietnam action would be an evil or greater evil than what they think can still be won by force of arms. And, of course, the way you described the first group also fits: they are thinking of the people who are suffering and being destroyed, but they do not think as alertly about the alternatives to the present, admittedly chaotic situation.

How one is to assess the comparative justice of whole regimes is admittedly a most difficult if not quite incorrigible problem. And one's judgment about the justness of the cause, which is one of the criteria of the just-war theory, is not as easy to use as a test as the whole tradition has thought. Reinhold Niebuhr once remarked, ironically, that he thanked God for having put him on the just side of three different wars in one lifetime. But I do remember that as World War II approached, and U.S. participation in it approached, one thing was often proposed as a not insignificant test or check: we should look to see which way the refugees were going. It was a movement of refugees in one direction only. And the fact that many German refugees and self-exiles had taken the astonishing step of breaking roots with their native land was taken to be a sort of judgment of comparative justice. Well, I think it's not unimpressive to note the millions of refugees from North Vietnam who voted with their feet. These are a goodly number of judgments as to justice and injustice. Moreover, these people certainly didn't think that they were walking into the twentieth century. They knew they were walking into what we call a traditional, lethargic society, ruled maybe by rascals, certainly by inept men. Still they judged that the regime of North Vietnam, which was squaring itself off for a launching into the industrialized twentieth century, was a regime that was so inhumane as to be intolerable.

I pick up Ramsey's reference to the just-war doctrine and ask him a number of questions I had asked O'Brien directly and a number of other people less directly. I am particularly interested in how he would see "necessities of state" limited by the doctrine and, with Vietnam in mind, how he would apply the principle of proportionality, and what status he would accord to the "inviolability of noncombatants." But first I ask to whom the just-war doctrine is addressed, who is expected to profit from it.

RAMSEY: I would say, Jim, that the just-war concepts are primarily a body of teachings addressed to statesmen and citizens, that is, to people in their political capacities. So I think it's a body of political teachings aiming to direct, guide, illumine or order in some fashion the way in which people think about politics at the point where it has resort to arms, or may have resort to arms.

Paul Ramsey

FINN: Do you think that in the modern political life of the United States, say in the twentieth century, just-war concepts have actually illuminated, clarified, and in some degree informed and modified actual practice?

RAMSEY: That's a very difficult question to answer. I think the answer generally would be no, but I would want that negative answer understood or qualified a bit. In the first place it's obvious that exactly this body of teaching, in all of its detail, has never been widely known and probably has not itself had any particular influence upon policy decisions and magistrates as they made their decisions. But it is undeniable, I believe, that general notions of justice that are in some measure the same as those expressed in the just-war theory have definitely influenced the American ethos. These notions of justice have shaped our understanding of the responsibilities of politics, and have entered in one degree or another into the general shaping of policy. Harlan Cleveland, for example, may not have made a study of the Church Fathers and what they said about the just war; but I certainly know that he, a man of considerable influence in our government, has certainly been affected by papal teachings, though he's not a Catholic. He certainly *has* been greatly influenced by the tradition of justice on which the just-war theory rests; he gives very great evidence of this in his recent book. This illustrates the way in which, it seems to me, American statesmen and political leaders, in one degree or another, are quite consciously influenced by certain general notions of justice. A good many of them have done some hard thinking about how this can actually be implemented, transcribed into law and institutions. This is not far from the just-war theory as a theory of statecraft.

FINN: Is there any reason, Paul, to expect, as some people apparently have, that the Christian bodies that are informed by just-war principles should be able to agree in terms of general ideas of justice about a particular war *apart from* their particular national allegiance? Is there any reason, for example, to have expected that Christians in Italy, Germany, France, England, the United States should have judged the Second World War in ways which were largely congruent rather than according to their national allegiance? As you know, this is one of the favorite questions asked by people who reject the just-war doctrine— Gordon Zahn, for instance.

RAMSEY: That opens up a mare's nest of questions . . . and even to answer one of them I have to presume that another one is already answered in some way. I mentioned a moment ago the extraordinary difficulty of assessing the overall justice of a regime or nation or total order of life, and then comparing it with another. In the few things that I have written, I have hesitated to go very much into the justice of the cause. I've concentrated rather upon the clarification of and analysis of *just conduct* in war. It seems to me to be something one can more readily grasp and make a judgment about. So it seems to me not unreasonable to expect or hope that Christians and all just men might come to an agreement about outstanding violations of just conduct in war. This was certainly not the case earlier in contemporary history. Obliteration bombing, and atom bombs on Hiroshima and Nagasaki, and the aiming of atomic weapons with real intent to use them upon the whole civil life of a nation—all these are illustrations of the fact that we have not known the meaning of just conduct in war. I should hope that Christians and people who think about the justice of political-military action should be able to agree about *that*. But as to whether there's any reason to expect that we would be in agreement about whether it's better for a nation to undergo a period of Communist domination with the hope that fifteen, twenty, thirty years will see liberalization, than for that nation to follow the slower process of development while maintaining a more liberal society—to judge which of these two different projects is *in toto* the more choiceworthy, if the latter can be secured only by resort to arms, is an extraordinarily difficult assessment to make.

Ramsey has said that the traditional doctrine is most helpful in coping with the justice of actual conduct in war. I ask him whether, according to that doctrine, necessities of state override, in moments of crisis, all possible prohibitions. Can the state, to ensure its survival, act without limitations?

RAMSEY: No, I don't think so. The just-war theory is, broadly speaking, specifically about war. It nevertheless expresses, in its teachings about the political use of violence, a certain view of statecraft. This view affirms that there are politically relevant, moral perspectives that should be assumed and can be made intrinsic to politics. If you're asking for a specific moral limitation upon what the state can do for itself, for its preservation,

Paul Ramsey

the chief illustration would be direct attacks upon civilian life; direct attacks upon those who are *not* the primary bearers of the force that one judges it just to resist. This is what the Vatican Council statement condemns in terms of acts of a war aimed indiscriminately at the destruction of entire cities and whole areas with their population.

FINN: Would this include Hiroshima and Nagasaki and other cities destroyed by obliteration bombing?

RAMSEY: Yes. Yes, I would say so. The Council asserted that there are limits upon the conduct of war and that such acts of war aimed at cities are violations of clearly knowable limits.

FINN: What does it mean to say "indiscriminately"? Can you have discriminate attacks on these cities and civilians?

RAMSEY: Certainly there can be justified destruction of an entire city that is an indirect consequence of the destruction of a military installation. The destruction of a city may be a collateral effect, an accompanying, unavoidable result of bombing military targets. That is, it would not be proper to characterize such an act as "bombing cities." Such an act of war might be the bombing of the SAC headquarters in Omaha, Nebraska, accompanied by destruction of Omaha; or the bombing of those underground headquarters in the Rocky Mountains near Colorado Springs and the destruction of a whole area named Colorado Springs.

FINN: And the Pentagon, even if Washington as a city were destroyed?

RAMSEY: Yes. So far as the principle of discrimination alone is concerned, yes.

FINN: But the principle of proportionality must also be applied?

RAMSEY: That's right. In other words, instead of saying that no nation can in its politics act in accord with the theory of just war, what I think you must say is that the principle of proportion puts upon our modern weapons and upon any realistic statecraft much more severe limitations than does the principle of discrimination. In an age when there are military installations fifty miles in diameter, where the way in which nations are organized for war means that they have mutually given one another legitimate military targets which would have unavoidably associated with their destruction the destruction of large numbers of people, then the overriding question is the question of the greater or lesser evil.

FINN: Well, the only limitation that seems absolute, as you phrase it, is that cities cannot themselves be regarded as military targets, but if their destruction is an unavoidable consequence of the destruction of significant military targets, then it is acceptable.

RAMSEY: Within these terms, yes. As I said earlier, the just-war theory purports to be a theory addressed to responsible statesmen and responsible citizens. It is *not* a department of ethics and politics addressed to such matters as the need for strengthening the U.N. or reconstructing the international system. The theory is addressed to a much narrower question. It aims to show how one *could* responsibly, as a last resort, make political use of violence. And thus it is justifying something. This is not a scheme for making world peace by discrediting wars one by one as unjust. It is rather an attempt to show the tolerable moral limits within which resort may be had to the use of armed force.

FINN: Bill O'Brien, as you know, is developing what some people would regard as a revisionist theory of just war in which the inviolability of noncombatants is not a cardinal principle, one in which noncombatants can, under some conditions, be just targets in war. That is, of course, contrary to your stated position. In your opinion how essential to just-war theory is the principle of inviolability of noncombatants, and how historically rooted is it?

RAMSEY: Well, when you ask how historically rooted it is, the first thing that occurs to me is that a number of historians of the just-war theory have made very much of the purely historical point that the formulation of this theory was the work of late medieval schoolmen. They have therefore spoken as if the moral and political substance of this theory is a late development, not long enduring in the Christian West. And of course, strictly speaking, that is correct. But what went into the finally constructed theory—especially the principle limiting direct attacks upon combatants and attempting to surround noncombatants with moral immunity while allowing their unavoidable involvement in damage of war—these moral principles and this

Paul Ramsey

analysis go back certainly to Thomas Aquinas. He, of course, was not a formulater of the just-war theory; but this principle of discrimination is there in his writings. My first response, then, would be an historical one, namely that if you're talking about how historically rooted this principle is, you need to look not simply at the treatises on just-war theory; you need to see all the reflections of Christians on moral problems involved in the conflict of people with people, of life with life that went on since the days of Augustine. My further response would be to defend the principle of discrimination by showing how rooted it is in certain very fundamental principles of moral action.

FINN: In discussing the means that are allowed or permitted by just-war concepts, we haven't said anything about individual acts of torture. What kind of limitations are placed upon torture by developed just-war theory, or is it even developed enough so that there's much agreement about it?

RAMSEY: I don't know the literature on this. It may be that there isn't much. I think the general inclination of those who, for example, would say that a soldier who has ceased to be a fighter or any part of the legitimate target is immune from being put to death, would also say that he should be immune from inhumane treatment or torture. To torture a prisoner would be to regard him still as a legitimate object of attack, in this case attack short of death. Or else it would be wanton cruelty.

FINN: I find it difficult to conceive of any war, certainly the limited wars that are most likely in modern times, taking place without the torture of individual prisoners who are captured. Let me quote something and ask your comments. Major General J.F.C. Fuller wrote a little foreword to this book by S.L.A. Marshall. Fuller says: "As a human creature man is rational and emotional, but at the cutting edge he is animal framed in a struggle for existence. His and his opponents' lives are at stake, and in the clinch both are hurled back into the jungle age of history, in which survival values replace peacetime morality. Everything that helps a soldier to survive is good. Everything that does not is evil. Thus it has always been in war and there's no getting away from it." * Comment of a fighting man and a theorist. And Marshall himself mentions an instance in which, after a particular battle, the men were appar-

* *Battle at Best* (New York, Pocket Books, 1965), p. ix.

ently so caught up in killing that they killed some animals who
had been staked out on a hill, in a completely irrational fashion.
Marshall says it was an irrational act, but so is war. Now these
are theorists on war, but they are also people who have participated in war. And one of the problems for anybody who theo-
rizes in just-war terms is to see how relevant the theory is to the
actual practice. Has it *any* meaning for the person who *actually*
enters into combat?

RAMSEY: I certainly disagree with the basic premise stated
by the quotation you read. The basic premise I will not take up,
namely that the fighting man is an animal. Instead, let's look at
another point. Fuller says "Survival values replace peacetime
morality." The basic premise there is that peace is one total
state of affairs and war is another total state of affairs. This I've
always identified as the American ethos which holds that there
is such a thing as morality during peacetime, but when war is
thrust upon us by some evil then anything goes. Certainly the
whole just-war tradition has been built upon the premise that
peace and war are not wholly different conditions, the one human, the other inhuman. And so what should be criticized in
that statement is not *only* its understanding of the state of war
as having in it no moral ingredients or limits, but equally its
understanding of the state of peace. The political tradition of
the West is precisely contained in the fact that it has been the
understanding of our whole civilization, with the exception of
only a few political philosophers, that when men are in a "state
of nature" in relation to one another, this is *not* a state of the
war of all against all. The state of nature is a moral state of
nature. What is lacking, terribly, tragically lacking, is any insti-
tutionalization of these moral values that *do* pertain to the state
of nature between nation states as well as to domestic society
within the states. The movement from the state of nature into
a civil state is a movement not from a non-moral or an amoral
or an immoral condition into a condition where you have morality. It's a movement from a moral state of nature into a domestic political life where you have civil institutions, where the
rights of man are guaranteed, where there's just adjudication,
where there's somebody to decide conflicting cases and to prevent the outbreak of war, and so forth. Thus are the moral principles in the state of nature clarified, implemented, institutionalized or given legal status. Now the nation-state system is in a

Paul Ramsey

state of nature, the nations in relation to one another are in this state of nature. But to hold that this is a state of war in the sense that it's an animal condition where there are no criteria other than sheer survival is, it seems to me, to break with the main tradition of political philosophy in the West.

If you take the notion that war is an extension of politics in other form and that politically embodied justice may, as a last resort, arm itself, you either have to say that *all* politics is a mere matter of animal survival or you have to say that peace and war are not all that radically different. Some pacifists and some realists seem to agree that politics in peacetime is governed by moral criteria while politics in war is not governed by any moral criteria. The just-war theory entails a theory of statecraft that has in it certain reference to the finalities of man, man as being a final end in himself, in his values; not being wholly reducible or subsumable to a totalitarian way, to reasons of state. It is an account of peace *and* war which refuses to make this radical distinction of ethics in the one condition and non-ethics under another.

Now to push on. From that quotation, you asked about how men actually do perform in war. Now here I suppose people who have been influenced by and find themselves in some sense committed to the general teachings of the just-war tradition would divide into two groups. And it's important to note this division. Some would say that if a war is unjust in any respect, it is wholly unjust and no Christian should participate in it. Now the case can be made for this view, if you have in mind the two, three, four, or five principle tests of the justice of war. If a war fails to be just in terms of one primary criterion, it has to be judged unjust, even though it passes the other tests. For example, if the cause is unjust the war is not justified because it's being conducted justly. But when you talk about what men actually *do* in the fury and fog of war, you're talking about the irrationality and the conditions to which they are driven. This raises a different question that does not so deeply affect the justice of the war in general.

One has to raise the question of whether the injustice that is admittedly done in all wars is peripheral, however abundant, or whether it's part of the central design of the war. The question one would ask concerning torture, for example, is whether the war is designedly being conducted, in significant measure, by the deliberate use of torture. This is the way to frame the most important question. There might be morally sensitive men who hold that they should not participate in a war when they know that in war torture does take place. I myself would not think it right to draw that conclusion about something that is not a necessary part of the principal design of war. Now this still leaves you with a very grave question, the question of whether insurgency and counterinsurgency warfare can be successfully conducted without torture being something more than incidental, however frequent, or whether torture must be accepted as a very definite part of the designed conduct of the war. And judgment as to this has to depend upon the clearheaded prosecution of findings of fact. If this is the nature of this form of war, it has become a morally intolerable institution in this respect.

This is, as Ramsey says, a very grave question, for whatever differences exist between the war in Vietnam and the "other Vietnams" anticipated in other countries, the way in which the wars are fought will be similar. If the present war is judged "morally intolerable," the others are likely to receive the same judgment.

We have covered, in very general terms, most of the issues that divide those who differ about the justice of the war in Vietnam, from the justice of the cause to the methods of prosecuting the war. I ask Ramsey, as one who generally supports U.S. policy in Vietnam, what activities fall outside of an acceptable range of activities for those who protest the war in Vietnam. How does he judge the politico-moral aspects of protests that range from signing petitions, to refusing to pay taxes, to attempting to stop troop trains?

His first response—to dispose of a relatively simple matter—is that "we should defend morally—and perhaps by legal institution"—the possibility of what is called selective conscientious objection, what Ramsey himself refers to as "just-war objection." A man would then be able to say "that this particular war is in his conscientious opinion so fundamentally unjust that he cannot participate in it." Ramsey then turns to the range of protest activities I had mentioned.

RAMSEY: It's hard for me to address those particular questions without first saying something in general about "direct

Paul Ramsey

action." First, it seems to me, one must affirm that there's such a thing as justifiable revolution. No political society defines a right of revolution; it's not a legal right. But there surely is a moral right of revolution against the whole of an organized society in order to overturn it. Now on anybody's view the conditions that would justify revolution would be very extreme indeed. Whether or not one can take direct nonviolent, revolutionary action, to force one's society and its institutions in a given direction, depends very much upon and varies inversely with the possibility of entering into the formation of public opinion, into law-making procedures, into social due process by which one's society is persuaded or not persuaded that some present policy is unjust or wrong or unwise. Now it does seem to me that in recent direct-action movements we have failed to make the vital distinction between things that fall within social due process and things that do not. The justification for those that do is different from the justification of those that do not. Freedom of assembly is one thing, but freedom to assemble in Times Square another. The right to protest to one's governors, and to exercise the right of free assembly, are precious rights; but to use that language to justify what is designed primarily as a form of social obstruction seems to me to be quite illicit.

It's a precious right and indeed a fact that—not having a declaratory constitution—it's a very definite part of our social due process that one has to violate a law in order to get a test case, to invoke the adjudicating processes of the society in the courts. To get a determination of justice one must violate law. But that, I think, falls within social due process; it is a part of our constitutional system that this be done. But to try to use the power of a nonviolent direct-action movement in order to stop troop trains from running, lying across the rails in Oakland, California, while using the language of social protest, seems to me an effort—however nonviolent the means—to impose the will of the protesters upon the national policy; to thwart, to impede, to tie up the movement that the country has undertaken. Now the justification for that would come close to what would be required for any sort of revolution. This raises the question of whether one has had a chance in the public forum to make his view clear, to enforce it as much as possible by persuasive means, by signal dramatic assemblies, and in all sorts of ways to get this point of view into the processes by which a nation's policy is made. But no one should say that simply because the nation's policy has not agreed with him he then has a right to thwart the policy he disagrees with because he sees so clearly the justice of that for which he stands. That would require such a clogging of due democratic processes as to come close to the condition of affairs that would justify violent revolutionary activity. The choice between violent or nonviolent revolutionary activity would then be simply a question of economy of means. I think these distinctions have been obscured by the moral value placed upon nonviolent direct action as over against violent direct action. That doesn't mean I approve of violence. But when it's a question of imposing your will upon the commonweal, what would be required to justify a nonviolent revolution or nonviolent obstruction is exactly what would be required to justify a violent revolution or violent obstruction. Both require a tyrannical situation, a state of affairs from which social due process for change had been excluded. Such tyranny, such a clogging of the processes of getting consideration for points of view that should be in the market place, does not seem to me to exist in the United States, either in regard to civil rights (because our Federal system allows for appeal to higher law) or in regard to U.S. policy in Vietnam.

COMMITMENT
WITHOUT LABEL

FREDERICK FRANCK

Frederick Franck is an artist whose drawings are in the collections of over two dozen museums and institutes, the author of nine books, and a dentist who no longer finds time for his practice. I first heard of him as a man who was so captivated by Pope John's opening address at Vatican Council II that he decided on an impulse to go to Rome to draw the event. Impulsive because he went neither as a Catholic, a theologian, a professional journalist or an observer, and he had no pull or inside connections to help him along. It is a mark of his many-sided talents, artistic, intellectual and social, that he covered all four sessions of the Council, wrote in *Outsider in the Vatican* one of the most pointed and personal accounts of Vatican II, and that he was awarded the Medal of Pope John's Pontificate for his drawings of the first session.

I visit Franck in his second-story studio that looks out over Bleecker Street and Father Demos Square in Greenwich Village. Off the large studio is a smaller room with a desk, filed stacks of paintings, books, a small bed. The whole thing had once been a Republican headquarters and Franck says that over the smells that drift up from the stores below "fish here, chicken there, vegetables over there"—over all this hovers the Republican smell. "We've never been able to get rid of it."

At least partially because I know Franck's reluctance to be labeled, I first ask him bluntly if he is a pacifist.*

---

* Some idea of his attitude about labels comes through in this partial self-description.

"Religiously, I am perhaps a unique ecumenical phenomenon: I was

FRANCK: Yes, well, you know my attitude toward labels and trying to avoid them. I think we always misrepresent as soon as we label ourselves—either politically or religiously or racially. I think we immediately start these separations; we are simply what we are. If you ask me am I a pacifist then I think, "Well no, no. It is not Franck *equals* pacifist." I'm not, and I don't belong to pacifist organizations. But of course I think that most of my attitudes are pacifist attitudes. They could hardly be different because I have a complete conviction in the unity of man—not as an ideal, not as a command, but as a physical fact.

FINN: How do your pacifist attitudes influence your judgment about *any* particular thing on the contemporary scene?

FRANCK: Are you thinking now of our contemporary little wars?

FINN: Little wars or even our major deterrents, the nuclear weapons system.

FRANCK: Well, the nuclear deterrent is one of the great tragedies of our whole technological attitude toward our lives, and our belief in purely technological solutions to our problems in general. I deplore them—I don't say condemn—I deplore them. I know they are part of our reality and I would do anything to avoid their use. And I don't think there's any justification at *any* time, at *any* time, for the use of these weapons.

I feel that we are still suffering now under the karma of

educated agnostically, but was deeply influenced by the Catholic culture of that southern tip of Holland where I was born. I can proudly boast a Calvinist uncle, a liberal Protestant aunt and another who is Jewish. Unfortunately my devout Catholic aunt recently died in a convent. My son, although baptized a Lutheran, is now an Episcopalian choir boy. A cousin of mine seems to head a liberal Protestant sect in Holland, where my brother-in-law exercises the honorable profession of being a Jesuit. I myself am a totally inactive Protestant, partly Jewish in ancestry, a member of the Buddhist Society, with strong Catholic leanings. . . .

"Culturally, I am the product of that border country between Holland, Belgium and Germany, an extremely fertile ground where hybrids of French, Flemish, Dutch and German mixture have borne their fruit without anyone worrying much where the chromosomes originally came from. . . . We all speak French, German and Dutch plus the local dialect, a kind of Burgundian, and our swear words are Walloon or Flemish. We speak French with a Belgian accent, German with a Rhinelandish accent, and our Dutch pronunciation is judged to be ludicrous by the people of the north of Holland, a country so small that the terms 'north' and 'south' are euphemisms or mere terms of courtesy."

Hiroshima. And, of course, a karma as such has a tendency, has a law, to become heavier at each turn of the wheel, so the wheel has to be stopped somewhere.

FINN: I remember talking with you about your attitude before the Second Vatican Council. You said you were filled with —maybe despair is too strong a word—but at least you were being . . .

FRANCK: Prepared. I was prepared for the end, is that what you mean? We have to be prepared for this kind of end because we are, I think, in the hands of the insane. Now this sounds a little bit . . . umm . . . apodictic perhaps, but in my mind there's no doubt that in our system of government—I mean not only the American—that those people get power who crave power. And I don't think that, unless they are born again somewhere along the line, they are able to wield this power with wisdom.

FINN: You're saying that's true of all governments?

FRANCK: Oh yes.

FINN: And when you say we're in the hands of the insane, it's these people you're talking about?

FRANCK: Exactly. Who that isn't paranoid would like to be the President of the United States? [laugh]

FINN: Well, this is an expression, as I recall, of the mood you had when you first read Pope John's fairly buoyant address.

FRANCK: And quite fantastic, quite fantastic optimism at that point of the Cuban crisis, to talk about prophets of doom who somehow surmised that the world was coming to an end. Pope John apparently had a clearer view, was probably not motivated by fear—as would be in character—and saw a long future ahead of us and planned, as it were, for this future. Anyway, he made the basic decision that I think we make at any moment when we think now about the future. That is, all our efforts are of course doomed *if* we are blown to smithereens. So the very fact that we are still working *at* some things, still striving for something, presupposes a reservoir of hope in us that goes beyond the rational.

FINN: This statement of Pope John, and everything that followed, has changed your own attitude?

FRANCK: Yes. Yes, at that moment it gave me faith that maybe there *was* a future, and Pope John's updating of the Church, as I understood it, was that the *core* of the Church and the Church's teachings, the Church's content, had a permanent, persistent, eternal validity; that it was the *formulations* in which it had bogged down. And I thought then of course that all the outcry about the death of God is nothing more than an outcry of people who despair about the formulations, not about the core. I also feel increasingly—but I think I already felt it dimly at that time—that the so-called indifferentism of the masses that the Church complains about, the Churches all complain about, is a sheer alibi, it's a phony, because I feel—especially in the so-called noncommitted, religiously noncommitted people—I feel an enormous hunger for spiritual content and spiritual values. I find that they rummage into anything that promises them a solution to their insoluble problems of emptiness, of existential vacuity. And the alibi doesn't hold. It only means that the Churches have no exit visa, they can only talk within their own little semantic conventions, and the indifferentism there is to their impotence to express verities, the verities they represent, into understandable language.

FINN: Do you think that this applies to the conditions which allow war or make it more of a likelihood? Do you think the Church has failed to say what it could say in this area?

FRANCK: Oh certainly. Oh certainly. During the Second World War, the utterances of Pope Pius XII were always ambiguous. I mean, you never mentioned aggressors by name, you always just talked about your heart bleeding; I mean, this heart has been simply oozing with tears and blood for . . . not exactly indicating who it was bleeding for. The Church certainly has been most ambiguous in its utterances on war. And even during the Vatican Council. It seemed now to me that after the soul-searching of the Vatican Council that it would be *very* difficult for anyone who was part of it to still *defend,* under certain conditions even, the use of these absolute *horrors.*

If you ever think of the Holy Spirit, then what could be more of a sin to the Holy Spirit—not only exploding bombs over people's heads but even exploding them on an uninhabited island in the Pacific, in the atmosphere or in the water. I have such a feeling—and I share this I think with many thoughtful people—that this is a sin against the crust of the earth of which we are a product. The violence done to the development of even the lower organisms in this earth crust is staggering. We don't know what we are unleashing and what we are getting at. So there's no justification *ever* to explode this device.

FINN: You talked about the leaders of countries as being almost necessarily paranoid, at least given the conditions today, but Pope John reached a position of eminence and undoubted authority and even *power,* and I presume from what you say that you wouldn't put him in the same category.

FRANCK: No. You see, he didn't climb up. He was somehow passively moved from one step to the other without demurring and accepted what was put on his shoulders. And then I think that Angelo Roncalli 1918 and Angelo Roncalli 1962 were totally different people. I think something happened to this man which made him disregard his own position and become totally aware of his human condition, his own essential humanity, until the very moment of his death. This was a man who, I think, was under the direct sway of the Holy Spirit, and John had disappeared and the Pope had disappeared. He was Man with a capital M in reacting to his fellow men. And he did not struggle for power—I mean, he *had* the power. He wielded it, but in a totally different manner, in a manner of extreme gentleness and only through the power of his own insights, I think, and his innocence.

FINN: Do you think that Pope John's spirit and even attitudes were sufficiently evident in the statements that came out of the Council as they dealt with war?

FRANCK: The Council can't be judged by its documents. The Council has to be judged by the spirit it generated and demonstrated. And the Council produced or gave body to a true spiritual revival—and I do not say a religious revival—a becoming conscious of man as a spiritual being. And I think that we see some results in this country, for instance—but *everywhere*—suddenly Catholics have to be what we call pacifists; they are no longer paralyzed, as they traditionally were, by the weight of the hierarchy.

FINN: What about the hierarchy itself? Has it felt this spirit that you're talking about? The bishops have not talked out.

FRANCK: It would be a very big step, wouldn't it, for bishops, because after all, they have somehow a tradition of siding with the haves and those in power and the government. If a bishop doesn't, he becomes somewhat of a maverick like Archbishop Roberts.*

FINN: Right. Well, there are bishops in England and Australia who have made large protests, and in Holland.

FRANCK: Holland of course is different. You see, Holland has a tradition of protest; that's why it used to be a Protestant country.

FINN: Do you think the lack of protest also has something to do with the fact that the United States is, after all, *the* strongest power and is the one engaged? Does this curb protests that might otherwise be here?

FRANCK: I don't think so. I think it's probably just a tradition of conformism. That's my feeling.

FINN: I presume you don't find the same strong conformism among Catholics generally today.

FRANCK: No. But this happens in the, shall we say, in the people of God. This does not happen yet at the top, anywhere . . . practically.

FINN: What about Pope Paul's statements?

FRANCK: Ah! I think that Pope Paul has an obsession about peace—which is by the way not a reproach; it's the noblest obsession one can have. It has become very obvious that he's deeply troubled, and I think it's one of the most attractive features of Pope Paul. Here he has *not* Pope Paul'd at all. You know what I mean.†

FINN: You spoke very strongly about your own abhorrence of nuclear weapons. Is there any kind of a dividing line that you recognize which separates violence, even massive organized violence, which is acceptable from that which is not, or even a gray area that separates these two?

---

* Thomas D. Roberts, S.J., former Archbishop of Bombay, has spoken out strongly on questions such as nuclear war and contraception.
† A reference to the reputation Pope Paul has gained of not landing forcefully on either side of a debated question.

Frederick Franck

FRANCK: Of course it's a very deep search, self-search, that one has to conduct there in answering this question. I can only answer a question like this existentially: what is my own re-action? I think I would be capable of violence, under stress, as long as it would be a reflex action. I cannot conceive of using physical violence consciously. However, this does not mean that I necessarily condemn violence in others. One thing we always forget, that the Church has forgotten—or maybe never *knew,* where it is decidely inferior to religions like Hinduism and Buddhism—is the frank recognition of different levels of consciousness in which people live. I haven't been able to find any-one who somehow could clearly state that the Church recognizes different levels of realization or consciousness. This of course tends to make dogmas, pronouncements, immutable, not in their essence but in their formulation. People have been burned at the stake and banished and God knows what, not because they were unbelievers, not because they even disbelieved a par-ticular formula, but because they happened to believe it accord-ing to their own level of understanding—which might sometimes exceed the level of understanding of the persons who formulated it.

Now I think there are plenty of people who are quite willing to do violence, do it with pleasure. I don't see that violence can be avoided. I think that if you have a violent situation, we have to have some people who are willing to use guns, or fire hoses or truncheons. Somehow this violence has to be stopped. It's not *my* function. We have to be very clear about our own func-tion, and we don't necessarily have to generalize from that. I cannot walk in demonstrations. I feel silly. Foolish. Even dis-honest. However, I built *Pacem in Terris.* This is my chapel. And this was my demonstration of what I understood about peace and my placard which says "Let's stop killing. Let's stop killing each other."

The "chapel" to which Franck refers is a remarkable struc-ture; next to his small house in New Milford, New York there was an old dilapidated ruin of a grist mill. From the stone ruins, the old mill-wheels, scraps of stained and plate glass and surplus scaffolding, he has transformed it, according to his own design and largely by his own hands, into a place of quiet and medita-tion. Although called *Pacem in Terris* and dedicated to Pope John, Franck says that "it is not dedicated to any religion in particular, but to all and to none. It grew in the trust that it may speak to all those who refuse labels, but nonetheless share the basic human search for wholeness. It is meant for inwardness, stillness and freedom." *

FRANCK: I have formulated my picket sign: I call this place an experiment in communication. We have to try, if we *really* desire to communicate, not to pontificate. Then we have to find the formulation which avoids the other person getting violent reactions—idiosyncratic or allergic reactions to what we are saying. In my placard I consciously tried to say everything I wanted to say, but in such a manner that it doesn't give hives to exactly those people I would like to talk to most intimately.

FINN: Could you be a little more particular about the chapel? I remember that there are not only statements from various people but references to contemporary events like Hiroshima.

FRANCK: Yes, I built the chapel as a sign of peace, a testimony to peace—when I say peace here I mean interreligious, international, interracial. Although I think of it as completely interfaith or nonfaith, still I dedicated it to Pope John as the prophet of human solidarity. As you know, there's a big statue of Pope John, and he's confronting a rather horrendous-looking angel, the angel of death, the angel of the apocalypse, who threatens us all. And he stops him—now I mean this also very individually—he really stopped death; he stopped hatred *within himself,* which is the only way to stop it in someone else. And look at the tremendous response to that, as if all the healthy factors, all the non-death wish factors in this world, rallied around him.

Now then I think I used traditional symbolism. One of the windows has in it the wheel of Buddhism and the seven-branch candelabra of Judaism and the many crosses of a fractured

---

* Simply to satisfy his curiosity about who visited the chapel and where they came from, Franck had a book for visitors to sign. They added spontaneous tributes such as these:

"Simple, primitive, yet beautiful and inspiring."

"This place is a brick in building a society of peace. Thank you for having the courage to make people stop and think."

"Peace be with all of you who visit here."

"Lord make me an instrument of Thy Peace."

"A wonderful monument to the good in all mankind."

Christianity. The only slight change I made there, I put the crosses topsy-turvy. The chapel is sort of a theological doodle too, you see, in stone and wood. Actually, the thing that says it all is this enormous hand of Christ sticking out of the earth, with the stigma in it. And it has on it, on the thumb, "They know not what they do," and it says "Guernica"—where the misery started for our century, or let's say after the First World War anyway—"Guernica, Lidice, Dachau, Auschwitz, Hiroshima, Alabama and Mississippi and South Africa." Of course you could go on forever, but to me these are the enormous and unforgivable sins against man, and hence against the Christ principle in man, that our century has produced, and this is my way of indicting . . . also myself by the way. I'm not proud of the fact that I'm not walking with placards and so on, that I'm so much of a snob or God knows what, a sensitive Pollyanna. I'm not proud of that. I respect it greatly, greatly in others. But we have our own way to walk.

FINN: Would Vietnam be added to that list if you'd gone on?

FRANCK: Oh certainly. The only reason why I haven't added Vietnam yet is it is too big an atrocity. You know, I feel that there must be some village, which will probably be called something like Quong Quong or so, where *really* everybody has been mutilated or killed, for no other reason than there *might* have been a Vietcong sitting somewhere. Last week when this bomb went off in Saigon and our soldiers and marines started shooting from both sides and were shooting each other—isn't that like a symbol of the whole madness that's going on? Vietnam is a *monstrous,* a monstrous mistake that we are making, and it has been fairly clearly proven that it is rather illegal, that it's an undeclared war and it goes on and it swallows human lives.

But it may have one very great plus. It has killed Babbitt totally. He's one of the victims. I spoke last week for the Catholic Library Association in a town in New England. I saw it in front of me: they would look, of course, exactly the same as the Episcopalian Library Association and the Jewish Library Association of East Orange. And I saw in my mind's eye a lot of silly women in flower hats, inverted flowerpots. Now when I walked in they *were* flowerpotted ladies and we *had* chicken à la king, or something like that, *but* when I talked about the Vatican Council, I felt such a response from this audience that

I started to talk about the chapel and completely deviated from what I had more or less prepared.

Then there were questions about demonstrations and what they did to these people. I felt here, as I say, that Babbitt was dead and Christ was rising. I felt that in these very ordinary small-town people from Springfield, Massachusetts—of course they're not ordinary, you know, they are quite extraordinary, but one is tempted to see them as ordinary—that *everything* had been stirred up and that under their well-dressed bourgeois Catholic library exterior were human beings in turmoil and that *everything* was being called into question.

And so I feel that Vietnam and the demonstrations have brought things to the surface. The consensus was, "Well, you know, the demonstrations are all very upsetting, but they're better, after all, than silent conformism." This is a new America speaking to me. This is no longer what we usually think of as the Elk and Legion of Decency and American Legion country. Something else is happening. I think this has happened through the suffering, the anguish, the internal uncertainties created by Vietnam. Vietnam has given us, has exteriorized, the deep feelings of guilt that were first felt after Hiroshima. It has brought them to the surface, I feel, in many people. And so it has made us human.

FINN: I'd like to bring together two things that you said. You spoke earlier about the people who actually obtain positions of high political prominence as being almost necessarily, given the conditions of the political process, paranoid, and you spoke also of Pope John conquering that kind of fear and hatred which can exist in the individual. Now do you see the possibility of a political process which would bring to the top people who do not have that driving ambition which you associated with paranoia? And do you see any possibility of *most people* conquering that kind of hostility and fear so that they will be able to control and direct their aggression in a more proper form?

FRANCK: Our whole political systems in general are so constructed that I do not think that representatives of the . . . shall we say those who suffer consciously in their minds, struggle with the realities of their own lives, would easily drift to the top. I think it an exceptional situation when a person already at the top gets converted, maybe through some trauma, and

Frederick Franck

bestows blessings instead of bringing pain and damnation on his followers.

We have seen, however, that general public opinion could *mitigate* and could *change* the expression, could make the so-called leaders more careful. And, after all, they want to be loved and respected and get votes. If the reverse happens, and anger takes over, then we get a general unbalanced situation where the worst features of the paranoid are going to be stimulated, and then we get Hitlerism. And the typical end of Hitlerism—which is *clearly* formulated in the Gospel, I feel, as a law of human behavior—he will be destroyed by the sword that he took up. But, of course, that means immense suffering ensues for untold numbers of individuals.

FINN: What effect do you think the peace movement—to use this broad umbrella term—is having in this country? Do you think it's doing something helpful, or is it being neutralized?

FRANCK: I think it has taken on such proportions, is growing so fast, that it is going to have one of two effects. One possibility is bringing the nation's leaders to their senses, making them act less automatically, less as reflexes on hurt feelings. That's a possibility. The other possibility we already see in principle; in reaction to the peace movement there may be a resurgence of a kind of McCarthyism. And I think that the momentum of reflection and criticism is greatest in that section of the population which has to bear the brunt of all this, and that's the students. And here, I think, we see a real revolution. Don't forget, I was a student in Europe and in Europe students were radicals. And I went to school here too, I went to university here too, and I thought that the students here were more conformist than retired businessmen.

Now not only the flower hats, or what is underneath them, have been shaken up, but we now have students who are radical and students who are talking back, students who do not just swallow all the ready processed nonsense they are being fed. And I think that this is of *immense* importance, *immense*. This, in fact, promises a different America. I think that in America now—if I compare the America of when I first came here twenty years ago—the revolution in taste, the revolution in attitudes toward cultural fulfillment, I think that we are perhaps once more going to be the great revolutionary country that America once was. There are so many symptoms of that. Kennedy recognized this, or rather, Kennedy was part of it. The present team certainly is not, has no contact with this at all. They are still the representative of the Elks.

FINN: I think that it's clear that you have pacifist attitudes without being labeled a pacifist, and that they operate here.

FRANCK: You say that I started out saying I'm not a pacifist but I have pacifist attitudes. I think this is perhaps very typical of a growing majority in this country. People see themselves as ordinary loyal Americans but just do not like much of what we do. There's a great danger in this, a great danger for our position of power. I think that as soon as we begin to feel guilty, from the point of view of domination, we are lost. The Church too, you know. We are lost. I think that as soon as we become rather conscious of our crimes, then we don't perpetrate them any more with so much gusto.

FINN: The danger you talk about is a danger you think we should risk.

FRANCK: Oh definitely. It's the danger of getting mature, maybe also of dying. But there may be some dispensations that I don't know of. Maybe also this is the only way to be constructive in the world.

TOM T. STONIER

It may be that Tom Stonier does not belong to that group of professors and intellectuals whose opinions are discounted by the President and a number of his advisers. For Mr. Stonier is a scientist, a biologist whose publications have titles such as "Radioautographic Evidence for the Intercellular Location of Crown Gall Bacteria," "Preliminary Attempts at Obtaining Mixed Fragmented Tissue Cultures," and "The Morphology and Physiology of Plant Tumors."

Tom T. Stonier received his Ph.D. from Yale in 1955, having done work on his thesis at Brookhaven National Laboratory. He was on the staff of The Rockefeller Institute for a number of years before he accepted a position at Manhattan College, where he is engaged in biological research. He is a consultant to Living Science Laboratories and the Hudson Institute, has lectured to many scientific and medical groups, and has presented expert testimony to subcommittees of both the Senate and House Armed Services Committees.

Mr. Stonier is also the author of *Nuclear Disaster*, the first study that attempts to assess the total consequences of a nuclear burst on a large modern city, to project the interaction of the physical, biological, psychological, economic and social effects both in short- and long-range terms. And the lessons Stonier has inferred from that study carry him quite beyond the realm of scientific research and plunge him into the center of contemporary political debate. Stonier is fully aware of the "unrealistic" nature of what he would propose in order to avoid nuclear disaster, for he states that it is necessary to change "certain fundamental social attitudes." One of these is a negative attitude, "the suspicion that anyone who advocates disarmament and peace is either a subversive or a lunatic idealist unable to grasp the realities of today's world." Positively, Stonier writes that "a preoccupation with peace is not only eminently reasonable and respectable, but in our generation has become imperative."

Stonier intends to see that his own preoccupation does not fall into the ethereal or ephemeral. When I meet him he, Robert Christen and other members of the Manhattan faculty are in the process of establishing a "Pacem in Terris" Institute at the College in order to construct a continuing program for peace. I ask Stonier how, as a biologist, he had become so deeply engaged with political and social issues. "It was more or less an accident," he says, because ten years earlier "I never poked my nose out of the laboratory." But at The Rockefeller Institute he had become friendly with a group of physicians who frequently gave talks to groups that wanted information about fallout, radiation and mutation. The demand for their services grew so great they enlisted their friends in the cause. Stonier resisted but they said, "Look, you're concerned about these matters, you have the information, and you can provide a real public service. Now put up or shut up." And, said Stonier, "I've always found it difficult to shut up, so. . . ."

The talks, however, took an unexpected turn. Stonier was prepared to give reams of factual information, but sooner or later the questions directed to him required political, social and moral considerations, "things I hadn't thought about before." "I haven't been quite the same since, because I realized two things: first, that I had a greater responsibility than just sticking to the laboratory; second, that I did more than recognize the problem, that I had something to contribute." Out of that group and Stonier's own commitment there was formed the Scientists Committee for Radiation Information, which has since become the Scientists Committee for Public Information. And out of questions directed to that Committee about the effects of nuclear war there grew a memorandum, a technical report and finally *Nuclear Disaster*. "It's absurd in a way that a relatively obscure biologist goes on to become an expert in nuclear war," but

Tom T. Stonier

Stonier knew of no one else who was going to draw together all the relevant information.

Since his initial engagement with the facts of nuclear disaster over ten years ago, Stonier has become progressively and deeply involved in the political and social consequences of modern war. I ask him to define what now are his general working assumptions.

STONIER: War is now an anachronism. It is an anachronism because of modern military and physical technology. The world has shrunk and just as it's now considered an anachronism for cities, for New York and Philadelphia, to go to war, it will become an anachronism for nations. The time, if not ripe immediately, will be within the next generation or two, and we must work for this. There is an urgency in the matter because of the existence of nuclear weapons. We know that irrational forces appear—sometimes an irrational leader, sometimes simply irrational social forces, the dynamics of which we still do not understand. So we're living in a very risky world. In addition, there's always the possibility of plain technical accident. We saw a few months ago the loss of four bombs, of which three were recovered, two of which had burst. The last one fell in the Mediterranean.

If one looks at the whole problem of accidents in the atomic energy industry, in the missile industry, if one looks at submarines like the *Thresher* going down, if one looks at any of the support systems, if one looks at the fact that three men in a thousand in the military forces are psychotic—this is lower than the civilian average, but it's a real factor—if one looks also at the fact that the history of major accidents has always been unpredictable—like the power failure last November—then one begins to get the feeling that the question is not *will* one of these nuclear weapons explode one of these days, but *when*. I mean, in spite of the very elaborate, ingenious and apparently foolproof systems that exist to keep a nuclear weapon from going off, the fact exists that weapons are *designed* to go off and that the engineering for not having them go off is secondary.

There are now five nuclear powers and there will be more. So there's a spread of nuclear weapons geographically, and in terms of who has the trigger on the finger. More and more tactical weapons go to lower- and lower-echelon personnel, and the chances of somebody doing something stupid or insane become ever greater. So between having these weapons around and having irrational components in our politics—and we are as susceptible as is anybody else—the dangers are great. The thing to do is get rid of these damn weapons.

FINN: So we're back to the social conditions that are necessary for disarmament.

STONIER: Yes, but let me finish stating the position. I think it is absurd to consider all wars immoral, particularly those of the past. I'm inclined to think almost all wars are an anachronism from here on in. There must be a better way of solving conflict situations than that. Certainly there will not be an absence of conflict; I think much good derives from conflict *if* it is kept within nonlethal bounds.

Military technology has made life so dangerous that the term "Defense Department," for example, is also an anachronism. The Defense Department cannot defend us against a determined major power.

The policy of deterrence has worked, and it's the only policy we have at the moment. But we must also recognize there's a time limit on this thing. You cannot run the world indefinitely on deterrence, because deterrence always assumes that the other side understands you completely, that you understand it completely, that you will never push *it* to the point where it considers war justified, and that they will never push *you* to a point where you think war is justified. But both sides have forces within them which do not recognize that a large-scale nuclear exchange would be absurd.

FINN: You yourself would reject as a logical enterprise all forms of nuclear war today?

STONIER: Yes. Absolutely. I cannot envision any system that is so evil that I wouldn't rather subvert it. Well, I'll quote: "It is a sign of the immature man to die for a cause and the sign of a mature one to live for it."

Stonier's position has been labeled "nuclear pacifism." I had just read an article criticizing this position by William R. Kintner, deputy director of the Foreign Policy Research Institute at the University of Pennsylvania. He would agree with Stonier

Tom T. Stonier

about the importance of modern military technology, but not with his conclusions. I ask Stonier what he thinks of one brief section which I quote: "Nuclear pacifism offers no escape from our dilemma. The balance must be struck between the defense of values and the defense of life. Pure physical survival cannot be raised to the Number One value of humanity, for we must be concerned not only for life itself, but also for the quality of life." *

STONIER: I consider that verbiage. I consider it absolute nonsense, because the quality of life has as its prerequisite the existence of life, and I think these people do not understand . . . well, they understand that if nobody were alive then any of these ideological disputes become academic. What they do not understand is that by permitting a nuclear war, they create conditions where life is even more intolerable than they think it would be if a nation simply submitted. He's just second-rate in his analysis of the situation. He does not understand the fundamental problems involved, the nature of modern warfare, the nature of modern society. All he can think of is in simplistic theological values without understanding the basis from whence they derive.

FINN: He also says, and these are conclusions of his article and labeled as such: "Since there is no possibility of repealing the nuclear age, the human race must learn to live with immense destructive power." Now you've suggested otherwise.

STONIER: Well, it depends what he means by living with it. What I call living with it, is to close the gap that currently exists between the physical technology and social technology. I can envision maintaining nuclear weapons under United Nations command. I can envision that this may be a very good device to assure everybody that nobody can cheat. In any case, one guarantee would be that the United Nations forces would constitute a nuclear military force which would be so in excess of anything that some nation could hide off in a little corner somewhere that it would be clearly unprofitable.

FINN: In a recent research study performed for the Arms Control and Disarmament Agency, Arnold Wolfers, who was

* "The Relation Between Power and Values in the Nuclear Age," *The Intercollegiate Review*, March-April 1966, p. 304.

really in charge of the project, wrote that "a drastically disarmed United States might find its interests jeopardized unless it enjoyed the protection of an international military force. But," he said, "if such a force were controlled by the United Nations it would offer little comfort to the United States and might indeed render the safety of many vulnerable American interests more precarious." Now I don't know what the international agency would be if it's not the United Nations.

STONIER: Well, this is exactly one of the key problems. You never get something for nothing in this world. I think this is true at a personal level as well as an international level. The question is what are we giving up?

Stonier points out that when he talked with East and West Europeans at a recent disarmament seminar in Italy, at which he was the only American, more than one person thought his own country had gained through the loss of former colonies. The Dutch, particularly, said that their initial reactions to the "loss of Indonesia" had later been reversed. Stonier adds that he would put national interests into two large classes, the economic and the ideological. An international police force would develop along with it the means to compensate for expropriations or losses.

The ideological component is clearly more complicated, he said, but we should learn from the last twenty years that much ideological zeal is generated by economic interests and will change with them. Further "we must begin to understand, as de Gaulle says, it is not a bad thing for some countries to go through a communist phase, or some phase of a controlled economy."

STONIER: We must not expect these countries to follow our lead just yet. At the same time, I feel that if Vietnam, all of Vietnam, had gone communist, it would be much less of a problem for us *now,* because I think Ho Chi Minh is the kind of a man who would've become a Tito. And Yugoslavia, although we may not like its economic system, is politically much closer to us than many of our NATO allies are, particularly if you look at Spain and Portugal. And I think in Vietnam there would have been an evolution; the answer for us is not to fight communism there and kill Communists. Rather, let the society fulfill its own need, including dabbling with communism for a generation or two, and let them evolve and let us help them speed up the evolution.

FINN: You talk as if you see communism as a temporary phase.

STONIER: Exactly. I think it's a temporary phase in moving from a backward agrarian society into a modern automated society, and that actually we have some things to learn from it. And I think we have totally misassessed communism. We are so busy pinning the label of evil on communism that we really fail to understand its strength and therefore are surprised that it's doing as well as it's doing in Vietnam. I mean, why do these people keep coming back? Do they like to see their villages napalm-bombed? Do they like to have their children maimed? Do they like to spend their life's blood in fighting us? Is it simply because they're interested in some nefarious quest for power? Or is it because they're convinced that the only way they can achieve social justice is through the devices that communism offers them?

So, on one hand we totally underestimate the strength of communism, and on the other hand we totally overestimate it. We feel that if we let the world go, it would be engulfed in communism and there'd be another Dark Ages for five hundred years, when in reality the thing wouldn't last twenty-five or fifty years and would immediately become subverted by indigenous forces.

FINN: I presume from what you said—I may be wrong here —that your own judgment about the reasons for U.S. policy in Vietnam would be that it's following an ideological component. The United States is not, in your terms, attempting to expand, to develop an empire.

STONIER: No. No. My explanation, and I think I got this across to the Eastern European colleagues. . . . I said "Look here, you've got to understand that the last traumatic experience for the United States was World War II. And this was true for most of the countries of the world. And there was a general feeling that World War II could have been nipped in the bud at Munich, and that the lesson of Munich was, 'You don't make a bully more moral by giving in to him. You only make him stronger.' Now if you view, as we view, communism as a kind of a bully, then the worst thing in the world for us would be not to challenge him at every point. And we did this in Berlin and we did this in Korea and we're doing it in Vietnam."

FINN: Did they understand and accept this?

STONIER: Yes, and when the Yugoslav reviewed the Cold War, he brought this in. And he came out with what I consider the most objective history of the Cold War that I've ever heard. The delusion that we're capable of, however, is that once you buy this Munich analogy then you can have a war and escalate in the name of peace, because you can say, "If we don't do it here and now, it's going to have to happen later and it'll be worse."

FINN: What is your own judgment of this analogy? Is it logical?

STONIER: It is absolutely logical, it's internally consistent. The flaw lies in the assumption. Is this another Munich? In my assessment it's not. I was willing to buy Korea as another Munich. I solidly supported the Administration at the time on the Korean war and I still do. But in Vietnam you are not dealing with a Hitler deliberately trying to take over another country. You're dealing with an indigenous revolution attempting to achieve social justice in a particular situation. We support the wrong end of a revolution; I think there has been a myth for years that the National Liberation Front is entirely controlled by the Communists with no other voices in it; that the Communists in South Vietnam are controlled entirely by Hanoi; that Hanoi is controlled entirely by Peking; and it used to be that Peking was controlled by Moscow. And nobody believes this anymore.

I'm always struck by statements of two people who have helped me come down very hard on my present position: the sooner we can settle and get out, the better off everybody will be, even if it means that the country goes completely communist. The first was a man who had been in the area as an AID official in the mid-fifties. And he was completely misinformed by State Department briefing. And he said this is characteristic. He thinks our government bumbled into the situation out of sheer ignorance and out of sheer misinformation. And I think this is the tragedy. If we had insisted upon the '56 election—I mean free elections seem to be fine when they're going our way, but when they don't go our way we can suppress them and the right of holding free elections.

This is part of the illusion which each side can create about itself. When *you* do something it's all right because you've got high motives, and when they do the same thing it's because they're aggressive and sneaky and so forth. And this, of course, is always the problem when two sides are in conflict. Well, anyway, if we had let them go, I think by now they would be as neutralist as Burma—and Burma's a good example. I think we have a narrow, nearsighted reliance on the military, and it's extremely dangerous. I think ultimately if we keep this policy up we'll get into dozens of Vietnams.

Instead of spending sixty billion dollars a year in our Defense Department, I would cut this in half and use the other thirty billion a year for what I would call international social reconstruction, because *therein* we will develop a stable world community and *therein* lies our real defense, not where the answer to communism is to kill Communists. That's a primitive and I think pretty ineffective and *terribly* inefficient way of doing it, not to bring in the moral problems involved.

FINN: This brings us back to what we've talked about earlier. You said there were social prerequisites to disarmament and you put it in four steps.

STONIER: Well, the disarmament negotiations at Geneva are not going to produce any real serious disarmament until the people there get instructions from their home government. They're not going to get instructions from their home government until there's been a change in policy. There's not going to be a change in policy until there's been a change in attitudes, because no government can move beyond the mores and norms of a particular society. And our society at this point—and this is even more true for American society than Soviet society— cannot envision living comfortably in a disarmed world. We would feel *terribly* uncomfortable. And with good reason, because all our values, all our assumptions, indicate that the dumbest thing in the world we could do is to relinquish the power we have and give it to some other agencies where we wouldn't even have the dominant voice. But these attitudes must be changed by realizing that what we're giving up is not as much as we think we're giving up, and that the main reason we're afraid of giving them up is because we have a stereotype image of "the enemy," which is basically quite unrealistic. What is not recognized is that the success of the communist society sows its own seeds of political change.

FINN: You talked about the AID man who helped to change your own attitude about Vietnam, but you didn't mention the second man.

STONIER: The AID man convinced me that the Administration was acting largely out of ignorance about what was going on in South Vietnam. The second person who had a profound impact on me was Donald Duncan, the Special Forces Green Beret man who quit. He himself had initially joined the Special Forces as a dedicated anticommunist. He quit because he came to believe that what we were doing to the Vietnamese was not for the Vietnamese. It was not that we were giving them a choice between communism and democracy. We were merely giving them a choice between communism and anticommunism. And I think this particular concrete statement on the basis of somebody who had been there, who, as a member of the military, would be under such immense psychological pressure not to admit this even to himself—and frankly at first I thought maybe he was a kind of a neurotic. I mean very often the only persons who escape from this kind of social trap, from a sociological and almost anthropological cultural group-thinking, are people who are themselves neurotic. However I heard him interviewed on the radio, and I was so very impressed with his general concepts and his general thoughtfulness about the matter, that I felt he really had crystallized in my own mind something which had been bothering me all along, which came out simply through the newspaper reports. In other words, when one looks at the Diem regime, when one looks at the Ky government, in either case one does not feel that these people are vigorously trying to bring about the change in social conditions which make communism almost an imperative. It strikes me on the basis of the information I have—and I'm always looking for other information—that Duncan's statement is basically correct; that we are more interested in beating the Communists than in defeating the circumstances which make communism inevitable. And I consider that the height of folly; that all we can do by our approach is increase the need for communism and the attractiveness of communism in that area, and at a tremendous

Tom T. Stonier

loss to us. And even if we *do* impose our will at this point, even if we pour in two million men and get the thing completely under military control, I think what we gain in Vietnam will not be worth a candle. Our victory will be very hollow and will leave a very bitter taste in everybody's mouth—including our own.

JOAN BAEZ

The president of the Institute for the Study of Nonviolence, a small school in Carmel Valley, California, is Ira Sandperl, the vice-president Joan Baez. The brochure announces that the Institute is a response to a "need of our time." The need "is to understand the nature, principles, and assumptions of nonviolence; its practical, psychological, personal, social, political, institutional and economic applications. It is the aim of the Institute for the Study of Nonviolence to explore every facet of this strange though commonly held assumption, namely, the extolled orthodoxy of international murder."

The general daily schedule is from one to five P.M., which allows time for exercise, lunch, meditation (no books, music, conversation, cigarettes) and seminar discussion. The usual length of a session is six weeks. Readings for discussion and meditation are drawn from the works of de Tocqueville, C. Wright Mills, Erich Fromm, Joan Bondurant, Tolstoy, Krishnamurti, Thoreau, Gandhi, Camus, Jerome Frank and others whose comments on violence or society or both seem relevant to the purposes of the Institute.

Since the school is small and its programs limited, it would have gained little attention without the presence of Joan Baez. More accurately, it would not have come into existence without her. Miss Baez was born in Staten Island in January 1941, of an English-Scottish mother and a Mexican father. As her father, now a consultant for UNESCO, accepted different teaching assignments, she was raised and educated in various parts of the country. After dropping out of Boston University, she sang in coffee houses around Harvard Square—enough to prepare her for the Newport Folk Festival of 1959. The records she made after that rapidly and firmly established her as a top folk singer to whom young people especially gave almost unrestrained homage. She cared about what she sang, and what she sang interested them. She accepted very few of the concert dates that were offered, but she did become a familiar figure at civil rights marches and protests on Vietnam.

Apparently confident of her own attitudes, she decided to get the intellectual support that a study of the tradition of nonviolence provides. Hence the school, of which Ira Sandperl is the principal tutor.

The one characteristic that apparently everyone who has met Joan Baez agrees on, even the most skeptical reporters, is her honesty. One fine writer with a sharp eye for sham spoke of "her most striking characteristic, her absolute directness, her absence of guile. She has a great natural style and she is what used to be called a lady." Because we could not arrange to get together, Miss Baez consented to the very trying procedure of a telephone interview. I said that I regretted being unable to visit the school and asked what she thought of the reports of other people who had visited.

BAEZ: I think most of what we talk about is a little rough for somebody who just walks in—that's because we tell the truth. I think it takes a couple of days of meditating, which most people have never done before, to settle down enough to even begin to know what's going on here. There are several ways to describe what's going on. Maybe the best thing is simply that we raise questions, and that the students are allowed to raise questions in relation to their lives, how their lives relate to the country and the world, and what they're going to do. And most of the people who have come here so far have been sympathetic to what they think nonviolence is about, but haven't known anything about nonviolence. The students learn, of course. After about a week they have a pretty good idea of what we're trying to do. But the people who come to observe really don't know anything, unless they're here for one or two days. And that's the pity about most of the articles that have been written.

FINN: When the school's successful—when people stay there long enough to learn from it—what should it ideally do?

BAEZ: Well, at this point, the school, as I see it, is in the embryonic stages for *any* degree of a nonviolent society. What I would like, and what I think is the only thing that will keep the world from blowing itself up, will be huge changes in the society. And right now what's frustrating is that we can do just so much. For instance, to work with only twenty people at a time and to read just so many books, and to do just so much talking—it's so complicated . . . my feeling is that I have a realistic outlook on the world, and that we have about one one-thousandth of a chance to live very long. I think that that's realistic. So with this in the back of my mind, I start a school anyway, which I think has contained in it somewhere some of the answers to the only realistic approach to make use of that one one-thousandth of a chance. So when somebody says, "Do you think you're a good school?" I answer, "Yes, I think we're really first-rate." I think that some of the students who've left have made real changes in their lives, and have found some real answers to some of their questions. It's all still very minute, but I think it's one of the very few possibilities that exist.

We discuss briefly the kinds of books that are studied, and then I ask Miss Baez if she thought she was, as others have described her, "politically naïve."

BAEZ: The last time this came up was in the Hearings when they were trying to take the permit [to operate the school] away from us. One of the men—he's from this right-wing board of supervisors—said, "Well, Miss Baez is very sweet and all that, but she's very politically naïve." He also said I was being led down the primrose path by the lunatic fringe, and a bunch of other things. And it dawned on me that of course I'm very naïve, and that's why I started the school, but so are all the leaders of the world or we wouldn't be having wars all the time, and riots, and seeing so many people starve.

FINN: I suppose the man who said this thought that he himself was politically sophisticated.

BAEZ: Well, that's the trouble. Because it may just get down to boring old semantics. I mean if politics means that you know how to connive and be sharp and deal with nations and sort of con people in general—well, that's not what I think that poli-

Joan Baez

tics means. I would think that a good politician would have a real concern for the rest of the people in the world. But when he said politics I'm sure he meant, for example, that President Johnson's a good politician because he keeps America first in the war race, and that kind of thing.

FINN: Well, are there any politicians in office that you particularly admire or think better than others?

BAEZ: No, not particularly admire. There are some that I would obviously prefer above others, but the way I feel about it, I wouldn't put any of my energies into any people who are in office now. I've been asked to campaign with people, and I just don't think that that's any good at all.

FINN: Even for the peace candidates?

BAEZ: Well, I just feel that once a person gets into that rat race . . . I've met, from the President on down, a variety of different people who are in politics, and it seems that the farther they get in, no matter what their intention was to begin with, the farther they get away from people or from anything that really could change the situation for the better.

FINN: You sound rather pessimistic about the possibility of improvement.

BAEZ: Well, I'm pessimistic about the possibility of something being done from inside the system. I mean it's so obvious that when the civil rights movement was good, everything was being done from outside the general political system. By the SNCC's and so forth. This is an aside, but I think that the reason the civil rights movement is in the process of going to hell right now is precisely because people knew a little bit about tactical nonviolence, and some of them knew a lot about it, but very few of them really cared about real nonviolence.

FINN: You mean they accepted it simply as a tactic, but not as a principle.

BAEZ: Yes, because they knew that in dozens of situations it would work better than violence. And this is a conflict, because obviously I would prefer as a tactic that nonviolence is used, but I also feel that if you don't really have a basis and don't really know what nonviolence is all about from inside out, that eventually you're going to lose it. You're going to resort to something you think is quicker or smarter or faster—namely, violence. And that's what I think has happened. It's quicker, not smarter, and it's a dead end.

FINN: Well, your own stand, of course, is that nonviolence should be adhered to; it's not simply a tactic, but should be a principle, in civil rights today as well as in the past.

BAEZ: Yes. And the trouble is that it's never really been accepted as that. It has by some people, but it hasn't been organized that well. And that's the huge conflict. I think that people have to be reached the way we're trying to do at this school. And yet the question is: is there enough time to reach enough people to make a good solid difference?

FINN: Among the problems for people who are themselves trained in and believe in nonviolence, is that they are called upon to participate in some movements, some actions they really approve of, but then to cooperate with people who are not pacifists, and do not even accept it as a tactic.

BAEZ: That's right. That's where another conflict comes for me. For instance, I don't feel that I should be politically inactive simply because I don't agree with what everybody says. On the other hand, I refuse to take part in a march where they haven't even decided ahead of time whether or not they're going to be nonviolent. That's why Ira and I dropped out of the VDC [Vietnam Day Committee] altogether. I mean when people are sitting around and discussing whether or not to carry lead in their picket signs, I think it's time to try to do something else.

FINN: Well, how effective can absolute pacifists be if they don't cooperate with what is, of course, most of the people in the country?

BAEZ: I think at this point an absolute pacifist realizes he may not be very effective at all.

FINN: Well, how much of an effect do you think the school has on people who do not themselves attend it? I mean there are clearly a number of people who do know of you and respond to your attitudes. Maybe not deeply, but at least they're aware of them and to that extent would be interested in trying to find out why you think the way you think.

BAEZ: Actually, I don't even receive letters now unless they're personal, so I don't know what the response is. But I know there's a definite response. Ira and I had a big fight about this because I refused to answer that question about a year ago, and he said it was false modesty; that I knew I made a difference and I simply didn't want to think about how many people I affected. I really don't know. It is hard for me to judge, but I do remember people like the Fort Ord woman who wrote me a furious letter last year and said that her husband was going to Vietnam. This year she wrote back and said she'd had a complete switch. Either he went, or she found out more about Vietnam, and now she's in a total state of flux and wants to come to the school to find out what the hell's going on. And that kind of thing. I mean there are lots of those that I think are very important. I really think the school is making a slight difference and has the potential to make a huge difference.

The school is one way that Joan Baez attempts to make her views effective. But another and more publicized way is to speak out at large rallies. At a SANE Emergency Rally on Vietnam that was held in Madison Square Garden on June 8, 1965, she said, before she sang:

"I would like to say one thing. This is mainly to the young people here, but really to everybody, and that is that ultimately you can listen to only one thing, and that is not your President, not your many misguided leaders, save a few, and not the Communists or the Socialists or the Republicans or the Democrats. But you must listen to your own heart, and do what it dictates. Because your heart is the only thing which can tell you what is right and what is wrong. And after you have found out what you think is right and what is wrong, then you must know that you can say yes to what is right and no to what is wrong. And that you young men, for instance, if you feel that to kill is wrong and to go to war is wrong, you have to say no to the draft. And if you young ladies think it is wrong to kill, and war is wrong, you can say yes to the young men who say no to the draft. Because it is not the leaders and the dictators, it is not God who is going to get us out of the bloody mess we are in. It is only you and only me."

When I recall this she says that "Ira can talk to these boys" better than she can and that there are agencies in the area—CCCO and AFSC, for example, to provide counsel. She does think every boy about to be drafted should be aware of the alternatives he faces. And, she adds:

BAEZ: I won't say anything unless I'm asked, because that means they really want to know my opinion. But for a girl to sit around and tell a boy, "You know, you really shouldn't go in the Army. You should sit in jail for five years,"—I don't think it's exactly fair.

FINN: Do you think it's because you've made such statements that some people have called you—and I'm quoting—"a pawn of the protest movement"?

BAEZ: Well, I think probably for a long time—when? let's see, starting at about seventeen or eighteen—I would do things that I *thought* were good ideas. I think I was more politically naïve then than I am now . . . but everybody will call me that anyway, simply because I sing. And they think that the people are going to use me because I sing. They figure some big meanie dragged me there and I was too stupid to know the difference, and so I just stood up there and sang.

FINN: Right. Like Jeanette MacDonald. Have your experiences tended to confirm your pacifism rather than to put doubts in your way at this point? Pacifists are frequently given a pretty rough time today.

BAEZ: Well, I think it's only fair to say that, partly because I'm protected by whatever the image is that's set around me from the music and also because I'm a female, I've never run into a situation where it was close to kill or be killed, hit or be hit. I know I've been in dangerous situations, like in the South when I sang and there were bomb scares and things like that, but nobody's ever really come up to me and put me on the spot.

FINN: You mentioned that you were tired of talking about the songs, but do these two parts of your activities, your singing and your nonviolent activities, come together for you?

BAEZ: For the last two weeks I've been really trying to figure our how separate the worlds are and how together they are. And at this point I feel that aside from the very few times when I've been singing something like "God on Our Side" to an audience, the worlds are almost entirely separate. And I've gone up a couple of times. I went to see the Rolling Stones concert and I went to a dance at the Filmore with the lights and so forth. And I'm beginning to feel that the more the music has to do with the stomach—I mean just rock and beat and all that —the farther away it seems to me to be from truth, whatever that means. And these are only words, and just beginnings of what I'm finding out, but I feel that in my life they're very separate right now. It's been hard for me to try to figure out what to do about it.* All I can do right now is cease worrying. I mean I've stopped singing, I've stopped concerts for the year, because that was the part that confused me. I just made a rock and roll record which I don't like terribly much. It's probably O.K., and I don't know whether I'll put it out or not. And a Christmas record, which I like very, very much, which is baroque. Oh, it's with all the ancient instruments and old carols and stuff. I think it's beautiful. I've sort of taken care of the music for this year [laugh], but I don't know what I'll do next year.

FINN: Do you think that artists—say painters, poets, artists all together—have a special role? Do they play a different role in society than other people?

BAEZ: Well, I think they certainly *could* play a role. I don't think many of them do. I think the poets are the most active right now.

FINN: But I'm not sure how effective they are in changing attitudes.

BAEZ: You know, it's so hard to tell who's effective, or if anybody can possibly be effective enough. I just feel that everybody has to take some kind of a stand, and the more people who realize that they have to take a stand the better. There's an awful lot of copping out. For instance, Hollywood is just

* A couple of weeks after this conversation I sent Miss Baez a copy of the transcript so that she could fill in blank spots lost by a bad phone connection. When she returned it, she had noted in the margin that she had found at least part of an answer in something Gandhi had written—that he couldn't accept art for art's sake, that it must relate to the truth and elevate the soul, or he rejected it. Even in that brief note it was apparent that she was uneasy about invoking grand, capitalized terms, but it was also clear that they meant something to her. For example, the rock 'n roll record she mentions is not going to be released.

hopeless. You would think some of these people could afford to take a stand 'cause they really have everything. But I guess that the opposite happens; they're afraid they'll lose all the stuff that they have, and so they don't want to take a stand on anything. But then I shouldn't distinguish between them and the average businessman who is afraid of losing his job.

In discussing some of the problems raised, today and in the past, for those who advocate laying down arms, Miss Baez says that Hitler could not have blossomed in a nonviolent society. He would not have been made into a hero. All of her actions now are to work toward a nonviolent society where such heroes cannot develop. Is it realistic to look forward to, to work for, such a society?

BAEZ: One of the ironic things is that when a soldier is handed a gun and sent off to the battlefield, he's certainly given no guarantee he's going to come back alive. But when somebody speaks to a nonviolent soldier, or myself, he wants guarantees, *proof* that what we're saying is going to work. And we don't have it any more than a conventional soldier has it.

FINN: The number of people who are going to be persuaded to nonviolence is likely to be small, so that the *individual* pacifist is frequently going to be caught in this kind of a bind, and be called on to answer such questions.

BAEZ: When the Negro revolution was nonviolent and was good, I think something like three percent of the Negroes in the South were involved. I mean they'll also say, "Well, you don't expect to change everybody in the country," and of course I don't. It would be nice, but I don't think I'm that idealistic either. I would want enough people to make a difference politically, but I also think that those people could show—if they were really good pacifists—could show other people how to live. And it wouldn't take the whole country, a great giant conversion, to make us change foreign policy.

MITCHELL GOODMAN AND
DENISE LEVERTOV

LIFE AT WAR

The disasters numb within us
caught in the chest, rolling
in the brain like pebbles. The feeling
resembles lumps of raw dough

weighing down a child's stomach on baking day.
Or Rilke said it, 'My heart . . .
Could I say of it, it overflows
with bitterness . . . but no, as though

its contents were simply balled into
formless lumps, thus
do I carry it about.
The same war

continues.
We have breathed the grits of it in, all our
        lives,
Our lungs are pocked with it,

the mucous membrane of our dreams
coated with it, the imagination
filmed over with the gray filth of it:
the knowledge that humankind,

delicate Man, whose flesh
responds to a caress, whose eyes
are flowers that perceive the stars,

whose music excels the music of birds,
whose laughter matches the laughter of dogs,
whose understanding manifests designs
fairer than the spider's most intricate web,

still turns without surprise, with mere regret
to the scheduled breaking open of breasts whose
    milk
runs out over the entrails of still-alive babies,
transformation of witnessing eyes to pulp-fragments,
implosion of skinned penises into carcass-gulleys.

We are the humans, men who can make;
whose language imagines *mercy*,
lovingkindness; we have believed one another
the mirrored forms of a God we felt as good—

who do these acts, who convince ourselves
it is necessary; these acts are done
to our own flesh; burned human flesh
is smelling in Viet Nam as I write.

Yes, this is the knowledge that jostles for space
in our bodies along with all we
go on knowing of joy, of love;

our nerve filaments twitch with its presence
day and night.
nothing we say has not the husky phlegm of it in
    the saying,
nothing we do has the quickness, the sureness,
the deep intelligence living at peace would have.

Denise Levertov

Mitchell Goodman and Denise Levertov are two of the many
writers who have joined in protest against the war in Vietnam.
Mitchell Goodman was born in New York in 1923 and grew
up in Flatbush when, he said, "it was trees, homes, open lots
and Depression." His studies at Harvard, which he attended on
a scholarship, bracketed a stint in the stateside army. He
abandoned his economic studies in 1947 when he went to Europe. It was there that he met and married Denise Levertov.
After living in France and Italy they came to the States.

Mitchell Goodman and Denise Levertov

Goodman's war novel, *The End of It,** was published in 1961. This story of a young American's introduction to violent death and life in Italy was praised by Norman Mailer, William Carlos Williams, Sir Herbert Read and other critics.

Denise Levertov was born in London in 1923. Her father was a Russian Jew who converted to Christianity at a German university and became a well-known Anglican clergyman. Since her mother was Welsh, Denise Levertov grew up in an atmosphere permeated by the Bible and Hasidic legends, Jewish jokes and Welsh folklore. Because she was a voracious reader she was allowed to educate herself at home, and the only school she attended was a ballet school. Her first poems were published when she was sixteen, her first volume, *The Double Image,* when she was twenty-three. Since then she has published five more volumes to increasing critical acclaim. Kenneth Rexroth, for example, has said that "She is the most subtly skillful poet of her generation, the most profound, the most modest, the most moving." She is preparing another volume when I visit the Goodmans in their apartment in lower Manhattan, close to the great markets through which funnel all the fruit and vegetables for the city.

When I ask about the extent of their commitment to the peace movement, to the protest against the war in Vietnam, they tell me how Miss Levertov initiated the Writers and Artists Protest. In 1964, Henri Percikow, whom she has yet to meet, wrote to ask if she would help him organize a protest. She replied that she would be willing but she didn't know how to go about it. The idea faded but the seed had been planted. When, contrary to her expectations, no one else shouldered the task within the following year, she wrote to a small group of friends and asked them to meet and consider the idea. Among the people who responded, they recall, were Muriel Rukeyser, Grandin Conover, George Kirstein, Paul Blackburn, Warren Miller, Jerome Rothenberg and Neil Kleinman.

This group was united in their opposition to the war, but Kirstein was more "cautious than most of us" and the statement the group drew up, which was finally accepted by over

* (New York, Horizon.)

five hundred other writers and artists and run as an ad in the *New York Times,* was a "fairly mild statement." But the committee thought the weight of many well-known names under a statement that started "WE PROTEST" would have effect. That ad appeared in the spring of 1965, and Goodman is confident that a similar ad today would be much more forceful and cogent.

GOODMAN: A comparison between the simple-minded protest we made and the recent ad put out by SANE shows how much the peace movement has developed in a year. The SANE ad was very cogent, really. They're thought to be a very middle-of-the-road group and a lot of people in the peace movement have very little use for them. But that was a darn good job and they really put it together. Well, it's a sign of how much people have progressed, have been educated by the facts of the war; that in less than a year they should have moved to that point of cogency and clarity. The earlier ads—ours and that of the clergymen and teachers—were really comparatively weak because we didn't know the situation and we hadn't educated ourselves.

FINN: Was there anybody in your initial group, or many people in the group, who really had worked at educating themselves, who had a solid grasp of the necessary information?

GOODMAN: No. I think it's a remarkable fact, given how long the Vietnamese war has been going on in all its phases, how the professional community in this country—all the way from writers, artists, teachers to physicists—how remarkably little, up to very recently, they've done to educate themselves, and therefore how inarticulate and relatively ineffective they've been.

FINN: So if you were picked up by someone who supported government policy, especially someone in government who had obviously informed himself, you would have been hard put to make a case.

GOODMAN: Yes, we'd have made an emotional, moral argument.

LEVERTOV: Well I *still* would be hard put really, because I don't have the kind of mind that marshals all the historical facts, but I don't feel that that matters too much because it seems to me such a very basic moral issue anyway.

Mitchell Goodman and Denise Levertov

GOODMAN: And also, if one looks back on it, I think that initial reaction of simple outrage was a particular necessary phase of the protest; at one stage all the different kinds of professional people organized to put ads in the newspapers; and in every case, I think—or almost every case—they've educated themselves and have gone on to more active and more organized kinds of protest. Certainly the read-ins that the writers were doing last spring arose from this initial effort.*

Miss Levertov then says that she thinks her involvement in the peace movement consists of two things: first, her work in initiating and organizing the committee; second, her discussions about the war in Vietnam with the students she has the opportunity to meet both at the poetry read-ins and at the schools where she teaches. Goodman adds that many of the writers they know teach part time and almost all of them talk to students about Vietnam.

GOODMAN: And these students are just waiting for older people who are willing to engage with them on these issues. I

* The poets taking part in these read-ins, at various times or places, are: Daisy Aldan, David Antin, Roger Aplon, Marvin Bell, Carol Bergé, Paul Blackburn, Ed Blair, Robert Bly, Paul Carroll, George Chambers, Robert Creeley, Harold Dicker, Alan Dugan, George Economou, Lawrence Ferlinghetti, David Ferry, Edward Field, Stuart Friebert, Barbara Gibson, Morgan Gibson, Allen Ginsberg, Allen Grossman, Donald Hall, James Hazard, Robert Hazel, Anthony Hecht, George Hitchcock, Daniel G. Hoffman, John Hollander, William Hunt, David Ignatow, Harold Jaffe, Donald Justice, X. J. Kennedy, Milton Kessler, Galway Kinnell, Stanley Kunitz, Tuli Kupferberg, Richmond Lattimore, Denise Levertov, John Logan, Robert Lowell, Walter Lowenfels, Jackson MacLow, Lenore Marshall, Eve Merriam, Robert Mezey, George Montgomery, Toby Olson, Joel Oppenheimer, Peter Orlovsky, Rochelle Owens, Henri Percikow, Mark Perlberg, Robert Peterson, Allen Planz, Paul Plummer, George Quasha, David Ray, Ishmael Reed, Franklin Reeve, Adrienne Rich, I. A. Richards, Jerome Rothenberg, Jon Roush, Raphael Rudnik, Muriel Rukeyser, Vern Rutsala, Ed Sanders, James Schevill, Dennis Schmitz, Armand Schwerner, Eric Sellin, Anne Sexton, Grace Shulman, Karl Shapiro, Philip Silver, W. D. Snodgrass, Louis Simpson, Peter Simpson, Barry Spacks, George Starbuck, Lucien Stryk, Robert Sund, Louis Untermeyer, Robert Vas Dias, Diane Wakoski, Peter Weiss, Richard Wilbur, James Wright, David P. Young, Marguerite Young, and Harriet Zinnes. Poets who have been unable to attend but have sent messages or poems in support of the protest are: Charles G. Bell, Richard Eberhart, W. S. Merwin, Henry Rago, Alastair Reid, and William Stafford. (*Poetry,* August 1966) think that they no longer respect the teacher fully who won't commit himself in some way on such a question.

LEVERTOV: And by the same token, even if they don't agree with one, the fact of seeing a person of the teacher's generation *be* committed to something makes them think. They respect commitment even if they question its particular grounds.

FINN: Most of the students that you talk to, if they're representative of the student group across the nation, support the Government position, I presume.

LEVERTOV: That is *certainly* not true of mine.

GOODMAN: No, that's not true of mine. Let's see, we've taught during this period at C.C.N.Y., Denise was teaching at Drew last year and I'm teaching there this year, and now she's at Vassar. And I was at Hofstra for a while. And then I was, for a week, in the Midwest at Knox College as a writer in residence. And everywhere one goes, there is no active support that one can see among students for the Government position. There's at least doubt and a very tentative feeling. The students are very mixed up about the thing. Here and there one finds an articulate exponent of the Government position, but they're pretty rare.

LEVERTOV: I should say that my experience is pretty special because, until this year, I have taught only poetry workshop classes, and the kind of kids that enroll for a special class of that kind in poetry are apt to be against war.

GOODMAN: The most significant and most definite sign of where they stand is that there are hundreds of thousands of students who are deliberately and consciously—and they make no bones about this—staying in college to avoid the Army, to avoid the war. Their action speaks for a very definite kind of objection.

FINN: Well, they don't want to get involved themselves. I read just the other day, and this may not be typical either, that Bobby Kennedy was speaking at Seattle University about Vietnam and he got some slight applause when he was slightly critical of our present policy. But when he asked whether we should escalate the war, go North, almost all the students responded "Yes." But when he was critical of deferment because of student status they all objected; they liked the deferment.

Mitchell Goodman and Denise Levertov

And then one of his aides said the students wanted escalation without participation. They didn't want to get involved but they were quite happy to have other people involved.

Seymour Lipset said that most of the students are *not* involved.* The ones you hear from, who express opinions, are a minority. Certainly the students who express strong opinions seem to be opposed. But the ones who do not voice opinions apparently are willing to go along. You mentioned that the kind of students you teach and the people you invited here, the artists and writers, all were critical of U.S. policy in Vietnam, almost without exception. Why is this so? It's not true of any other groups you can think of. It's not true of the clergy, of lawyers, of political scientists.

LEVERTOV: I know an awful lot of poets and I can really think only of one, among those I know, who is a supporter of Government policy. And I can think of very few who have not committed themselves by now at least to the extent of signing a protest and reading at a read-in. I can't tell you why this is so.

GOODMAN: I have a thought about why. I think the most significant, underlying fact about this war is that it is being fought ten thousand miles away in a country that people here have no conception of. They have not even the *beginning* of an idea of what these people look like, what their gestures are, what their speech is, how they walk—*nothing* about these people. They are unreal. And the whole situation is unreal. And the general population—and I include a great many educated people—simply don't have the imagination to visualize what this thing is. And the writers and the artists *have* this kind of imagination. This is what they live by.

FINN: You mean you can imagine what's happening to the particular person who's undergoing this experience of war.

GOODMAN: Yes, and I think certain very important underlying relationships. For example, they can recognize, their feeling tells them, that an important element in this war is that it is a kind of race war; that it wouldn't be the brutal, terrible thing it is if these were not Orientals. And the American population is willing to put up with their extermination because basically they cannot imagine them as fully human. And I think the

* Seymour Martin Lipset, "Doves, Hawks and Polls," *Encounter*, October 1966, pp. 38–45.

writers and artists do feel their humanity and won't allow themselves to underestimate that humanity. I've said over and over
to students, "You know, the imagination is the basis for compassion. Unless one can imagine what these people are and
what they've lived through for twenty years now, then there's
no possibility of compassion." Thank God, evidently the artistic
community has that imagination.

LEVERTOV: And along with imagination, I think that artists
in general have developed in them, by virtue of being artists,
that zest for life, for living, which is dormant in all human beings but isn't developed in all human beings. It's sometimes very
highly developed in very, very simple people who are not
artists. But artists as a class, with all their craziness, with all
their hang-ups, psychological problems and the things which
they're perhaps better known for, have a very highly developed
zest for life, the knowledge that one can't live one's life and
be happy and thriving in the world along with other created
things unless other created things are striving too. This is a
human knowledge which, however, is apt to be more highly
developed in people engaged in creative activity.

FINN: Do you think this war is different from others in this
sense? You certainly have writers and poets who engaged in
the First World War and Second World War, and really engaged in it—I suppose maybe Hemingway would be the prime
example of someone who found that a zestful activity. And
there have been, of course, through periods of time, people who
celebrated, in their poetry and writing, the very act of war.

LEVERTOV: This war is different from all those other wars in
that it was possible for people of intelligence to believe, some
of the time at least, that there was a high ideal for which those
wars were being fought. And it is quite impossible for any sane
person, in my opinion, to believe that there is a high ideal for
which this war is being fought, and for any sane person to suppose that even if there were a high ideal, it justified the completely filthy way in which it is being fought.

GOODMAN: Another thing is that imaginative writers live by
their perceptions; they live by their eyes and ears. And they
have highly developed ears. When they hear the debased
voices of the politicians, in all their vapid, banal explanation
of what this war is about, they register the falseness of it very

quickly and I think very accurately. I think that there's something very important connected with this. The peace movement in this country, as you said before, certainly does break down into a number of overlapping segments, and they tend to remain rather fragmented. I think this is basically a very healthy sign, because it means that sectors of the society are expressing themselves each in its own way and are not being taken over by a monolithic organization for articulation of protest—which is, for example, the old Left-wing method. People remain allied to their own necessity to speak, and to speak in their own ways. And I think out of this kind of diversity of opinion and expression has come a very, very healthy peace movement and a very effective one in preventing the formation of a simple-minded consensus.

FINN: I gave Denise that little poem of W. B. Yeats that you may know, which raises the question of the proper direction or function of an artist: the whole problem of whether he should be engaged with political activity or whether he should, in the tradition of Joyce and Flaubert, commit himself to his work. And the poem by Yeats suggests that he should commit himself to his work.

LEVERTOV: My personal feeling about this has changed gradually and rather radically in the last few years. Of course Yeats said, on being asked for a war poem, "I think it better that in times like these / A poet's mouth be silent, for in truth / We have no gift to set a statesman right." And a few years ago the *Chelsea Review* was going to do an issue of political poems, and the editor of the issue asked me for a political poem. I said, "Well, I don't think I know what a political poem is, and I don't write on commission, and so I don't think I can supply you with one." Then I thought about it and out of trying to decide what a political poem was I did write a poem. What I came up with was three meditations, the first of which took as a theme a quote from Charles Olson that said, "The only object is a man, carved out of himself, so wrought he fills his given space, makes traceries sufficient of others' needs (here is social action, for the poet, anyway, his politics, his news)." And that was the sort of first stance that I took on a political poem; that the politics of a poet was being as fully poet as possible, and it seemed to imply at least *not* engaging in direct action.

The theme of the second of these three poems was a quote

from Ibsen: "The task of the poet is to make clear to *himself,* and thereby to others, the temporal and eternal questions." Well it does say the *temporal* as well as the eternal questions, but that his obligation is to make them clear to himself and only *thereby* to others.

And the third poem was on a theme from D. H. Lawrence saying "And virtue? Virtue lies in the heroic response to the creative wonder, the utmost response." Well, I think that in the poems that I wrote on those three themes there are seeds, as it were, of a more engaged point of view.

Well, by 1965, although I hadn't really written any political poems in the meantime, I had written a couple of poems that I have called didactic poems, and by the time I wrote "Life at War," I couldn't write anything *but* a political poem because this was what was on my mind night and day. Since writing that one I've written several other quite explicitly political poems.

And I think this has been the history of many other poets in the last five or six years; our lives are so permeated with the knowledge of this war, that it is not only terrible in itself but is such a threat to the continuance of life on earth, that we are inevitably led into the writing of engaged poems. And I don't think that at this time most poets feel as Yeats felt at the time he wrote that, that in truth poets have no gift to set the statesman right. It isn't so much that we think we can set the statesman right as that, because we are verbal people, we have the obligation to be the spokesmen for humanity, and that it can't be left to the statesmen, whether they're honest statesmen or dishonest statesmen. . . .

GOODMAN: Yes, it's like that saying, "War is too serious a matter to be left to the generals." But you see, I think in a way Yeats makes a mistake here too, where he says "We have no gift to set a statesman right." The effort certainly of the writers in acting against the war today is no longer an effort to set the statesman right. Our hope is to set *ourselves* right, as Ibsen put it, to get clear, and in the process to help to set our fellow citizens clear and right.

FINN: This does raise a question. There's apparently a problem of communication between the politician, the statesman, the people actively employed by the Government, and artists and writers particularly. There is not much dialogue or ex-

Mitchell Goodman and Denise Levertov

change, and maybe you can just not expect it. For instance, I would presume they would want to talk in political terms and ask, "What is the basis of your moral outrage? What would you suggest as an alternative in Vietnam? Where did we go wrong? And what would you have done?" And, you suggested, these are not the terms that you or most of the people in that group would want to deal with.

GOODMAN: But there's a difference between now and a year or two years ago. That's what I meant by this education. We *have* come clearer. I would be perfectly willing to discuss with a member of the Department of State very specific political questions, absolutely. But I think that our hope basically has always been to try to alert the population to the dangers. And my own feeling has been that one of the great costs of this war has been the opportunity that is given to a man like Johnson, who is basically a manipulator, to debase consciously or not the democratic process.

Goodman then listed and discussed in some detail a number of incidents which should, he asserted, at least raise questions about U.S. policy in Vietnam and the men who continue to support them without reservation or question. Then he turns to what he regards as a symbol of the entire war, the use of napalm.

GOODMAN: In spite of what we know about the Nazi experience and how the German people allowed themselves to be led by the noses into these horrors and then claim to know so little about it, we've now used napalm in Vietnam, used it very widely, the use of it is mentioned on television, radio, in the newspapers every day, and Americans still seem either consciously or unconsciously not to know or not to *want* to know what this is. And I talked this summer in Maine to two groups of Rotarians and they simply didn't know what napalm is. That it is a broadcast weapon that burns out whole areas, whole villages, that it was a wholesale effort to burn people alive, was shocking to them. But the use of napalm is really the *sign* for me of this war. I mean if people ask me, "What do you mean by the dirtiest war this country's ever been in?" I think this is what defines it.

Goodman then tells how his own political inertia was overcome by his sense of the degradation of the Vietnam war and
his feeling that simply to retain a sense of self-respect one had
to belong to a community that would speak out.

GOODMAN: It finally led me to join a group which calls itself
the Veterans and Reservists to End the War in Vietnam. It's
not really typical, but it stems from the kind of action groups
that were invented by organizations like CNVA. We have a
more diverse political background than the rather straight pacifist position held by most of those people. But we've learned
a lot from them. We decided what we needed was to try to
wake up the population as far as we could by way of direct
actions. And we've conducted, I think, a remarkably large number of very successful actions. We had, for example, a solemn
march from Columbus Circle, right along the edge of the park
into the Plaza and down Fifth Avenue. And we carried this
coffin that we've made with a very simple sign that just said
the number of casualties in the war. And the girls were dressed
as kind of Buddhist nuns with these marvelous masks representing grief that Peter Schumann made. But this demonstration
of ours was very inventive and it had a very good impact. The
people who saw us in the streets were really moved by it; there
were all kinds of signs that they were. That's only one of the
things we've done.

FINN: Let me shift to another question. When I was talking
to Rabbi Heschel the other day, he had read a review of Saul
Bellow's new play. And he thought, on the basis of the review,
that it had dealt with a fairly trivial subject—at least trivial compared to Vietnam. And he said, "Now why doesn't Saul Bellow,"
whom he respects as an artist and who he knows has been
critical of Vietnam, "Why doesn't he, when he turns to his
own work, pick this as a topic? This is very important."

GOODMAN: There's a basic mistake here—I don't know if the
Rabbi realizes it—but Bellow is the one important figure in the
literary community in this country who a lot of us recognize as
a *fink* in relation to this war. He has *not* taken a strong position.
He has wavered. He's backed up.

FINN: Well, let's leave him aside as maybe not the best example. There is still the question that Dr. Heschel posed. He

Mitchell Goodman and Denise Levertov

was suggesting that an artist should take Vietnam as a topic to deal with if he's concerned with what's important, *rather than* what appeared, at least to him, to be trivial.

LEVERTOV: Well, I think that that is to put it in too simple a way. The fact is that an artist, even if he wants to, may not be able to. At least my belief concerning the writing of poems is that you don't first have a formulated idea or feeling and make a decision to write about it. A good poem is only written *when* that thought or feeling or complex of thoughts and feelings and experiences makes itself known *within you as words*. And one can't *make* this happen. And in my experience one has complexes of thoughts and feelings which do *not* make themselves felt in one as words, even if they are very strong—or not at the time. One cannot find words for them until later. If one does, then one has an obligation to write them.

If one doesn't, if one is aware of them in some other way, as some verbal thinking process perhaps, but not the words of a poem, one has to do something else with them. Then one goes to demonstrations and one signs a protest and one sends money and so forth. But one can't *make* the poem . . . one can't use poetry in that way. One is used by poetry; one is at the service of poetry. It so happens that if these preoccupations are very full and heavy, the likelihood is that sooner or later they *will* emerge in the form that is one's form. But one can't make it happen. So I don't think I would ever accuse a writer of not having dealt directly with these problems. If he feels strongly about them, I'm sure he wants to deal with them. There are many writers I'm sure who want to write something about these problems and haven't yet found *their* way in.

Most of the people Mitchell Goodman and Denise Levertov mentioned were people who have not been greatly interested in politics. But there are a number of other writers who have been. For example, when John P. Roche, President Johnson's new assistant, chose to castigate American intellectuals who are critical of the United States policy in Vietnam, he covered with his scorn a number of people for whom the *Partisan Review* has been a forum for intellectual exchange. Political discussion is a staple of the journal and the war in Vietnam is, inevitably, part of the present discussion. There is no *Partisan Review* consensus, for the divisions that exist in the country are reflected in the journal. But a number of the editors and regular contributors were in sufficient accord to sign the following statement, "On Vietnam and the Dominican Republic."

We do not think that the present or past policies of the United States in Vietnam are good ones, and we lament the increasing and often self-defeating military involvements which those policies require. We have not heard of any alternative policy, however, which would actually lead to a negotiated peace in Vietnam or promote the interests of the people of Southeast Asia. This is not to say that the critics of American actions in Vietnam are therefore required to propose a specific policy. But it is not unfair to ask that their criticism be based on more than the apolitical assumption that power politics, the Cold War, and Communists are merely American inventions. Most of the criticism of Administration policy at the teach-ins and in the various petitions we have been asked to sign has simply taken for granted that everything would be fine if only the Yanks would go home. It is not clear whether these critics think Asia will not go Communist if American troops are withdrawn or whether they don't care. Nor is it clear whether they really care what happens to the people of Southeast Asia so long as America gets out.

The creation of a world in which free societies can exist should be the goal of any international policy. Our policies in Vietnam do not promote that end, even though it is claimed that they are justified because the United States is preventing a Communist take-over. Nor do the policies of North Vietnam, Communist China or the Vietcong, however they are explained. As for our policies in the Dominican Republic, they cannot be justified even on the grounds that the United States is preventing a Communist coup. They are a disastrous violation of any democratic principle, a violation likely to alienate the people of South America, especially the youth, or even drive them into an alliance with precisely those Communist forces our government claims to be combatting.

The fiasco in the Dominican Republic illustrates, we think, what is basically wrong with our policies. So long as we are not able to understand the political and economic problems of rapidly changing countries, and to support democratic revolutionary groups, we are bound to find ourselves in a false dilemma, always having to decide at the last minute whether to intervene, as though that were the only solution. Military

Mitchell Goodman and Denise Levertov

> action can be a substitute for political foresight only if we
> propose to police the whole world, and to imagine that we can
> do that is to lack even hindsight.
>   Obviously, the time has come for some new thinking. And
> some of it has to be about what's happening in different parts
> of the world, regardless of what the United States does or
> fails to do.*

The statement, in its backing and filling, seemed almost designed to draw strong response, and it did. The next issue contained brief comments by a number of intellectuals. The following quotations will not do justice to the arguments they presented but they do indicate the range of opinion.

Lionel Abel: "I do not think the statement in PR either clear
or forthright. . . . Must we who protest the President's policy
indicate as our credentials for such criticism how a negotiated
peace in Southeast Asia could be arrived at? I think the stipu-
lation preposterous. Very probably a negotiated peace in Vietnam cannot be arrived at. Our past policies have taken care
of that alternative. Very probably all that we can do now is step
up the war, which is what the President is doing, or get out.
Where does PR stand on the matter?"

Norm Fruchter: "Why should men of such calibre publish
such crap? Why should men of such calibre bother to backbite
the increasing student protest about our war in Vietnam? I
share the views of 'the critics of American actions in Vietnam'
but my assumptions about the Cold War and American responsibility for its inception, escalation and continuance are hardly
apolitical. . . . Our troops and resources are destroying the
economy and society of both North and South Vietnam, in the
name of a democratic alternative we have helped to destroy, in
the service of a freedom substantial numbers of American
citizens do not and have never enjoyed. . . . All of us who
want an end to our war have a responsibility to maximize our
protest, not to draft alternative policies."

Paul Jacobs: "I think the basic conception of the statement
in PR is faulty, for it makes a separation between American

* This statement, which appeared in the Summer 1965 issue of *Partisan
Review*, was signed by Eleanor Clark, Martin Duberman, Irving Howe,
Alfred Kazin, Bernard Malamud, Steven Marcus, William Phillips, Nor-
man Podhoretz, Richard Poirier, and Richard Schlatter.

policy in Vietnam and in the Dominican Republic. I am convinced that both cases represent the carrying out of the same basic policy, the same view of the world and the U.S. role in it."

Christopher Lasch: "The attack on the teach-ins is both unnecessary to the argument . . . and inaccurate. . . . In the second place, the suggestion that we should support democratic revolutions is too harmless and vague. It is unimpeachable, but it doesn't take you very far toward a policy for Vietnam, where the choice is not between a democratic revolution and an authoritarian one, but between an authoritarian one and no revolution at all."

Jack Ludwig: "I believe that sad reality fixes itself on actions, just or not just. If Bolingbroke became King illegally, he was no less King in reality. So with American involvement in Vietnam. Though I might not have approved of that involvement when it began I look on it as real, and certainly connected with our heroic, and sometimes quixotic, attempt to meet Communism (or anything which looks a little like it) move by move, head-on or obliquely. The 'domino' analogy is a sweet knuckleheaded oversimplification. . . . I would take the Vietnam confrontation as serious enough in and of itself, and would welcome a truce, an end to the fighting, even if that end came at the price of a settlement as unsatisfactory as the one we all live with in Korea at the present time."

Dwight Macdonald: "I didn't sign the statement in PR because, despite a formal impartiality—much to be said against both sides—it asks American intellectuals to reopen a question many of us have come to consider closed: whether there is any justification, moral or in terms of national self-interest, for President Johnson's recent military adventures in Santo Domingo and Vietnam."

Norman Mailer: "Three cheers lads. Your words read like they were written in milk and milk of magnesia . . . our present policy in Vietnam which the editors gloomily, glumly, *inevitably* (they are liberals after all) proceed to defend, is in fact a policy which is the antithesis of the previous policy. The previous policy, the policy in effect just before escalation, was the unstated policy to lose quietly in Vietnam, and get out. There were better countries to defend. It was a practical policy which

Mitchell Goodman and Denise Levertov

might in practice have worked or not worked, but the new policy is a radical policy . . . right out of the naked lunching heart of the Wasp in his fevers."

Herbert Marcuse: "The statement is outspoken in its opposition to the American policy while at the same time making assumptions which all but invalidate this opposition. . . . Here are these assumptions:

"1. If one advocates the withdrawal of American troops, one does not consider, or does not care about a Communist take-over.

"2. If one does not care about a Communist take-over, one does not care what happens to the people in the respective countries.

"No matter how one answers, the reply must appear as 'un-American' according to the current usage of the term."

David Riesman: "In Vietnam to begin de-escalation by stopping the bombings and offering to deal with the Vietcong would take great courage, too. It might not open the way toward immediate solution; but it would eventually make other changes possible, moving in the direction of a settlement. Otherwise, by polarizing the world and seeking goals beyond stabilization, he [Johnson] may prepare the very defeats he fears."

Harold Rosenberg: "Read casually the statement seems unobjectionable . . . upon closer examination what comes through is the intellectual format of the polarizing anti-Communist *Realpolitik* of the McCarthy days. In actual fact, the statement is a reactionary defense of the policy it seems to attack and its call for 'new thinking' is silly."

Susan Sontag: "As someone who has signed many of the petitions and ads from which the 'Statement on Vietnam and the Dominican Republic' in the last PR wishes to distinguish itself, I found that statement quite mysterious. What were you trying to say? Whom were you trying to appease? Is it people like McGeorge Bundy and Chancellor Erhardt, who have complained lately about the impertinence and irresponsibility of intellectuals and writers shooting their mouths off in public about politics and disturbing the national consensus? I doubt if the carefulness of the statement in PR will reassure them."

W. H. FERRY

"There are times in public life as in private life when one must protest, not solely or even primarily because one's protest will be politic or materially productive, but because one's sense of decency is offended, because one is fed up with political craft and public images, or simply because something goes against the grain. The catharsis thus provided may indeed be the most valuable of freedom's uses."

A number of people would agree with this sentiment of Senator Fulbright, and W. H. Ferry is one of them. What distinguishes "Ping" Ferry even among these people is the frequency with which he sees "times . . . when one must protest." He is, in fact, the kind of man who gives gadflies a good name.

While his voice is raised on many issues and his name attached to many more, he is far from being a prickly nitpicker or a social malcontent whose private life and personality are submerged beneath a host of "causes." As one of his friends told me, "If I had my life to live over, Ping Ferry is one of the people I would try to emulate. He seems to me to lead a more balanced and satisfying life than anyone else I know." The impression he gives as I talk to him in the New York offices of the Fund for the Republic supports that judgment. He is going over an address he is to give soon, checking an article that is soon to be published, and answering phone calls with easy efficiency. As usual his clothes seem almost a deliberate rejection of the "ivy league" cliché which he could have legitimately adopted.

Mr. Ferry is a vice-president of the Fund for the Republic

W. H. Ferry

and staff administrator of the Study of the Economic Order at the Center for the Study of Democratic Institutions. After graduating from Dartmouth College in 1932, Mr. Ferry worked both as an editor and reporter in newspapers in the U.S. and South America. He has worked with Eastern Air Lines, the International Labor Office, the OPA, the CIO Political Action Committee and, in a civilian advisory position, with the Army Air Force. Much of his work has been in public relations and he was for nine years a partner of a public relations concern, Earl Newsom and Company, before he joined the Fund for the Republic.

In addition to his many articles, he has written a number of booklets published by the Center including the *Economy Under Law, Caught on the Horn of Plenty* and *Mass Communication,* and has contributed to a recent book *The Corporation Takeover.*

Ping Ferry has been critical of U.S. policy in Vietnam for a long time. In late 1965 he was moved to write a letter to President Johnson.

"I am so ashamed and dismayed by the actions announced by you in the past several days that I am today withdrawing from the Democratic Party. Neither our honor nor security are involved in Vietnam. But your policies there have become more abhorrent and inhumane; and it is clear now that you intend not to diminish our reliance on violence but to increase it indefinitely. Therefore, I must, after more than thirty years as a Democrat, get out. This is a weak way of expressing my total disagreement with programs that call themselves peace but are war. It is the only way I know of dissociating myself from actions that provoke disgust and apprehension all over the world."

I ask him if he has found in the year which has elapsed since he wrote that letter any reason to regret it, to change his mind.

FERRY: Yes, in this respect. I should have done it a lot earlier, and I should have done it a lot louder. You know, I didn't intend this to get a lot of publicity. I was just plain fed up when I wrote that letter to the President. I sent a copy to a friend of mine who was on the newspaper in Santa Barbara, and they published it as an open letter to Johnson. It sort of went out the back door and through the shrubbery and ended up in lots of publications. No, I haven't had any reason whatever to change my mind.

FINN: My own impression is that a number of things that you said in that letter are being increasingly supported now. For instance your early emphasis upon what you called the hypocrisy of the statements coming out of the present Administration regarding the war.

FERRY: Every editorial writer in the country, hawk or dove, says it's a damn shame that none of us can believe anything that comes out of Washington.

FINN: I'm not sure it's general. Apparently most of the people still support the Administration policy.

FERRY: Well, in a way, I hope they would. And the President's following is *not* unexpected. That's what leaders are for. They're supposed to lead. And if Lyndon Johnson said tomorrow, "Folks, changed my mind. I'm turning around. I'm going smack in the other direction. I'm gonna get the hell out of there just as fast as I can. I'm satisfied now that we are wrong to be in Vietnam. No sense in our boys getting killed. No sense in us killing off those people there, either; it's no way to settle anything. We're packing up and getting out as fast as possible." He could make this switch and the polls would come out *exactly* the same way, except better. He'd have a much bigger following. This is what leaders are supposed to do. You know, there aren't many Ferrys and Finns. Most people are just not in the worry-about-peace business. My business is concern about issues of this kind. So is yours. Other people are selling garter belts and making a living, raising children, and they're insulated from the hot affairs of the world, at least far more than we are. They've elected the President, they expect that he knows what the hell he's doing—and they should. That's what the stability of the regime, of the country, depends on.

FINN: What kind of long-term effect do you think the admittedly widespread distrust will have if it's continued? I remember a column of Reston's in which he said this erosion of confidence would be even more important than the outcome of the war in Vietnam.

W. H. Ferry

FERRY: I think there isn't any question about that. I think that the disappearance of confidence in the leaders of a country is . . . a terrible thing, really. And I don't mean just disagreement, but the fact that today Johnson is regarded by many people not just as stubborn and self-regarding but as a dirty pool player, not to be trusted even by his best friends. This is rough stuff when you're talking about the Presidency.

FINN: This is something beyond the kind of reaction you expect during any crisis. This is different from the reaction to other past wars, Korea or the Second World War.

FERRY: Exactly right; this is a different thing. And *this* is where I get in arguments with student groups, and others. They say, why are you taking it so seriously? We've been in wars before. This isn't very pleasant, but it's just more of the same. But it *isn't* more of the same. I'm a prophet of historic disjunction in society; I believe we are at such a disjunction. I don't regard Vietnam as a cause; I regard it as a symptom. There's a malaise in Western civilization in general, showing itself in particularly acute ways in *this* country. It's a malaise choked with paradoxes. Powerlessness in the most powerful nation in the world. Here we are with all of this stuff, education, money, all kinds of sciences and talent. Still we've got poverty, we've got racism, we don't know really what the hell to do about our economy, we don't know what the purpose of the country is, and we've got this damn war going on. We can't win it; nobody can say anything sensible about it. Is *this* power?

I don't know quite what the explanation is. I *think* it is probably because there is nothing to worship. Men have always had some central object: science or God or man, or something of the kind. Now there isn't anything out there in the middle. Can't think of a time when men had so little to cling to. Maybe it's just temporary until we find something that can bring us together. I never had any faiths at all of that kind, and I suppose it's one of the reasons that I've had such a charmed life. I once had a sort of simple-minded enthusiasm for labor unions but it didn't run deep. I was an organizer for a little while in the thirties. But I never had the great conviction that might have led someone to say "There's a likely young fellow for the Socialist Party or for the Communist Party." Nobody ever asked me. Or even the Socialist Front. Nobody ever asked me to join or to do anything except to come and have a beer after the union meeting. Really. They must have perceived quite clearly that I didn't have *that* sort of commitment. And it wasn't out of caution. It was another sort of temperamental expression, not caution.

FINN: If it's temperamental it means you probably had to change. At least you got involved with some large if not spacious ideas with the Triple Revolution.*

FERRY: Oh sure. But not in the Theobaldian way. Bob Theobald's going to get rid of bunions, the Vietnam war, the remains of the Nazi Party and fill up all those dry lakes in Rumania at the same time. This is not my kind of outlook. The world needs crusaders. I'm very much for the Theobalds of the world. I'm just contrasting that with my own feeling. Now this may be the main difference between me and other people with whom I've been closely connected.

FINN: Well, your description makes you sound as if you're not an activist. But for someone who's not an activist, you've . . .

FERRY: I'm not an activist. I never have been. I'm a hit-and-run fellow, I guess. Dan Berrigan, for example, gets into things and stays with them. A. J. Muste organizes mobilizations, sits up night after night talking. Year after year he goes over the fences. I haven't any objection to going over fences except I'd rather stay home and practice Mozart. I can do my bit a lot better sitting at a typewriter. And every once in a while getting at something or writing something that will help A. J. and the other lovely people who move and act. None of these things are wrong. None is *better* than another. Nobody has ever, thank God, been able to measure cause and effect in such things. Nobody can say that the vigil in Port Chicago is a better thing to be doing than a quiet vigil that's being staged on Wednesday

* The Triple Revolution is a document that was intended, according to Ferry, "to startle readers into an appreciation of the increasing dominance of technology in respect to war, [race] prejudice and economic machinery. . . . In view of the basic alterations in every circumstance of the common life, the need for a radically new theory and practice of political economy is inescapable." The Triple Revolution concentrated on cybernation. But it did state that, "New forms of weaponry have been developed which cannot win wars but which can obliterate civilization." Among the thirty or so people who signed this document and sent it to President Johnson and Congressional leaders are W. H. Ferry, Gerard Piel, Gunnar Myrdal, Robert Theobald, Linus Pauling, A. J. Muste and Bayard Rustin.

noons in Santa Barbara. Kids lie down in front of napalm trucks. I don't. I write. I have a real bitter, dirty, nasty groin-gouging piece coming out in one of the big magazines, I hope. This form of protest isn't better or worse than direct action. One has to do what he can do in the way that he feels he can use his time best.

FINN: Well, this can cut you off from a lot of people who feel that they have a strong dedication and a pure position; someone like you is just lost, I presume, as far as they're concerned.

FERRY: I suppose. I'm not going to come to the meetings and I'm not going to show up for all the marches, and so on. I understand how they feel. It's hard work to organize these things. I send them money as I can, and my name has been used so much it's the most tattered piece of paper in the whole U.S.A. It's all right with me. I don't mind that. But when they say "It is your duty to be in Washington on such and such a day for mobilization," or "You're needed" for this and that, that's not the agreement, it's not the way I perform. When I'm around and they're starting these vigils and picket lines and so on—I take part. That's fine. I always put on my white shirt. (I always put on a white shirt for a vigil.)

FINN: You sound more diffident on this than I would really think you are. More than two years ago you had strong enough feelings about what was taking place in terms of our foreign policy; you made judgments about what we were doing and what we were saying. What first aroused not only your concern but your strong antipathy toward what we were doing?

FERRY: A good many years ago, Jim, I published a piece called "What Price Peace?" in which I predicted war in the sixties. (It was picked up and reprinted in lots of places—in the *Bulletin of the Atomic Scientists,* and so on.) This piece was a series of reflections on the nuclear business and on the kinds of arguments I had been involved in at the Center quite a long while. All the just-war experts, Father John Courtney Murray and others, had been telling us why we had to accept these weapons as a sort of larger firecracker. And it took me weeks to recover from Paul Ramsey when he spoke to us about modern war. But I couldn't see it their way. I saw and see the war question as a sort of universal folly which is really technological at the center; the infatuation with technology was apparent.

Well, "What Price Peace?" and also a speech I made advocating unilateral disarmament attracted some attention, and I've been holding down a seat in the peace game since. I had some hopes in 1964 for just a little while. But I should have perceived very soon after Johnson came into office that he wasn't a peaceful fellow—although I didn't vote for him, I didn't vote for Goldwater either. I wasn't for LBJ, but this just reflected an unbreakable anti-Southern prejudice I've always had. I should have recognized at once what in fact turned out to be the case, that the country had a hawk as a head, and there was no intention whatever of withdrawing or palliating the situation. And I was just too damn obtuse to see it right away. When I did, my protest took the form of resigning from the Democratic Party. You know, I'd run out of ways of objecting to Vietnam and the whole drift of affairs. I said, "Have I got one spade left in my hand? Just one?" "Yes, my membership card." Other people were tearing up their draft cards. I tore up my membership card.

FINN: You said Johnson was a hawk. A number of people—and Johnson is one of the foremost—say he's simply continuing the policy of the previous Presidents, and this includes Eisenhower and Kennedy.

FERRY: What the hell's that got to do with it?

FINN: Well, I was wondering whether if Kennedy hadn't been killed we would be doing what we're now doing. Was there a certain impetus here that no likely Administration would have halted?

FERRY: I don't know the answer to that. I don't know whether this would have gone on if Kennedy had lived. If it had I certainly would have resigned from the Party. These people are acting so anti-historically, un-historically. I can't really believe that Kennedy was as stubborn and vainglorious as this President. Kennedy was a student of mine when I taught at Choate, 1932. I kept in casual touch with this guy off and on for quite a long while thereafter, because he wasn't only a student. He and his brother Joe were in my charge. I was their housemaster the one year I was there. So I had a little investment in him,

W. H. Ferry

but no investment of the emotional kind that Abe Chayes and
Galbraith and Cogley, the rest of the fervent Kennedy people,
had. I never saw JFK in that way. You didn't know either that
Bob McNamara was for a long while one of my closest friends
in Detroit, and Mr. McNamara and I have not met now for
nigh on three and a half years. At our last meeting I took Bob
Heilbroner in to see him. That was the last time I ever saw the
Secretary of Defense. And he did something that night that
I won't forget, and neither will Heilbroner, I'm sure.

While we were talking, he was tossing something a little
larger than a couple of matchboxes up and down. I said, "What's
that?" He said "Haven't you ever seen this? I'm very proud of
it. It's the calendar that was given by President Kennedy to the
people around during the Cuban Missile crisis." It's gold, and in
raised platinum or something are the ten days, you know, the
ten crucial October days. And I was pretty shaken by this. That
crisis left a scar on me that I will never get over, as it scarred
a great many people.

You know, Bob and I never talked about these war and
peace matters because our ideas are so opposed. We had a kind
of compact. I said "If you ever want to talk about war-peace
questions you can open the topic. You know I'm dedicated to
putting you out of business as fast as possible. I'm a unilateral
disarmer." He said he knew it very well. "And I'm sorry you're
in there; you're too damn efficient for anybody's good." I was
the man who proposed him for the Secretary's job, at least according to Ken Galbraith.

I have been asked a good many times recently, "What about
your friend McNamara? Is this the McNamara you remember?"
And I have to confess it is not that man, standing up there on
the television screen and talking to Senate committees. It's not
the same man. I have a theory to explain what's happened—
and according to learned men to whom I've exposed it, it's an
absolutely preposterous theory. But I believe it's right.

My theory is the following: someone, or history or something,
has somehow persuaded Bob McNamara and the President that
it is inevitable that we should go to war with China; this is just
in the historical cards; war between East and West cannot be
avoided. The Secretary of Defense, being convinced of this, is
thus led to certain decisions and investments. The decision is
that if you're going to go to war with a country sooner or later,
you'd better be as close to it as possible and stand as loose

and be as flexible and as well prepared as possible. This means *numerous* and extensive bases near the periphery of China.

I regard Vietnam not entirely but chiefly as a huge camouflage operation while the United States secures permanent bases in Indochina. I think there's no intention whatever on the part of the United States Government of withdrawing from Vietnam, no matter what our offers to get out have been. If Ho said "I'll buy the whole American proposition," we would, I believe, find an instant reason not to agree. I think we're in there to stay, in Camranh Bay and Danang and other places, because McNamara and others believe that the finger of destiny points to our staying. We will *not* get out, we will find every excuse for not getting out.

I remind you that this theory came into being to explain McNamara, not to explain what's going on over there. Because he's too smart a man, he is too generous and decent a man, it seems to me, to persist in this awful inhumanity that we have been engaged in except for long-range prudential reasons of the kind I'm surmising. He's too sensible really not to look at himself in the mirror and say "Did you *really* make that statement yesterday? You humbug. You know damn well it wasn't true. You know damn well that the problems of the world are not the issues of communism and anti-communism; they have almost nothing to do with it." He knows better. At least in my judgment.

Bob McNamara cannot be that nuts about LBJ either, because he's never worn anybody's initial. He was always his own man. There was never a big F for Ford on his sweater, though he was a first-rate and loyal leader in that company. He's not that simple. All I can figure out is that there is some theory, some conviction that has deeply taken him and on which he is acting. There's a certain amount of evidence in support of my theory about his theory. It seems to me a strange proposition that the situation requires, for example, the construction of a fifty- or sixty-million-dollar headquarters building complex at Camranh Bay, in addition to three quarters of a billion dollars worth of base construction—and that's probably a fudged figure. It is so disproportionate and so permanent, considering the size of the Vietnam conflict.

It may just be American lavishness at work, of course. Vietnam is, after all, a WPA project as well as a war. We've got to keep the American economy going. I'm not speaking cynically.

W. H. Ferry

I'm not opposed to WPA's. I'd just like it to be a decent building up of a different kind, real public works, not killing works. I do have the feeling that we are committed to a holy crusade over there, finally against China, and time must be the major part of the consideration. He's a very prudent man, McNamara. He's a long-distance planner. My theory also explains why the Administration constantly has to fabricate different formulas for our presence and our activities over there. You know, first it's self-determination and then it's reprisals for the sneak attacks on Pleiku, and then it's something to do with dominoes. Then there's the "bestiality of the enemy" line. But McNamara's not as disorganized a man as would be indicated by the variety of rationales that've been offered.

FINN: You talked about this as a kind of WPA project. A number of people have said that we can have both guns and butter, and we can run this war at this level for years without really affecting our domestic economy or conditions in this country. I presume from what you're saying that you wouldn't agree with that.

FERRY: I don't believe it's true. I don't know about the economics of it. But it's kind of Keynesian. You remember what Keynes had said, that you could always employ people to dig holes and other people to fill them in. We could just keep on manufacturing war stuff and taking it out to sea and throwing it overboard. Why kill people with it? But if that is the extent of our political and economic imagination, you know, it's too bad. Maybe some people only feel happy manufacturing this stuff. But let's not take all the trouble of shipping these weapons overseas. Or let's ship them over without any bullets, throw all the propellants away before we send out the missiles; take tanks and artillery out in the jungle and let them rot.

I'd like to say one other thing about your main theme here. One of the reasons for the frailty of the peace movement is just people like me, the soloists and those who say, "Look, I'll do my part in my own way. Don't bother me." It's not possible to organize people who feel that way. That isn't the way the labor unions were organized by a long shot. So I am one of the contributors to the fragmentation in the peace business, which I deplore just like everybody else. When my resignation from the Democrats came out, many people wrote me and said "For shame! That's a terrible thing to do. You gotta work for the

Party, you gotta reform it, you gotta stay inside, use your influence." You know the argument.*

FINN: I think I would agree with you. But something more intangible may have very real effect, and that's the kind of climate of feeling and opinion that's created in a country either in support of a war effort or in criticism of it. And I think this is where it's fairly clear that the peace movement has an effect.

FERRY: I don't know that it is an effect so much as a result of Vietnam, because this *is* a different war. The unpopularity of Vietnam is where the peace movement gets most of its present strength; this is why it is more bold and is more listened to, why it's spread much more widely around the country than ever before. Going into little communities as I do to speak, in

---

* Arnold Kaufman is one of the people who would probably make this argument. In his article "Where Shall Liberals Go?" he asked, "What does an authentic liberal do when liberalism is perverted in this way by powerful men who are regarded as liberals? . . . One thing he may do is purchase immunity from the sickness of pseudo-realism by forgoing any prospect of effective political action. He can repudiate the system that breeds and sustains the evils he despises. Unfortunately, in rejecting the system he also forfeits access to institutional resources which he must control if liberal ideals are to be effectively pursued. Thus, he sacrifices the prospects of political success for the sake of his soul. He practices the politics of self-indulgence.

"When one prominent liberal, sickened by the Administration's Vietnam policy, decided to resign from the Democratic Party, he justified himself in the following terms:

" 'The major issue in most of the criticisms of my letter to the President has been whether leaving the Democratic Party makes political sense.

" 'Of course it does not. Anyone wanting to exert maximum political leverage would stay in the Party, organize dissenting precinct leaders and district leaders, and see that their protest appeared in newspaper columns and advertisement and, if possible, on the desk of the President himself. This is the kind of politics to which the President responds. *If I were of a different temperament I would have done just that.*' [my emphasis]"

"What interests me here is not the action itself: in balance, it may have been the right thing to do. What interests me is this liberal's implicit assumption that the indulgence of his peculiar temperament is a justification *in itself*. Others go a bit farther. They proclaim that their predominant concern is to achieve 'personal authenticity.' They also condemn as 'finks' liberals who refuse to participate in their projects of protest when those projects seem ineffective or counter-productive. But— and this is my central point—between 'finkdom' and violent revolution there may be only the career of noisy impotence, despair, and eventual absorption by the hated 'establishment.' "

Wisconsin, and Kentucky and so on, I've met quite a lot of people who say, "Count me out. This ain't right. Count me out." I didn't know what to do about it except stand back and cheer people like Dan Berrigan and A. J. Muste and others who are taking the lead in building up this feeling and giving it practical point.

FINN: In the elaboration of the letter you wrote to Johnson, you said that one of the worst things that war was doing was brutalizing our own society. As the war has continued, do you see evidence that this is happening?

FERRY: Everywhere. Everywhere. But people I respect—the psychologist Gerry Frank, for example—reject this thesis. Frank says war has always been a brutal affair and that societies recover from the brutalizations. Frank says Vietnam's no more brutal than any other war, and he says "I don't perceive the effects in the general population that you do." I read the evidence differently. It seems to me that when a whole country does, under the leadership of the President, commit itself to bullying a tiny nation as a national policy—bullying with fragmentation bombs and napalm and "high velocity" bullets, and with fleets of ships and planes—brutalization is a mild word for the public acceptance of such acts. It seems to me definitely brutalizing for Americans to ratify bullying on this order, and the burning and slaughter of civilians, and say "Yes, they're doing this in my behalf. I approve." I know World War I was atrocious and so was World War II; I think World War I was worse in many respects than World War II.

FINN: You said that you were for unilateral disarmament. What should follow from that? Would you be for an international police force to control conflicts that would spring up?

FERRY: Of course a world organization is needed. You've got a *de facto* world organization now. Every part of the world has demands on every other part of the world. It is preposterous, however, to think that you can run a *de facto* thing of this size merely on the basis of (a) tacit agreements; (b) the United Nations, which is praiseworthy but limited; and (c) the international trade network, which is responsive to profit but not to need. We need a world government with everything that must accompany effective government in modern times—including, of course, a police force. But no police force would have any imaginable use for atomic weapons. Nonviolence is at the heart of my belief. That's what leads to unilateralism and everything else, the conviction that nonviolence is the only practical as well as principled way of getting out of the ugly corner we've painted ourselves into with the armaments of genocide and the willingness to use them.

POLITICS AND THE
SPIRITUAL NOBILITY

There is no peace movement in America today. Although the term is a staple in discussions about Vietnam, the preceding conversations support what is evident even to the most superficial inquiry. There is much activity, intense emotion, acrimonious and fraternal debate, some study and research. But if the word "movement" signifies something positive, unified and cohesive, a peace movement does not exist. It is not enough, for example, to say that a desire for peace is what unites the various voices into one great chorus; Lyndon Johnson wants peace too, but given the terms in which he considers it, even the most voracious peace organization could not ingest him. The terms in which one thinks of peace, desires peace, works for peace are here all-important. If one understands that the label "peace movement" is simply a rhetorical umbrella under which are sheltered individuals and organizations, opinions and attitudes of great diversity, and uses it with that limitation, it can be a utilitarian term. To think of it otherwise is to increase the likelihood of misdirected plans and activities.

A number of highly informed and politically sophisticated people have proposed, in my opinion, just such plans. To take but one example: Richard Goodwin, a former special assistant to both President Kennedy and President Johnson, and the author of a book on Vietnam,* gave a speech late in 1966 in which, after acknowledging "enormous differences between the

* *Triumph or Tragedy: Reflections on Vietnam* (New York, Random House, 1966).

critics of the war" in Vietnam, he made the following logical and persuasive proposal:

> . . . our danger is so grave that those who fear the future even more than they distrust the past—a group which encompasses, I believe, the majority of the American people—must seek some common ground rather than dissipating energies in exploring the varieties of dissent. Without sacrificing individual views we must also shape a unified stand, a focal point of belief and action which can unite all who apprehend coming dangers. Only in this way can we create a voice strong enough to be heard across the country, bringing together men of diverse beliefs, adding strength to the views of those in government who share this apprehension. It must also be a clear and direct stand; one that fires response in those millions of our fellow citizens who glimpse through complexity, discord and obscurity the vision of something dark and dangerous.
>
> I believe there is such a position. . . . It is: No wider war. It is to oppose any expansion of the bombing. It is to speak and work against all who would enlarge the war in the North. . . .
>
> Such a rallying cry requires compromise, the willingness to seek less than is desired; but that is the basic necessity of those who seek not self-indulgence but to shape the course of this nation.*

To implement this admirable goal there should be, for example, "the organization of a national committee against widening the war." Mr. Goodwin's proposal was widely praised as a soundly based, politically feasible and morally adequate program. The committee he proposes may be desirable and, if erected, might be as effective as some other existing organizations; but those who would expect it to accomplish more have been led astray by an analysis that is unrealistic and therefore politically unsound. In terms of the current protest, Goodwin has given point to the saw that "orthodoxy is my doxy and heterodoxy is my neighbor's," for divisions run deep within the peace movement and many people would find it impossible to join Mr. Goodwin's committee even at the risk of being labeled self-indulgent. To discern these divisions, to grasp their essential

* "What We Can Do About Vietnam," *The New Leader,* November 7, 1966, p. 12.

causes and possible consequences, is to learn much about our society.

The divisions and the problems within the major religious communities as they respond to the questions posed by modern war are today so severe that it is difficult even to describe them without indicating partisanship. For modern war has questioned in a particularly acute form the relation which obtains between religion and the public order.

Do religious spokesmen or organized religious groups have something particular to say, for example, about the conflict in Vietnam, something that distinguishes them from other groups that address themselves to the same question? When they petition the President, "In the name of God, stop it!" are we to assume that they have a right, superior to that of other citizens, to speak in the name of God? Does the criticism voiced by these religious groups have some special quality denied to other protesting groups? If so, what is it and from what does it derive? If not, is the strength of religious groups to be judged only statistically, in terms of their political weight? Are these groups simply using the prestige of the churches to power their own highly fallible and partisan political judgments? These are some of the questions that trouble those who attempt to distinguish the voice of religion in the general clamor of protest over the war in Vietnam.

There are, of course, those who state that Christian ethics and political ethics are incompatible. Christians who are convinced that this is the case would seem to have the choice of withdrawing from politics or of ignoring Christianity as a source of political illumination. Others are content to say that there is no relation between the two, that "to introduce religious overtones into political discussion is to prostitute religion or corrupt politics or both." *

The major intellectual tradition of biblical religion has accepted neither of these views. It has insisted that there can be no political decision without moral responsibility and that the moral character of political action is open to investigation and

* Quentin P. Hogg, M.P., *Spectator*, May 6, 1966, p. 564.

judgment. It has also insisted that political society is under God, who is sovereign over all the world, and that nations are under His providence and judgment. It has further insisted that "the brotherhood of man under the Fatherhood of God" is more than rhetoric, that it implies concrete obligations in the social order. And where some would assert a radical disjunction between the moral obligations that govern individuals and those which operate among nation states, this tradition asserts the continuity of those obligations.

In positing this as the major religious tradition, I have already cut off significant groups whose formulations would challenge or modify these—but the end of division is not yet. Much of the weight of traditional Western thinking about the relation of man to the world and to God rests firmly upon a distinction between the sacred and the secular, the latter clearly subordinate to the former. The distinction was intended to establish, both in theory and practice, that man was not wholly encompassed by or to be entirely understood in terms of his political life, his social relations. Again, it was for long accepted that the churches would enunciate general principles which the individual would apply in the specific manifestations of public life. Now the distinction between the sacred and the secular is under serious attack, and a significant number of religious people have rejected the idea that the churches should speak in generalities of unspecified application. A number of these people wish to commit themselves fully to the secular order, and they urge religious communities to make specific judgments on specific issues.

This general ferment is fed by many streams which do not always mingle readily: for example, Teilhard de Chardin, the Jesuit paleontologist; Dietrich Bonhoeffer, who has been called the martyr-theologian of the German Resistance; C. Wright Mills, a sociologist who first spoke of the New Left and who wrote "A Pagan Sermon to the Christian Clergy," in which he berated Christians for their moral insensibility to modern war and for their failure to engage the "moral issues of politics"; and Albert Camus, who said, "What the world expects of Christians is that Christians should speak out loud and clear, and that they should voice their condemnation in such a way that never a doubt, never the slightest doubt, could rise in the heart of the simplest man. That they should get away from abstraction and confront the blood-stained face history has taken on today. The grouping we need is a grouping of men resolved to speak out clearly and to pay up personally."

How have the religious communities actually responded when the specific issue was war? They have responded much as the general public, and the tendency of the American people, only now being modified, is to fluctuate between extremes: to abhor war until it is initiated, but, once entered, to renounce almost all restraint. It is to the credit of the Clergy and Laymen Concerned about Vietnam, for example, that some of its members are attempting to make politico-moral discriminations that are essential to sustained and informed debate about the nature of the Vietnamese conflict. It is because such efforts were absent during World War II that, in retrospect, one is forced to say that the religious communities failed sadly to live up to their own proclaimed ideals and traditions.* But when the religiously concerned person today attempts to avoid that failing, he must cope with the same problems as other citizens. With the possible exception of those who find in religion the basis for a radical pacifism—John McKenzie, S.J., Steven Schwarzschild, Paul Peachey and Gordon Zahn, for example—the religiously committed person who has joined in the protest movement seems to be politically indistinguishable from his neighbor, and so, too, are many of his slogans, arguments and activities. It is a sign of the deepest division in the religious communities that some people regret this development and attempt to counter it while others regard it as the proper, desirable, even necessary path of the future.

Amid such large generalizations it may seem inappropriate to remark on a trend whose development is still uncertain, but the growing interest which American Catholics have in pacifism and activities for peace—an interest for which they were not previously noted—cannot go unremarked. Nor can the increased questioning and frequent rejection of the just-war theory, which

---

* In his admirable book *The Irreversible Decision,* Robert Batchelder records the reactions of Americans, with particular attention to organized religion, to the development of nuclear weapons and their employment on Hiroshima and Nagasaki.

has been the intellectual grounding for most Catholics who have considered the problem. The pacifists were almost alone in noting when Alfredo Cardinal Ottaviani, the great conservative, said in 1947 that modern war is such that the conditions which justify war and make it permissible are never present. When, in the context of the Vietnam war, Bishop John J. Wright questioned the present usefulness of the theory, the impact of his comments was, for Americans, greater. What I would stress, however, is not this reconsideration among Catholics but the *context* in which it is made. The nuclear weapons systems have been for years at the center of thought and concern about modern war, but the issue may be decisive for many at the other end of the scale; it will not be the thought of mass destruction but the knowledge that individuals are being killed by fragmentation bombs and napalm, by torture and terrorism, that will determine the question.

It is in times of danger and stress, before a country is caught up in a war that concentrates all its energies, that pacifism exerts its greatest attraction and pacifists their best efforts. Those familiar with the history of peace movements know that it is a melancholy and dispiriting affair and that, with marked exceptions, peace movements follow a pattern of enthusiasm and growth, impasse and apathy, and a general decline into political ineffectiveness. Pacifists burdened with this knowledge must act with a dedication born of high hope and low expectation. But even those who are borne along on youthful enthusiasm must be discouraged with the response they so often encounter. What can pacifists hope for when John P. Roche, later to become an assistant to the President, writes: "Let me make it perfectly clear that a pacifist can on principle argue that the use of force in international affairs is immoral. . . . But a pacifist is thus forbidden by his moral imperatives from having any favorite wars."

While it is likely that the number of people who have favorite wars will always, mercifully, be small, what is there to prevent the pacifist from saying, with others, that no wars are favorite, but some are more unfavorite than others? Pacifists are capable, in other words, of making political discriminations as neatly as

Politics and the Spiritual Nobility

any political scientist. It is true that they will then make judgments that will distinguish them from the nonpacifist. But that,
as both Jack Bollens and Paul Peachey said, is where conversation, if there is to be any between pacifists and nonpacifists,
should begin. And as a number of pacifists in this book argue, I
think quite convincingly, the benefits would not accrue only to
themselves.

Joan Baez said that she and others withdrew from activities
of the Vietnam Day Committee when some members began to
discuss whether they should put lead in their picket signs—an
anticipated departure from nonviolence—and this act of withdrawal could stand as a symbol of one division in the peace
movement. The pacifists do form a hard core, they do carry on
a tradition, and they are a source of inspiration and ideas when
crises arise. But when a peace movement gains size and momentum the pacifists are, once again and still, a minority. The
general reader and popular journalism may blur the distinction
between the pacifist and the average protester, as David Reed
pointed out, but those in the movement will not.

Still, the greatest problem for the pacifist is not with the nonpacifist in the movement but with himself and other pacifists.
The problem was, I think, accurately stated by David Mc-
Reynolds: "What is required by pacifism and what cannot be
given up is the ability of people to make individual judgments.
But that also mitigates against its becoming an effective political
force." It is at least partially this which makes it impossible to
have a "politics of pacifism" even when the peace movement
is of significant proportions. There is in pacifism, however, a pull
toward some form of politics. At the moment its major expressions are a nostalgia for a recent past when it seemed to
exist in embryo and a longing for a future, not yet in view, when
it might develop under propitious circumstances. Until the early
years of this century the term "pacifism" was defined less narrowly than it is now, and it was understood to embrace both a
personal commitment to nonviolence and an internationalism
which placed great trust in agreements between nations that
would ensure international peace. These two aspects have been
sundered into separate elements, one emphasizing the value
of individual protest and personal political salvation, the other

the value of international organizations designed to inhibit war. As the world now moves, neither aspect can nurture a "politics of pacifism," nor does either seem capable of coping adequately with the problems of contemporary revolution. The latter charge may seem less harsh when we recognize that the failure is generally shared. Nevertheless, it is clear that pacifists, though a minority, are seriously divided in their approach to social order.

In no area of the peace movement is the question of the relation between domestic policies and foreign policy posed more starkly than in those groups labeled the New Left or the New Radicals. The accuracy of the designation may be questioned, since it almost immediately invites qualification and classification, but the label has been certified by usage and may outlast some manifestations of what it is intended to describe. In his rapid tour over the complicated and shifting terrain of the Radical Left, Jack Newfield pointed out many significant features—the persons, the organizations, the ideas, the journals, the activities—but there were two major landmarks, SNCC and SDS. In spite of many changes in organization, membership and tone, they remain the most important groups. Different as they are, the two organizations share a radical critique of American society and a vision of transforming it into a society in which the dispossessed and disenfranchised have a voice that is heard. Julian Bond described the changes SNCC was undergoing, reflecting its student origins less and less and working more and more with young people from the black ghetto. SDS continues to achieve successes important to itself but of yet negligible importance to the country.

Beneath the protean manifestations of these organizations is a firm conviction that the relation between foreign and national affairs is not accidental. Both sets of policies, they argue, will reflect the society within which they are developed. John Lewis, for example, spoke of "the Movement," reluctant to separate it into the civil rights movement and the peace movement. For the evils to be attacked had a common source, and so should the efforts to eliminate them.

It was much easier for the Southern civil rights worker, particularly the Negro, to resist the rationale for U.S. intervention in Vietnam than it was for most critics of U.S. policy; they could identify with the enemy. As Howard Zinn wrote, there was "a raw and simple feeling, drawing a line straight from southern Vietnam to the southern part of the United States." They had learned for one thing to distrust the U.S. government, to regard it as the guardian of established disorder, and they knew the cost in beatings and deaths and publicity before some small, and possibly temporary, victory was achieved. They found it easy and natural to ask why a government could expend so much to defend the rights of people in South Vietnam and so little to defend the oppressed in this country, why it could send so many troops to Vietnam and so few federal law enforcement officers to the South. It was easier to see the U.S. government as a strong, misguided, white oppressor in each case. It led easily to Martin Luther King's judgment that "the United States is the greatest purveyor of violence in the world." And Negroes who had seen the power of nonviolence achieve success in domestic problems asked: why was such violence necessary in foreign affairs? Although the new leadership of SNCC has moved in other directions, nonviolence is still an active and potent ingredient within the civil rights movement. It is, in fact, one of the things on which the civil rights movement is divided, as it is also divided on the question of supporting U.S. policy in Vietnam.

For the equation which I have been drawing is reversible and the question has been posed: if violence is sometimes necessary to attain justice abroad when other means have proved unavailing, are there times when it is equally necessary at home? The riots which exploded across the states during the summer of '67 are one positive response to that question. As Julian Bond said after these riots, "The American way of politics and appeals to conscience have been tried but they have not worked." He added that violence would not work either, but that the angry Negroes saw it as the only avenue left.

The relation between violence at home and violence abroad is seen not only by the angry Negro but by responsible white leaders. Robert Kennedy, for example, said after the riots, "If we as a nation say that it is justified in killing thousands and thousands of people 12,000 miles from our own country, then it becomes a

rather more acceptable instrument for change within the United
States itself."

There are still close ties between the civil rights movement
and the peace movement—they depend upon many of the same
people who share many of the same long-term goals—but this
is a weakness as well as a strength, for the divisions within one
tend to reflect themselves in the other. And as the Vietnam war
lengthens, some of the inherent difficulties become more pronounced. For national and foreign affairs do have different con-
stituencies and do have quite different levers of power. There
are still some things to be accomplished in one area even by
those who feel, with good reason, that they are ineffectual in
the other. But people in what used to be the "Movement"
divide sharply on strategy and tactics. Should one cooperate with
the government in its foreign policy—at least to the extent of
softening one's criticism—in order to get government support
for needed domestic reforms? Should one try to work with a
loose grouping of labor unions, religious groups and middle-class
liberals without pressing for total agreement on Vietnam in order
to achieve domestic reform? Is coalition politics a corruption of
the dream or a step toward the desired goal? The different
response given to such questions by, for example, Roy Wilkins
of the NAACP, Julian Bond, Martin Luther King, Robert
Pickus, Bayard Rustin, Staughton Lynd, and Stokely Carmichael
reveal the deep divisions that have appeared.

Another division within the Radical Left has been defined
in terms of generations. It is as if the new radicals would reverse the familiar saying so that it would read, now in political
rather than sexual terms,

> "If the young were able;
> If the old but knew"

For what the old radicals do not know, they are told, is that
the Cold War has ended and that their anti-communism is an
historical drag and a present handicap; they do not realize the
extent to which liberalism is corrupted and corrupting; they do
not understand all that is positive and constructive in the stance
of a Castro or a Nasser or even a Tito; they deliberate about
policy for Vietnam instead of saying simply that the U.S. should

withdraw. But the young radicals, whose perception of reality is apparently uncluttered by conceptions designed for another age, do not have power. If they were able they would move the country toward authentic democracy, "participatory democracy" in which every citizen would have a voice in making decisions that a society must make. The person, in these terms, would be re-established at the center of a system which he would use, rather than on the periphery of a system which uses him. Are these ideas the consequences of the new radicals' "unrestrained impulse to moral integrity," to use Arnold Kaufman's phrase? Their near allies, who are also their sharpest critics, say yes, and add that when the romanticism sloughs off the young radicals, they too will be forced to deal with the elements of power and learn the terrible art of political compromise.

The difficulties of forging an effective coalition between various groups on the Left—New Left students, Old Left radicals, civil rights organizations, anti-war groups, black militants and radical labor—was dramatized by the National Conference for New Politics which met in Chicago during the first week of September 1967. The result was a shambles. The dangers of participatory democracy became as evident as the advantages of political power, as the Conference wavered between anarchy and elitism. The Conference served mainly to expose and exacerbate the differences which divide those on the left.

The role played by intellectuals, artists and academics in the protest movement is one of the most interesting, revealing and puzzling, and it is not at this time played to its completion. Traditionally intellectuals and academics are expected to discern and articulate the issues with which the country is, should and will be concerned. And among artists there will be some who shape, from the material of the present movement, works that will allow us to apprehend more nearly the conditions in which we live. In terms of the present crisis, the performance of these groups has been curious. The teach-in movement is now moribund, having perhaps served its purpose. To take the place of the teach-ins, the academics now publish advertisements containing many thousands of signatures opposing the war in Vietnam.* But this is clearly a falling back, if not a retreat, from a hard-gained vantage point. The artists, particularly the poets, have been most remarkable in the protest movement. As Denise Levertov noted, almost every known poet has raised his opposition to U.S. policy in Vietnam. And they have sustained an interest in read-ins and group protests. There is rarely any political leverage in what they do; it becomes primarily a matter of pitting prestige, where it exists, against power, and of communicating with as large an audience as possible. As for the intellectuals, whether in or out of academe, they give the impression frequently of curdling in isolated frustration. The sections quoted from the *Partisan Review* are a fair indication of what takes place in other journals; the writers who protest are as critical of each other's ideas as they are of the policy they all reject.

It would be difficult to exaggerate the anguish with which at least some intellectuals regard their present ineffectual state, and it would be difficult to express it more poignantly than George Steiner has. Mr. Steiner is a critic of formidable erudition, at home in several languages and cultures. Greatly distressed by the apparent inability of intellectuals to discharge their responsibility, he wrote:

> The present Administration and Congress do appear to represent the duly expressed views of a majority of our fellow-citizens. We are committed to the full rights and power of that expression. Not *one* Congressman has been elected on a true anti-war platform. We feel with anguish that we know better, that an elite of conscience and insight must be heard. But how, and in what politically active form? If we cannot act politically, or only very slightly, what then can we do personally, *now*, in our professional and private lives? How can we help subvert the ugly, inhuman coexistence of a brilliant intellectual and artistic culture with a simultaneous Vietnam policy which many of us find self-defeating and abhorrent? †

* Such an advertisement appeared in the *New York Times* of March 12, 1967, containing 6,700 signatures.

† In the *New York Review of Books* for February 23, 1967, Noam Chomsky wrote a long article entitled "The Responsibility of the Intellectual." Mr. Steiner's sympathetic response and question appeared in the review's issue of March 23, 1967.

I am not certain how other members of the protest movement would describe this view, which is not an isolated view, but it would not be "participatory democracy." Nor would Mr. Steiner's attitude serve to unite a divided protest movement.

It is on the basis of these divisions and differences—and it is more difficult to become fully aware of them than it is to exaggerate their importance—that I have said there is no peace movement. But there is some impulse that unites all those who are, in various ways, opposing the war in Vietnam, those who picket and march, wear buttons and carry slogans, write books, articles, plays and poems, attend teach-ins and poetry read-ins, burn draft cards and attempt to obstruct troop trains, sign ads and write letters to the editor. They are not united in their political allegiance, or their political sophistication, their education, background or dedication, their religious commitment, their proposals or their hopes for success. They are united only in protest to the present military policy of the U.S. in Vietnam. The distinction between a peace movement and a protest movement is not merely verbal. Those who say that the U.S. should withdraw its military forces at once can hardly claim that, as a happy consequence, peace would descend upon that tortured land. They can mean at most that in the ensuing conflict the U.S. would not be an agent and that the conflict would be less horrible. They are choosing not between peace and war, but between two kinds of war, one of which they judge to be less evil than the other. Despite all the positive and valuable aspects to the movement, its unity is one of protest, not affirmation.

Charles Péguy wrote that everything begins as *mystique* and ends in *politique*. There is a sense in which the protest movement in America exists between these two poles. It appeals to both, draws resources from both and, when the crisis is over, will fragment and disappear into both. To make this statement convey fully what I mean requires some elaboration of the polar terms.

Relying heavily upon the authority and legacy of Aristotle, I use "politics" to mean something quite limited and precise. The definition is neither arbitrary nor neutral and it will set me at intellectual odds with other views expressed in this book. Politics, as I will use the term, is that process within a community by which groups with different interests and commitments compromise their differences in order that they may share in some measure in governing that community. It is an activity intended to ensure that all real interests are represented and that no single interest is paramount. Given this definition, politics is not only an ongoing but an essential activity in the American system of governing; since it requires the active expression of different interests, it exists in a diminished form, if at all, in a theocratic state or a police state; since it depends upon a stable order in which differences can be compromised, it can exist only imperfectly in the present state of international affairs.

As the present conditions of our country indicate, the activity of politics does not lead ineluctably to an ideal order. For as critics of this theory of politics have correctly pointed out, it allows injustices to be inflicted upon those who cannot readily introduce their interests into the political system. Since it depends upon the interaction of "groups with different interests," those people who do not recognize the interests they share with others, who cannot act as a group, and who have little power to make conflicting groups compromise—those people are subject to rather than participants in the political order. The race riots of 1967, for example, can be read as an attempt by some Negroes to show that there is a final power they do have—the threat of violence. But, even more important, the riots can be seen as an attempt to forge a tight self-recognizable group with shared interests. The plight of Negroes in this country is that they must struggle to get the power they do not have in order that, with that power, they may enter the political process in order to gain the exercise of rights they are presently denied.

The activity of politics will include all the acts of compromise, conciliation and patronage that many find offensive. It is an activity in which, contrary to some politicians, a theory of values is inevitable and in which, contrary to many critics, experience seems necessary for real mastery. It is an activity of great value—not least because it allows other activities essential to man's nature and well-being to develop within their proper autonomy, without imposing itself upon them or demanding tribute from them.

Politics is not competent to regulate, if I may use the term

Politics and the Spiritual Nobility

broadly, that which is spiritual in man: religion, art, the intellectual life. But if politics is inadequate or abused it constricts the freedom proper to the spiritual life; and, whether they are political or not, those most sensitive to this constriction will protest and complain. Nor will their protests always be cast in terms that the policy maker will find relevant or even applicable. In noting the various levels of abstraction at which discussions of foreign policy take place, Charles Burton Marshall has said:

> To any proposal, pronouncement, criticism, or communique concerning foreign policy I like to apply the test of trying to translate it into intelligible and effective instruction. If its terms are such as would readily lend themselves to being put into language appropriate to guide the officers of this government in upholding its interests and purposes and put other governments on notice regarding our intentions in specific situations, then I regard the instrument favorably. If, on the other hand, the terms are airy and highly general so that it is difficult or even impossible to see how to translate them into practicable instructions and specific propositions of action, then I look askance. Foreign policy is generated by what governments do to affect situations beyond the span of their jurisdiction. Verbalizations about foreign policy that are deficient in giving us a key to what is intended or recommended in specifics are likely to be valueless if not even mischievous.*

This formulation sets a worthy standard, probably essential to those who advise on policy and those who make the decisions. If applied to the protest movement it would deflate many balloons and dispense much of the chaff. But it would leave untouched much that is instructive in the movement. Acknowledging the difference between domestic and foreign affairs, the example of the civil rights demonstrators is apposite here. The racism endemic to our society had allowed unjust laws and customs to stand and just laws to go unfulfilled. The channels normally open for redress and correction were clogged. With no long-range program or strategy and with only the most sketchy of tactics, a small group challenged the structure of injustice. It

---

* "Aggression and National Self-Interest," *Christian Ethics and Nuclear Warfare,* Ulrich S. Allers and William V. O'Brien, eds. (Washington, D. C., Georgetown University, 1961), p. 25.

did not immediately fall but it rang hollow. The sight of young people getting burned and clubbed because they sat at a segregated lunch counter exposed the foul conditions that racism imposed as previous rhetoric and legal action had not. And it was protest, not positive program. The Negro was able to say, "I don't want the white man to give me the shirt off his back; I just want him to get his foot off my neck." The effect of this action was to awaken much of America from a moral torpor, to stimulate both black and white Americans to participate in greater protest, and to bring about changes in the political and social order. Racism and its injustices are still with us, and the war in Vietnam has directed energies and attention away from them, but those early acts of protest illumine our society still, and they took place outside of politics.

Many of the people involved in the protest movement are acting outside of politics, some unknowingly but some consciously and deliberately. Joan Baez, for example, not only thinks that the civil rights movement was most effective when it operated outside the political system but she recognizes clearly the limitations absolute pacifism places on political effectiveness today. A number of other people would agree with her: Frederick Franck, Jim Forest, David McReynolds, Paul Peachey, W. H. Ferry. But they do not conclude that to be apolitical condemns one to inactivity. They find it worthwhile to insist on exactly those values which politics is not equipped to handle and which war tends to diminish: the value of each man, regardless of color, nationality or belief. When an organization declares in an advertisement "They are our brothers whom we kill," it can be dismissed as a simple-minded slogan. It certainly provides no levers for the politician. But we frown on the practice of killing brothers, and truly to think of the Vietnamese in such terms helps to restore them to that full humanity which is always a casualty of war.

Mitchell Goodman spoke of the special ability of the artist to feel compassion for those who live at a geographical and cultural distance and, by an act of imagination, to communicate that feeling. But most artists do not expect to be acknowledged legislators of the world. During the week of "The Angry Arts" in which writers, artists, poets, dancers, actors, musicians and film makers protested American policy in Vietnam, the critic Harold Rosenberg said, "What can art do in politics? Nothing except say, 'I'm against this war.' But to expect that you can produce a result is a dumb idea."

To dismiss the protest movement as unpolitical, as some have done, is to be mistaken on two counts. The first is that a number of influential people who are critical of U.S. policy in Vietnam are quite political. Who would deny that, for example, Hans Morgenthau, Reinhold Niebuhr, George Kennan, William Fulbright, Kenneth Galbraith or Edwin O. Reischauer are political —and they are critics of the policy. Second, many of the protesters are apolitical, but their comments and activities are extremely pertinent. By insisting on the difference between America's promise and its attainment, they make complacency about U.S. foreign policy more difficult to condone. By insisting that truth has a positive value superior to any activities it is intended to serve, they show that a shifting rationale for the war and constantly renewed progress reports cannot safely bridge the credibility gap. It is true that some protesters, like a number of their critics, have confused or rejected the relation between *mystique* and *politique,* between morality and policy. They have attempted to ignore an iron rule which I have previously formulated in this way: A moral solution to a political problem that is not also a political solution is no solution. The protesters may frequently have failed to see ideals of truth and justice in perspective, but they have constantly kept them in focus and have impelled them into public attention. They, more than their critics, have been aware of the political consequences of nonpolitical action.

It is in the area of *mystique,* rather than *politique,* that those on the radical Left and the radical Right come together. It is here that the conservative Young Adults for Freedom can meet and momentarily join forces with the Students for a Democratic Society. Positively, they agree on the dignity of the individual and on the need to interpret political action in moral terms; negatively, they agree that the present political system is not designed to acknowledge either.

W. E. Hocking has written that "the state depends for its vitality upon a motivation which it cannot by itself command."

It would be arrogant to deny that the people in our government cannot be and are not a source of that vitality, but we have no right to expect it from the political activity itself. That vitality will derive from those who have a true concern for the spiritual life of the nation, for the inward depths and potential glory of man. Those who are a source of that vitality—and I am contending that a number of them are in the protest movement—have a right to be called the spiritual nobility (though the phrase would sicken some of them). I believe their protests will stand in our national history as redeeming acts.

I began my investigation of the protest movement with the hypothesis that it differs significantly from previous efforts and that reflection on those differences will not only illuminate the present situation but better prepare us for the future. This hypothesis derives from three major assumptions; for two of these I would anticipate general agreement. In the most skeletal terms these are the three assumptions.

First, the decline of colonialism, the accompanying rise of nationalism, and revolutionary ferment among long-suppressed peoples combine to make armed conflict within and between countries a long-term probability. Where these conflicts and the concomitant upheavals do not actually invite participation by the great world powers, they make such participation easier. As the war in Vietnam illustrates, the label one applies to these conflicts depends less upon empirical observation than upon the socio-political framework that is employed. It is likely that these conflicts will continue to be variously described as civil wars, revolutions, wars of national liberation and wars of aggression. Granting the characteristics that are unique to Vietnam and the variables that exist in Asia, Latin America and Africa, the first assumption is, briefly, that these continents are the seeding ground for other "Vietnams."

Second, the conditions under which these conflicts occur suggest that they may be particularly brutal and widely reported. A general nuclear war remains a possibility, but leaders of the major powers have publicly repudiated it as a rational enterprise, and the threat of such a war apparently inhibits conventional war between them. The wars in which the major powers engage are, therefore, likely to be "limited," i.e., nonnuclear. But

Politics and the Spiritual Nobility

if introduced into an area where the indigenous forces are prepared both by necessity and design to fight with guerrilla tactics, the conventional forces of a major power will be engaged in a particularly ugly struggle whose terrible and sensational aspects will receive world-wide attention. If America is involved, there will be maximum exposure by press, radio and television. As the conflict is protracted the difficulties for the major power will be compounded.

Thirdly, the present foreign policy of the United States is interventionist and commits the U.S. to oppose Communist aggression in vast areas of the world, by military force if necessary. The authority for this statement derives from Secretary of State Dean Rusk, who has stated his concept of U.S. policy with admirable clarity and directness. Appearing before the Senate Foreign Relations Committee, Dean Rusk said that in the event of an aggression against a territory covered by a treaty to which America is a signatory, the U.S. has an obligation to oppose that aggression regardless of what the other signers do. Since the U.S. has commitments with over forty countries strung along the periphery of the Communist world, it has taken on obligations of unparalleled proportions. As long as this is U.S. policy the possibility of U.S. participation in other Vietnams is considerable. It is the wisdom of this policy that is, I assume, questioned by all the disparate elements in the protest movement.

If the U.S. does engage its military forces in "other Vietnams" there is every reason to believe that America will again be the scene of large-scale protests. Each instance of intervention must be judged on its own terms, but there are many Americans who are united in one large dissent; they find it increasingly difficult to believe that such acts, justified in the name of countering communism and fostering security, are serving the cause of our national interest, world order, or some higher, transcendent values.

In a book which depends so much upon the ideas and words of others, it may not be inappropriate to end with a prayer from John Stuart Mill: "Lord, enlighten thou our enemies, sharpen their wits, give acuteness to their perceptions, and consecutiveness and clearness to their reasoning powers: we are in danger from their folly, not from their wisdom; their weakness is what fills us with apprehension, not their strength."

Bibliography

The following bibliography is limited to works which deal with the relation between ethics and political affairs. It has been selected from a much more extensive bibliography compiled by Quentin Quade, Department of Political Science, Marquette University, and is used with his permission.

An excellent bibliography of books on "war, pacifism, non-violence and related studies" has been compiled and edited by William Robert Miller. It is included in *The Pacifist Conscience*, Peter Mayer, editor. New York: Holt, Rinehart and Winston, 1966.

Addison, James Thayer. *War, Peace, and the Christian Mind*. Greenwich, Conn.: The Seabury Press, 1953.

America (periodical). *Between Two Cities*. Chicago: Loyola University Press, 1962.

Angell, Robert Cooley. *Free Society and Moral Crisis*. Ann Arbor: University of Michigan Press, 1958.

Bainton, R. H. *Christian Attitudes Toward War and Peace*. Nashville, Tenn.: Abingdon Press, 1966.

Barth, Karl. *The Church and the Political Problem of Our Day*. New York: Charles Scribner's Sons, 1939.

Barth, Karl. *The Church and the War*. New York: The Macmillan Co., 1944.

Batchelder, Robert C. *The Irreversible Decision: 1939–1950*. Boston: Houghton-Mifflin Co., 1962.

Bennett, John C. *The Christian As Citizen*. New York: Association Press, 1965.

Bennett, John C. *Christian Ethics and Social Policy*. New York: Charles Scribner's Sons, 1946.

Bennett, John C. *Christian Realism*. New York: Charles Scribner's Sons, 1941.

Bennett, John C., editor. *Christian Social Ethics in a Changing World.* New York: Association Press, 1966.

Bennett, John C. *Christians and the State.* New York: Charles Scribner's Sons, 1958.

Bennett, John C. *Foreign Policy in Christian Perspective.* New York: Charles Scribner's Sons, 1966.

Bonhoeffer, Dietrich. *The Communion of Saints.* New York: Harper and Row Publishers, 1963.

Bonhoeffer, Dietrich. *Ethics.* Glascow: William Collins' Sons & Co., Ltd., 1964.

Bonhoeffer, Dietrich. *Prisoner for God: Letters and Papers from Prison.* New York: The Macmillan Co., 1954.

Bookes, E. H. *Power, Law, Right, and Love.* Durham, N. C.: Published for the Lilly Endowment Research Program in Christianity and Politics by Duke University Press, 1963.

Booth, A. *Christianity and Power Politics.* New York: Association Press, 1961.

Bosley, Harold A. *Doing What Is Christian.* Nashville, Tenn.: Abingdon Press, 1960.

Brunner, Heinrich Emil. *The Divine Imperative.* London: Lutterworth Press, 1937.

Brunner, Heinrich Emil. *Justice and the Social Order.* London: Lutterworth Press, 1945.

Canham, Erwin D. *The Ethics of United States Foreign Relations.* Columbia: University of Missouri Press, 1966.

Carlson, E. M. *Church and Public Conscience.* Philadelphia: Muhlenberg Press, 1956.

Cogley, John, editor. *Religion in America.* New York: Meridian Books, Inc., 1958.

Croce, Benedetto. *Politics and Morals.* New York: Philosophical Library, 1945.

Cronin, J. F. *The Catholic As Citizen.* Baltimore: Helicon Press, Inc., 1963.

Dawson, Christopher H. *Beyond Politics.* New York: Sheed & Ward, 1939.

Dawson, Christopher H. *Religion and the Modern State.* New York: Sheed & Ward, 1935.

De Boer, Cecil. *Responsible Protestantism.* Grand Rapids, Mich.: Wm. B. Eerdmans Publishing Co., 1957.

Devlin, Patrick. *The Enforcement of Morals.* New York: Oxford University Press, 1965.

Dewart, Leslie. *Christianity and Revolution.* New York: Herder & Herder, 1963.

Dodd, Charles H. *Gospel and Law.* New York: Columbia University Press, 1951.

Duff, Edward. *The Social Thought of the World Council of Churches.* New York: Association Press, 1956.

Bibliography

Durkheim, Emile. *Professional Ethics and Civic Morals*. London: Routledge & K. Paul, 1957.

Eliot, T. S. *The Idea of a Christian Society*. New York: Harcourt, Brace & Co., 1949.

Falk, Richard A. *Law, Morality, and War in the Contemporary World*. New York: Frederick A. Praeger, Inc., 1963.

Finn, James, editor. *Peace, the Churches, and the Bomb*. New York: Council on Religion and International Affairs, 1965.

Fletcher, Joseph F. *Situation Ethics*. Philadelphia: Westminster Press, 1966.

Forell, George Wolfgang. *Ethics of Decision*. Philadelphia: Muhlenberg Press, 1955.

Friedrich, Carl Joachim. *Transcendent Justice*. Durham, N. C.: Duke University Press, 1964.

Geyer, Alan F. *Piety and Politics*. Richmond, Va.: John Knox Press, 1963.

Giannella, Donald A., editor. *Religion and the Public Order*. Chicago: An annual review of church and state and of religion, law and society, published for the Institute of Church and State, Villanova University School of Law by the University of Chicago Press, 1964, 1965, 1966, 1967.

Gilby, Thomas. *Between Community and Society*. London: Longmans, Green & Co., 1953.

Ginsberg, Morris. *On Justice in Society*. Ithaca, N. Y.: Cornell University Press, 1965.

Goerner, E. A. *Peter and Caesar*. New York: Herder & Herder, 1965.

Gordis, Robert. *Politics and Ethics*. Santa Barbara, Calif.: Center for the Study of Democratic Institutions, 1961.

Gordis, Robert. *The Root and the Branch*. Chicago: University of Chicago Press, 1962.

Graham, Aelred. *Catholicism and the World Today*. New York: David McKay Co., 1952.

Hallowell, John Hamilton. *The Moral Foundation of Democracy*. Chicago: University of Chicago Press, 1954.

Harding, Arthur Leon, editor. *Religion, Morality and Law*. Dallas, Tex.: Southern Methodist University Press, 1956.

Hill, Norman Llewellyn and Lund, Doniver A. *If the Churches Want World Peace*. New York: The Macmillan Co., 1958.

Hodges, H. A. *Christianity and the Modern World View*. New York: The Macmillan Co., 1949.

Holloway, Vernon H. *Christians and the World of Nations*. Boston: Pilgrim Press, 1948.

Hughes, Emmet John. *The Church and the Liberal Society*. Notre Dame, Ind.: University of Notre Dame Press, 1961.

Hyma, Albert. *Christianity and Politics*. Philadelphia: J. B. Lippincott, 1940.

Jack, Homer A., editor. *Religion and Peace.* New York: The Bobbs-Merrill Co., 1966.

James, Walter. *The Christian in Politics.* New York: Oxford University Press, 1962.

Jerrold, Douglas. *The Future of Freedom: Notes on Christianity and Politics.* New York: Sheed & Ward, 1938.

Jones, Rufus Matthew, editor. *The Church, the Gospel and War.* New York: Harper & Bros., 1948.

Kaplan, Abraham. *American Ethics and Public Policy.* New York: Oxford University Press, 1963.

Kelley, Alden Drew. *Christianity and Political Responsibility.* Philadelphia: Westminster Press, 1961.

Kendall, Guy. *Religion in War and Peace.* London: Hutchinson & Co., Ltd., 1947.

Knight, George Angus Fulton. *Law and Grace.* Philadelphia: Westminster Press, 1962.

La Noue, George R. *A Bibliography of Doctoral Dissertations Undertaken in American and Canadian Universities, 1940–1962, on Religion and Politics.* New York: Published for the Department of Religious Liberty by the Office of Publication and Distribution, National Council of the Churches of Christ in the U.S.A., 1963.

Latourette, Kenneth Scott, editor. *The Gospel, the Church and the World.* New York: Harper & Bros., 1946.

Leclercq, J. *Christ and the Modern Conscience.* London: Geoffrey Chapman, Ltd., 1965.

Leclercq, J. *The Christian and World Integration.* New York: Hawthorn Books, 1963.

Lee, Robert and Marty, Martin E., editors. *Religion and Social Conflict.* New York: Oxford University Press, 1964.

Lefever, Ernest W. *Ethics and United States Foreign Policy.* New York: Meridian Books, 1957.

Loos, A. William, editor. *Religious Faith and World Culture.* Englewood Cliffs, N. J.: Prentice-Hall, Inc., 1951.

Macgregor, G. H. C. *Relevance of an Impossible Ideal.* Nyack, N. Y.: Fellowship of Reconciliation, 1941.

MacIver, Robert Morrison, editor. *Conflict of Loyalties.* New York: Published for the Institute for Religious and Social Studies, Jewish Theological Seminary of America, by Harper & Bros., 1952.

MacIver, Robert Morrison, editor. *Integrity and Compromise.* New York: Published for the Institute for Religious and Social Studies, Jewish Theological Seminary of America, by Harper & Bros., 1957.

Malik, Charles. *Christ and Crisis.* Grand Rapids, Mich.: Wm. B. Eerdmans Publishing Co., 1962.

Maritain, Jacques. *Christianity and Democracy.* New York: Charles Scribner's Sons, 1944.

Maritain, Jacques. *Man and the State*. Chicago: University of Chicago Press, 1963.

Meiklejohn, Alexander. *Inclinations and Obligations*. Berkeley: University of California Press, 1948.

Meyer, Donald B. *The Protestant Search for Political Realism, 1919–1941*. Berkeley: University of California Press, 1960.

Micklem, Nathaniel. *Theology of Politics*. New York: Oxford University Press, 1941.

Miller, Robert Moats. *American Protestantism and Social Issues, 1919–1939*. Chapel Hill: University of North Carolina Press, 1958.

Miller, William Lee. *Piety Along the Potomac*. Boston: Houghton-Mifflin Company, 1964.

Miller, William Lee. *The Protestant and Politics*. Philadelphia: Westminster Press, 1958.

Moody, Joseph N. and Lawler, Justus George, editors. *The Challenge of Mater et Magistra*. New York: Herder and Herder, 1963.

Morgenthau, Hans J. *Politics Among Nations*. New York: Alfred A. Knopf, 1961.

Morris, Philip. *Christianity and the World of Today*. London: Epworth Press, 1961.

Munby, D. L. *God and the Rich Society*. New York: Oxford University Press, 1961.

Munby, D. L. *The Idea of a Secular Society*. New York: Oxford University Press, 1963.

Murray, Albert Victor. *The State and the Church in a Free Society*. Cambridge: Cambridge University Press, 1958.

Murray, John Courtney. *We Hold These Truths*. New York: Sheed & Ward, 1960.

Nagle, William J., editor. *Morality and Modern Warfare*. Baltimore: Helicon Press, 1960.

Niebuhr, Helmut Richard. *The Responsible Self*. New York: Harper and Row, 1963.

Niebuhr, Reinhold. *Christianity and Power Politics*. New York: Charles Scribner's Sons, 1940.

Niebuhr, Reinhold. *Man's Nature and His Communities*. New York: Charles Scribner's Sons, 1965.

Niebuhr, Reinhold. *Moral Man and Immoral Society*. New York: Charles Scribner's Sons, 1932.

O'Brien, William V. *Nuclear War, Deterrence and Morality*. Westminster, Md.: Newman Press, 1967.

Odegard, Peter H., editor. *Religion and Politics*. New York: Oceana, 1960.

Petry, R. C. *Christian Eschatology and Social Thought*. Nashville, Tenn.: Abingdon Press, 1956.

Pike, James A. and Pyle, John W. *The Church, Politics, and Society*. New York: Morehouse-Gorham Co., 1955.

Powers, Francis J., editor. *Papal Pronouncements on the Political Order*. Westminster, Md.: Newman Press, 1952.

Ramsey, Paul. *Christian Ethics and the Sit-In*. New York: Association Press, 1961.

Ramsey, Paul. *Deeds and Rules in Christian Ethics*. Edinburgh and London: Oliver & Boyd, Ltd., 1965.

Ramsey, Paul. *War and the Christian Conscience*. Durham, N. C.: Duke University Press, 1961.

Raven, Charles Earle. *Theological Basis of Christian Pacifism*. Nyack, N. Y.: Fellowship of Reconciliation, 1951.

Regan, Richard J. *American Pluralism and the Catholic Conscience*. New York: The Macmillan Co., 1963.

Schilling, Sylvester Paul. *Methodism and Society in Theological Perspective*. Nashville, Tenn.: Abingdon Press, 1960.

Schneider, Herbert Wallace. *Three Dimensions of Public Morality*. Bloomington: Indiana University Press, 1956.

Schneider, Louis, editor. *Religion, Culture and Society*. New York: John Wiley and Sons, 1964.

Scott, M. L. *The Christian and Social Action*. Philadelphia: Presbyterian Board, 1948.

Spann, John Richard, editor. *Church and Social Responsibility*. Nashville, Tenn.: Abingdon-Cokesbury, 1953.

St. John-Stevas, Norman. *Life, Death and the Law*. Bloomington: Indiana University Press, 1961.

Stahmer, Harold, editor. *Religion and Contemporary Society*. New York: The Macmillan Co., 1963.

Stratmann, Franziskus Maria. *War and Christianity Today*. Westminster, Md.: Newman Press, 1956.

Sturzo, Luigi. *Church and State*. Notre Dame, Ind.: University of Notre Dame Press, 1962.

Thompson, Kenneth W. *Christian Ethics and the Dilemmas of Foreign Policy*. Durham, N. C.: Duke University Press, 1959.

Thompson, Kenneth W. *The Moral Issue in Statecraft*. Louisiana: Louisiana State University Press, 1966.

Thompson, Kenneth W. *Political Realism and the Crisis of World Politics*. Princeton: Princeton University Press, 1960.

Tillich, Paul J. *Love, Power, and Justice*. New York: Oxford University Press, 1954.

Tucker, Robert W. *The Just War*. Baltimore: Johns Hopkins Press, 1960.

Wilmore, G. S. *The Secular Relevance of the Church*. Philadelphia: Westminster Press, 1962.

Index

Abel, Lionel, 477
Acheson, Dean, 32, 35, 159–60, 235, 237
Acton, Lord, 333
Ads, as form of protest, 465–67, 503–4
Alfrink, Bernard Cardinal, 63n
Allers, Ulrich S., 507n
Americans for Democratic Action (ADA), 211
American Civil Liberties Union (ACLU), 61, 235, 397
American Pax Association, 180
Angry Arts week, 508–9
Aptheker, Herbert, 224, 300n
Aquinas, Thomas, 402
Arendt, Hannah, 113, 127–28
Armstrong, Donald, 117n

Baez, Joan, 238n, 454–62, 499, 508
Ball, George, 89, 133n
Barnett, Frank R., 118n
Batchelder, Robert, 497n
Bellow, Saul, 474
Bennett, John C., 3–16, 23, 113, 211, 416
    influence of, 30
    limitations of pacifism and, 41, 253
Benson, David, 266
Berle, Adolf, 315n
Bernardin, Bishop Joseph C., 44n
Berrigan, Daniel, S. J., 72, 141–54, 183, 484, 491
    integrity of, 120, 169
Berrigan, Philip, S.S.J., 72–82, 120, 141, 144, 188

Bettelheim, Bruno, 113, 114–15, 116, 128
Blackburn, Paul, 465, 467n
Black Muslims, 285
Black Power, 285, 293
Blocker, Joel, 75n
Bollens, Jack, 246–56, 499
Bond, Julian, 290, 292–309, 310, 500–2
Bondurant, Joan, 454
Bonhoeffer, Dietrich, 496
Booth, Paul, 320, 321
Boyle, Kay, 206
Bray, William G., 187n
Brown, H. Rap, 293n
Browne, Malcolm W., 267n
Brzezinski, Zbigniew, 343n
Buber, Martin, 118
Bundy, McGeorge, 343, 345, 479
Bunker, Ellsworth, Jr., 314n
Brodie, Bernard, 219n–20n
Buchanan, John, viii
Burdick, Eugene, 144
Buswell, Bishop Charles A., 89n
Butterfield, Henry, 66

Caffrey, Judge Andrew A., 267–68
Câmara, Dom Helder, 147
Cameron, J. M., 43
Camus, Albert, 454, 496
    influence of, 281, 282
    dispute with Sartre, 343–44
Carmichael, Stokely, 285, 287, 293, 502
Carroll, Bishop Mark K., 89n
Carthage, 117n–18n
Carver, George, 366

Catholic Association for International Peace (CAIP), 180
Catholic Peace Fellowship (CPF), 176–78
Catholic Worker movement, 72, 180, 188, 189, 358
  influence of, 372–76
  purpose of, 184
Center for the Study of Democratic Institutions, 123*n*, 481
Center for War/Peace Studies, 247
Central Committee for Conscientious Objectors (CCCO), 73, 260, 385
Chaney, James, 299*n*
Chapman, G., 144
Chayes, Abraham, 487
Cherne, Leo, 343*n*
Chomsky, Noam, 504*n*
Church, Frank, 92
Church Peace Mission, 29, 42, 73
  sponsoring groups of, 36*n*–37*n*
Civil Rights Act (1964), 227, 228
Civil rights movement, 143, 227–28, 234, 310
  foreign policy and, 302
  moral awakening due to, 28, 507–8
  nonviolence and, 143–44, 203, 311–12, 331, 457, 501
  peace movement and, 311–13, 502
  politics and, 279, 230–31
  racial outlook in, 302–3
  SNCC and, 284
  strength of, 334–35, 358–59
  Vietnam war and, 121–22, 203–4, 302–4, 317–18, 500–2
  violence and, 299
  See also specific civil rights organizations
Clark, Eleanor, 477*n*
Clausewitz, Karl von, 408–10
Clergy Concerned about Vietnam, 142, 379
  usefulness of, 89–90, 137, 158, 163–66, 174–75, 497
Cleveland, Harlan, 419
CNVA, *see* Committee for Nonviolent Action
Cody, Archbishop John P., 156
Cogley, John, 487

Cohen, Mitchell, 280*n*
Collins, Judy, 238*n*
Committee for Nonviolent Action (CNVA), 27, 72, 113, 183, 206, 247, 474
  effectiveness of, 28
  nature of, 269–70
  peace movement and, 273–74
  reaction to protest by, 26
  Reed and, 257, 263–65, 268
Congress for Racial Equality (CORE), 72, 188, 302*n*, 305, 328, 331
Conover, Grandin, 465
Conscientious objectors (COs)
  Catholics as, 62, 69, 177–82
  government and, 8–9, 51
  impediments to becoming, 189–90
  irrelevancy of, in nuclear age, 209
  Jews as, 95–97, 106–7
  just war and Catholic, 180–81, 190
  Lynd and, 224–27
  moral right of, 88
  problems of, 385–94
  Reed and, 258–60
  Rustin on, 337–38
  selective, 108–9, 176–77, 202–3
CORE, *see* Congress for Racial Equality
Corbin, Martin, 374, 379
Cornell, Thomas, 176, 183–92, 373
COs, *see* Conscientious objectors
Coser, Lewis, 230*n*
Coughlin, Charles E., 254
Council on Religion and International Affairs (CRIA), 29
Cousins, Norman, 150
Cox, Harvey, 34
Cunningham, Adrian, 193*n*
Curtis, Bishop Walter W., 89*n*
Cushing, Richard Cardinal, 44*n*

Davidon, William, 195*n*
Day, Dorothy, 132, 184, 185, 372–82
Deats, Paul, 17–35, 417
Decatur, Stephen, 44*n*
Declaration of Conscience, 233
Declaration on the Threat of Bom-

bardment of Civilian Centers, A, 89*n*
de Gaulle, Charles, 448
Dellinger, David, 120, 199, 206, 213, 214
Deming, Barbara, 188, 195*n*, 206
de Tocqueville, Alexis, 168, 283, 454
Dewart, Leslie, 33, 85
Dibble, Ernest F., 132
Dodd, Thomas J., 320
Dolce, Danilo, 216, 381
Donahue, Bishop Hugh A., 89*n*
Dougherty, Bishop John, 44*n*
Douglass, James, 85, 120, 183
Draft-card burnings, 186–87, 189, 221, 257
  Bond's support of, 296
  Reed and, 264–68
  SNCC and, 308
Draper, Theodore, 349*n*
Dresden, bombing of, 13, 14*n*, 65, 403*n*
Duberman, Martin, 477*n*
DuBois Clubs, 207
Duncan, Donald, 28, 132, 542
Dylan, Bob, 281, 282, 284

Eisenhower, Dwight D., 78, 80, 370, 486
Esmond, David, 280*n*
Ethics
  just war and, 13–14, 67, 120
  limits imposed by, 365–66
  means and ends in, 30–31, 369–71
  nations and, 53–57, 159–60
  nonviolence and, 5–7
  nuclear weapons system and, 85–86
  order as basis for, 34–35
  policy evaluations and, 11–12, 349–53
  Ramsey and, 15, 34, 375, 399
  torture and, 14–15
  two traditions in, compared, 31–33

Fall, Bernard, 343*n*, 350
Falk, Richard A., 400
Fanon, Frantz, 80, 282

Farland, Joseph, 315*n*
Farmer, James, 318
Fellowship of Reconciliation (FOR), 17, 38, 72, 112, 183, 194, 328, 358, 378
  churches affiliated with, 176
Felt, Admiral Harry, 348*n*
Ferry, W. H. "Ping," 480–92, 508
Fesquet, Henri, 181
Fischer, John, 342
Fishel, Wesley R., 343
Flacks, Richard, 320
Flaubert, Gustave, 471
Fletcher, Joseph, 15
Ford, Gerald, 87
Ford, John C., S. J., 405, 408, 508
Forest, Edgar C., 266
Forest, James, 9*n*, 125, 137, 176–92
Forrestal, James V., 19
Forst, Bishop Marion F., 89*n*
Fortas, Abe, 315*n*
Fosdick, Harry Emerson, 20
Fox, Robert James, 85
Franck, Frederick, 431–43, 508
Frank, Jerome, 29, 278, 454, 491
Frankel, Max, 343
Freedman, Monroe H., 293*n*
Free Speech Movement, 281, 289
Fromm, Erich, 246, 454
Fruchter, Norman, 477
Fulbright, J. William, 8, 27, 51, 79, 147, 353, 360, 509
  on arrogance of power, 201–2, 313, 399
  on protest, 270–71, 480
  on war fever, 276, 289
Fuller, J. F. C., 423, 424
Fund for the Republic, 480, 481

Galbraith, John Kenneth, 487, 509
Gallup Poll, 43, 106
Gandhi, Mohandas K., 102, 122, 181*n*, 294, 454
  goodness of man and, 331
  influence of, 256, 315, 375
  military action and, 215
Gendler, Everett, 111–23, 174
German Catholic Peace Union, 60
Gibbon, Edward, 55
Gilbert, Arthur, 94–110
Gilmore, Robert, 207, 246

Goldberg, Arthur J., 48, 105, 106, 299
Goldwater, Barry, 87, 240, 396, 486
Goodman, Andrew, 299n
Goodman, Mitchell, 376, 463–79, 508
Goodman, Paul, 206, 282
Goodwin, Richard, 493–94
Grimmelsman, Bishop Henry J., 89n
Gruening, Ernest, 92, 360
Guernica, 156, 439

Hale, Dennis, 280n
Hallinan, Archbishop Paul J., 44n
Hamburg, bombing of, 13, 403n
Hanh, Thich Nhat, 154
Harrington, Michael, 188, 230n, 281, 283
Harriman, Roland, 315n
Harris, Bob, 281
Hartigan, Richard S., 408n
Hartke, Vance, 360
Hayden, Tom, 224, 281, 300n
Hatfield, Mark, 355
Hearst, William Randolph, 254
Heidbrink, John, 183
Heilbroner, Robert, 487
Hemingway, Ernest, 470
Hentoff, Nat, 194n, 206
Hershey, General Lewis, 264, 387, 390, 398
Heschel, Abraham Joshua, 154–62, 166, 474
Higgins, Monsignor George G., 180
Hiroshima, 14n, 402, 406, 420, 421, 433, 439
Hocking, W. E., 509
Hogg, Quentin P., 495n
Honey, P. J., 343n
Hooft, Visser 't, 38, 164
Hook, Sidney, 218, 289
Hoover, J. Edgar, 289
Howe, Irving, 230n, 233, 288, 289, 326, 477n
    on New Left, 280
HUAC (House Un-American Activities Committee), viii, 287
Hughes, H. Stuart, 207, 283
Hugo, John, 376
Huizinga, John, 343n

Ibsen, Henrik, 472
Institute for the Study of Nonviolence, 454
Inter-Religious Committee on Peace, 89
Inter-University Committee to End the War in Vietnam, 356, 358, 362
Irving, David, 14n
Isolationism, pacifism and, 4–5, 20–21, 22, 254

Jack, Homer A., 89n
Jacobs, Paul, 280n, 477
James, William, 335
Jewish Peace Fellowship (JPF), 95–97, 106, 108, 112
Johnson, Lyndon B., 35n, 68, 204, 228, 277, 299, 316, 396, 498
    basis for action of, 370–71
    limitations of, 196–97
    racism of, 300
    Vietnam war and
        call to impeach, 222
        deception and, 49–50n, 168
        democratic process and, 473
        dissent and, 27, 307, 355
        escalation and, 240, 348n, 350
        Ferry and, 481–83, 486, 488, 490n, 491
        intellectuals and, 342, 353n–54n, 478
        Jews and, 105
        negotiations and, 7, 28, 87, 133, 493
        Neuhaus and, 168, 171
        weapons development and, 52n
John XXIII, 71, 176, 378
    greatness of, 435
    hope offered by, 433
    influence of, 147, 177, 192, 377, 387, 431
    just war and, 63, 74n, 83, 203
    as prophet of solidarity, 438
Jones, LeRoi, 290
Joyce, James, 471
Just-war theory
    Catholic Church and, 176–77
    Catholic clergy and, 67–68
    Catholic COs and, 180–81, 190
    Catholics and, 62–63, 401–2, 497–98

Index

criticized, 30, 31, 52–53
ethics and, 13–14, 67, 120
explored, 399–414, 418–28
Jews and, 97–99
John XXIII and, 63, 74n, 83, 203
limiting nature of, 152–53, 170–71
in nuclear age, 86
stated, 7
Vietnam war and, 93, 142, 176–77, 296–97, 403, 413–14

Kahn, Herman, 29, 113, 169
Katzenbach, Nicolas de B., 320
Kaufman, Arnold S., 342–54, 376, 490n
Kazin, Alfred, 477n
Keating, Edward, 355
Kemble, Penn, 230n
Kennan, George, 12, 235, 509
    as ethical realist, 32–33
Kennedy, John F., 348n, 396, 442, 493
    Ferry and, 486–87
    missile crisis and, 218–19
    traits of, 370, 371
Kennedy, Robert, 147, 501–2
Keynes, John Maynard, 489
King, Martin Luther, 121, 203, 313, 329, 502
    Day on, 375, 381
    influence on SNCC of, 294–95
    southern Negro and, 285
    on U.S. violence, 501
Kintner, William K. ,447
Khrushchev, Nikita, 218, 219
Kleinman, Neil, 465
Kustein, George, 465

Landau, Saul, 280n
Lane, Mark, 281
Lasch, Christopher, 478
Lasserre, Jean, 113
Lawler, Justus George, 84–93
Lawrence, D. H., 472
League for Industrial Democracy, 319, 326
Lens, Sidney, 206
Levertov, Denise, 463–79, 504
Lewis, John, 305, 310–18, 500
Linowitz, Sol, 35

Lipset, Seymour Martin, 467
Lorenz, Konrad, 162n
Lowell, Robert, 154, 467n
Lubell, Samuel, 240
Ludlow, Bob, 376
Ludwig, Jack, 478
Lynd, Staughton, 187n, 206, 207, 214, 223–45, 281, 300n, 502
    influence of, 362–64
Lyttle, Bradford, 195n

McCarthyism
    Millet and, 365
    resurgence of, 290, 339, 441
McCormick, Robert R., 254
Macdonald, Dwight, 478
McIntyre, James Francis Cardinal, 376
McKenzie, John L., S. J., 43–58, 182n, 497
McKissick, Floyd, 302n
McNamara, Robert S., 19, 307, 370
    Ferry and, 487
    nuclear war and, 66, 169
    on security, 25n
    traits of, 487–89
    universal conscription and, 325, 398
    Vietnam war and, 87n, 299, 348n
McReynolds, David, 206–22
Mailer, Norman, 290, 465, 478–79
    influence of, 281, 284
Magnes, Judah, 118
Malamud, Bernard, 477n
Mao Tse-tung, 400, 401
Mansfield, Mike, 320, 348n, 350
Marcus, Steven, 477n
Marcuse, Herbert, 479
Maritain, Jacques, 381
Marshall, Charles Burton, 507
Marshall, General S. L. A., 409n, 423, 424
    on American fighting man, 392n–93n
Marty, Martin, 163
Marx, Karl, 213
Mattison, Lindsay, 133n
Mauriac, François, 381
Maurin, Peter, 184, 185, 372, 374, 379–81

Maximos, Patriarch, 82
May 2nd Movement, 207
Mayer, Milton, 400
Meerloo, Joost A. M., 334
Meredith, James, 299, 302-3
Merton, Thomas, 85, 143, 144
Meyer, Donald, 39
Meyer, Karl, 195n
Mill, John Stuart, 511
Miller, Arthur, 154
Miller, David, 176, 183-92, 373
Miller, Warren, 465
Millet, Stanley, 343n, 355-71
Mills, C. Wright, 80, 454, 496
  influence of, 59, 282, 287
Moore, Marianne, 142
Morgenthau, Hans, 27, 137, 313,
    343n, 509
  as ethical realist, 32, 33, 235-37
  influence of, 12
  on intellectuals, 353n
  on national interest, 31
Morse, Wayne, 147, 360
Moses, Bob, 284
Mott, William C., 118n
Murphey, Thomas M., 266
Murray, John Courtney, S. J., 400,
    401, 485
Muste, A. J., 120, 193-205, 206,
    274, 330, 381, 484
  importance of, 216
  influence of, 188, 207, 331, 491
  as marginal figure, 358
  New Left and, 282
  pre-World War II positions of,
    20, 21, 23
Myrdal, Gunnar, 484n

Nagasaki, 14, 402, 420, 421
Nagle, William J., 400
National Association for the Ad-
    vancement of Colored
    People (NAACP), 302, 502
National Conference for New Poli-
    tics (NCNP), 503
National Coordinating Committee
    to End the War in Vietnam,
    234
National Inter-Religious Confer-
    ence on Peace, 44n
Neff, John C., 118n
Negotiation Now, 44n

Nelson, John Oliver, 154
Neuhaus, Richard John, 163-75
Newfield, Jack, 279-91, 319, 500
New Left, 150, 246n, 270, 496
  influences on, 282, 283, 288
  morality of, 358-59
  old left and, 23, 237, 502-3
  participatory democracy and,
    271, 339-40
  peace movement and, 213
  traits of, 149, 280-84, 286-91,
    324, 500
  Vietnam war and, 289-91, 502-3
Newman, John Henry Cardinal, 86
Niebuhr, H. Richard, 20, 131
Niebuhr, Reinhold, 4-5, 20, 331,
    509
  criticized, 41, 131
  as ethical realist, 32, 33
  on Muste, 194-95
  view of national interest by, 12
Niemöller, Martin, 244-45
Nonviolence
  basis for, 152
  Bond on, 295-96
  civil rights movement and, 143-
    44, 203, 311-12, 331, 457,
    501
  Day on, 374-75, 380
  effects of, 462
  ethics and, 5-7
  Ferry and, 492
  Gendler on, 121
  Jews and, 100, 103-4, 115-17,
    128
  legitimacy of, 241-42
  limitations of, 145-46
  Lewis on, 310-12
  nuclear weapons system and, 195
  problems posed by, 458
  Reed and, 262-63, 272-74
  revolution and, 199-200, 214
  Rustin and, 330-31, 334, 336
  SNCC and, 294-95
  value of, 455-57
  World War II and, 185-86
Nuclear weapons system, 498
  dangers of, 10-11, 13
  Deats on, 24-25
  Franck on, 432
  immorality of, 85-86
  irrationality of, 51-52, 217-19

Index

Israel's development of, 120–21
just war and, 407–9, 411, 413,
  414
nonviolence and, 195
Reed and, 260–61
Rustin on, 333–34
Schwarzschild on, 135
SDS and, 327
Stonier on, 445–47
support for, 130
Tatum on, 397
use of, 65–66, 77–79

O'Boyle, Archbishop Patrick H., 68
O'Brien, David, 266
O'Brien, William V., 136, 399–414,
  422, 507
O'Connor, Patrick, 197*n*
Oglesby, Carl, 314*n*
Olson, Charles, 471
Osgood, Charles, 26, 29
Osgood, Robert E., 401
Ottaviani, Alfredo Cardinal, 82,
  498

Pacifism, *see* Conscientious objectors; Nonviolence; Peace
  movement; *specific pacifist
  organizations*
Page, Kirby, 20–21
Parks, Rosa, 381
Pauling, Linus, 484*n*
Paul VI, 63, 64, 83, 176, 387, 406
  peace and, 436
Peace movement
  absolute pacifists in, 214–15
  Catholics in, 71
  civil rights movement and, 311–
    13, 502
  CNVA and, 273–74
  development of, 471
  divisions in, 206, 230, 238*n*, 243,
    489
  during World War II, 185
  function of, 168–69, 441
  influence of, 211–12, 216, 283,
    379–80, 493
  Lynd and, 227, 233–34
  nature of, 193
  New Left and, 213
  political realities and, 252–53

problems of, 198–99, 498–500
Reed on, 273–74
Rustin and, 227, 229, 336, 337
social situation and, 212–13
strength of, 355–60, 490–91
in the thirties, 253–54
Vietnam war and, 215–16, 308,
  317–18, 330, 337, 356–57,
  360–63, 490–91, 493–94,
  508
See also Conscientious objectors;
  Nonviolence; *specific peace
  organizations*
Peachey, Paul, 36–42, 253, 497,
  499, 508
Peguy, Charles, 505
Percikow, Henri, 465, 467*n*
Phillips, John, 28, 266
Phillips, William, 477*n*
Pickus, Robert, 207, 214, 246, 502
Piel, Gerard, 484*n*
Pike, Douglas, 366, 367*n*
Pike, Bishop James, 313
Pius XII, 63*n*, 83
Podhoretz, Norman, 477*n*
Poirier, Richard, 477*n*
Pomfret, John, 353*n*-54*n*
Powell, Adam Clayton, 285
Protest, *see specific forms, for ex-
  ample:* Draft-card burnings;
  Read-ins; Teach-ins
Protest movement, viii–ix, 493–511,
  see also Civil rights move-
  ment; Peace movement

Radford, Admiral Arthur W., 78
Ramsey, Paul, 29, 403, 415–28, 485
  ethics and, 15, 34, 375, 399
RAND Corporation, 219*n*
Randolph, A. Philip, 328, 329
Read-ins, 467, 504
Reed, David, 113, 257–78, 499
Reed, Sir Herbert, 465
Reed, Bishop Victor, 44*n*
Reischauer, Edwin O., 509
Religion and International Affairs,
  Council on (CRIA), 29
Reston, James, 49*n*-50*n*, 168, 313,
  347, 482
Rexroth, Kenneth, 465
Riesman, David, 28, 246
Rivers, L. Mendel, 187*n*

Roberts, Archbishop Thomas D., S.J., 85, 436
Roche, John, 289, 475, 498
Romney, George, 345
Roncalli, Angelo, *see* John XXIII
Roosevelt, Franklin Delano, 21
Roosevelt, Theodore, 194
Rosenberg, Harold, 479, 509
Rosenthal, Benjamin S., 166
Rossi, Mario, 349n
Rothenberg, Jerome, 465, 467n
Rotterdam, 156
Rukeyser, Muriel, 465, 467n
Rusk, Dean, 28, 35, 41, 172, 231, 299
    deception and, 166–67
    misconception of, 354–55, 371
    on teach-ins, 343, 344
    U.S. policy and, 511
Russell, Franklin, 162n
Russell, Bishop John J., 89n
Rustin, Bayard, 206, 328–41, 484n, 502
    Communist peace groups and, 207
    influence of, 209, 216
    Lynd's criticism of, 227–33
    New Left and, 286, 288

Sahlins, Marshall, 346
St. Augustine, 401
Sandperl, Ira, 454, 455
SANE, 72, 211, 274, 356, 358, 362
    Vietnam and, 466
SANE Emergency Rally on Vietnam, 459
Sartre, Jean-Paul, 243, 244, 282
Scalapino, Robert A., 343n
Scheer, Robert, 281, 343n, 355, 360
Schelling, Thomas, 25
Schexnayder, Bishop Maurice, 89n
Schilpp, Paul, 20
Schlatter, Richard, 477n
Schlesinger, Arthur Jr., 133n, 343n, 345
Schomer, Howard, 30
Schumann, Peter, 474
Schurmann, Franz, 133n
Schwarzschild, Steven S., 105, 120, 124–38, 174, 497
Schwerner, Michael, 299n

Scientists Committee for Public Information, 444
SCLC, *see* Southern Christian Leadership Conference
Scott, Peter Dale, 133n
SDS, *see* Students for a Democratic Society
Seeger, Pete, 268
Sevareid, Eric, 349
Shannon, Bishop James, 44n
Sheen, Bishop Fulton J., 44n
Shehan, Lawrence Cardinal, 44n, 377–78
Sheinbaum, Stanley, 355
Sibley, Mulford, 115n, 206
Silone, Ignazio, 245n
Simon, Ernst, 127
Sit-ins, 263, 284
Smith, General Walter Bedell, 314n
Smith, Gerald L. K., 254
Sontag, Susan, 479
SNCC, *see* Student Nonviolent Coordinating Committee
Southern Christian Leadership Conference (SCLC), 72, 138, 286, 302, 305, 329
Southern Conference Educational Fund, 302, 305
Speck, Robert, 319–27
Spellman, Francis Cardinal, 44n, 142, 287
Spock, Benjamin, 141
Steel, Marshall, 20
Stein, Walter, 67n
Steiner, George, 144–45, 504–5
Stonier, Tom T., 75, 443–53
Students for a Democratic Society (SDS), 206, 224, 233, 281, 289, 331, 509
    background of, 319–21
    importance of, 500
    Jewish affiliation with, 118
    politics of, 271, 286, 324–27
    prospects for, 283
    Reed and, 259, 262, 269, 270
    return of McCarthyism and, 290
    Vietnam war and, 320–24, 326–27
Student Nonviolent Coordinating Committee (SNCC), 72, 113, 268, 281, 289, 381

Index

civil rights movement and, 284, 457
critical of foreign policy, 312
evolution of, 293–95, 309, 331, 363, 501
importance of, 138, 500
Jewish affiliation with, 118
Lewis and, 311
participatory democracy and, 271
prospects for, 283–86
and SDS, compared, 319–20
Vietnam war and, 292, 304–7
Student Peace Union (SPU), 206
Sullivan, Terry John, 108
Sylvester, Arthur, 48
Symington, Stuart, 87*n*
Szold, Henrietta, 118

Tamaret, Aaron Samuel, 112, 114, 116
Tanham, George, 366
Tarlov, Malcolm H., 105
Tatum, Arlo, 73, 385–98
Taylor, General Maxwell, 277, 348*n*
Teach-ins, 342–48, 351–52, 382, 503
Thant, U, 48, 349
Theobald, Robert, 484
Teilhard de Chardin, Pierre, 169, 496
Thomas, Norman, 141, 207, 246
Thoreau, Henry David, 122, 283, 294, 363–64, 454
Thurber, Sherry, 195*n*
Thurmond, Strom, 320
Tinder, Glenn, 342
Tokyo, 13–14*n*
Tolstoy, Leo, 454
Torres, Camillo, 80–81
Torture
   as corrupting, 14–15
   legitimacy of, 136
   Lynd's view of, 242–44
   necessity for, 413
   Ramsey on, 423
Truman, Harry S, 402
Tucker, Robert, 410–12
   just-war view of, 30, 31, 35
Turn Toward Peace (TTP), 118, 207, 246, 248–51

U Thant, 48, 349
Urban League, 72
Un-American Activities Committee, House (HUAC), viii, 287
United Nations, 76, 77*n*, 447–48
Urofsky, Melvin, 353*n*

Vatican Council, Second, 9, 406, 407, 421, 431, 433
   conscientious objectors and, 177, 179
   Day and, 377, 378
   effects of, 435
Veterans and Reservists to End the War in Vietnam, 474
Vietnam Day Committee, 458, 499
Vietnam war, 5, 18, 21, 22, 32, 40, 68, 79, 252, 455
   D. Berrigan and, 147–50
   Catholics and, 44*n*, 51, 64, 68–69, 82, 89*n*, 90, 93, 132*n*, 191, 377–78, 380
   COs and, 391–94
   development of protest against, 464–66
   Ferry on, 481–91
   Franck and, 439–40
   indiscriminate violence in, 52*n*, 86–87, 156–58, 350, 473
   intellectuals and, 342–43, 476–79, 503–5
   isolationism and, 254
   Jews and, 104–7, 133–35, 154–55
   Johnson and, *see* Johnson, Lyndon B.—Vietnam war
   Lewis and, 315–18
   Lynd and, 227, 229–33, 235, 239–41
   McNamara and, 87*n*, 299, 348*n*
   Millet on, 364–71
   misinformation and, 48, 49*n*–50*n*, 166–67
   Muste and, 196–98
   Neuhaus and, 163–68, 170–73
   poll on (1966), 43
   power structure and, 359–62
   Protestants and, 7–8, 15, 27–30
   Ramsey and, 417–18, 426–28
   Reed and, 257–61, 263–65, 275, 277–78

religious communities and, 495, 497, 498
responsibility for, 161, 299–300
Rustin and, 229–30, 330–31, 335, 338–41
Stonier on, 448–51
torture and, 243, 413–14
U.S. role in, 133–34, 200–1, 225, 488
world opinion and, 75
writers and artists and, 469–73, 474–75
See also Vietnam war *under* Civil rights movement; Just-war theory; New Left; Peace Movement; SDS; SNCC; *and also specific techniques of protest*
Violence
civil rights movement and, 299
as dead end, 458
domestic, 501
Franck on, 436–37
Gendler on, 121
Gilbert on, 103
immorality of, 57
inevitability of, 23, 146–47, 200, 297–98
Jews and, 102
justified, 80–81, 200–1
just-war theory and, 152–53
Lewis on, 311–12
limitations of, 195–96
Merton's view of, 144
as a minority position, 152
new approach to, 204–5
modern compared to past, 155–56
Reed on, 270
roots of western, 211
SNCC and, 309
Vietnam war and, 52n, 86–87, 156–58, 350, 473
See also Torture; War

War
anachronism of, 445
basis in nations for, 159
Bennett's view of, 15–16

Catholic Church and, 81–82
Day on, 379
Ferry on, 485–86
impossibility of, in nuclear age, 75–76
individual decision and, 108–9
Jewish views on, 76–100
irrationality of, 45–47, 53
man's nature and, 145n
Millet on, 368–69
religious communities and, 495–98
Rustin on, 339
See also Just-war theory; Nuclear weapons system; Vietnam war
War Resisters International, 385
War Resisters League, 112, 206, 207, 260, 385
Warren, Earl, 68
Waskow, Arthur, 287
Weber, Adam R., 392–93
Weber, Max, 238n, 283
Wilkins, Roy, 304, 318, 502
Williams, William A., 343n
Williams, William Carlos, 465
Wilson, E. Raymond, 246
Wilson, Harold, 301
Wolfe, Robert, 324n
Wolfers, Arnold, 447
Women Strike for Peace, 206, 358
World Council of Churches, 34, 38, 164
Wright, Bishop John J., 44n, 379, 498
Wright, Quincy, 145n
Writers and Artists Protest, 465

Yeats, William Butler, 471, 472
Youth Against War and Fascism (YAWF), 199, 207
Young, Whitney, 318
Young Peoples Socialist League (YPSL), 206

Zahn, Gordon, 59–71, 85, 108, 181, 497
Zelnik, Reginald, 133n
Zinn, Howard, 302, 501

ABOUT THE AUTHOR

JAMES FINN is Editor of *worldview* and Director of Publications for the Council on Religion and International Affairs. He was previously an editor of *Commonweal* and he has taught at a number of universities, including the University of Nebraska, the University of Chicago and New York University. The author, who was educated at the University of Chicago, saw combat as a private in the infantry in World War II. Among the publications to which he has contributed are the *New York Times, Christianity and Crisis, Dissent,* and the *National Catholic Reporter.*

Mr. Finn, who was born in Gary, Indiana, now lives in New York with his wife and five children.